IMAGINING WOMEN'S CONVENTUAL
SPACES IN FRANCE, 1600–1800

Women and Gender in the Early Modern World

Series Editors:
Allyson Poska, The University of Mary Washington, USA
Abby Zanger

The study of women and gender offers some of the most vital and innovative challenges to current scholarship on the early modern period. Now approaching its tenth anniversary, "Women and Gender in the Early Modern World" is an established forum for presenting fresh ideas and original approaches to the field. Interdisciplinary and multidisciplinary in scope, this Ashgate book series strives to reach beyond geographical limitations to explore the experiences of early modern women and the nature of gender in Europe, the Americas, Asia, and Africa. We welcome proposals for both single-author volumes and edited collections which expand and develop this continually evolving field of study.

Titles in the series

Dominican Women and Renaissance Art
Ann Roberts

Education and Women in the Early Modern Hispanic World
Elizabeth Teresa Howe

Intertextual Masculinity in French Renaissance Literature
David P. LaGuardia

Women, Imagination and the Search for Truth in Early Modern France
Rebecca M. Wilkin

English Printing, Verse Translation, and the Battle of the Sexes, 1476–1557
Anne E.B. Coldiron

Imagining Women's Conventual Spaces in France, 1600–1800

The Cloister Disclosed

BARBARA R. WOSHINSKY
University of Miami, USA

ASHGATE

Published by
Ashgate Publishing Limited
Wey Court East
Union Road
Farnham
Surrey, GU9 7PT
England

Ashgate Publishing Company
Suite 420
101 Cherry Street
Burlington
VT 05401-4405
USA

www.ashgate.com

British Library Cataloguing in Publication Data
Woshinsky, Barbara R.
Imagining women's conventual spaces in France, 1600–1800: the cloister disclosed. – (Women and gender in the early modern world)
    1. Monastic and religious life of women – France – History – 17th century. 2. Monastic and religious life of women – France – History – 18th century. 3. Convents in literature. 4. Nuns in literature. 5. Human body in literature. 6. Literature, Modern – 17th century – History and criticism. 7. Literature, Modern – 18th century – History and criticism.
    I. Title II. Series
    809.9'33827190044–dc22

Library of Congress Cataloging-in-Publication Data
Woshinsky, Barbara R.
  Imagining women's conventual spaces in France, 1600–1800: the cloister disclosed / by Barbara R. Woshinsky.
    p. cm.—(Women and gender in the early modern world)
  Includes bibliographical references and index.
  ISBN 978-0-7546-6754-4 (alk. paper)
  1. French literature—16th century—History and criticism. 2. French literature—17th century—History and criticism. 3. Convents in literature. 4. Space and time in literature. 5. Women in literature. I. Title.

PQ239.W67 2010
840.9'35844028—dc22

ISBN 9780754667544 (hbk)

2009052899

Mixed Sources
Product group from well-managed forests and other controlled sources
www.fsc.org Cert no. SA-COC-1565
© 1996 Forest Stewardship Council
FSC

Printed and bound in Great Britain by
MPG Books Group, UK

Contents

To Bill

Acknowledgements

This book could not have been completed without the aid of many individuals and institutions. I wish to thank the Five Colleges Women's Studies Center, Mount Holyoke, MA, for their sabbatical support; the University of Miami, for research grants furthering this project; Dean Michael Halloran and Associate Dean Perry Lee Roberts of the College of Arts and Sciences for helping to defray the cost of reproductions; the members of the Writing Group on Gender in the Early Modern World, especially Anne C. Cruz, Laura Giannetti, Pam Hammons, Maria Stampino and Mihoko Suzuki, for their encouragement and helpful suggestions; Matt Lubeck, for his willing technical aid; Dora Romero, for tracking down recalcitrant references; the staff of the Bibliothèque nationale de France reproductions department, especially Franck Bougamont, for locating illustrations. Thanks as well to Francis Assaf, André Bourrasa, Tom Carr, David Ellison, Donna Kuizinga, Sara Melzer, the sisters of the Monastère Ste-Claire and my husband Bill Turner, for his unfailing faith in my work. Finally, I offer my appreciation to Erika Gaffney, editor at Ashgate Publishing, for her patience and support.

I gratefully acknowledge permission to reprint in this book materials that have appeared in an earlier form elsewhere: "Desert, Fortress, Convent, Body: The Allegorical Architecture of Nervèze's *L'Hermitage de l'Isle saincte*." *Cahiers du XVIIème* X.1. (2005), 67–74, by permission of the editor; "On the Mirror's Edge: Imagining the Body in Pierre de Croix's *Miroir de l'Amour divin*." *Seventeenth Century French Studies* 25 (2003), 37–49, by permission of the editor; "Spatial Ambiguities and Conventual Openings," *Biblio 17* 131 (2002), 113–20, by permission of the editor; and "Convent Parleys: Listening to Women's Voices in Madame de Villedieu's *Mémoires de la vie de Henriette-Sylvie de Molière*." In *Convent Voices*, ed. Thomas M. Carr, Charlottesville: Rookwood Press, EMF, Studies in Modern France 11, 2007, 167–85, by permission of the publisher.

List of Figures

Foreword

We crossed the deserted plateau of the Massif Central in two cars. Little was to be seen; even the sheep seemed to be hiding in the woods. After following the winding, narrow roads for half an hour, we turned onto a farm track leading uphill to a closed gate. Everyone got out: the six guests from the convent hostel and the three nuns. All were dressed in bulky coats and caps to keep out the cold—in the nuns' case they were worn over their religious habits. As we climbed for twenty minutes, I was struggling against the icy wind and puffing from the unaccustomed climb. Finally, in the distance, I spotted a rough structure, almost like a lean-to, built into the hill. This deserted shepherd's hut was our destination—a cloistered space within a landscape the seventeenth century would have called "un désert."

I had arrived in the small town of Mur-de-Barrès a few days earlier. As I was beginning my research on women's conventual spaces in early modern France, I felt the need to experience those spaces from the inside, or as close to the inside as possible. So I started looking for a women's convent that had existed in the same buildings since the seventeenth century. This turned out to be a tall order; a small disturbance had intervened called the French Revolution. But after some searching, I found the perfect place: le monastère Ste-Claire. This establishment had been originally founded by the Clarisse order (Poor Clares) in 1651.[1] They had been expelled from the building in 1792, but another group of Clarisses returned in 1868 and nuns of this order still remain in residence there. I was attracted not only by this architectural continuity, but also by the secluded location and the welcoming tone of their statement. Convent guests stayed in a hostel, a seventeenth-century building a few doors away from the convent itself, and ate their meals in a dining hall run by the sisters. After explaining my project, I had obtained an interview with the *soeur archiviste* who gave me much of the information I have used here. A few days later, we received a special invitation. The convent was located in the center of town, with little space for the sisters to walk. So the abbess had asked and received permission from the local bishop for two nuns at a time to retreat twice a year to a *buron*, or shepherd's hut, lent them by a local doctor. We were invited to accompany the nuns who were about to begin their weeklong retreat. Since the *buron* is considered part of the convent enclosure (*en clôture*),[2] this invitation was a mark of confidence.

---

[1]   The Poor Clares, the female order associated with the Franciscans and founded by Saint Clare of Assisi, celebrated its 500th anniversary in 1993. See *Sainte-Claire en Rouergue*.

[2]   In *clausura* or cloistered space. The concept of *clausura* will be discussed in the Introduction.

We proceeded gingerly across a field populated by cows, and even a bull, which the nuns restrained. The *buron* was a simple two-story structure. Downstairs were the kitchen and cellar; the nuns ate their meals outside under a roofed terrace (Fig. F.1). The same enterprising abbess had also designed a "modern" flush toilet. The nuns proudly showed me how it operated from a cistern above. The upper story contained a room with a simple altar and two curtained cells. Aside from the cistern, there was no running water and no electricity.

This visit upset my basic, almost unconscious preconceptions about conventual spaces, preconceptions I refer to as "architectural literalism." The most important of these are that cloistered nuns live in convents with cloisters, and that nuns must stay within a closed, unitary space delimited by walls, locks, grills and gates. Here, the conventual space was reduced to a nearly symbolic minimalism. Basic signifiers of convent practice were provided: the altar, the cell. As the sisters ate their simple meals, prayed, meditated and walked in the fields, conventual life was carried on miles from the convent.

The next day, I received a note from the archivist: we had apparently passed a further test and were to be admitted *plus en clôture*, into the area of the convent restricted to nuns. We toured the dining room, workrooms, gardens—in fact, the whole convent property. This visit again upset my preconceived ideas. Ste-Claire never occupied a structure built for monastic purposes, and does not contain features traditionally associated with monastic life, such as a beautiful medieval cloister like the one found at the Abbaye de Fontenay (Fig. F.2).

Indeed, until recently it had no cloister at all. As Fig. F.3 shows, the nuns could walk on an upper terrace, but because the convent is built into a hill they were exposed to the view of outsiders—somewhat like the nun in the *Religieuse portugaise*, though the actual Portuguese convent where its fictitious heroine is enclosed does not possess a gallery with a view (see Chapter 6).

The new cloister at Ste-Claire (not shown), originally part of a shed, is non-traditional in design: rather than an open arcaded square, it is an enclosed L-shaped room with large picture windows, more practical in the rude mountain climate. Other modern features of the convent also deviate from "conventional" ideas of construction. The parlors are simple rooms with no separation between the nun and the visitor; both sit at the same table. The effect of simplicity and openness at Ste-Claire can be felt more strongly if one compares it with a medieval monastery church, such as St-Michel de Frigolet, located near St-Rémy de Provence (Fig. F.4).

Is the Monastère Ste-Claire typical? Yes and no. A few wealthy women's convents such as Fontevraud, built by the Bourbon family, were constructed on a traditional Benedictine plan with a cloister. But like the Victorian women's colleges immortalized by Virginia Woolf, women's orders often occupied, and still occupy, buildings which were not designed for that purpose. As Marie-France Hilgar has shown, even St-Cyr, founded in 1682 as "La Maison royale de St-Louis," was not built to a monastery plan. One proposed site of a seventh-century Benedictine convent was rejected in favor of a château

Fig. F.1   *Buron*-retreat for nuns from Monastère Ste-Claire, near Mur-de-Barrès, France. Photo: B. Woshinsky.

formerly belonging to the Sieur de St-Brisson. The château received extensive and costly renovation and refurbishing which made it, according to one observer, "the image of earthly paradise" ["l'image du paradis terrestre"]; but according to its architect, Mansart, the result was "neither a palace nor a convent" ["ni un palais ni un couvent"].

In contrast, the humble and checkered history of Ste-Claire is perhaps closer to the norm for women's convents. It was founded in 1651 in order to supply "l'éducation nécessaire" for the bourgeois girls of an isolated provincial town. The convent's sponsor, François d'Humières, initially gave the nuns two houses. The monastery was probably built around one of them; but a major fire in 1809, and years of neglect and misuse during and after the Revolution, make it very difficult to discern its original plan. Even leaving aside major political upheavals and natural disasters, the history of the successive renovations and alterations to the buildings is extremely complex. For example, an addition built in 1768 to house two parlors is now the location of the dining room and hostel. Only the vast vaulted cellar remains relatively untouched. A building or collection of buildings being remodeled through time is certainly a common occurrence in lay architecture; but it does not fit our architecturally literal model of historically significant, religiously immutable church buildings.

These observations lead directly to my point of departure for this book. Women's convents are, by definition, female spaces. Because of the disparities in wealth and power between men's and women's orders, women often occupied, and made do with, buildings not designed for their use. But this "making do" also enabled the transformation of the conventual space into a place suited to their needs. In this project, the nuns were perhaps aided by a grasp of the symbolic (spiritual in their terms) meaning of *clôture*, which allowed them to negotiate a space within the patriarchal ecclesiastical structure.

The non-literalness of *clôture* is apparent in a work by Teresa of Avila, founder of the Carmelite order. Teresa's *The Interior Castle*, published in 1557, is a direct contemporary response to the Council of Trent's imposition of strict enclosure on women:

> Considering the strict enclosure and the few things you have for your entertainment, my Sisters, and that your buildings are not always as large as would be fitting for your monasteries, I think it will be a consolation for you to delight in the interior castle since without permission from the prioress you can enter and take a walk through it at any time. (195)

Teresa's suggested walk is, of course, allegorical; but the work of the twentieth century nuns of Ste-Claire also demonstrates in a concrete sense that "walls do not a convent make."

Fig. F.2   Cloister, Abbaye de Fontenay. Photo © Adrian Fletcher, www.paradoxplace.com.

Fig. F.3   Rear view, Monastère Ste-Claire. Photo: B. Woshinsky.

Fig. F.4   Eglise St-Michel de Frigolet. Photo: B. Woshinsky.

Introduction/Opening

"A whole history remains to be written of spaces—which would at the same time be the history of powers (both of these terms in the plural)—from the great strategies of geopolitics to the little tactics of the habitat."
—Michel Foucault, "The Eye of Power," in *Power/Knowledge* 149

"… the poet's mastery of enclosed spaces …"
—Alfred Habegger, *My Wars are Laid Away in Books: The Life of Emily Dickinson*. New York: Random House, 2001, 550

In 1563, the Council of Trent issued an edict imposing strict enclosure on women's convents. By 1792, the French Revolutionary regime had closed all monasteries in France and expelled all the religious living within them. These tumultuous changes, occurring over little more than two centuries, fixed the contemporary imagination on enclosed women's spaces. Always an object of fascination, they were regarded with greater intensity than perhaps ever before. This book examines the representation of conventual spaces in seventeenth- and eighteenth-century France within a multi-disciplinary framework of post-Tridentine religious thought, architecture and history. In a larger sense, it seeks to delimit the place of women's enclosure in the early modern imaginary and in our own. I choose to speak of "conventual space" rather than "the convent" because this study includes other female sites of retreat, from the private room or "closet" to the women's refuge, which build on monastic features or functions. The conventual space, as I envision it, is both a real and a symbolic enclosure—a structure encompassing and expressing the religious, political and social powers that affect women's lives, women's responses to these forces, and their active role in shaping their own surroundings. The conventual space is thus a dynamic and dialectical one. Is this space public? Private? Sacred? Is the convent prison or refuge? Does it signify inclusion in the body of the church,[1] or forced enclosure? Or is a prison/refuge dichotomy too narrow? Finally, to what degree, in what sense, could early modern writers achieve the "mastery of enclosed spaces" attributed to the reclusive poet Emily Dickinson in the second epigraph above? These are some of the questions this book addresses.

On the negative side of the refuge/prison dichotomy, the image of the cloister can certainly evoke feelings of constraint, imprisonment, even (etymologically) claustrophobia. Molière's heavy fathers threaten their daughters with the convent if they refuse to marry the man selected for them. The entry for "couvent" in Furetière's 1696 dictionary confirms this social usage: "It is said in threatening a disobedient girl, that she will be placed in the depths of a convent in spite of

---

[1]   As literally constructed by the anchorage: see below, 18–20.

herself, to mean that she will be made a nun against her wishes; that she must marry a suitor offered her, or [enter] a convent" ["... on dit en menaçant une fille désobéissante, qu'on la mettra dans le cul d'un couvent, pour dire qu'on la fera religieuse malgré elle; qu'il faut qu'elle épouse un parti qu'on lui propose, ou un couvent"]. *Aut maritus, aut murus.* In Spanish religious communities as well, according to Concha Torres Sánchez, cloistered life had more in common with physical and mental sacrifice than with earthly paradise ["tenía más de sacrificio fisico y psiquico que de paraiso terrenal," Torres Sánchez 193].

However, I do not concur with Alvin J. Schmidt's global assertion that nuns were all cloistered against their will by a sexist church (*Veiled and Silenced: How Culture Shaped Sexist Theology*). Rather, the convent offered an alternative for women, a feminine space where they were sometimes able to achieve a degree of agency and autonomy—sheltered, if never wholly free, from the male gaze and male control.[2] Conventual enclosure also bore some practical benefits. When women are locked in, men are also locked out, curbing voyeurism and the abductions that really took place from convents, especially in the early Middle Ages.[3] In addition, the cloister afforded women practically their only alternative to the often oppressive institution of marriage.[4] This situation may not have changed significantly in early modern Europe. As Elizabeth Rapley affirms: "it is therefore reasonable to suppose that many of the women who became nuns ... did so as an alternative to marrying" (*Les Dévotes* 19).[5] The exemplary case from Spanish Colonial history is that of Sor Juana Inés de la Cruz (1648?–95). A member of the court of the viceroy of New Spain (Mexico), Sor Juana chose at the age of 20 to enter the convent of San Jerónimo in order to escape marriage and

---

[2]   Barbara B. Diefendorf puts this point well: "However foreign these convents may be to our present sensibilities, we need to try to connect imaginatively with the goals of those women who, far from being forced to spend their life behind a convent's high walls, sought this seclusion as necessary to their spiritual ambitions and, in the course of pursuing these ambitions, discovered a leadership role usually denied the female sex" ("Discerning Spirits" 245).

[3]   Nuns were actually abducted from convents during the Middle Ages, which was a motive given for their enclosure at that time. See Johnson, *Equal in Monastic Profession* 125, 130. In the early modern period, the argument that strict *clausura* protected women from the violence of the age was also commonly used. See Rapley, *Dévotes* 27.

[4]   As Elizabeth Robertson observes, "Given the quality of medieval married life, it does not seem unreasonable to think that women might find the religious life ... an attractive alternative to marriage. Nuns at first had had educational opportunities unavailable to women elsewhere. They could even write religious works themselves" (170).

[5]   Torres Sánchez makes a similar observation concerning Spain: "The so-called 'brides of Christ' in the Spanish tradition were women who preferred entering a convent to marrying under unequal circumstances" ["Las llamadas en la tradición española 'esposas de Cristo' eran las mujeres que preferían profesar en un convento antes que casarse en condiciones desiguales," Torres Sánchez 80].

be able to continue her studies and writing.[6] In the convent, she composed not only religious works but secular love poetry, and carried on an extensive social life and correspondence. According to most accounts, Juana enjoyed this freedom for 25 years until, in 1693, she was forced to sign a new profession of faith and was stripped of all her personal possessions, including her 4,000-book library (Harvey 120).[7]

Nevertheless, the convent was no "feminotopia" in an idealized sense of the word.[8] Despite its isolation, the cloister constituted in some ways a microcosm of the larger society, replicating its power structures, economic strictures and social hierarchies. Thus, a study of the convent can contribute to the "history of spaces—which would at the same time be a history of powers" called for by Michel Foucault in the first epigraph to this chapter. Convents were governed internally by a monastery council, usually consisting of the superior or abbess, the sub-abbess, the mistress of novices and three more nuns appointed by the abbess. The only decision in which the whole community was allowed to participate was the election of a new superior. In Teresa of Avila's *Constitution for the Descalced Carmelites*, the abbess was accorded very broad powers to govern the convent "in spiritual as in temporal matters. Teresa advises, "With a mother's love, seek to be loved in order to be obeyed" ["así en lo espiritual como en lo temporal, con el amor de madre. Procure ser amada, para que sea obedecida," Teresa of Avila, *Constituciones*, Chapter 9, in *Obras completas* 832]. The constitution employs the word "mother," which was indeed spoken by nuns in addressing their superior; the official term "abbess," still used in French convents, comes from the word "abbot," or father. In the Benedictine rule, the monks are told to obey their abbot as a father; and as in the patriarchal family, the mother (or abbess) of the women's convent has considerable delegated authority over her household.[9] Yet again, despite a hierarchical structure congruent with their times, convents were "feminotopic" in the etymological sense of "women's places" as well as in the Foucauldian one of alternative communities.[10]

On an economic level, the convent also participated in the realities of the surrounding society. To maintain the house financially, new postulants, as "brides of Christ," were asked to pay a dowry. The distinction between the upper-class

---

[6]   Juana had first entered a Carmelite institution, but found the discipline too restrictive.

[7]   This has recently been challenged by Mexican historian Elías Trabulse. See *La muerte de sor Juana*. Mexico, D.F.: Centro de Estudios de Historia de México Condumex, 1999.

[8]   I invented this word partly as a play on "heterotopia," Michel Foucault's term for alternative spaces on the fringes of the social network. See Foucault, "Of Other Spaces," *Diacritics* 16 (Spring, 1986), 24–7. I have since seen it used by other writers to denote an ideal female society. In my sense, however, a feminotopia is not necessarily utopic; rather, it is a community wholly or largely composed of and/or governed by women. To distinguish between the two, I call a utopic female space a "femin*u*topia." See Chapter 3.

[9]   For more on the power of the abbess, see Chapter 6.

[10]   As Helen Hills argues, "participation in religious life gave [nuns] access to a 'public' space at a time when such spaces were generally inaccessible to women" (*Invisible City* 8).

nuns who were dowried and those who were not was marked by an architectural metonymy. Women who could afford the dowry became *religieuses de choeur*, or choir nuns, with full privileges. Those who could not afford to pay were taken in as *soeurs converses* or lay sisters. The *soeurs converses* performed the role of servants; they were not allowed into the choir, or sanctuary, to pray, but sat in the nave of the monastic church (Torres Sánchez 128; Johnson 178). In her reform of the Carmelites, Teresa tried to eliminate, or at least soften, this stratified system, but was unable to do so, for reasons of social entrenchment or financial necessity. Nevertheless, with all its faults, the convent offered a possibility of self-realization for women: because of the respect accorded the religious life, nuns held a social status superior to that of single women, and equal to that of wives. Indeed, according to Hills, "Despite [the] picture of uniform ecclesiastic repression, the general consensus is that in convents women were freer, more independent, and better educated than in any other sphere open to them" (*Invisible City* 9).

The ambiguities of convent life would take many books to tease out; but the apparent contradiction between prison and refuge can be, if not resolved, at least reframed, by placing conventual enclosure within the larger context of the power struggles taking place within the patriarchal ruling structure. The Council of Trent, by enforcing the enclosure of women in convents, safeguarded the family patrimony and found an "honorable" way to dispose of the demographic surplus of marriageable young girls.[11] The council of bishops who ordered convent gates to be locked in the late Renaissance seemingly had little in common with the Revolutionary government which forced those gates open two hundred years later; but both acts represent efforts to control women by removing them from participation in the public sphere. Conventual enclosure breaks women permanently away from their families, for whom they are legally dead,[12] and places them under the control of the Church; in

---

[11]   Torres Sánchez remarks in reference to Spain: "Seventeenth-century society encouraged female enclosure as a *means to control the mechanisms of honor and to safeguard family patrimony*, and, above all, to channel the excess young girls impossible to marry off according to this code of honor. Such enclosure could not be accomplished in just any way, but rather within established norms which, moreover, confirmed it as what it was: *an instrument of power*" ["La sociedad del siglo XVII fomentó el encerramiento femenino como *forma de controlar los mecanismos de la honra y salvaguardar el patrimonio familiar* y, sobre todo, para encauzar el excedente de doncellas imposibles de casar según este código de honor. Pero este encierro no se podía hacer de cualquier manera, sino dentro de unas normas establecidas que, además, lo confirmaban como lo que era: *un instrumento de poder*," 140; italics added]. While family honor was perhaps not emphasized so explicitly, in other respects Torres Sánchez's analysis holds true for France, as the institution of "civil death" indicates (see n12).

[12]   Upon contracting solemn vows, monks and nuns entered a state of civil death, making them "non-persons in secular society" (Rapley, *The Dévotes* 39). This status was actually demanded by wealthier families, who did not wish their cloistered daughters suddenly to return and claim succession rights or—even worse!—marry, complicating the family inheritance and causing endless lawsuits.

fact, one of the papacy's motives for convent reform was to wrest them away from the aristocratic families who sometimes held them as a kind of fiefdom. Convent abolition, on the other hand, by restoring women to their "natural" roles of wife and childbearer, strengthens the husband's authority as model and foundation of the bourgeois state. It is no coincidence, in my view, that Diderot, whose *Religieuse* prepared ideologically for the end of conventual enclosure, also wrote popular "bourgeois dramas" that emphasized the importance of the *père de famille*.[13] Thus, diametrically opposed changes in religious structures can reflect attempts, whether by church, government or family, to contain women. The shifts of power from Divine Right absolutism to Revolutionary regime to bourgeois monarchy brought about changes in the manner, not the fact, of their containment—or attempted containment—whether in the home or within convent walls.

With Diderot, we have moved from the realm of history to that of fiction. In this book, I have chosen to study, not the women's communities themselves or even the writings of convent women, but the place of these communities in the cultural and literary imagination. After a period of neglect, the first two topics—convent history and writing—are now the object of intensive research. Torres Sánchez has correctly remarked that the 1980s and 1990s produced a "veritable avalanche" of historical studies on women's religious life (10). The reader will find many of these works cited in the bibliography and discussed in the text and notes. The writings of cloistered women have also been subjected to intense scrutiny, notably in Nicolas Paige's *Being Interior* (2001). To my knowledge, however, no one has systematically studied the relationship between women's convents as architectural and social institutions and their depiction in early modern French literature.[14] Bernard Beugnot's *Discours de*

---

[13]   Johnson sees this shift from aristocratic to bourgeois ethics as already affecting the status of women during the Middle Ages. "The public/private dichotomy was paralleled by ecclesiastical authorities' efforts to subject nuns to more rigorous cloistering. The good nun was the cloistered nun whose purity reflected well on the church, just as the good wife reflected well on her husband" (Johnson 256–7).

[14]   Although explorations of gendered space in early modern literary studies have generally lagged behind these other disciplines, there are some exceptions. The title of Joan DeJean's *Tender Geographies* reposes on the spatial construction of Mlle de Scudéry's celebrated *carte du tendre*, the allegorical map from her novel *Clélie*. In a chapter entitled "Women's Places, Women's Spaces," DeJean presents the salons as private spaces controlled by women. Similarly, in the first chapter of *Cartesian Women*, entitled "Gender and Discursive Space(s) in the Seventeenth Century," Erica Harth contrasts female *ruelles* with male *cabinets*. In closer relation to the topic of this book, Peggy Kamuf investigates "fictions of women's enclosure" and "[woman's] attempt to make a space for her erotic experience" (*Fictions of Feminine Desire* xv, 8). Spatial studies of individual works, such as *La Princesse de Clèves*, have also begun to appear (see Chapter 4). However, the relation between material and metaphorical space in critical works concerned with early modern women is sometimes confused and contradictory. In *Louise Labé, Marguerite de Navarre et Madame de Lafayette: trois voix féminines et espaces féminins retrouvés*, Mahdia Ben Salem says of Lafayette: "She offers her heroine a *symbolic textual space* of freedom to allow her to analyze her feelings. She proves that the young woman possesses a private place to hide …" ["Elle offre

la retraite au dix-septième siècle, while giving an excellent overview of how retreat was talked about in the seventeenth century, touches only briefly on actual *spaces* of retreat and even less on the position of women within those spaces. In contrast, I seek to illuminate the unique place the convent occupies in the early modern imaginary, in the context of space, gender and power.

My approach to this multifaceted topic applies, within a metonymic framework, elements of spatial analysis derived from recent research in the social sciences. Like Roberta Gilchrist's work on the archaeology of convent architecture, this book concentrates attention on openings, passageways, and places of encounter—which are also main features of literary construction. As well as an analytical tool, metonymy supplies the organizational principle and a pivotal point for my study, allowing me to move back and forth from buildings to (women's) bodies to books. The works chosen fall into three main categories: canonical texts which have not been closely read from the perspective of conventual representation; several rare texts which help fill in the general trends of this representation; and finally, works by women authors, known or unknown, that sometimes contest these general trends. By placing the reductive and allusive device of metonymy in a central position, I wish to emphasize that the aim is not to analyze the works chosen as so-called reflections of historical conditions, but to discover how they dance around, diverge from, even contradict, those conditions. Further, it is often these points of divergence which illuminate most clearly the ideological lines of the texts and the surrounding culture. This introductory chapter will now proceed with a brief history of monasticism and the material forms it has taken. I will then explore philosophical and social concepts of space and further develop my own approach to a theory of gendered spaces, and a method for studying them. Finally, I will outline the book's structure and content.

The History of Women's Monastic Enclosure

Women have always played a prominent role in monastic life. Early Christian congregations contained ascetics of both sexes; women were frequent visitors to Egyptian monasteries, and some, such as the Melanias, founded convents of their own (Derwas 65–6). In Roman Gaul, female monasteries existed at Apt, Marseilles and Arles, as well as in Anglo-Saxon England. During the seventh-century Merovingian dynasty, double monasteries like Chelles grouped men's and women's establishments under the rule of an abbess. In fact, according to Gold, "In this early period of Christian monasticism, cooperation between monks and nuns seems to have been the norm" (78). By the High Middle Ages,

---

un *espace textuel symbolique* de la liberté à son héroïne pour lui permettre d'analyser ses sentiments. Elle prouve que la jeune femme jouit d'un endroit privé pour se cacher … ." 172]. In two consecutive sentences, Ben Salem moves from a symbolic to an architectural view of space without any satisfactory transition. What is needed in literary studies is an approach distinguishing the material from the metaphorical while incorporating both.

however, the male church hierarchy had restricted the power and autonomy of convent women. Monastic confession, which previously could be heard by an abbess, was abolished in the thirteenth century. After that date, penance had to be imposed by a priest, which meant admitting a man into the conventual space. Further, double monasteries ruled by abbesses had mainly disappeared from France by the end of the eleventh century.[15] The new, exclusively female convents that replaced the double monasteries were smaller, poorer and more subject to the jurisdiction of male ecclesiastics: Gilchrist notes that at Thetford in Norfolk, "A site considered inadequate for three monks was supporting at least twenty-six nuns in the thirteenth century" (44). Women's establishments took two main forms. In the closed or reformed convents, which sometimes contained cloisters as an architectural feature, the inhabitants led rigorous lives cut off from the world. An example is the first Cluniac convent, founded at Marcigny by St Hugh in 1056, and called a "jocund prison" by Peter the Venerable (Lawrence 220). Because they could no longer go around soliciting lands or money like abbots, women under strict enclosure became more economically dependent on the bishop or other clergy, and the chronic financial and numerical disparities between male and female monasteries increased: in late medieval England, nunneries had become outnumbered by male monasteries by six to one (Gilchrist 61).

Although strict enclosure is the defining factor for both women's conventual life and its representation in the early modern era, in the context of the long history of Western monasticism this practice was both recent and short-lived. More precisely, while the principle of clausura had always existed for both male and female religious, it was rarely implemented fully. However, the Tridentine directive for strict female enclosure draws on a long tradition of such pronouncements. The first attempt to formalize the enclosing of French nuns was made by Caesarius, Bishop of Arles (468/70–542). Of the 73 articles in his *Regula ad moniales*, nineteen deal with regulations for full clausura. Caesarius's *Rule* for monks has neither the detail nor the strictness of his rule for women, in which we find all the characteristics of modern enclosure; Pope Boniface II drew on it in composing his influential bull, *Pericoloso*. By the eleventh and twelfth centuries, "we see a great variety of

---

[15]   Exceptions to the decline of women's houses and double monasteries in the late twelfth century generally resulted from the intervention of French monarchs. Such was the case for the convent of Poissy near Paris. In 1298, the same year the bull *Pericoloso* was issued, the Capetian King Philip the Fair (Philippe le Bel) had the old Augustinian monastery at Poissy transformed into a Dominican priory, to honor the canonization of his grandfather Louis IX (St. Louis). The convent was generously provided with endowments and privileges and richly decorated in the manner of the Royal Abbey at Royaumont. Louis IX's heart is buried at Royaumont, but Philip consigned his heart to Poissy. The convent is described in a detailed poem, *Le livre du dit de Poissy*, written by Christine de Pizan after a visit to her daughter who was a nun there (Labarge 111). The vast Royal Abbey of Fontevraud also opened its doors at a time when most double monasteries directed by women had already been closed. Gold argues that Fontevraud was not a double monastery in the strict sense, but a monastic complex (101–2). See below, 16–17.

evidence in the sources of growing concern, even perhaps obsession, with the need for rigorous, unbroken active enclosure for women religious" (Schulenberg 63). This trend culminated in 1298 in *Pericoloso*. This papal pronouncement mandated total clausura in order that "the nuns be able to serve God more freely, wholly separated from the public and worldly gaze and occasions for lasciviousness having been removed, may most diligently safeguard their hearts and bodies in complete chastity" (*Periculoso*, quoted in Makowski 30). *Periculoso* represents an attempt by Boniface II to reassert the power of the papacy at a precarious time when kings like Philippe le Bel were challenging its authority, and growing religious movements were embracing evangelical ideals of renunciation of private possessions and life in common, but not necessarily in clausura (Lawrence 164).[16] In Makowski's view, *Periculoso* was also an effort to control "unruly women" for whom Boniface felt a personal "antipathy" (40). This papal bull would in turn serve as the basis for the Council of Trent's enclosure of nuns in 1563, during another period of challenge to Catholic orthodoxy.

The dialectic of opening and closing, innovation and reform described above repeated itself throughout the later Middle Ages and much of the Renaissance: despite the plethora of ecclesiastical edicts and rules enjoining it, strict enclosure was never fully enforced.[17] According to Penelope Johnson, "the nunnery walls served communities as permeable membranes rather than watertight seals" (152). As stated above, it was imperative for abbesses or nuns to leave their convent at times, in order to conduct business necessary to its very survival. The rules for Fontevraud imply that clausura there was not absolute: "one provision, for example, ordains that the cloistered nuns should always maintain silence, except for those who attend to business on the outside" (Gold 99). The lay community seemed to accept this reality. Some laxness in the observance of enclosure did not trouble people unduly; the brunt of the criticism came from priests and the church hierarchy (Johnson 150–63). Even the 1298 edict of Boniface II was a "counsel of perfection" rather than an order. Hence, some unreformed convents remained where women could live in uncloistered retreat, able to receive visitors, read, and instruct themselves. Although few in number, and often only an option for upper-class women, it can be said that these houses kept the idea of convents alive as a model affording women some degree of dignity and autonomy.

The definitive tightening up on women's religious institutions did not take place until the late sixteenth and early seventeenth centuries, as part of the Counter- or Catholic Reformation.[18] In response to the challenges of Protestantism as well as to

---

[16]   Clausura denotes both the practice of enclosing monks or nuns and the cloistered space restricted to the religious within a monastery.

[17]   For more on the historical debate surrounding the enforcement of medieval clausura, see Jane Tibbets Schulenburg, "Strict Active Enclosure," 69 ff.

[18]   The semantics of "Catholic-" vs. "Counter-Reformation" have been debated for well over a hundred years. The term "Counter-Reformation" was coined by Leopold von Ranke, a nineteenth-century German Protestant historian. Ranke viewed the actions taken by the

internal pressures for change, the Catholic bishops held council at the Italian city of Trent (Trentino). One of the issues taken up was monastic reform. The Council reaffirmed Pope Boniface VIII's thirteenth-century imposition of strict enclosure on women, with all the force of the Church behind it: those who broke their vows were threatened with excommunication, eternal damnation and "calling in the help of the secular arm if need be," presumably to recapture escaped nuns (Makowski 128). These stern edicts were not necessarily implemented at once. As Elizabeth Rapley observes, "The half-century after Trent was a period of hesitation. It was not immediately certain that the Church would enforce in practice what it had laid down in law" (*The Dévotes* 28). In Spain, Teresa de Avila's reform of the Carmelite order had brought strictly enforced enclosure. But in France, where the wars of religion were still raging, the Catholic Reformation did not begin to take hold until the early seventeenth century, and the decrees of Trent were not accepted by the French Assembly of Clergy until 1615 (Rapley 21). The continuing fluidity of conventual spaces will have its affect on their representation: accounts range from lascivious openness to penitential strictness, depending on the writer's anxieties or fantasies. Before entering into an examination of these accounts, it is necessary to determine what we mean by "space" in an early modern context, and how postmodern approaches might help open up the conventual space to our gaze.

Catholic Church, such as the reorganization of the Inquisition in Italy in 1542, as attempts to counter Protestant advances. Later in the century, another German Protestant historian, Wilhelm Maurenbecker, "discovered significant [Catholic] reform efforts antedating 1517" (Birely, *The Refashioning of Catholicism* 5). For this reason, Maurenbecker suggested the alternate term "Catholic Reform." In his foundational study "Catholic Reformation or Counter-Reformation?" Hubert Jedin attempted to reconcile the two views by confining Catholic Reform to issues specifically addressed by Trent. In my view, it is impossible either to limit the scope of Catholic reform to the edicts of Trent, or to make a sharp distinction between what happened inside and outside of it. Though the Council of Trent is a response to the changing world of early modern Christianity, it is also part of an ongoing cycle of reform recurring periodically throughout Catholic history. For Birely, the upsurge in piety, spirituality and the founding of new orders in the sixteenth and seventeenth centuries were "little directly related to Trent and Tridentine reforms" (250). For this reason, Birely refers to "Early modern Catholicism" as an overarching phenomenon of which Catholic Reform and Counter Reformation are parts (Birely 3). On the other hand, while many decisions to counter Protestantism and propagate Catholicism were taken outside the context of Trent, some grew out of Tridentine principles. I find all of these terms useful, depending on the context. In this book, "Catholic Reformation" refers to the internal, grass-roots changes that took place in early modern Catholicism, and "Counter-Reformation" to the more reactive, even combative, actions of the Church, from verbal polemics to coercion and forced reconversions of "heretics" (Jedin 41). Sometimes these terms overlap: thus, while the Council of Trent was convoked in order to "counter" Protestant reform, the changes following upon Trent can be seen as manifestations of both the Catholic Reformation and the Counter-Reformation. On Counter-Reformation and Catholic Reform, see also Jean Delumeau, *Catholicism Between Luther and Voltaire* (London: Burns & Oates, 1977).

Spatial Explorations: Spaces and Places

According to Anthony Vidler, "Space, in contemporary discourse, as in lived experience, has taken on an almost palpable existence" (167). But this "existence" is rife with ambiguities that dictionary definitions can exacerbate rather than clarify. For example, the Robert dictionary defines *espace* as "a more or less circumscribed place where something can be located" ["lieu plus ou moins délimité où peut se situer quelque chose"]—an affirmation that raises more questions than it answers. For instance, does space exist independently, or only in relation to "something else?" What lines can be traced between philosophical, scientific and spiritual concepts of spatiality? How do notions of space and place intersect, collide or dialogue?[19] Finally, what congruences or incongruences appear between contemporary and early modern spatiality, and how best can we understand early modern spatial concepts while maintaining (of necessity) our own conceptual perspective? In order to clarify these issues, it is necessary to make some distinctions between contemporary and historical notions of space.

The current proliferation of spatial language rests on a transformation of the definition of space with Kant at the end of the eighteenth century. Kantian space is not just a material but, more important, a mental structure underpinning our perceptions of the world—"an a priori form of our (external) sense knowledge" (Brugger 383). Kant maintains that space and time are not objective entities; rather, space is performance, "a [mental] activity as opposed to a property or relation attaching to objects themselves" (Melnick 383). It is this imagined space-representation, rather than real extension, which underlies current usage. The post-Kantian definition of space as a *cosa mentale* informs Merleau-Ponty's phenomenology, Bachelard's "poetics of space," Bourdieu's "schemes of perception and thought" (15), the geographers' *espace vécu*, as well as ubiquitous contemporary coinings like "social space," "inner space" or Blanchot's *espace littéraire*, which hover between metaphor and mental construct.[20] This perceptual framework also supports the notion of models or "archetypes" that structure our imagining of spatial relations (Zumthor 112, 338–9).[21]

---

[19]   Distinctions between space and place can become severely blurred in post-modern discourse. For Linda McDowell, "places are contested, fluid and uncertain … . It is socio-spatial practices that define places," not a set of coordinates on a map (McDowell 4). An extreme version of this identification of terms comes from Mona Domosh's *Putting Women in Place*. Domosh overrides any distinction between spatiality and locality, saying space "refers to the three-dimensionality of life—to its material form;" places are "spaces invested with meaning … we might say that 'spaces' become 'places' when we have some personal association with them" (Domosh xxii).

[20]   Without crediting any philosophical origin, the geographer R. Brunet echoes Kant's view of space as a product of human activity (*Les mots de la géographie*, s.v. "espace géographique").

[21]   In a somewhat critical review of Georges Matoré's *L'espace humain*, Gérard Genette distinguishes between "the light poetic touchings of a deep reverie" and "a socialized 'zone'

Premodern spatial models, however, lacked these figurative extensions. Plato conceived of space as "pure, unsupported extension" existing independently of the bodies within it (Aristotle, *Physics* xxviii). Aristotle's more relative view, however, was dominant throughout the Middle Ages.[22] Following upon Galileo's discoveries at the end of the sixteenth century, French classical discourse conflated space (*espace*) with extension (*étendue*); it was perceived as an astronomical, almost abstract, void. Furetière's dictionary affirms this view, stating that "space signifies in general an infinite extension of place" ["espace signifie en général, estendue infinie de lieu"]. Hence, classical space lacks the figurative richness the term holds today: definitions of it are generally brief and dry. Hatzfeld's *Dictionnaire générale de la langue française du XVIIe siècle jusqu'à nos jours* does give one metaphorical example from Mme de Sévigné: "you have given too much space to your imagination." However, most metaphorical usages of *espace* in French classical language are not spatial at all, but temporal, such as in the expression *espace de temps*, "duration, passage of time" (Dubois and Lagane).

However, this lack of a classical spatial imaginary is only apparent. Looking deeper, one discovers a richly developed realm of inner spiritual spaces, expressed through a different lexicon. Whereas Galileo or Descartes construed space in an objective, scientific sense, seventeenth-century spiritual vocabulary frequently employs the word *intérieur* or other metaphors of internal extension. In a kind of Baroque mirror image, these metaphors open up a limitless interior space. As Nicolas Paige states, "Human insides acquire here characteristics more commonly associated with the outside—vastness, openness, infinite expansion— as if characteristics of the divinity had been transferred onto and introjected into the subject" (*Being Interior* 3). Thus, while they would not have used such a phrase, intimations of an "inner space," containing or comprehending physical extension, are central to early modern spirituality.

This three-dimensional expansion of the *intérieur* is accentuated by expressions denoting depth: for example, Mère Anne du Saint-Sacrement Viole is said to have

---

... a sort of social rhetoric of space" ["les affleurements poétiques d'une rêverie profonde (et) une 'zone' ... socialisée ... une sorte de rhétorique sociale de l'espace," *Figures* 104]. Without denying the importance of this distinction, I contend that on a deeper level the Kantian notion of subjective space supports both.

[22]   For Aristotle, space (and void, which the philosopher treated similarly) were not meaningful terms. This view (or, more precisely, non-view) so dominated the Middle Ages that to a large extent, medieval thought lacked any spatial concept at all: in old French, the word "espace" was rarely used (Zumthor 51). In the Renaissance, however, scientists developed a cosmology of space closer to both the Platonic and the modern vision. For Pico della Mirandola, space is "something that exists independently of the physical world" (Sorabji 28): a void to be filled with, or perhaps transformed into, the substances contained within it. Newton will agree: "Space had existed without properties until, at the time of creation, God bestowed properties on it" (Sorabji 39). Finally, refuting the Aristotelian reduction of space to place, Descartes argued in his *Principles of Philosophy* that there is only one extension, viewed alternately as space or body.

"penetrated the depths of the soul of her young protegee" Madame de Combalet, who came to her for spiritual guidance (Diefendorf 255). In *Le fond du coeur: Figures de l'espace intérieur au XVIIe siècle* (1991), Benedetta Papasogli exhaustively analyzes the role of these "architectural metaphors" in the moral philosophy of the time (9n3). Finally, seventeenth-century figures of cells, as well as expressing spiritual depth metaphorically, also suggest a continuity with the pre-modern spatialization of memory: Aristotle portrayed memory as a "storehouse," and Dante's gloss of the *Aeneid* reads Aeneas's visit to the underworld as a descent into the "cells of memory" guarded by Proserpina.[23] In contrast to these classical borrowings, other early modern metaphors cited by Papasogli show a reaction to new astronomical and geographical explorations: the interior is a "small world," "new world" or "region of new discovery" ["petit monde," 148; "nouveau monde," "région de nouvelle découverte," 233].

While metaphorical evocations of space and extension in seventeenth-century discourse are expressed, for the most part, through indirection and allusion, a figurative weight falls directly on the lexicon of localization: *endroit, lieu, place*. The words *endroit* and *lieu* (English "place," "spot," "location") convey some spatial associations: thus *lieu*, like English "place," can designate an empty space. Yet French notions of place remain true to the medieval/Aristotelian concept: place must be occupied, or at least defined, in relation to its occupancy (as in *place vide*).[24] Moreover, unlike space, place is by origin and usage a social and architectural construct: its etymology, like that of the Italian "piazza," is from the Latin *platea*, a wide public thoroughfare. The very extensive entries for "place" in both classical and modern French dictionaries lay out the boundaries of a semantic structure which ranges from the physical to the metaphoric. For example, Littré's definition, "the space occupied or occupiable by one person" is first illustrated literally by "une place au théâtre" [a theater seat], then figuratively by "une place au soleil" [a place in the sun] and "tenir une grande place" [to occupy a high social position]. If, according to Aristotle, "place is the measure of positioning," the seventeenth century understands this definition in a social context (Sorabji 208). Thus, classical discourse of place explicitly encompasses social meanings drawn from, and taking precedence over, the physical. Aristotelian claims that "each thing moves to its own place … everything remains naturally in its proper place" (*Physics* IV.1 208b10–12), meant as descriptions of the physical world, are recast as social metonymies, congruent with the ideals of a hierarchical society. This sense of social positioning, carried over into English, still remains in formulae like "it's not my place to say anything" or "he's afraid he'll lose his place." While such phrases appear dated in modern English usage, similar spatial representations of a

---

[23]   On this topic, see John M. Kerr, *Proserpinan Memory in Dante and Chaucer* (Dissertation, University of Notre Dame, 2001). On Aristotle's spatialization of memory, see Frances Yates, *The Art of Memory* (Chicago: University of Chicago Press, 1966), 34.

[24]   In Aristotelian philosophy, place [*topos*] is defined as the location of an object: in Richard Sorabji's words, "something in which it is possible for there to be body" (Sorabji 132).

hierarchical society are central to seventeenth-century writing, as the description of the court in *La Princesse de Clèves* witnesses.

To summarize the preceding analysis, *espace* in the seventeenth century is generally confined to the scientific realm of extension "out there"; *place* holds many of the metaphoric social connotations of our "social space"; and inner experience is connoted by a metaphorical or metonymic *intérieur*. While keeping these earlier meanings in mind, as denizens of our own time we need to accept some of the current metaphorical usages of "space" and "place" as both inevitable and useful. My own work is "modern" in that it falls into a general effort to integrate a spatial dimension into fields that have traditionally been historical and diachronic. For clarity, in this book I consider "space" as "space within" and "place" as "place where." In other words, place is primarily architectural or geographical location: the convent of Fontevraud or the Tate Modern are places. Space, on the other hand, is social and subjective: in Michel de Certeau's terms, "space is a practiced place" created by human activity (117). In the context of my work, conventual space implies someone inside, or someone outside looking in (or trying to look in, or imagining they are looking in)—witness the complex narrative visualizations of the *Lettres portugaises*. While the classical age might not have used the terms in exactly the same way, the issue of positioning without or within was certainly paramount in their social consciousness, just as the modern usage of "inner space" connects to a spiritual *intérieur*.

Beyond the lexical plane, how can current discourse be reconciled with, or accommodated to, early modern spatial concepts? In a scientific sense, even following the discovery of relativity and sub-atomic particles, Cartesian space is still familiar territory to us; but in other respects their space is not ours. An apparent counter-example may help clarify this point. In two sentences from Pascal's *Pensées*, the word *espace* seemingly acquires a mental and spiritual dimension as literal, astronomical extension is evoked within the subjective framework of the narrative voice. The first example, placed under the rubric "Roseau pensant," magnifies the power of thought: "By space, the universe surrounds and engulfs me like a point; through thought, I comprehend it" ["Par l'espace, l'univers me comprend et m'engloutit comme un point; par la pensée je la comprends," *Pensées* Sellier 143]. In a play on the word *comprendre* difficult to convey in English, the infinite universe first surrounds the passive self ["me comprend"], swallows it ["m'engloutit"] and finally reduces it to a one-dimensional point. In the second segment of the sentence, "par la pensée je la comprends," the tables are turned: the narrative "I" has become the speaking grammatical subject that contains the universe by understanding it, in the two senses of *comprendre*. While the above quotation is balanced and rational, the second example—"these infinite spaces frighten me" ["ces espaces infinis m'effraient," Sellier 233]—speaks directly from and to the heart. Despite his resistance to Descartes, Pascal's incorporation of spatial vocabulary into a subjective context maintains a Cartesian distinction between space, still pre-existing objectively "out there," and our inner understanding or reaction to it. The twenty-first century play on the words "inner and outer" space would not have been possible three or four centuries earlier. Thus, I argue that the classical analogy, and possible origin, of our subjectivized "inner space" is not Cartesian *espace* but spiritual metaphors and metonymies of the *intérieur*. For instance, the expression "le fond de mon coeur," which was common currency in seventeenth-century spiritual language (Paige 58), is still present in contemporary usage: viz. the popular song of the mid-twentieth century entitled "I Love You— From the Bottom of my Heart." As we tread the inner spaces of song, fable, Jungian myth or our own dreams, perhaps we are, all unknowing, walking in our spiritual ancestors' footsteps.

Sacred Spaces: Desert and Cloister

We will now turn from abstract definitions to the concrete sacred spaces at the origin of the early modern convent. Sacred localities have existed in all cultures. Many, like Jerusalem, Mecca, Lourdes or Mount Fuji, have been sanctified by historical or legendary events; others form part of the natural world. For the religions that sprang up in the Middle East, the most significant sacred spaces were the garden and the desert, or deserted (wild) place. Like many religiously charged spaces, the desert has an ambivalent meaning: in the Hebrew Bible, it is the place of wild beasts, evil spirits and death; but it is also the place of the covenant with Israel. According to George H. Williams:

> the wilderness or desert will be interpreted variously as a place of protection, a place of contemplative retreat, again as one's inner nature or ground of being and … as the ground itself of the divine being … in its negative sense the wilderness will be interpreted as the wasteland, and as the world of the unredeemed, and as the realm or phase of punitive or purgative preparation for salvation. (6)

He continues, "the desert was, in effect, for the ascetics as for the biblical Israelites at once the haunt of demons and the realm of bliss and of harmony with the creaturely world" (41). Following in the footsteps of the Jewish ascetics, early Christian anchorites fled to the Egyptian desert and other wildernesses to seek in solitary reclusion the God who had spoken to Jacob, Elijah, John the Baptist and others.[25] Even when, in the fourth century, Egypt and Palestine were centers of organized monasticism, small groups of hermits continued to live largely isolated existences. Some of these hermits and wanderers were women. The most celebrated anchoress was probably Mary of Egypt (344–421), who lived in solitude near the Jordan River for 47 years. Another legendary figure is Theodora, a married woman who abandoned her husband and, disguising herself as a man, dwelled in a monastery

---

[25] St. Anthony, the prototype of the Christian hermit, went out into the Egyptian desert in 270 C.E., where he first lived in a tomb, then in an abandoned fort. St. Simeon the Stylite allegedly stood for 36 years on a pillar, becoming something of an architectural monument himself.

outside Alexandria. Syncletica, who lived in a tomb not far from Alexandria, "has the distinction of being the first Christian heroine to be the subject of a biography" (*Catholic Encyclopedia*, "Eremitism" 140). For such religious seekers, the ideal monastic space was a *désert* in the classical French sense, a social void to be filled with God's presence. The Greek word *monasterion*, which we think of as a structure for a religious community, originally designated the isolated dwelling of these single recluses, who flocked to the desert in the fourth century.

The New Testament teaches us to closet ourselves in a private chamber in order to examine our souls and hold converse with God;[26] but at the same time, the developing Western church came to perceive solitary asceticism as overly individualistic and excessive. The *Encyclopedia of the Early Church* complains that "numerous solitaries escaped all organized discipline, preferring to wander in wild and desert places, leading a primitive and eccentric life" ("Monasticism," 1035). As C.H. Lawrence states in a significant metaphor, this "wildness" of early monasticism "had to be *domesticated* and brought under the *roof* of the institutional Church" (17; italics added). The monastery as a historical and architectural construction was created in response to these opposing imperatives of solitude and order. The first common dwellings of coenobites, which developed in the Egyptian and Palestinian deserts in the third and fourth centuries C.E., comprised a series of separate buildings, connected by porticos and arcades. Despite these built connections, the inhabitants' lifestyle remained largely independent and hermitical. With St. Benedict in the sixth century, monasticism received both a rule and a single "roof," a distinctive architecture. Benedict's hilltop community at Monte Cassino took the form of a Roman country villa. There, the Benedictine monks proffered a vow of stability, committing themselves to staying within the same walls for the rest of their lives. While the Benedictine rule does not specify a building form, the introverted courtyard design of the villa would give rise to the most characteristic feature of the monastery: the cloister, a quadrilateral structure consisting of four roofed passages enclosing a courtyard. The cloister walk formed by these passages typically had a gallery of columns facing the courtyard side. Medieval cloisters were generally built of stone and roofed with wood; if the cloister roof was vaulted, a second story could be built out over it, saving space (Vitruvius 210).

Cloisters usually extended along the side of the church, following the main axis from east to west. This East-West orientation of the church also holds an allegorical meaning. As Zumthor lyrically states, "It deploys a spiritual geometry. ... according to the compass points traced by the obscure North, the East of the dawning day, the apotheosis of noon and the West of the end of time" ["Il en déploie la géométrie spirituelle. ... selon la rose cardinale tracée par le Nord obscur, l'Est du jour naissant, l'apothéose du Midi et l'Ouest de la fin des temps," Zumthor 99, 101]. On a more earthly and practical plane, in northern countries the

---

[26] "When thou prayest, enter into thy closet, and when thou hast shut thy door, pray to thy Father which is in secret" (Matthew 6:6).

cloister was usually situated on the southern side for protection from cold winds, whereas in southern regions it adjoined the north side of the church to receive shade from the sun. The typical Mediterranean arrangement of porticos and arches was retained in the medieval cloister, but the central structure of the medieval monastery was a single self-enclosed unit rather than a series of separate buildings connected by covered walkways, as had been the case in the ancient Middle Eastern monasteries. Eleventh-century Benedictine cloisters were relatively small: the average enclosure measured about 100 feet square, though some, like Cluny, attained enormous dimensions (Zumthor 99). In medieval times, the segment of the cloister appended to the church was the inmates' only zone of communication with the world.

What forms did sacred enclosure take for women? Of the many beautiful medieval convents still standing in Europe, some were built by and for women's orders. In thirteenth-century England, the countess Eta of Salisbury, a widow and mother of eight children, decided to found a nunnery of her own on her manor of Lacock. She sought and received the necessary authorizations, obtaining the foundation charter in 1230. The convent buildings occupied a 20-acre meadow bordering the Avon. Abbey buildings included a beautiful cloister in the high Gothic style. Lacock was basically a small family house, designed to shelter the founder and any of her descendants who wished to embrace the religious life. Eta of Salisbury's female descendants maintained the convent into the fourteenth century. Another English house for women, the Benedictine abbey of Wherwell, was much rebuilt and improved by a thirteenth-century abbess, Euphemia, who repaired the buildings and created a pleasant open walk for the sisters. Euphemia was able to increase the number of nuns from 40 to 80 at a time when women's convents were shrinking, and even designed a basic but effective privy system (Laberge 110–11).

In France, by far the most extensive women-ruled convent was the Royal Abbey of Fontevraud. Fontevraud was founded in 1101 by Robert d'Abrissell, with the support of the French and Anglo-Norman royal and noble houses: Henri II, Richard the Lion-Hearted and Aliénor of Aquitaine are all entombed in its church. Of its 36 abbesses, 16 were of royal blood. The four youngest daughters of Louis XV were educated there. Fontevraud probably survived, where other women's orders did not, because of these illustrious connections; but it is also important to note that Robert d'Abrissel's rule institutionalized an exceptional relationship between the sexes, "with the women the focus of the community, and the men there to serve the women."[27] Since the inclusion of women was formally written into the legislation of the order, they could not be seen as peripheral and forced out, as happened in many other monasteries that had originally harbored women (Gold 111–12).

Another factor distinguishing Fontevraud from other women's convents is that royal patronage provided ample funds to build; and its isolated location in the

---

[27] To my knowledge, the only other twelfth-century order to subordinate men to women was Paraclete, a monastery founded by Abelard where Héloise was abbess.

désert of the western Loire valley afforded the establishment plenty of room to expand.[28] Rather than a single house, Fontevraud was a large monastic domain, consisting of several buildings within its walls as well as a number of dependent priories in France, England and Spain. The main building, *le Grand Moutier* or Great Minster, was dedicated to virgins and widows "who had led an irreproachable life in the secular world" (Melot and Joubert 11). Other buildings included the men's house, Saint-Jean de l'Habit (now in ruins), Saint-Lazare for lepers (now a hostel for visitors to the Abbey), Sainte-Marie-Madeleine for repented (female) sinners and the Monastère de Saint-Benoît for old or invalid nuns, which later became an infirmary. All of these establishments, including the men's monastery, lay under the jurisdiction of the abbess.[29] This veritable monastic "city" spread over 34 acres, seven of them covered by buildings, making it the largest monastic complex still preserved in Europe (Colleu-Dumond and Rondeau 46). The cloister of the Grand Moustier, the largest in Europe, was rebuilt in the sixteenth century under the abbesses Renée and Louise de Bourbon, conserving the proportions of the original Romanesque structure.

As in Benedictine houses, the cloister at Fontevraud provided the main means of communication from place to place. The location of the various living areas also followed a Benedictine plan, with the church to the north, the sacristy, chapter-house and community hall to the east, and the refectory to the south. Interestingly, Gilchrist has found a significant variation from this practice: in one third of the medieval English convents she studied, the cloister is located to the north of the church rather than the south. The reasons for this inversion seem to be symbolic: first, the north side of the church is identified with the feminine; second, it reflects the iconographic tradition of the Virgin sitting on Christ's right hand (140). This example reveals how differences in gender roles assigned to men and women can express themselves in architectural form.

More broadly, the architecture of the women's convent had to adapt to simultaneous and contradictory demands which were not placed on male communities: demands to be both penetrable and inaccessible. On the one hand, as Lowe points out, women sometimes had to let men in: "while monasteries could function at all levels without employing women, convents were required to avail themselves of the services of male priests and confessors, and spatial arrangements had to be adapted to conform to this imperative. On the other hand, the requirements for clausura made architectural arrangements for nuns "crucially

---

[28]   In my view, its relatively isolated location is a major factor preventing the government-supported Centre Culturel de l'Ouest at Fontevraud from developing successfully. The modern visitor to Fontevraud is struck by the enormous size of the community, but also by its rather neglected and "deserted" air.

[29]   This subjection to female authority led to a decline in the number of monks at Fontevrauld and a male "revolt" during the seventeenth century. See Michel Melot, "Le pouvoir des abbesses de Fontevraud et la révolte des hommes" in Kathleen Wilson-Chevalier and Eliane Viennot, eds. *Royaume de fémynie: pouvoirs, contraintes, espaces de liberté des femmes de la Renaissance à la Fronde* (Paris: Champion, 1999), 135–45.

different to those of monks and friars ... . The combination of functionality and spatial arrangement was decisive for the lifestyles of the inmates in these all-female institutions ..." (124).

While the classic Benedictine cloister was stretching itself to accommodate the requirements placed on medieval religious women, other, less traditional options were also becoming available to them. As noted above, an upsurge of religious fervor in the thirteenth century, almost rivaling that of the late Renaissance, led many people of both sexes to seek the religious life. Men could join the new mendicant orders, the Dominicans and the Franciscans, but women were not allowed to roam about in this free and easy way. At the same time, for both financial and misogynistic motives, most male regular orders wanted nothing to do with the supervising of women religious, or *cura mulierum*—even St Francis, reputedly so fond of animals and birds, refused to admit the nuns of St. Clare into the Franciscan order, writing that "God has taken away our wives, and now the devil gives us sisters" (quoted in Bolton 151).[30] This lack of official outlets led some women to choose less traditional options. Two important alternate forms of religious dwelling, the anchorhold and the béguinage, underscore the ambiguities and variations in female enclosure central to this book.

The word "anchorite," or "anachorite," comes from the Greek for "one who retires from the world." The Desert Fathers used the terms "anachorite," "hermit" and "monk" almost interchangeably to describe a religious solitary, in opposition to the coenobites (followers of a common life) who lived together in community (Chitty, 90). In the Middle Ages, however, these usages became distinct: while a hermit lived in a remote location or else wandered about from place to place, the anchorite's dwelling, or anchorhold, would typically be located adjacent to a church or religious center so her or his material needs could be attended to. According to Geoffrey Shepherd, "The life of the recluse was obviously particularly suited to women" (xxx), presumably because they would be protected from the dangers and rigors of an isolated hermitic life—and kept under the eye of the clergy. In contrast, the anchorage also attracted those who wished to be free from the dictates of traditional female communities. In "An Anchorhold of her Own," Elizabeth Robertson suggests that it might have offered a preferable alternative for women to a regular convent, given the impoverishment and strict control these establishments experienced following the Norman Conquest of England. Supporting this assertion, Margaret Wade Labarge gives the example of Loretta de Braose, the widowed daughter of a powerful lord, who was enclosed in a village near Canterbury Cathedral. Her choice of becoming an anchoress may have been influenced by her

---

[30]   Clare was converted by Francis in 1212 and immediately gave away her property to live in poverty, following the Franciscan model. But when Clare established her community in the church of St. Damian of Assisi, it did not follow any recognized monastic rule. In 1216, Innocent gave her his support and a special dispensation from the property regulations normally imposed on convents. Thus the Poor Clares received, and with some struggle maintained, a special "rule of their own" outside the Franciscan purview (Bolton 148–53).

insecurity as a childless widow, her high social status and "perhaps disinclination to accept another's rule" (Labarge 127). For over 40 years, Loretta continued to exercise public influence from her cell, even interceding with the king for her neighbors. Robertson calls into question the degree of autonomy an anchorhold could actually afford most women, since they were subject to control and even visits by male clergy (170–71).[31] This ambiguity is apparent in the semantic evolution of the term itself. The Middle English word for anchorite is *ancre*; while there is no etymological connection, this form invites contagion with the word "anchor," "something that serves to hold an object firmly" (*Webster's 3rd New International Dictionary* definition 3). Similarly, the word "anchorhold" contains the old English suffix "-hold," meaning "shelter" or "protection." In Middle English, after the Norman Conquest, "hold" also came to mean "possession, land or property," as in the word "holdings." Thus, the anchorhold is an enclosure for a (female) recluse, "anchored" to the wall of a church, as well as the "hold" of/for a woman who is both sheltered and held as property.

The rites performed at the enclosure of an anchoress emphasized her putative isolation: a twelfth-century order of service included a mass for the dead, not only because she should "live as one dead" to the world, but also because she might not be able to receive these final offices once she had been walled up. In the thirteenth and fourteenth centuries, however, the period of the anchorages' greatest dissemination, the anchoress's life became linked to the world in surprising ways. Often built onto a church wall, her dwelling typically included two rooms— a bedroom and a parlor—and two windows: one a "squint" facing the church altar and the other (covered by a curtain) facing the outside.[32] Anchorholds were also attached, limpet-like, to city or castle walls and gates, and even to the Tower of London (Labarge 122). Anchoresses often had a servant, and sometimes were allowed to keep a small garden to help support themselves. Like hermits, they were venerated as wise, and people often sought them out for advice.

The temptations of this "window on the world" stimulated a series of guides for anchoresses, the most famous being the *Ancrene Wisse* or *Ancrene Riwle*, composed in 1215 for three sisters living in an anchorhold near Wigmor Abbey in Herefordshire.[33] These guides laid down a "rule for one," prescribing the prayers to be recited and their frequency, the work to be done and so forth. But they also regulated the anchoress's contact with the outside world. In a twelfth-century text, Ailred of Rievaux "warns his sister not to behave like the contemptible anchoresses he describes who became local gossips and business dealers" (Robertson 171). He also puts her on guard against "those [visitors] who install themselves at the window, and after a pious word or two by way of introduction, will settle down to

---

[31]   This situation is dramatically portrayed in the 1993 film *The Anchoress*.

[32]   In English churches, the openings cut into chapel walls to create a view of the altar are still called squints.

[33]   For more on this subject, see Linda Georgianna, *The Solitary Self: Individuality in the 'Ancrene Wisse'* (Cambridge, MA and London: Harvard University Press, 1981).

talk of worldly affairs, interspersed with romance, and so spend a sleepless night" (Robertson 174). The *Ancrene Wisse* even counsels the recluse against the use of her cell as an inn! (Shepherd xxxv). Both Ailred and the author of the *Ancrene Wisse* give attention to the physical setting of the anchoress as well as to her behavior. Ailred urges her to remove all but religious objects and decorations from the anchorhold. As much as possible, every object is assigned a religious meaning: the *Ancrene Wisse* allegorizes the parlor window as an "eye" that can provide an entrance for sin (Robertson 176). Thus, anchoritic practice opened a space onto the world, a space which the guides attempted to eliminate or reduce through an allegorization of the body. The early modern allegories analyzed in Chapter 1 show a similar strategy, pursued with a greater or lesser degree of success.

The béguinage, which developed around the same time as the anchorhold, offered a very different mode of religious life. While anchorites were often women of upper-class origins who did not wish to submit to the rule of a regular monastery, béguinages served a population of lower nobility, bourgeois or poor women. And rather than solitary recluses, the Béguines lived in community. They followed no definite monastic rule, though they did take a private vow of continence and simplicity (Bolton 144–5).[34] Most significantly, they were not bound by vows of stability to remain within a convent enclosure. More will be said about béguinages in Chapter 5 which explores the convent "parlor," or social connection to the outer world.

While such *via media* or middle ways were often chosen by the bourgeoisie, French aristocratic families, with some exceptions, remained faithful to the traditional enclosed convent (Gilchrist 170). The large numbers of women destined for a religious life during the Catholic Reformation created a great pressure for convent building and expansion. In Naples, "The number of convents swelled dramatically through the seventeenth century, until squares, streets, and whole neighborhoods were dominated by them" (Hills, *Invisible City* 4). A census taken just before the Revolution counted more than 300 women's religious communities in Paris alone, numbering 2,500 members (Biver, frontispiece). Architectural design for these new women's convents came under a number of powerful social and economic influences, some of them conflicting. On the one hand, the tightening of the rules for clausura directly affected convent construction. According to Lowe, "Much of the rhetoric driving stricter enclosure for women both before and after Trent focused on inventing ways of curtailing women's control of themselves and their own convent space, so that women could be entirely cut off from outside view" (125). This task was complicated by the fact that convents had evolved beyond the early medieval model to comprehend numerous points of contact with the outside: not only doors and windows, but confessionals, turnstiles, parlors and gates for distributing alms to the poor.

---

[34]   According to Lemoine, the gates of the béguinages were locked at night, but this was also a sensible security measure (Lemoine, 266). See also 2n2.

The Council of Trent dictated concrete security measures to enforce clausura at these vulnerable threshold points. Bars should be placed a specified distance apart; parlor windows were to be covered with fine mesh, double grills and curtains. Individual orders sometimes added their own requirements: for example, Chapters 13–18 of the Rule of the Poor Clares set out in detail exactly how many keys should be in circulation, and how many bars must be attached to doors (Makowski 36). Teresa of Avila's rule for the Discalced Carmelites also specified who should have keys, and what precautions must to be taken for the entry of doctors, confessors and other men into the convent (Torres Sánchez 147). Other orders prescribed prison-like procedures: the convent door was double locked, with two different nuns having the keys. Two or three senior nuns, their faces covered by veils, always accompanied male visitors (Lehfelt 143). The convent of Santa Chiara in Naples pushed this obsession with security a notch higher: spikes were attached to the grill separating the nuns' choir from the church nave. Helen Hills's photograph of this grill shows a hand-written sign impaled on the spikes, reading "attenzione agli occhi" ("be careful with your eyes") (*Invisible City*, Fig. 31, following p. 148); "care of the eyes," or avoiding looking at others, is prescribed in convent rules.

Paradoxically, in contrast to these moves toward retrenchment and enclosure, the early modern period was also one of dispersal and opening in monastic design. The creation of multiple religious *benefices*, or ecclesiastical livings, sometimes led to the fragmentation of the conventual unit: each abbot, prior, cellarer or porter came to have her or his own buildings, dependencies and income. Renaissance abbesses built elegant galleries and monumental stairways, similar to those found in the châteaux of the time. The high status of royal monasteries also spurred the construction of elaborate abbatial residences. In 1670, Gabrielle de Rochouart had an abbatial palace built on the grounds of Fontevraud which entailed a rearrangement of the whole monastery entrance. All these innovations tended to explode the traditional Benedictine cloister in both form and spirit (Melot 7). Another opening influence on convent life was the Catholic Reform policy of placing new houses not in remote locations, as in the Middle Ages, but in urban centers. According to Torres Sánchez, "Reformed orders after Trent manifested their urban vocation above all" ["Las ordenes reformadas después de Trento manifiestan su vocación urbana por encima de todo," 106]. In *Instructiones fabricae ecclesiasticae*, Bishop Borromeo of Milan's treatise on monastery building published posthumously in 1599, the Bishop suggests that women's convents be built in affluent neighborhoods where their presence could influence the neighbors to greater piety (but as far as possible from male monasteries).

However, land shortages and costs of property in urban areas like Paris often caused religious orders to take over and modify existing buildings rather than undertake new construction. An example from the high end of the social scale was the Couvent du Carmel de l'Annonciation, or "Grand Carmel de la rue St Jacques." This first Discalced Carmelite convent in France would become the mother house for 63 other convents established in the country between 1615 and 1618 alone;

its Spanish founding mothers would then move on to create an even greater presence in Flanders. The location chosen for the new Paris convent was the priory of Notre Dame des Champs.[35] This eleventh-century priory belonged to the Religieux de Marmoutier, of whom only three or four still remained in residence in 1600. This is still a highly desirable address, located on the Left Bank near Montparnasse and the Latin Quarter. In the seventeenth century, the area also housed the convents of the Feuillantines, Val-de-Grâce and Port-Royal.

The social importance of the reformed Carmelite order in early and mid-century France will be further explored in Chapter 3. In the architectural context that occupies us now, it is interesting to note how the original plan of the Paris house departed from the Benedictine model. The space in clausura comprised two wings attached to the right side of the church and a main building block (*corps de logis*). The courtyard or cloister was adjoined on three sides by a wing of the convent facing the rue d'Enfer, the house of the *tourière*,[36] and a block of rental properties belonging to the order.[37] To quote Bivert's description of the cloister more fully: "The cloisters were attached to the church and to the claustral buildings, instead of being incorporated into them, as is customary. That is because they did not exist at the outset" ["Les cloîtres étaient adossés à l'église et aux bâtiments claustraux, au lieu d'y être incorporés, selon la coutume. C'est qu'ils n'existaient pas au début"]. Another indication that the cloister was an afterthought and did not follow the Benedictine model is that "these cloisters did not form a perfect square, but a rectangle" ["Ces cloîtres ne formaient pas un carré parfait, mais un rectangle," Bivert, 266–7]. Some of these irregular features are evident in Fig. I.1.

According to Gilchrist, it was not uncommon even in the Middle Ages for cloisters to be added to women's convents after the necessary domestic spaces, such as the dormitories, refectory and chapter hall, had been completed (121). Thus, while the cloister metonymically represents the convent in the Western imagination, both for its beauty and its meaning as an inward-looking, closed space, it was not the most essential element of women's convent design. More will be said below on this disconnect between symbol and practice.

---

[35]   The convent was razed during the Revolution. Its former entrance can still be seen on the rue St-Jacques. See Chapter 4.

[36]   Or extern sister; this was sometimes a paid position.

[37]   Housing and land rents were among the main sources of convent income during the *Ancien Régime*. Philip T. Hoffman observes: "Like other major religious institutions in early modern Europe, Notre Dame owned a staggering amount of agricultural property …" (*Growth in a Traditional Society*, 53). Well-established monasteries thus were absentee owners of enormous amounts of land, a fact that contributed to their unpopularity and the eventual abolition of monasticism. However, newer urban convents, especially the women's houses established in the seventeenth century, were more likely to buy city property nearby for investment or expansion. The taxation of monastic property begun in the late seventeenth century seriously undermined the stability of women's convents. See Chapter 6.

é de N.D. des CHAMPS, autrefois selon l'opinion commune le Temple de Mercure, de Ceres; fut vn Prieuré de l'Ordre de St. Benoist, dependant de l'Abbaye de ... nouſtier, et depuis en l'année 1601, a efté donnée aux Rehäcules Carmelites de la Reformée de S. Thereſe, pour y eſtablir le premier Mönaſtere de cette St. en ... ... de la Reformée de S. Thereſe ...

Fig. I.1   Couvent des Carmélites de la rue St-Jacques. Drawn and engraved by Pierre Mariette, chez Jean Marot. Paris, BnF.

A final impetus for the creation of women's religious communities in the seventeenth century was the need to educate the daughters of the rising bourgeoisie— a role assumed by new orders such as the Ursulines, Filles de la Charité, Dames de St-Elisabeth and many others. These congregations took girls into the convent as day pupils or boarders, or sometimes even went outside the cloister to teach. Thus, enclosure was called into question at the same time it was being imposed with unprecedented rigor. More generally, the effects of modernity and the Catholic Reformation on the spaces, spirit and perceptions of women's convents constitute one of the main foci of this book. We will now explore how contemporary theory can contribute to an understanding of these early modern phenomena.

Space, Language and Gender

If diverse disciplines now share a common interest in space, it is partly because they also share a concept of language existing simultaneously and interdependently on the social, material and symbolic levels. In this view, material objects, social structures and verbal/literary representations form an interlocking, ever-shifting pattern of signifiers: not only words, but material and social structures as well, communicate meaning. Within this system of signs, as Shirley Ardener observes, much of social life is "given shape" by spatial language, and "appreciation of the physical world is in turn dependent on social perceptions of it" (11).[38] Complementing this spatial perspective is Michel de Certeau's concept of *l'art de faire*—social practice that cuts across esthetic and social boundaries. In a book dealing more with representations than with social "realities," practice, in a sense, must be subsumed under discourse—it is really discourse about practice. But at the same time, discourse is in itself a social practice that contributes to and changes social and spatial structures. Moreover, with the evolution of cultural studies, architecture is being seen more and more as a language to be interpreted, along with other signs, within a larger semiotic system. Especially central to my work have been the contributions of feminist architects, archaeologists and geographers. As feminist literary critics had done for written language starting in the 1960s, feminist approaches to architecture are demolishing the generic (male) concept of space and replacing it with a gendered view. In *Discrimination by Design*, Leslie Kanes Weisman reveals a "gender-based understanding of space as a language" (9) which, like any other language, is not neutral (or neuter) but socially charged. Social distinctions literally compartmentalize and construct a spatial environment, a symbolic built universe which we then take for reality. After all, what is more "real," and more deceptively so, than brick and mortar? Thus, we both form, and are formed by, the rooms (or cells) we inhabit.[39]

---

[38]   See also Hillier and Hanson: "The ordering of space in buildings is really about the ordering of relations between people ... . Society already possesses its own intrinsic spatial dimension" (2, 28).

[39]   Research on gendered spaces in social geography has also grown exponentially. Among the studies I have found most germane are David Bell ed., *Mapping Desire:*

Until recently, the element of space was largely ignored in convental studies. As E.J. Soja asserts, there has traditionally been "an implicit subordination of space to time" (*Postmodern Geographies* 14). Studies of religious orders generally spent a great deal of time discussing the rules that governed the arrangement of time, and devoted very little space to the actual spaces in which the religious lived.[40] Certainly, one of the ways that the founders of monasteries distinguished monastic from ordinary existence was by marking the passage of hours with prayers (*heures*); books of hours, some lavishly illustrated, circulated among secular readers as well. But if time is perceived differently within and without the convent walls, this difference is dependent on its isolated location. Thus, convent life is compounded of special time lived in a special place. As Daphne Spain points out, "Although space is constructed by social behavior at a particular point in time, its legacy may persist (seemingly as an absolute) to shape the behavior of future generations" (6). The former spatial void is now being filled by studies of the early modern period examining the materiality of religious construction from a gendered perspective.[41] *Architecture and the Politics of Gender in Early Modern Europe*, edited by Helen Hills, explores "the relationship between the architecture of modern Europe and the bodies it was built to represent or to house ..." (3).

Geographies of Sexualities (1995), which examines the relations between place and the gendered body; and Nancy Duncan ed., *Body Space: Destabilizing Geographies of Gender and Sexuality* (1996). A number of other recent volumes on the "geography" of the gendered body have been published by Routledge. These include Paul Rodaway, *Sensuous Geographies: Body, Sense and Place* (London, New York: 1994); Heidi Nast and Steve Pile, *Places through the Body* (1998); Ruth Butler and Hester Parr, *Mind and Body Spaces* (1999); Elizabeth Teather, *Embodied Geographies* (1999); and Robyn Longhurst, *Bodies: Exploring Fluid Boundaries* (2001). Among general collections on feminist geography are John Paul Jones, Heidi Nast and Susan Roberts eds, *Thresholds in Feminist Geography* (Lanham, MD: Rowman & Littlefield Pub., 1997); and Nina Laurie, *Geographies of New Femininities* (Harlow, UK: Longman; New York: Pearson Education, 1999). Articles include Elizabeth Grosz, "Bodies-Cities" in I.B. Colombina, *Sexuality and Space* (1992), 241–53; and Sue Best's "Sexualizing Space" in Grosz' edited volume, *Sexy Bodies* (1995), 181–94. See also the journals *Gender, Place and Culture: A Journal of Feminist Geography*; and *Society and Space*.

[40] A striking exception to this generalization is attributed to Ste-Beuve in Philippe Sellier's introduction to "Port-Royal et la Vie Monastique," *Chroniques de Port-Royal* 37. Sellier quotes Ste-Beuve: "There were, almost without interruption, the cloister, the sanctuary, the cell and the alms gate, the Christian practice of morals and the inviolable interior of certain souls, the poor, silent study, the desert and the [Port-Royal] Conference Grotto ..." ["Il y eut, presque sans interruption, le cloître, le sanctuaire, la cellule et le guichet des aumônes, la pratique chrétienne des moeurs et l'intérieur inviolable de certaines âmes, le cabinet d'étude pauvre et silencieux, le désert et la *Grotte des Conférences* ... ," 15].

[41] Italian scholars have been in the forefront of early modern convent studies. Recent books include Helen Hills's *Invisible City: the Architecture of Devotion in Seventeenth-Century Neapolitan Convents*, and Anabel Thomas, *Art and Piety in the Female Religious Communities of Renaissance Italy* (Cambridge: Cambridge University Press, 2003).

As mentioned above, Roberta Gilchrist's *Gender and Material Culture: The Archaeology of Religious Women* (1994) focuses on gender and space in terms of power, calling nunneries "extreme gender domains" which accentuate the gap in status between men and women (167). However, convent plans can also be seen as "collective spatial gestures" (79) which give women an opportunity to display and reinforce their group identity. Examining how encounters are controlled through architectural boundaries and entrances, "access analysis" reveals the "depth"—levels of accessibility—built into architectural design. Applying this method, Gilchrist found that compared to men's houses, the plans for women's convents showed an extra degree of separation: four levels instead of three. She also discovered a gender difference in the hierarchy of accessibility: whereas in male monasteries, the least accessible level is reserved for the chapter hall, in nunneries it is the dormitory (164–5). Access analysis informs my readings of Diderot's drawings and fiction in Chapter 6.

The research outlined above merely confirms a situation of which we are instinctively aware. In our everyday lives, we exist and move through different spatial realms; and in each setting, variations in spatial features, such as area, height, openness and accessibility, are often tied to differences in social and gender status. For example, the most "upscale" apartments and executive suites are located on the top floors of skyscrapers.[42] But when the variable of gender is introduced, the correlation between height and status is affected in significant ways. If the locus of power is on the ground, then displacement occurs on the vertical plane: women are relegated to upper galleries in some orthodox synagogues, Greek orthodox churches and, until as late as 1942, the British House of Commons (Rodgers 53). As in traditional fairy tales, the isolation of women through "elevation" can also reinforce their enclosure. In the old Casbah of Algiers, women occupied the top floors and roofs of buildings—prime real estate in New York—because the street was a male domain (Çelik, "Gendered Spaces in Colonial Algiers," *Sex in Architecture* 130). This distinction persists in English usage in the contrasting expressions "man in the street" and "woman of the streets."

Like height, accessibility and contact with the outside are ambiguously coded features in building design. On the one hand, the number of windows an office-holder possesses is precisely calculated in relation to her or his position in the organization. On the other hand, privacy—the control of access to one's personal space—is a mark of power and status. Devices designed to create an effect of privacy through "visual occlusion"—screens or partitions—are an unsatisfactory substitute for real barriers. Thus, unlike ordinary workers, CEOs possess offices with complete walls and doors that shut—a luxury Suzanne will lose in Diderot's *Religieuse*. Privacy must be balanced, however, with accessibility or focality: in traditional Egyptian and Sudanese houses, the women's entrance and quarters are found in the back, which makes them private but also "out of the way." And the beautiful carved *mashrabiya* screens covering the windows of women's quarters

---

[42]   On the gendered design of skyscrapers, see Weisman, *Discrimination* 37–42.

were designed to let in air, but block visibility both in and out. Women behind them could hear, but not see or be seen. The fundamental ambiguity of the female space is revealed through this dialectic of containment and privacy. Women only briefly and partially control their own space; and the history of the convent, like other aspects of women's material history, reveals a constant movement from space to space as these dialectics of control shift. These are the movements whose traces we will follow.

Bodily Thinking

The interpenetration of gender and structure comes directly to the fore in the architectural analogies drawn between buildings and bodies. Vitruvius's vision of bodily proportions inspired Michelangelo's famous drawing of the ideal male figure (Fig. I.2). Inscribed in a square and a circle, symbols of geometric perfection, the Vitruvian man became a model for neoclassical architecture. Claude Perrault's influential translation of Vitruvius's *Ten Books on Architecture* reads: "It is certain that the number of man's fingers is at the origin of all other numbers, and that there is a proportional relation between the parts of his body and the whole" ["il est constant que le nombre des doigts de l'homme est à l'origine de tous les autres nombres & qu'il y a rapport de mesure entre les parties de son corps & le tout," Vitruvius, Perrault trans. 62]. Following this analogical pattern, the names for segments of buildings or furniture were often taken from body parts. Expressions such as "table leg" or "chair arm" remain in use, though *précieuse* and Victorian usage found them too graphic. Eighteenth-century architectural vocabulary in English, however, was rich in colorful bodily metonymies, including nose, bust, joint, limb and buttocks (*Builders Magazine*, London, 1774, quoted in Frank 230). In an architectural supplement to the French *Encyclopédie* edited and annotated by Diderot, we find the words *col* (neck or collar), *panse* (belly) and *galbe*, signifying "outline" or "profile" (Fig. I.3). Throughout his commentaries, Diderot emphasizes the primacy of proportion in creating beautiful structures— proportions drawn from the ideal masculine form.

Figures of buildings as bodies, or bodies as buildings, were also employed by philosophical and religious thinkers as a way of representing the relation between body and soul or mind. This relation has always been as problematic as the definition of space itself: thus, Aristotle construed mind both as a substance which occupies no space and as a "place of ideas" [*topos eidon*] "housed" within the body [*De anima* 429a].[43] The connection between buildings and bodies underwent a major change through the allegorization of discourse central to medieval Christian hermeneutics: Aristotle's house-as-body becomes the "temple of the body" in John 2:21. Conversely, the cruciform outline of the church is likened to a body,

---

[43]   Deepening this ambiguity, even though Aristotle states that the soul is not "'in' the body in the same way as a thing is in a vessel or place" (*Physics* III 201^b 32), his denial itself implies an idea of housing or enclosure.

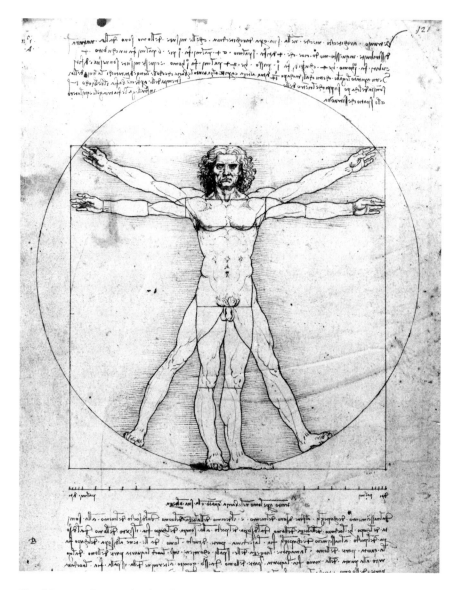

Fig. I.2   Leonardo da Vinci, *Vitruvian Man*, ca. 1492. Accademia, Venice, Italy. Alinari/Art Resource, NY.

arms outstretched, lying on the ground (Zumthor 101). This embodiment of buildings has also played an enormous part in the representation of women.

The construct of the body as a temple for the soul, like the injunction to cloister oneself, was perhaps initially made irrespective of sex; but in a world structured by gender roles, they could not be left out for long. Whereas all bodies

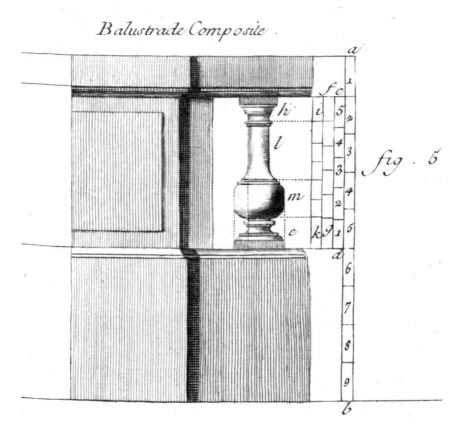

Fig. I.3   *Balustrade composite*. Diderot, *Encyclopédie. Recueil des planches sur les Sciences les Arts libéraux et les Arts mécaniques*. "Architecture et parties qui en dépendent." Plate IX (Balustrades et Balustres relatifs aux cinq Ordres), Fig. 5. Minneapolis, University of Minnesota, Special Collections and Rare Books.

are allegorized as buildings, women's bodies are also specifically constructed as enclosures—buildings with courtyards or cloisters, so to speak. And while the open cross follows the shape of Christ's (male) body—or the body follows and becomes one with the crucifix—the closed forms of the circle or the square are sometimes identified with the female.[44] This construction pervades many cultures

---

[44]   Zumthor's relation of archetypal forms to gender is suggestive but unsystematic. At some points, Zumthor trades gender distinctions for generic statements: "human space is lived as closed" ["le lieu humain est vécu comme clos," 58]. But he later describes the "inner space" (*espace interne*) of the church as "feminized in some way because it contains God as did the womb of the virgin" ["féminisé en quelque sorte parce qu'il contient Dieu comme le fit le sein de la vierge," 100].

of African or Middle Eastern background, including our own. Woman is the *hortus conclusus* of the Song of Songs, a closed garden of erotic delight which only her lover can enter. The Christian conceit of the garden as allegory for the chaste, intact body of the Virgin Mary is expressed in an anonymous Renaissance motet published by Ottavio Petrucci in 1503–04. "Inviolata, integra et casta es Maria / Qui es effecta fugida caeli porta" ["Immaculate, pure, and chaste you are, Mary / You are the shining gate of heaven"]. The translations of *inviolata* as "immaculate" and *integra* [whole] as "pure" are abstractions of the very physical sense of intactness—*virgo intacta*—which allows Mary to become the "gate" of Paradise, open only to the Holy Spirit. Janice Boddy reports that similar terms are used in the Sudan to describe and justify the practice of radical genital infibulation which keeps girls "pure," "smooth," "white" and "clean": "through occlusion of the vaginal orifice, her womb, both literally and figuratively, becomes a social space: enclosed, impervious, virtually impenetrable" (321). Gilchrist argues in contrast that the nun's chaste body becomes a private space dedicated only to Christ, her mystic Husband (Gilchrist 19). Yet this body is locked up with other female bodies in a "holy harem," so to speak, a social space shared by all Christ's brides.[45]

In sum, enclosure is built into our mental and social construction of the female. The spatial oppositions we have identified, such as accessible/removed, open/closed, inside/outside, roof/street, and front/back, all reduce themselves to a single imperative: containment to achieve or maintain intactness. This construction is still very much a part of Western thinking. The mid-twentieth century psychologist Erik Erikson claimed that woman's "inner space," and her need to maintain its inviolacy, profoundly affect her personality. Contemporary women writers also conceptualize the body as a container in which the female consciousness is lodged. The novelist Mary Gordon explores this relationship in *The Rest of Life*, asking herself "what it's like to live in a female body." It is impossible for her, however, to "go outside" into a male body: "To be larger, not to be afraid of being raped … . No I can't imagine it yet" (Interview with Mary Gordon, *New York Times Book Review*, August 8, 1993, 25).

Cloister as Discourse

Reentering the cloister after these peregrinations, we can now see how the concentricity characteristic of convent architecture (enclosed spaces within enclosed spaces), while not originally created by or for women, simulates and reinforces feminine gendering. The convent is a walled, enclosed space containing women's bodies, which in turn contain that primordial space, the womb. Even the word itself becomes feminized in the late eighteenth and nineteenth centuries, no longer conjuring up a place of the religious (undifferentiated as to gender) but a site consecrated to women and girls. The 1881 edition of the Littré dictionary gives as

---

[45]   I thank Anne Cruz for this metaphor.

the third sense of the word: "a boarding school run by nuns for fashionable young girls" / ["pensionnat tenue par des religieuses pour des jeunes filles du monde"].

Linguistic and built constructions stand apart in other ways. Our survey of convent architecture has indicated that the "classic" Benedictine cloister disappeared or was radically altered in the seventeenth and eighteenth centuries—not that it was ever the absolute rule for women's monasteries. In a divergence from actual building practice, the new dictionaries appearing in the late seventeenth century re-erected the cloister in its traditional architectural form. For example, in Furetière's 1696 dictionary we find: "cloister also refers more specifically to the *main part* of a closed convent, which is a square formed of buildings and surrounded by four galleries" ["cloistre, se dit encore plus particulièrement de la *principale partie* des lieux reguliers, qui est un quarré de bâtiment compris en quatre galleries"; italics added]. Furthermore, the cloister is taken to represent the whole convent metonymically: "Closed dwelling where canons or religious live" ["Habitation fermée où logent des Chanoines ou des Religieux"]. The eighth edition of the *Académie française* dictionary (1932–35) further builds on this metonymic dimension: "convent enclosure, grill that separates the religious from the world, and by figurative extension, separation from the world ... . It is often used by extension for Monastery" ["clôture d'un couvent, grille qui sépare les religieux du monde, et par extension figurée séparation d'avec le monde ... . Il se dit souvent par extension pour Monastère"].

As seen above, the word *clôture* is often used as a synonym for *cloître*. *Clôture* can be translated, depending on the context, as "enclosure" or "cloistering." This ambiguity partly stems from etymological confusions among related French words. Although *cloître* and *clôture* both originate in the Latin verb *claudere*, "to close," their specific etymologies later diverge: *cloître* deriving from the classical Latin *claustrum*, enclosed space, and *clôture* from the popular Latin *clausitura*, "barrier that closes," or "enclosure [formed] by walls or hedges" ["barrière qui clot ... enceinte de murs, de haies," *Dictionnaire de l'Académie française*] which can more accurately be translated as "enclosing barrier or fence." To complicate things further, the word *cloître* is itself a hybrid, altered by the influence of the Old French *cloison*. It thus combines the semiotic loads of enclosure and separation. The French nuns I interviewed referred to their own conventual space as "clôture" or "en clôture," not "cloître," but the two terms are conjoined (rather confusingly) in English, and sometimes in French as well, to designate interchangeably any place devoted to religious seclusion. Thus in the *Petit Robert*, *cloître* is defined as "part of a monastery off limits to lay persons and enclosed by a barrier" ["partie d'un monastère interdit aux profanes et fermée par une enceinte"]. A signpost at the Frigolet Abbey (Fig. I.4) confirms that monastery walls are meant to keep the public out, not to keep the religious in.

In a subtle variation, the *Robert* describes *clôture* as the "walled-in enclosure of a monastery, forbidden to lay persons, where the religious live a cloistered life" ["enceinte d'un monastère, interdite aux laïcs, où les religieux vivent cloîtrés"]. The sociolinguistic basis of these terms is highlighted if we compare these

Fig. I.4   "Accès réservé aux religieux." St-Michel de Frigolet. Photo:
               B. Woshinsky.

definitions with those found in English dictionaries. While *cloître* and "cloister" are cognates coming from the same Old French root, their meanings reflect divergences in national history and social attitudes towards religious enclosure. Thus, the English verb "to cloister" is first defined in the *American Heritage Dictionary* as to shut away from the world, and secondarily to provide a building with a cloister. The evolving social meanings of *clôture* and *cloître* will be further examined in Chapter 5, "Cells I." Whenever possible, I follow Elizabeth Rapley's example and refer to the cloistered space by the Latin term *clausura*, which means both the principle of enclosure and the space reserved for the religious within the convent (Rapley, *Dévotes*, glossary 203).

An entry from the *New Catholic Encyclopedia* entitled "the cloister in canon law" supplies a final important perspective on claustral discourse. "Cloister, from the Latin *claustrum* meaning bar, signifies that part of a religious house as well as gardens and recreational areas, reserved for the exclusive use of the religious" ("Canonical Rules for Cloister," 959). While the *Encyclopedia* description of the cloistered space includes concrete references to gardens and recreational areas, the etymological sense emphasizes not the enclosed space per se, but the barrier (bar) surrounding it. The entry goes on to state that this bar is more discursive than physical: "In the formal sense, cloister denotes the *body of laws* governing egress and ingress to the enclosure. In both the Latin and Oriental churches, the law of enclosure is obligatory in all lawfully established religious houses." Thus, cloistering is constitutive of the religious house, establishing its very legal existence: in a canonical sense, the rule *is* the roof. Most important, canon law implicitly acknowledges that cloistering is an abstract principle, not necessarily tied to any one architectural form or solution. In considering the cloister, it is thus important to avoid "architectural literalism"—clausura is not only, not even principally, a material "thing," but a symbolic and semiotic category. As such, neither the space nor the language of the cloister is neutral; both exist within an overlapping network of social meanings. And these meanings press down harder upon women.

If social and religious imperatives lead to architectural modifications—enclosure entails cells, walls, locks, curtains, grills—the built environment is clearly a *perceived* environment as well, a place in the mind. And the language of architectural design, like human speech, relies on figures. As a number of examples show, the demarcation of sacred space is often as figurative as it is real. Hence, in the Shinto religion, the entry to the other world is marked off by a free-standing torii gate (Fig. I.5).

During the early history of the Fontevraud convent, the limits of enclosure were indicated by a simple cross placed in front of the church door. In the convent of Ste-Claire described in the Foreword, the wooden grill which separated the convent chapel from the main altar in earlier centuries has been replaced by a glass wall (Fig. I.6); the heavy old wooden grills lie disused in the convent garden. The practical reason I was given for replacing them with glass was so that the sisters could better observe the mass being performed behind the church altar. But "Claire" ("Clara") also means "clear" or "bright" in both Italian and French; the luminosity

Fig. I.5   Torii gate, Tokyo. Photo by permission of David Woshinsky.

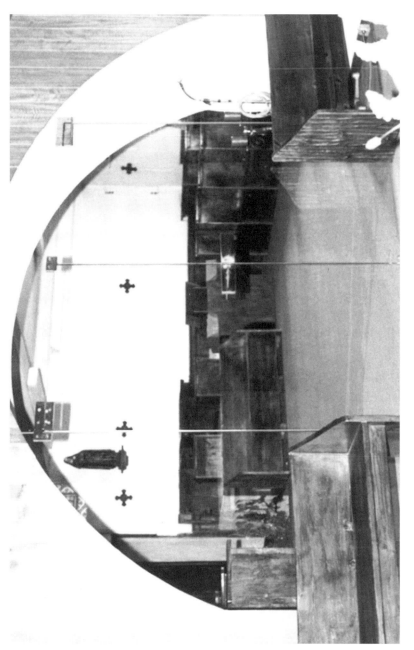

Fig. I.6   Altar and nun's chapel, Eglise Ste-Claire, Mur-de-Barrès. Photo: B. Woshinsky.

and openness of the setting is part of their spirituality, and makes a statement about how the nuns of Ste-Claire perceive themselves and their relation to the church and to God. The glass wall still figures their *clôture*; but where this separation previously rendered the nuns invisible, the separation itself has now become so.

From the Language of Architecture to the Architecture of Language

It should now be abundantly clear that figures drawn from the spatial and architectural domains combine with verbal signs to form a hybrid language.[46] This figural language of building is the key that opens the door to textual analysis, allowing one to move back and forth from buildings to (women's) bodies to books. Writings, like buildings, incorporate ideas, and the literary structure, like the architectural one, employs a vocabulary of closure and disclosure. In terms of structure, frame stories and paratexts—frontispieces or forewords—constitute a "verbal portal" to the text;[47] critical language defines stories as "closed" (having a neat ending) or "open." Sometimes closure is coincidental with enclosure: at the end of Racine's *Britannicus*, the woman Nero is pursuing enters the convent-like Vestal Virgins to escape from him. In non-theatrical genres, the choice of inside or outside views for narration or setting helps determine whether the conventual space is perceived by the reader as prison or refuge. Is there a male character outside, looking in? A female inside, looking out? Or is a male narrator usurping the female subject position? On the level of imagery, as stated earlier, the key figure for my study is metonymy. While it as often construed in a limited way as taking a part for the whole—for example, a torii gate representing a whole barrier—metonymy can also denote an association between two related things, such as shelter and clothing. In a 1629 Abraham Bosse engraving of a woman in church, perhaps in mourning, her voluminous black garb is depicted like a cloister surrounding her body (Fig. I.7).

The *Constitution de Port-Royal* gives explicit expression to the metonymic relation between clothing and architecture. In a section concerning the rules for new construction at the convent, it requires that "the [religious] house, as much as religious dress, display signs of Evangelical simplicity and poverty far removed from worldly customs: *For the House is a kind of exterior and common garment,*

---

[46]   According to Zumthor, architectural and other creative activities "speak the same language and embrace the same gesture of the body and spirit" ["parlent le même langage et embrassent du même geste l'espace du corps et celui de l'esprit," 93]. And in his chapter "Walking in the City," Certeau finds a "homology between verbal figures and the figures of walking" (100). Drawing from J.-F. Augoyard, Certeau assigns to urban locomotion the basic figures of synecdoche and asynedon (101). Like Certeau, I concentrate on metonymic figures that "leave something out." In contrast, where Certeau considers movement as a necessary constituent of figures, I see their dynamic and static aspects as equally important.

[47]   I owe this expression to Jeffrey Peters's participation in the "Paratexts" session of the Kentucky Foreign Language Conference, November 1999.

Fig. I.7   Abraham Bosse, *femme de dos*. Paris, BnF.

like the Monastery's habit" ["la Maison porte autant les marques de la simplicité et pauvreté Evangélique très éloignée des moeurs du monde, que les habits des Religieux: *Car la Maison est une espèce de vêtement extérieur et commun et comme l'habit du Monastère*," *Constitution* 9, quoted in *Chroniques de Port-Royal* 37, 135; italics added]. Analogously, the wearing of loose clothing and head coverings by orthodox Jewish or Muslim women may be an expression of their religiosity or their desire for privacy, rather than a sign of their oppression.[48] Conversely, the abandoning of religious habits by nuns signals a closer connection to the world *extra muros*. A summary of the book will elucidate how metonymy supplies its architectural principle.

Organization of the Book

Conventual Spaces is organized both diachronically through historical progression and synchronically through a series of metonymic focus points. Without following a strict chronological sequence, the book encompasses four main moments. First, the Tridentian decree of strict enclosure, along with the general upsurge of religious fervor following the Catholic Reformation, stimulated a wave of religious writings in early seventeenth-century France. These writings are the subject of the first two chapters. Chapter 1, "Hermitages of the Soul," examines gender, retreat and the body in three allegorical works from the beginning of this period. In a long poem found in Pierre de Croix's *Miroir de l'amour divin* (1600), the Song of Songs is coded allegorically as the marriage between the soul and the Holy Spirit, a common topos in devout literature. To complicate matters, however, the soul and the Spirit each occupy bodies of the opposite sex. In Antoine de Nervèze's illustrated allegorical meditations, *Le Iardin Sacré de l'Ame Solitaire* (1602) and *L'Hermitage de l'Isle saincte* (1612), retreat is represented both literally and figuratively. On a literal level, solitary characters wander through the wilderness like the early desert hermits. But the didactic aim of his work is to spur readers into following St. François de Sales's practice of *retraite intérieure*—a kind of cloistering within the self also recommended by St. Teresa. The illustrations contained in Nervèze's texts carry further a problematic aspect of allegory found in Pierre de Croix's poem: what happens when one gives the soul a body. And in all these works, issues of gender—whether souls inhabit male or female bodies, whether they themselves are male or female—can lead to consequences unforeseen by the authors and contrary to their apparent intent.

Chapter 2, "Living Temples," further develops the allegorical and apologetic thrust of the Catholic Reformation through a study of the polymath and controversial Bishop Jean-Pierre Camus, whose lively and sometimes violent writings are attracting new critical attention. In addition to performing his Episcopal functions and carrying on long-term feuds with fellow religious, Camus found the time to

---

48   The complex and evolving meanings of Moslem women's dress are forcefully expressed in Ayaan Hirsi Ali's memoir, *Infidel* (New York: Free Press, 2007).

write over fifty "anti-romans" whose aim was to counteract the effects of secular novels and to inspire people—particularly women—to choose a religious life. But the Catholic Reform movement was not, of course, limited to men. In Elizabeth Rapley's words, an upsurge in piety spurred a veritable "conventual invasion" by women in the seventeenth century, as well as the creation of alternative forms of religious community (Rapley, *Les Dévotes* 21). The attempts of orders like the Soeurs de la Visitation to leave the convent and work in the world caused controversy for much of the century, and revealed the paradoxical misogyny of some authors, like Camus, who ostensibly wrote for a female audience.

Chapter 3, "Thresholds," marks a transition from the strictly religious representations of conventual spaces to a more secular and feminocentric view. It considers three works by women, writing in three different genres. In 1658–59, Mlle de Montpensier, Louis XIV's cousin, laid out in correspondence with another lady of the court an imagined community which emulates, but does not imitate, a conventional cloister: Montpensier will accept "gentlefolk of both sexes" ["honnêtes gens de tout sexe"], provided they are not married. In contrast, Margaret Cavendish's closet drama *The Convent of Pleasure* (1668) constructs a feminutopia where women, locked securely away from men's importunate demands, happily partake of the innocent joys Nature offers. The chapter concludes with an analysis of Lafayette's *La Princesse de Clèves* (1678), until recently one of the handful of women authors included in the seventeenth-century French canon. The novel's conclusion presents another variation on the "threshold" space: the heroine chooses to end her life in a retreat that possesses a definite religious dimension, while remaining outside the formal restrictions of convent profession.

By the latter decades of the seventeenth century, the world has radically encroached on the conventual space; rather than an alternative setting, the cloister is represented as part of the social network and implicated in the turnings of real and novelistic plots. These plots are drawn out in the real-life memoirs of Hortense and Marie Mancini (1674–75) and Villedieu's fictional *Mémoires de la vie de Henriette-Sylvie de Molière* (1671–74), which influenced Marivaux's better-known *La Vie de Marianne*. I will examine these works in Chapter 4, "Parlors." Beginning at the end of the seventeenth century and extending into the eighteenth, Counter-Reformation fervor gives way to a more earthly (or earthy) view, involving the attraction of the forbidden and the eroticism of enclosed female spaces. Whereas in convent ritual, the postulant's crossing of the boundary between world and cloister is an occasion for solemn ceremony, in erotic literature the imagined breaching of this boundary from outside is a source of voyeuristic excitement. The convent has always been a site of predilection for satiric and erotic narrative (often present in the same work); but what distinguishes conventual representation from this time is heightened eroticism combined with heightened anti-clericalism. Significantly, the 1682 novel often considered the precursor of the eighteenth-century *roman érotique* is Barrin's *Vénus dans le cloître, ou la nonne éclairée*—the enlightened nun. These erotic and satiric views of the convent are glimpsed in Chapter 5 ("Cells I"). In contrast with the lesser-known works considered in Chapter 5, Chapter 6 ("Cells II") analyzes the two most famous portrayals of involuntary monachization in French literature, Guilleragues's *Lettres portugaises* (1669) and Diderot's *La Religieuse* (1790). In both of these novels, first-person narration enables the author/narrator to penetrate the convent walls and to "in-habit" the nun's persona. The *Lettres portugaises* were presented as, and are still believed by some to be, the work of a passionate nun abandoned by her lover. In *La Religieuse*, Diderot adopts a nun's voice and a moral tone in order to exhibit her sufferings at the hands of corrupt convent superiors, while affording his readers (and himself) the voyeuristic pleasure of this exhibition—the pleasure being authorized by the moral tone.

The Revolutionary decree of 1790, in abolishing monasticism and expelling nuns from their convents, would seem to impose historical closure upon my project; but the gradual reopening of the convents, begun under Napoleon and continued after the Restoration, adds an important epilogue to the story, told in Chapter 7 ("Tombs"). In a historical introduction, this chapter reviews the situation of women's religious communities in the pre-Revolutionary era, the nun's reactions (and resistance) to the emptying of their convents, and the fascinating variety of uses to which the surviving buildings were put. A second part considers conventual representation after the Revolution. A "Restoration zeal," recalling the Counter-Reformation sentiment that reigned two centuries earlier, is expressed, along with more troubling emotions, in Chateaubriand's *René* (1802). The convent is also "restored" as an alternative space for women, like Claire de Duras's protagonist *Ourika* (1824), who have no other place of their own. Despite this partial restoration, the nineteenth-century conventual space is a metonymic "tomb": separated from the contemporary world, it harks back elegiacally to an irreclaimable pre-Revolutionary past. Once the cloister door has been forced open, things can never return to their former state. Yet the conventual space persists, whether as a real enclosure for women (some of whom still have memories of their own convent educations) or as a compelling image of female solitude and solidarity. Chapter 7 also examines some twentieth- and twenty-first-century narratives of life within the convent, whether in Karen Armstrong's metonymically entitled memoirs, *Through the Narrow Gate* and *The Spiral Staircase*, or within a convent-like women's refuge in Toni Morrison's *Paradise*. Finally, the chapter and book conclusion explores patterns of connection and disjunction existing between the conventual space and its manifold representations: the differences representation can make through historical asynchronies, narrative focus and gendered views. Imagining throughout the centuries a space they could not see, male writers mostly overlooked—and modern readers have mainly forgotten—the role that conventual spaces played in women's culture. Hence, the secrets disclosed by the cloister may be of an unexpected kind.

Chapter 1
The Body in Early Modern Religious Discourse (1). Hermitages of the Soul: Bodies as Allegorical Enclosures in Counter-Reformation Writing

> ... let the bishops diligently teach that by means of the stories of the mysteries
> of our redemption portrayed in paintings and other representations the people
> are instructed and confirmed in the articles of faith, which ought to be born in
> mind and constantly reflected upon; also that great profit is derived from all holy
> images ... .
>
> —*Canons and Decrees of the Council of Trent*, 25th session, 216

During its prolonged deliberations, the Council of Trent subjected nearly all aspects of the Catholic Church to critical scrutiny.[1] Its wide-ranging decrees touched on matters from the behavior of priests and the conducting of services to rules for entering monasteries and selecting superiors. Along with these internal reforms, the aim of Trent was to strengthen and increase the membership of the Church in face of Catholic disillusionment and Protestant incursions. These two separate yet interrelated goals are reflected in the dual terms "Catholic Reform" and "Counter-Reformation": the former referring to internal changes within the church, the latter to its external reactions against Protestantism.[2] The "interior" and "exterior" faces of Early Modern Catholicism complement other inner/outer oppositions, like those of buildings and (female) bodies, which we have already noted.

In its 25th session, before laying out the reforms of monastic enclosure that would dramatically change the lives of women religious, the Council of Trent had taken up the role of images and representations in the Church. Although idols and images "painted and adored with a seductive charm" were condemned unequivocally, Trent strongly reaffirmed the legitimacy and usefulness of religious images—a policy which, to this day, distinguishes Catholics from some Protestant denominations. In a broader context, artistic and literary representations were an integral part of the Counter-Reformation spirit as defined by Béatrice Didier: "The Counter-Reformation exalted at the same time interiority, but also

---

[1] Part of the material in this chapter was presented at the Annual Conference of the Society for Seventeenth-Century French Studies in September 2002. I wish to thank Professor William Brooks and all the participants for their encouragement and contributions to my work.

[2] On the meanings of "Counter-" and "Catholic Reformation," see the Introduction, n18.

externalization, the blatant and theatrical expression of religious sentiment, intransigent zeal" ["La Contre-Réforme … a exalté à la fois l'intériorité, mais aussi l'extériorisation, l'expression outrée et théâtrale du sentiment religieux, le zèle intransigeant," Didier 209]. During much of the Early Modern Period, the arts were central to Counter-Reformation campaigns to capture or recapture souls throughout the world. Twenty years before Trent, sixteenth-century missionaries in New Spain wrote and produced plays in Nahuatl, one of the indigenous Mexican languages (Birely 152)[3]. And as late as 1659, the Société des Missions Étrangères in Paris sent out an appeal for "some good laymen with interest and devotion who are knowledgeable in *some excellent art such as surgery, painting or music*" to embark on an evangelical expedition to the Far East (Jansen 32, n52; emphasis added). It is perhaps less well known that Catholic writers participated in a similar mission within France's very borders. This chapter will deal with authors whose efforts at conversion employ religious imagery centered on allegorical representations of the human body. This prism creates a way to examine the relation of building to body, body to soul in Catholic Reformation writing.

The role of art in the Counter-Reformation project is closely linked to the concept of the body in early modern spirituality: as Terence Cave points out, "'devotion'—for both Catholic and Calvinist—involved first and foremost the awareness of man's body and Christ's body" (303).[4] Religious debates of the period centered on whether the Eucharist meant the literal or figurative giving of Christ's body to humanity. Trent's reaffirmation of the literal meaning of transubstantiation led to a heightened "Catholic sacramentalism of the physical world" and our perceptions of it.[5] Whereas the medieval *Anchrene Wisse* enjoined the removal of all objects that might distract the soul, Ignatius of Loyola's instructions for strengthening the faith call for an "application of the senses." Baroque devotional art dramatically answers this call: in colorful, sometimes lurid detail, poets "make a concerted attack on the reader by a cumulative effect of horror … or … involve him emotionally and almost physically in a situation such as the Nativity or the Passion" (Cave 27). Bernini's celebrated *St. Teresa in Ecstasy* projects the site of mystical experience from the invisible interior onto the outward form of the female body, making a dramatic, sensuous impact on the viewer. This work, admired even by the anti-clerical Diderot, displays a strong "seductive charm" which seems to put into question the injunctions of Trent.[6] The difficulties involved in segregating

---

[3]   See also Viviana Díaz Balsera, *The Pyramid Under the Cross* (Tucson: University of Arizona Press, 2005).

[4]   Writing in the 1960s, Cave is using the expression "man's body" in a generic sense; in contrast, this chapter will investigate the differing representations of male and female bodies.

[5]   Andrew Sullivan, "The Saint and the Satirist." *New York Times Book Review*, May 30, 2004, p. 11.

[6]   According to Didier (209), Diderot sensed a natural affinity between the "fanatically" intense and dramatic style of Baroque art and his own esthetic. See below, Chapter 6.

"good" sensual impulses, of divine origin, from evil impulses associated with the Devil constitute a large part of this chapter.[7]

In contradiction to its intense corporality, Counter-Reformation thought continued to evidence a profound distrust of the body, inherited from earlier Christian tradition. One way early modern devotional writers attempted to reconcile these opposing tendencies was through an allegorical translation of the corporeal into the spiritual. Allegory occupied a significant place in the art, architecture, poetry and, especially, religious discourse of seventeenth-century France. Authors as diverse as La Fontaine, Sorel and d'Aubignac, to mention a few, shared a common allegorizing bent. Even Furetière, better known as an innovator in the modern dictionary form, authored allegorical texts.[8] Unlike unabashedly Baroque Spain, where allegory is considered part of the Baroque canon and intensively studied by scholars, French allegorical writing remained until recently relegated to a shadowy corner of the official seventeenth-century portrait.[9] This neglect was spurred by neoclassical critics like Jean Chapelain, for whom allegory represented at best a tool for rationalizing fable, in an oft-vain effort to rescue the old epics and romances from their "absurdités" (*De la lecture des vieux romans* 11).[10] The disavowal of allegory by nineteenth-century Romantics helped reinforce its occlusion, as well as that of seventeenth century spiritual writing (Van Dyke, 15).

---

[7] For more on the sixteenth-century debate surrounding the uses and dangers of the senses, see David Freedberg, *The Power of Images: Studies in the History and Theory of Response* (Chicago and London: University of Chicago Press, 1991), 368–71.

[8] Cf. La Fontaine's "Psyché" and "Le Songe de Vaux" and the allegorical illustrations in Jean-Pierre Collinet's edition of La Fontaine's *Oeuvres complètes* (Paris: Gallimard, 1991); also Furetière, *Nouvelle allégorique: Histoire des derniers troubles arrivés au royaume de l'éloquence* (1658; ed. E. Van Ginnekin [Paris: Droz, 1961]); Sorel, *La Solitude et l'amour philosophique de Cléomède* (1640) and *Relation véritable de ce qui s'est passé au royaume de Sophie, depuis les troubles excités par la rhétorique et l'éloquence. Avec un discours sur la Nouvelle Allégorique* (1659); d'Aubignac, *Macarise, ou la reine des îles fortunées* (1664) and *Histoire allégorique contenant la philosophie morale des stoïques* (1664).

[9] Principal initiators of the current interest in French classical allegory are Georges Couton (*Ecritures codées*) and Bernard Beugnot, "Pour une poétique de l'allégorie classique," in *Critique et création littéraires en France au XVIIe siècle* (Paris: Editions du C.N.R.S., 1977), pp. 409–20; reprinted in Beugnot, *La mémoire du texte* (Paris: Champion, 1994), pp. 171–86). Their initiatives remained relatively isolated until the 1990s. Since then, a number of studies on Camus and Nervèze have appeared, including those by Sylvie Robic-de Baecque, Max Vernet and Nancy Oddo. See also Chapter 2 n2 and Works Cited at the end of the book.

[10] In speaking of Homer, Chapelain states: "Judge whether the most subtle allegory can satisfy reason offended by such absurdities" ["Jugez si l'allégorie la plus subtile peut satisfaire la raison offensée par de telles absurdités"]. For an eighteenth-century critique of allegory, see Antoine Pluche, *Histoire du ciel ou l'on recherche l'origine de l'idolâtrie* (Paris: Veuve Estienne, 1740; 1st ed. of 1738 reviewed in the *Journal des savants* 1739, 418.) I owe this reference to Philippe Salazar.

While critics are again exploring the rich literature surrounding the Catholic Reform,[11] obstacles to interpretation remain. Those imbued with the rational ideology of French classicism may find it difficult to place themselves in the mindset of early seventeenth-century readers and writers, for whom a mixture of profane and sacred discourse seemed natural. Uncertainty over the status of so-called preclassical writers is reflected in the interrogatory titles of some recent criticism. Nancy Oddo asks: "Antoine de Nervèze: Pieux Protée ou caméléon mondain?" and Gabrielle Verdier simply inquires: "Lire Nervèze?" One entry into this unfamiliar world is through our common preoccupation—one might say obsession—with corporality, a subject which, as I have already suggested, was as compelling for early modern theologians as it is for contemporary geographers of the body. After exploring how spirits and their corporeal enclosures are imagined allegorically in Counter-Reformation religious discourse, and how women's bodies differ in their representation from men's, we will then assess the consequences of a concept of allegory that claims to separate spiritual from corporeal, male from female. For souls, however allegorical their depiction, remain stubbornly attached to bodies; and even in seventeenth-century writing, the body tends to escape from its assigned role as prison or hermitage of the soul to take on a troubling life of its own. This point will be examined through readings of three little-known allegorical productions from the early seventeenth century: Pierre Croix's *Miroir de l'amour divin* (1608) and two works by Antoine de Nervèze, *Le Iardin Sacré de l'Ame Solitaire* (1602) and *L'Hermitage de l'Isle saincte* (1612). Before passing to these texts, I will begin by defining allegory and tracing its implications for gender and corporality.

Though we can recognize and agree on specific instances of allegory, it often evades precise definition. According to Carolyn Van Dyke, the indefinability of allegory stems from its otherness: etymologically it denotes "other speech"—*allo goria* in Greek. This alterity is foregrounded by Roman rhetoricians. According to Quintilian, allegory is a trope that says something in order to say something else; for Augustine, "an allegory is nothing but a trope in which one thing is understood from another" (*De Trinitate* XV.9.15; *The Trinity* ed. John E. Rotelle 15.9, 407).[12]

---

[11]   Cf. for example John Lyons, *Embodied Thought from Montaigne to Rousseau* (Palo Alto: Stanford University Press, 2005) and his lecture "In Love with an Idea: François de Sales and the Inner Life" presented at the 2004 meeting of the North American Society for Seventeenth Century French Studies. More references to this subject are given in Chapter 2.

[12]   *De Trinitate* XV.9 also includes a second, slightly different definition of allegory: *quae sunt aliud ex alia significantia*, or "These things are signifying one thing from another" (*The Trinity* 406). But a close examination of the context reveals that rather than giving his own definition, Augustine is quoting the translators of Galatians, whom Augustine claims are ignorant of subtle rhetorical distinctions or writing for an uneducated audience. However, most Christian commentators (and their literary successors) seem to follow the gloss on Paul rather than Augustine's own definition. For example, Cassiodorus states: "Allegory is ... when one thing is said, and another thing signified" (see Whitman, 266–9). Part of the confusion regarding allegory arises from a tension between these two definitions. While it is obviously important to take into account the views held by later Christian exegetes, in my

While Angus Fletcher follows Quintilian (Fletcher, 2n), I prefer Augustine's *tropus ubi ex alio aliud intelligitur.* The difference in wording is subtle but important. While both Quintilian and Augustine emphasize the bivalence of allegorical discourse, in Quintilian's definition, the "something" is subordinated, if not totally evacuated, to leave room for the "something else;" for Augustine, however, both *alio* and *aliud* continue to coexist and interact, in a play of readerly understanding.[13] In modern architectural terms, allegory, though bi-level, is not split-level.

Medieval theory expanded these two levels into four.[14] The French classical view, while recognizing a four-part division in theory, remains strongly dualistic, even if the two layers can overlap in practice. My working definition of allegory emphasizes this duality: I define it as *bi-level* or *bivalent writing.* This bivalence is explicitly marked within the text, its paratexts and, when applicable, its illustrations.[15] The bi-level mode of writing and reading known as allegory has

---

view Augustine, with his rhetorical training and verbal sensitivity, shows a greater intuitive grasp of what happens in an allegorical text. More important, Augustine's work is essential to an understanding of the ensuing development of figurative language: as Colish points out, "St. Anselm, St. Thomas Aquinas and Dante all share the same verbal epistemology, an epistemology formulated first by St. Augustine in the West" (x). Augustinian theology is also the basis of the Jansenist vision, so important for seventeenth-century writing. Finally, and most directly relevant to this study, the "redeemed rhetoric" Augustine sketched in the latter part of his *Confessions* prefigured and served as a model for Counter-Reformation esthetics, suggesting the need for a counter- or Christian rhetoric to replace the beautiful but empty sounds—*flatus vocus*—of profane poetry with the message of God. Augustine stressed the "importance of learning and teaching through speech" (20). For him, the Incarnation redeemed language, which is indeed its main conduit: after all, words, through the preaching of St. Ambrose, brought God into Augustine's soul (*Confessions* V. xiv.24), and it is through words that redemption will take place: "For Augustine then, God creates the world and man through His Word, and He takes on humanity in the Word made flesh so that human words may take on divinity" (Colish 35).

[13] See also Van Dyke's refutation of "split-level" allegory (*Fiction of Truth* Chapters 1–2).

[14] The four levels of interpretation are the literal, allegorical, tropological or moral, and anagogic or spiritual. On fourfold interpretation, see Henri Lubac, *Exégèse médiévale: les quatre sens de l'écriture* (Paris: Aubier, 1959).

[15] In Maureen Quilligan's words, allegory "announces itself by a number of blatant signals" (Quilligan 163). What are these formal signals of allegory? According to Bede's eighth-century treatise *Concerning Figures and Tropes*, scriptural allegory manifests itself in two ways: *in verbis* and *in factis*. Allegory *in verbis*, the mode we are most familiar with, involves word play, extended metaphors and various figures of duality including paradox, oxymoron, simile and, most often, personification. Allegory *in factis*, on the other hand, extends beyond the level of trope to direct the structure and ordering of the narrative itself— its *inventio* and *dispositio*. Allegory *in factis* also includes narrative interventions telling the reader how to process the text. Thus bi-level, allegorical writing necessarily implies, and is accompanied by, a guided bi-level reading. That is, the allegorical mode carries with it its own *mode d'emploi*, a reader's manual for understanding the text. These basic aspects

been cast by Western philosophy and theology into spatial relations of outside to inside, container to contained. According to Aristotle, the mind or soul is a substance that occupies no space, but is nevertheless "housed" within the body; the Neo-Platonist Plotinus construes the material world as a microcosm of a transcendent order of being (Copeland, "Medieval Theory" 1). And for Macrobius, secular *fabulae* or plots can become containers of sacred messages, hidden under a "pious veil" of fiction (*Commentary* I.2.11, p. 85). Medieval authors like Alain de Lille replace Macrobius's terms *fabula* and *velus* with the generic *integumentum* (cloak, covering). By this move, the whole text becomes a cloak for divine truth.

Allegory, with its bivalent nature, is particularly suited to religious texts that juxtapose flesh and spirit. When Christian thought and imagination had to account for the dual mysteries of incarnation–the Word made Flesh (John 1:14)—and transubstantiation, the famous *hoc est corpus meum* (this is my body) of the Port-Royal logicians—it is not surprising that these doctrines were interpreted allegorically from an Augustinian perspective. According to the doctrine developed by Augustine in *De Trinitate* and *De doctrina christiana*, a sign is "something which, in addition to the impression it produces on the senses, causes something else to come to mind" (*De doctrina* II.2.1, p. 34). Augustine thus sees the sign as conceptually close to allegory, in which one thing is understood as and through another: *alio aliud*. In comparison with other signs, Biblical signs possess a double alterity since the "something else" also contains a hidden spiritual meaning. Thus, the Biblical sign can be seen as tripartite, containing signifier, signified and allegorical "other."

To interpret the divine messages hidden within Biblical signs, theologians turned to typology, the exegetic method according to which stories from the Old Testament, or even profane poetry, can contain figures and prefigurations of Christianity. In typological interpretation, spatial and architectural metaphors are often used to convey the links between body and soul or to spiritualize the corporeal: as we saw in the Introduction, the Aristotelian house of the soul is metamorphosed into a "temple of the body" (John 2:21). The divisions between body and spirit, literal and figurative meanings, and the associated typological method of interpretation, continue to inform Christian hermeneutics throughout the seventeenth century. The *Bible de Port-Royal*, published in 1701, contains, along with the Latin Vulgate version and Saci's French translation, a commentary on each passage's "literal and spiritual sense" (*sens littéral et sens spirituel*). Both Furetière and the Port Royal writers refer to this allegorical relation as *figure*. Pascal frequently uses the term *figure* in both the headings and the text of the *Pensées;* and in addition to Saci's translation and exegetical commentary, Port-Royal also

---

of allegory were recognized in seventeenth-century usage, though the signifieds were not always contained within the same signifiers. Thus, Furetière's dictionary locates allegory within the *in verbis* category as a kind of rhetorical ornament: "une métaphore continuée" (Couton, 10). Allegory *in factis*, or what I call structural allegory, persists as a form, but it is placed, following Macrobius, under the definition of "fable" (*fabula*).

published a 552-page *Figures de la Bible* with illustrations.[16] As Couton states, in scriptural interpretation "allegorical research is hence research into figures" ["La recherche allégorique est donc la recherche des figures," 23].[17]

As already stated in the Introduction, gender differentiation enters into the religious imagination of the body as into nearly all aspects of human thought, bringing with it intractable ambiguities. An example of such ambiguities is the doctrine that, since the Pentecost, the "mystical body" of God is incarnate in the Church (Colish 2). Viewed as a collectivity of believers, this religious "body" is neither specifically male nor female. But in an institutional and hierarchical sense, the Church body, as we well know, remains exclusively male. On a verbal level, the use of the male generic was, until recently, universal and unquestioned: 'Godtalk' dealt with the relation between man and a male deity. For example, in *De doctrina*, Augustine quotes from Corinthians 12:4: "*he* heard things that cannot be told, which *man* cannot utter." The quotation continues, "the condition of our race would have been much more degraded if God had not chosen to make use of *men* as the ministers of *His* word to their fellow-*men*" (4; italics added).

At first glance, allegorization might seem to offer an escape from this exclusively male discursive world: the words *église* and *âme* are grammatically feminine in both Latin and Romance languages, and often allegorized as such. Yet *le corps*, a masculine noun, is rarely represented as male; on the contrary, the allegorical construction of bodies incorporates an implicit sexual dualism whereby the female represents the natural, the male the spiritual. Woman re-enters the scheme of things through reference to the flesh—the material part of our nature, or nature in general, whereas the male is frequently dematerialized. Thus Pascal, whose discourse is less anti- than non-feminine, employs metaphors like "the ample bosom of nature" ["l'ample sein de la nature," *Pensées* L199] and "the veil of nature which covers God" ["Le voile de la nature qui couvre Dieu," lettre à Mlle de Roannez, *Oeuvres complètes* 267]. Once the burden of corporality is shifted onto the female, the male element can freely be spiritualized and dematerialized. Like the Church structure, this spirit-flesh/male-female dichotomy is hierarchical, with carnal knowledge seen as a lower, debased form of knowledge. To quote Augustine again: "Now it is surely a miserable slavery of the soul to take signs for things, and to be unable to lift the eye of the mind above what is corporeal and created ..." (*De doctrina* 86). While the soul is exalted, the body, and particularly the female body, remains a site of impurity and evil. And real women, who figure the carnal yet, for Christianity, possess souls as well, find themselves at a spiritual disadvantage vis à vis their

---

[16] *Figures de la Bible* was published in1670; it has been attributed by Couton to Saci or Fontaine (Couton 577).

[17] A similar ambiguity is implied in the notion of the mystical body as a body politic, as theorized by Michel de Certeau. On this topic, see Hélène Merlin, "Fables of the 'Mystical Body' in Seventeenth-Century France", in *Corps mystique, corps sacré: Textual Transfigurations of the Body from the Middle Ages to the Seventeenth Century. Yale French Studies* 86 (1994), 126–42.

male counterparts: the desexualized male body reflects the divine in ways the female cannot. "Only man, therefore, is fully [in] the image of God; woman is so only through her soul, while her body constitutes a permanent obstacle to the exercise of her reason" ["L'homme seul est donc pleinement image de Dieu; la femme ne l'est que par son âme, son corps constituant un obstacle permanent à l'exercice de sa raison," *Les Femmes au grand siècle* 15]. Gender inequalities go even deeper. It is often assumed that every human being possesses an asexual soul and a sexed body; but Augustine, in his allegorical interpretation of Genesis 2:11, divides the very soul into two genders: Adam represents *virilis ratio* and Eve the *pars animalis*. Thus, within each human soul there is a kind of marriage, by which the "virile" should guide and control the animal, female partner. Unfortunately (or fortunately), an analysis of Croix's *Miroir de l'amour divin* will reveal that in literature as in life, this marriage is not always so smooth, nor the domination of "virile reason" so certain, as Augustine portrayed them.

Pierre de Croix and the Mirror on its Edge

We will now examine how the ambiguities of religious allegorization affect the "marriage" of male and female bodies and souls in a perfect context for that purpose: the Song of Songs. Attributed to King Solomon in his youth, the Song is a lusty and sensual paean to the beauties of nature and the beloved. This erotically charged text has evoked a fascination mixed with wariness from clergy of all persuasions. In the first century of the Common Era, the rabbis who established the canon of the Hebrew Bible retained Solomon's poem, but with the stern warning that it should only be read as an "allegory of the loving relation between the Lord and Israel, his bride" (Steiner 29). With the advent of Christianity, the Song became a favorite source for a wide variety of writings, from the Latin commentaries of the early Middle Ages to the Puritan sermons of seventeenth-century Massachusetts. The Song was also mined for Christian meanings in early modern France: it was a popular subject among both Catholic and Calvinist poets, including Chassignet, Bèze and Belleau. M. Hamon, doctor for the Port-Royal convent, wrote an *Explication du Cantique des Cantiques* which appeared in 1708, after his death. Cloistered nuns also composed meditations on the Song, discussed by Mary Rowan in "The Song of Songs in Conventual Discourse." In such Christian allegories, woman is the *hortus conclusus*, the enclosed virginal garden exemplified by Mary. And the female body, amorous and erotic in the original poem, is salvaged as a figure of the Church or the Soul. Architectural allegory here takes on a gendered twist already familiar to us. While all bodies may be allegorized as buildings, women's bodies are more specifically constructed as enclosures: the female body contains the womb as buildings contain gardens, courtyards or cloisters (see above, Introduction, 29–30). Thus, through a process of allegorical transformation, "the potentialities of a style developed in a profane context are released into vernacular devotion; and once again, Biblical paraphrase has been the mediator" (Cave, 263–4). But once "profane" style has been "released" from its confines, the consequences may not be what the Christian allegorist would have wished. *Miroir de l'Amour Divin* is a case in point.

Le Miroir de l'Amour Divin, a collection of religious poetry by Pierre de Croix, Seigneur de Trietre, contains a striking Song of Songs allegory. Croix's collection existed only in its original Douai edition of 1608 until it was reedited by Lance K. Donaldson-Evans and published by Droz in 1990. Little is known of its author, beyond the fact that he was a gentleman of Lille whose devotion to God and to Ronsard is expressed with real talent.[18] Croix's *Miroir* is a literary device for "converting" Renaissance love poetry into a vehicle for religious expression and spiritual rebirth. The mirror was a central allegorical trope throughout the Christian Middle Ages and Renaissance—so central that a major medieval journal is called *Speculum*.[19] Their mirror was both an allegorical vehicle and an alternative, non-mimetic space. Unlike the neutral reflector of nineteenth-century realism, the pre-modern mirror does not reproduce what Stendhal called "the mud below and the sky above." Rather, like the magic looking glass of fairy tales, its shows us both how things truly are and how they could or should be. The archetype for this revelatory mirror is of course the Bible. According to Alcuin, "In the reading of the Holy Scriptures is the knowledge of divine blessedness. Man can consider himself in them as in a *mirror*; he can see what he is and what he aims at" (quoted in Bradley 102; italics added). Thus, the scriptural mirror has an exemplary and a transfiguring effect: by looking in it, one can become what one sees. Like these earlier examples, Croix's *Miroir de l'Amour Divin* opens an alternative space within which one hopes to see divine love revealed, not just a mimetic representation of it.

Croix attempts to convert Renaissance love poetry into a vehicle for religious expression and spiritual rebirth by applying typological interpretations to both Old Testament texts and pagan mythology (*Miroir*, Introduction 14). In the first book of *Le Miroir*, a series of stances and sonnets contrasts profane and divine love, in a sensuous style foregrounding Renaissance imagery (38). This mixture also characterizes Croix's allegorical meditation on the Song of Songs: sungods, cherubs, arrows, chains and flames mingle in peaceable poetic fusion with the shepherds, sheep and cedars of Solomon's pastoral landscape.[20] Most of the 31 sections of Book 3 are introduced by lines from the Song in the Vulgate Latin; but the poem also includes quotations from the Psalms and Isaiah. With these

---

[18] He calls Ronsard "le Prince de nos Poëtes" (*Au lecteur*, 27).

[19] Authors from Augustine to Marguerite Porete gave the title "mirror" to their works: cf. *De Scriptura sancta Speculum*, in *Patrologia latina*, ed. Jacques-Paul Migne [Paris: Migne, 1844–54. 32.887–1040]. Augustine also refers to the holy mirror in *Ennarratio in Psalmum* 103 (PL xxxii, 1338). *Le Mirouer des simples Ames: Margaretae Porete Speculum simplicium animarum* contains both the Latin and French versions of Porete's work. (Ed. Paul Verdeyen, Romana Guarnieri [Turnhout: Brepols, 1986].)

[20] *petites Amours, traits, chaisnes* and *flames*.

materials, Croix weaves a complex polyphony of voices: third-person descriptions, first-person narrative interventions and a "chorus" of girls of Zion who express themselves as "we." But in the main, the work is a first-person dialogue—or juxtaposition of monologues—between its two main characters, the Eternal Word (*le verbe Eternel*) and the Christian soul (*l'ame chrestienne*). This point of view, which enhances the exploration of intimate thoughts and feelings, is well chosen for tracing the dramatic ups and downs of an amorous relationship that is simultaneously spiritual and intensely personal: in his analysis of François de Sales's *Traité de l'amour divin*, John Lyons speaks of a "lover's quarrel" between "man" and God (*Traité* 424). And at the beginning of *Le Miroir*, the narrator reveals to the reader that the soul involved is *my* soul, "mon ame" (195, v. 2).

Croix describes his subject as "le sacré mariage du verbe Eternel et de l'ame chrestienne" (195). The Christian tradition of sacred or Mystic Marriage derives from pagan gnosticism, in which the figure of sexual union was used to describe "the relation between the individual soul and the Godhead" (Hills, *Invisible City* 58). This allegorical Marriage could link the souls of men and women alike to God. With the incorporation of a nuptial-like ritual into medieval profession ceremonies for nuns, the nature of the mystic marriage changed: from a joining with an impersonal godhead, it became a personal union between an individual *sponsa Christi* (Bride of Christ) and Jesus. As post-Trent Catholic spirituality became more sensorial, the union of Christ the lover and his beloved was expressed more and more "literally" (Cave 245). Rather than depicting the marriage of a nun to her Holy Bridegroom, Croix's poem describes a seemingly more abstract union of the soul with the Holy Spirit. Nevertheless, his paraphrase of the Song of Songs exhibits the concretization, gendering and sexualization characteristic of Counter-Reformation art in general and the representation of the Mystic Marriage in particular. Croix follows the grammatical and oratorical tradition according to which the Holy Spirit (or *Verbe*) is masculine and the Soul feminine. In addition to its grammatical gender, the soul possesses other so-called feminine attributes associated with youth and beauty: smallness, weakness and inconstancy. She refers to herself as "I, still a young thing, delicate and weak" ["Moy qui jeunette encor, delicate et debile," 213, v. 10], and "I, small and languorous in soul *and* body" ["moi d'ame *et* de corps chetive et langoureuse," 214, v. 17; italics added]. Thus, not only is the narrator's female soul contained within a male body and identity—his own—but the soul itself has a female body which both feels and arouses desire.

The oxymoronic figure of the sensual spirit, or spiritual body, is not unique to Croix's poem: it often occurs in works from the Catholic Reformation, including an anonymous Latin text set to music by the seventeenth-century composer Marc-Antoine Charpentier. The relevant passage begins: "Pierce through, O Sweetest Jesus, the *heart and body of my spirit* with the healing and cleansing wound of your love" ["Transfige dulcissime Jesu, *medullas et viscera animae meae* suavissimo ac suluberimo amoris tue vulnere"; italics added].[21] *Medullas*, "bone marrow," is translated here as "heart," and *viscera*, a word frequently found in religious discourse, becomes "body"; the French equivalent is the more concrete *entrailles* (see below, 53). The translation erases the corporality of the Latin original: unlike the conventional "heart and body," *medullas* and *viscerae* denote hidden, intimate and vulnerable parts of the human anatomy. This text was probably written to accompany the elevation, the part of the mass following the consecration of the Host where the body of Christ is offered up for communion.[22] In this context, *vulnere* refers to the wound made in Christ's side by the soldier's lance. In a profane context, it also recalls the wounds made by Cupid's arrows, allowing love to enter the heart. In this case, their purpose is to break down the barriers blocking human union with God. The narrator asks "that my soul may weaken and melt forever solely in the love and desire for You; / May my soul covet You and lose itself in Your dwelling place, may it desire to become one with You" ["ut languat et liquifiat anima mea solo semper amore et desiderio tui: / Te concupiscat et deficiat in atria tua, cupeat dissolvi et esse tecum"]. Strict body/soul dualism is exploded by the "embodiment" of the soul, lost in translation.

The amorous corporality of *Transfige* and other early modern Catholic texts is carried to a high intensity in Pierre de Croix's *Miroir*. Croix's representation of the Soul/Bride desiring her mystic Bridegroom contains a potent mixture of the sensual with the spiritual. For example, in part 2, an amplification of "kiss me with the kisses of your mouth" [*osculetur me osculo oris sui*] from verse 1 of the Song, the Espouse says: "I want the full enjoyment of your kisses, and the sweetest honey of their suavity" ["Je veux de tes baisers la pleine jouissance, / et le miel plus sucré de leur suavité," 202, vv. 86–7]. In part 4, the Espoux's "essence" permeates her entire body, like a perfumed oil that has "flowed into my bosom, my heart" ["Coulé dans mon sein, en mon coeur," 207, v. 3]. While the passage evokes the opening of the Song, "your anointing oils are fragrant," it also recalls the scent of perfume spread from the dining table throughout Simon's entire house in the Gospel story of Mary Magdalene. This perfume can be interpreted typologically as Jesus' grace (Duby 28). The typological meaning is reinforced in *Le Miroir* when the Espouse asks the Espoux: "Bring me this fragrance that perfumes me" ["Fay venir jusqu'à moy ceste odeur qui m'embasme," 215, vv. 61–2]. In an elegant quatrain based on Song 3:6, Croix depicts the Espouse rising above the desert to meet her holy Bridegroom:

> Oh who is this, who with an agile tread
> Leaving the world and its gaze far behind
> Like a fragrant and subtle plume of smoke
> Ascends from the desert to reach the Heavens?

---

[21]   M.-A. Charpentier, *Motet à cinq parties 'Transfige, dulcissime Jesu,'* performed by Les Chantres de la Chapelle de Versailles, Saturday, February 8, 2003, First United Methodist Church of Coral Gables, Florida. English translation from the program notes.

[22]   This information was given to me in a conversation with the director of the Chantres de la Chapelle de Versailles, Olivier Schneebeli.

Hé, qui est celle-cy qui, d'une traite agile
Laissant bien loing derriere et le monde et ses yeux
Comme un trait de fumée odoreuse et subtile
Monte par le desert, et donne dans les Cieux? (242.1–4)

Although the Espouse is imagined as disembodied and separated from the world, she still perfumes the air for those below: "With what exquisite odors of incense and myrrh / she perfumes the air and the fields all around" ["Que d'exquises senteurs et d'encens et de myrrhe / Elle emparfume l'air, et les champs d'allentour!"]. The next two lines, more suitable for a love poem, are not found in the Biblical original: "What graces and amiable attractions she breathes forth / Suffused with delight and burning with love!" ["Que de graces, d'attraits aimables elle respire / De delice entournee, et bruslante d'amour!" 242 vv. 5–8]. Even in her heavenly ascension, she brings the *delices* and *flammes* of love with her. Other references to oil, incense and perfume also heighten the text's carnal impact, as in "The radiant Sun of your mercy / Has melted these oils, and their fragrance overflows / With a delicious scent that, avidly, I pursue" ["Le Soleil radieux de ta misericorde / A fondu ces onguens, et leur odeur desborde / D'un flair delicieux qu'avide je poursui," 215 vv. 74–5], and "I run through shrubberies and bushes, immersed in its fragrance" ["Par halliers et buissons je cours en son odeur," 214 v. 48].

As she feels and enjoys desire, the Soul suffers from a consciousness of herself as body. The verses inspired by this theme depart markedly from the original. Some recall neo-Platonism: "Still subject to endless infirmities / Weighed down by the cowardly passions of the body" ["A mille infirmitez encor assujettie / Des lasches passions du corps appesantie," 214 vv. 25–6]; others employ the harsh terms of asceticism. L'Ame asks the Espoux: "What makes you in the enclosure of my heart / Search for your beloved domicile, as in some holy place? / …. Can your pure beauty / Find a pleasant spot in such a foul location?" ["Qui te fait rechercher dans l'enclos de mon cœur / Comme en quelque lieu saint ton aimé domicile? / …. Peut donc ta beauté pure / Trouver place agreable en un lieu tant infect?" 207, v. 15–18). The Soul also condemns "this corporeal being that binds me with earthly bonds / The proud and cruel tyrant that holds me trapped in its mire" ["Cet estre corporel qui de liens de terre / Fier et cruel tyran dans ses fanges m'enserre," 215, vv. 79–80]. The Espoux, for his part, uses the language of corruption to put the Soul in her place when she arrogantly seeks to rise too high, or know too much of her divine Husband: "For a bit of mud, ha! You presume too much. … For a meal for worms, it is far too great a hope. / Eternal is the honor of my omnipotence, / And you will rot and lie in the tomb" ["Pour un morceau de fange, ha! C'est trop presumer. … Pour un repas aux vers, c'est par trop d'esperance. / Eternel est l'honneur de ma toute-puissance, / Et tu vas pourriture en la tombe gesir," 232, v. 3, 10–12]. Perhaps sensing that this representation of divine wrath is less than sympathetic, the author intervenes at this point to reassure the reader that the Espoux's anger is merely feigned—a stratagem meant to test the Soul and make her worthy of his love. All will be forgiven, and the fructifying kiss of the Espoux will transform her "stench-filled entrails" ["entrailles ... pleines de puanteur"] into "a vessel of sweet herbs" ["un vaisseau plein de doux aromats," 204, v. 61, 64].

The preceding quotations demonstrate how frequently the female body is described in the poem as a container—a vase or vessel filled with corruption or perfume. Other enclosed spaces associated with the Espouse are *enclos*, *cabinet* (257–8), and, of course, *jardin*: "You have chosen me for a pleasure garden / Where free of all care, your spirit is refreshed, / For an amorous flowerbed where one's sweetest desire / Through countless pleasures frolics and plays" ["Tu m'as comme choisi pour jardin de plaisir / Où libre de tout soing ton esprit se recree, / Pour parterre amoureux où son plus doux desir / En mille voluptez s'esbat et s'agree," 242, vv. 25–8; see also 245]. Of all the images of enclosure found in the Biblical Song, it is interesting that Croix does *not* borrow the most common Christian conceit: the *hortus conclusus* of the Virgin's intact body.

The female body transformed into a "garden of pleasure" or "vase ... filled with vice" recalls familiar gender patterns. It is much rarer, however, to see the Verbe/Espoux embodied as a male who feels desire at the sight of the Bride. In Croix's poem, her "charms" (*appas*) shot out "amorous little flames ... and the spouse suffered a thousand breaches in his heart" ["amoureuses flamesches. ... et l'espoux en son coeur en souffrait mille bresches," 196, vv. 22, 24]; more concretely, he feels a "*burning heat* in his *entrails*" ["*ardeur* dans ses *entrailles*," 204, v. 69; italics added]. While the words *ardeur* and *entrailles* are often used allegorically in religious poetry, the intense inner heat of Croix's "amoureuses flamesches" gives these allegorical commonplaces an unusually erotic tone. As for the Espoux's body, while it is not depicted as a hollow space like the Espouse's, neither is it shown as an impregnable structure. The Bride's physical attractions break down—make breaches in—the Espoux's bodily integrity.

The mutual desire uniting the lovers is acknowledged by the Espouse when she asks: "Can I prevent you from taking pleasure / In the sought-after love of your humble servant" ["Pourroy je t'empescher de prendre les plaisirs / En l'amour recherché de ton humble servant," 256, vv. 49–50]. This reciprocity is highlighted throughout the poem by a recirculation of identical amorous vocabulary. Thus the Espoux "languishes" for his beloved: "Think of him who seeks you in this way / Think of the fervent *desires* of his *languishing* heart" ["Pense qui est celuy qui de sorte te cherche / Pense aux fervents *desirs* de son coeur *languissant*," 247, vv. 25–6; italics added]. In an indirect response, the Espouse implores the daughters of Zion: "Tell him how the pains of love I suffer for him / Pursue and importune me night and day, / Tell him how strong is the *desire* that tortures me / Tell him, I beg of you, for I *languish* with love" ["Dites luy que pour luy une amoureuse peine / Me poursuit, importune, et la nuict et le jour, / Dites luy la rigueur du *desir* qui me geine, / Dites-luy je vous pri', car je *languis* d'amour," 249, vv. 25–8; italics added]. Both Espoux and Espouse are compared to negligent lovers. The Spouse complains in rather tortuous style: "Ungrateful one, how can you see the one who, full of care, undergoes endless suffering in order to find you, / The one you should seek out despite myriad difficulties / And still neglect his anxious pursuit?" ["Ingrate, peux tu voir celuy qui soucieux / Tu devrais rechercher au prix de mille maux / Subir pour te trouver mille et mille travaux / Et negliger encor sa poursuite anxieuse?" 247, vv. 29–32]. The Spouse laments more simply: "When I most thought I could rely on him / Alas! He withdrew" ["Lors que plus je pensoy me reposer en lui / Las! Il s'est retire," 217, vv. 35–6].

Thus in the *Miroir*, allegorical lovers of both sexes suffer desire and its "mille et mille maux," and references are made to both male and female bodies. Nevertheless, actual depictions of the body, both negative and positive, are much less frequent and developed for the male than for the female. In other words, while both spirits have bodies (or both bodies have spirits), the male is not materialized as a full physical presence. Despite the reference to his "entrailles" in the example above, most descriptions of the Espoux focus less on his body than on how the sight or imagination of the Espouse's body affects him—a common way of representing masculine desire through transference. As a result, the Soul/Bride's corporeal beauty is detailed repeatedly and almost obsessively. Part 6, drawn mostly from the Song of Songs ["tiré de la plus part des Cantiques"], contains familiar Biblical comparisons: "Her nose is like the Tower of Lebanon which looks towards / Famous Damascus, and the fields around. / I compare her teeth to the whitest fleece / Of the freshly-shorn herds coming up from the washing, / To my flocks with a fresh whiteness about them, / All bearing twins with not a barren one among them" ["Son néz est comme la tour du Liban qui regarde / La fameuse Damas, et les champs d'environ. / J'accompare ses dents à la thoison plus blanche / Des troupeaux frais-tondus qui montent du lavoir, / A mes ouailles qui ont une candeur si franche / Toutes afruits gemaux sans de sterile y voir," *Cantique* 7:5; *Miroir* 209, vv. 23–8]. Augustine, also taken by the comparison of teeth to fleece, interpreted it typologically as "the teeth of the Church cutting off men from their errors and transferring them to her body, after their hardness has been softened as if by being bitten and chewed" (*De doctrina*, I.vi.7.37).[23] Croix's verses do not attempt such typological sublimation.

Other descriptive passages, belonging stylistically and lexically to the late Renaissance, rival or outdo the Biblical source in their use of graphic detail (Donaldson-Evans, introduction 13–16). Thus, part II constitutes a kind of *blason du corps féminin de l'âme* [coat of arms of the soul's female body], in the tradition of Belleau and Ronsard. Dressed in fine fabric and adorned with jewels, the Soul is detailed from the golden crown on her head down to her feet. Her "fine, wavy hair, unbound / Outshone the splendor and grace of gold itself. / This beautiful golden hair artistically loosened / From time to time fluttered back and forth, / Hidden within it, Cupid shot his arrows, / The spouse found himself caught in their wantonness. / A precious ruby adorned / her round, white, tender and delicate ear" ["cheveux primes, torts, deliez / De l'or mesme effaçoit la splendeur et la grace. / Ces beaux cheveux orins artistement espars / Çà et là voletoient à petites remises,

---

[23]   On this passage and Augustinian figures in general, see Woshinsky, *The Linguistic Imperative* (Saratoga, CA: Anma Libri, 1991), 110–14.

/ Amour qui s'y cacha tiroit de là ses dards, / L'espoux se trouva pris dedans leurs mignardises. / Un ruby precieux alloit enrichissant / Sa ronde, blanche, tendre et delicate oreille," 196, vv. 27–34]. On her bosom, "twin mounds, appeared two rubies, or two rosebuds" ["tertre jumeau … paraissoient deux rubis, ou deux boutons de roses"]. The adjectives "ronde, blanche, tendre et delicate," used in the preceding lines to describe the ear, carry over their meaning to the breasts. (And what does it mean for a soul to have nipples? Few allegorical manuals contain the answer to this question.) The passage's conclusion transposes this sensual imagery onto a metaphorical level, straining syntactic separations between individual lines: "In brief, all the most exquisite things the voluptuous / Orient hides in its Bosom overflowed upon her / Along with the scents of the pungent perfumes / In which happy Arabia opulently excels" ["Bref, tout ce qu'en son Sein l'Orient plantureux / Cache de plus exquis abondit dessus elle, / Et les senteurs encor des parfums odoreux / Dont l'heureuse Arabie opulemment excelle," 197, vv. 65–8]. The French language is unusually rich in words for perfume, and Croix exploits many of them.

To counteract the effects of this pre-Baudelarian exoticism, Croix employs a series of arguments fusing Petrarchan with Augustinian neo-Platonism. First, the narrator claims that the Espoux loves the Espouse for her inner beauty alone, of which her physical attractions are but a mirror: "Thus the many beauties ornamenting the outside / Were the portrait of the beauties within. / It was the true mirror of perfection" ["Aussi tant de beautez ornemens du dehors / Des beautez du dedens estoient la portraiture. / C'estoit le vrai miroir de la perfection," 198 vv. 103–4]. The narrator also insists on the reforming power of the Bride's virtue: "They [the virtues] increasingly inflamed him with completely new desires / Reforming the lowness of his first desires / And as refining gold in their sacred furnaces / Gave him access to more divine concepts" ["Elles (les vertus) alloient l'enflammant de desirs tous nouveaux / De ses premiers desirs reformant la bassesse, / Et comme or l'affinant en leurs sacrez fourneaux / Aux conceps plus divins luy donnerent adresse," 198, vv. 80–84]. However, these claims are no more convincing than such claims usually are when made by earthly suitors.

Finally, the Espoux's first-person intervention makes such excuses moot because he denies feeling any physical desire: "But however the beauty that charms me in you / Let it not be considered an earthly beauty. … However beautiful a body may be, it never caused me to love / I am not the prize of such a vile flame" ["Mais pourtant la beauté qui me ravit en toy / Qu'on ne l'aille estimer une beauté de terre. … Pour beau que soit un corps jamais il ne m'esprit / Je ne suis le butin d'une si vile flame," 35, vv. 41–2, 47–8]. Untouched himself, he has only used carnal language so that the human Bride may understand: "I only use earthly discourse / To make you understand my ideas better. / The earth that holds you clasped in its bonds / Makes it impossible for you to understand me when I speak of Heaven" ["Je me sers seulement de discours terriens / Affin de mes conceps te faire mieux comprendre. / La terre qui te tient serree en ses liens / Fait que parlant du Ciel tu ne sçaurais m'entendre," 235, vv. 49–52]. This final argument is even less convincing, since it contradicts the others: if the Espoux's use of profane love language is merely allegorical, why would he need to reform the *bassesse* of his desires?

More compelling than these explicit justifications, in my view, is the allegorical theory of mirroring and mutuality implicit in Croix's work. As we have seen, the narrator repeatedly emphasizes the reciprocity of the bond linking Soul to Bridegroom: "And with an equal effect acting on the Spouse / A reciprocal fire flowed into his soul" ["et d'un égal effet en l'Espoux agissant / Un reciproque feu luy couloit dedens l'ame," 198, vv. 91–2]. This reciprocity is based on a belief in the creation of man by God's hand and in his own image: "Man without contradiction is his most beautiful work, / Molded by his own hand, in his own image, / To unite him, immortal, to his divinity" ["L'homme sans contredit est son plus bel ouvrage, / Moulé de sa main propre, et à sa propre image, / Pour l'unir, immortel, à sa divinité," 252, vv. 50–52]. If, following the Platonic tradition, any love is a desire for one's other half—"L'aimée à son amant est un autre soy mesme" (255, v. 32) —how much stronger must God's desire be to complete Himself through union with his creature and mirror reflection? This union is expressed in the beautiful lines: "O perfect beauty, of the image, / Where I see myself my lovelier self as in a mirror" ["O parfaite beauté, de moy mesme l'image, / Où je vois mon plus beau comme dans un miroir," 244, vv. 115–16]. The allegorization of Man as a beautiful woman is the perfect expression of this godly/male desire.

In conclusion, *Le Miroir* has two linked aims, both dear to the heart of Counter-Reformation esthetics: to "convert" the literature of profane love and thereby to harness its erotic power for spiritual ends. As Croix says to the reader, "In short, I have described for you the love of a true Christian" ["Bref je t'ay descry les amours d'un vray Chrestien," 27]. It is this doubling of profane and sacred discourses that gives the work its seductive power, felt in lines like "Plunged again, engulfed in the sea of love" ["Replongee, abismee en la mer des amours," 208, v. 39]. Certainly, people throughout the ages have expressed their passionate longing for union with God; and Croix's devotion was convincing enough for his work to pass the muster of the Catholic Church. According to George Colveneere, Licencié et Professeur en la S. Theologie, visitor and censor at the University of Douai, "this book ... which contains nothing contrary to the Catholic faith, [and] thus is full of piety and devotion, therefore can be usefully published" ["Ce livre ... lequel ne contient chose contraire à la foy Catholique, ainsi est plein de pieté et devotion, partant se pourra utilement imprimer," 263]. In the spirit of Trent, imagery turned to the service of Christianity can be of "great profit."

Yet the very power of amorous language in *Le Miroir* subverts its pious aims. For this reader, Croix is much more effective when he describes erotic delights than when he glosses, and glosses over, them allegorically. Furthermore, given the bivalent and imbricated nature of allegory, his attempt to use figures to spiritualize or dematerialize the corporeal have the opposite effect of reinforcing the links between body and soul. To what extent writing religious poetry about allegorized female bodies reveals a disguised or displaced eroticism on the part of the poet is something we cannot know—nor, perhaps, did he. But the harder

Croix's narrator tries to sublimate desire and clothe the female body in holiness, the more mired he becomes in the *fange* of corporality—and of allegory. This dilemma prefigures similar difficulties Jean-Pierre Camus will face in transmuting the profane "body" of fiction into an *histoire dévote* (see below, Chapter 2). The reversibility of allegory was well expressed by Honoré de Balzac, who stated that when word becomes flesh, "flesh becomes word" (Miller, "The Two Allegories," 361). Croix's work attempts to reflect the divine in the human, the male in the female, the spirit in the body; but too often, the mirror turns on its edge to project a very different reflection. To paraphrase Balzac, when the Word becomes flesh, Flesh has the last word.

Retreat, Bodies and Gender in Antoine de Nervèze's Allegorical Meditations

> Our spirit finds its hermitage everywhere, and in the most crowded assemblies of men in the largest cities, I often find myself in the desert [Notre esprit trouve son hermitage partout, et dans les plus nombreuses assemblés des hommes des plus grandes villes, je m'y trouve souvent au désert].
> —François La Mothe Le Vayer, "De la vie privée," 147.

At the same time the Society of Jesus and other Catholic organizations were launching an ambitious expansion plan through missionary and apostolic expeditions, early modern Catholicism manifested an equally powerful trend toward withdrawal, in the forms of meditation, retreat and interiority. The origins of this movement are multiple. At the turn of the seventeenth century, the *topos* of retreat was very much in vogue in secular literature; Montaigne famously exchanged his public function for a private life in retirement. In Danièle Duport's words, "Against a background of wars and doubts, the conjoined influences of the definitions of happiness in classical writings call forth the dream of a pastoral and agricultural golden age" ["Sur un fond de guerres et de doutes, les influences conjuguées des définitions du bonheur chez les Anciens font surgir le rêve d'un âge d'or pastoral et agricole," Duport 89]. The secular expressions of "the popular fashion of retreat to the country" ["cette vogue de la retraite aux champs"] will be further examined in Chapter 2. Devotional and mystical literature also manifested a preoccupation with retreat, both in the literal sense of retirement from a corrupting world and the metaphorical sense of withdrawal into the self. St. Teresa of Avila's *Life*, which became popular in elite devout circles immediately after it was translated into French in 1601, gave impetus to a cult of interior mystical experience.[24] But the preoccupation with inner retreat permeated all doctrinal camps, even those hostile to mysticism: as Nicolas Paige points out, "Antoine Arnauld's *De la fréquente communion* (1643) contains 38 uses of variants of 'secret,' 21 of 'intérieur'

---

[24] For a general introduction to Teresa of Avila, see Patricia Ranft, *Women and the Religious Life in Premodern Europe* (New York: MacMillan 1996, 1998) Chapters 7–8. See also references to Benedetta Papasogli and Nicolas Paige in Chapter 1, 11–12, 14.

12 of 'caché,' 10 of 'profond' and 7 of 'invisible'" (*Being Interior* 250n86). Jean-Pierre Camus, glossing Montaigne on the sense of spiritual interiority, sees the essayist's self-study as an effort to "penetrate more deeply into the secret cells and recesses of the spirit" ["pénétrer plus profondément dans les secrets cachots et recoins d'un esprit," Camus, *Diversités*, quoted in Paige 42].[25]

Like spiritual writing, religious fiction from the early seventeenth century also explores varied forms of retreat—whether inner or outer, pastoral or conventual. It is tempting to see these early modern images as paralleling the historical movement from desert to social enclosure which took place in the formative centuries of the Christian era. Certainly, born-again Catholics turned to the writings and example of the Desert Fathers. And many *romans dévots*, like the popular pastoral romances of the time, chronicle the wanderings in deserted places of voluntary and involuntary exiles from society. For example, Lourdelot's *Courtisane solitaire* (1622) is set in the early Christian era in the desert of the Thébaïde, or southern Egypt. In this long, rambling work, multiple narrators recount a series of saints' lives flavored with romance. In the first episode, the hermit Hardouin tells the primary narrator how he came to choose a solitary life. As a young man, Hardouin had asked for the hand of Maxilende, but she wished to remain a virgin. Outraged at Maxilende's refusal, Hardouin stabbed her. This martyr's dying words so touched Hardouin's heart that he retired into the desert, where he lived for 77 years without encountering any other mortal than a few Anchorites (85).

Not all *romans dévots* show their heroes wandering in the desert. Rather, an early example of the genre, Antoine de Nervèze's *Victoire de l'amour divin sous la description des amours de Polidore & de Virginie* (1608), presents a model of monastic retreat. Nervèze (1570?–1625?) was both a successful courtier and an amazingly prolific writer in many genres. Secrétaire de la Chambre to Henri IV, he penned a *Guide des courtisans*, letters of consolation to the nobility and a funeral oration for the King. Between 1590 and 1610, he also published at least 50 novels and a number of pastorals. Even after he ceased writing *romans dévots* per se, Nervèze's religious writings continued to incorporate novelistic traits (Oddo 44n20).[26] At the same time, allegorical figures cross the boundary between Nervèze's purely allegorical works and his novels.

Two illustrated texts by Nervèze, *Le Iardin Sacré de l'Ame Solitaire* (1602) and *L'Hermitage de l'Isle saincte* (1612), represent through allegorical imagery the

---

[25]   Camus further develops the religious implications of Montaigne's interiority in his 1631 *Traité de la réformation intérieure*.

[26]   Among Nervèze's disparate works are: *Les religieuses Amours de Florigène et de Meliagre* (1601), *L'exercise dévot de la courtisane repentie* (1603), *Amours diverses* (1606) and *Le guide des courtisans* (1613). The most complete study of Nervèze's *romans dévots* is Oddo's, which also contains a thorough bibliography of his writings. See also Yves Giraud, "Parlez-nous d'amour: Roman et sentiment chez Nervèze." *Travaux de littérature* 6 (1993) 103–24; and M.-M. Fragonard, "La notion d'image: un confluent du discours théologique et du discours littéraire." *Figures* 5 (1990), 67–8.

Christian's seeking after a place of physical and spiritual retreat.[27] Like Croix's *Miroir*, Nervèze's *Le Iardin Sacré* is a series of first-person meditations (10 in all) inspired by the Song of Songs. But its relation to the Song is looser than that of *Miroir*: most references are introduced in the early meditations and recur only in part 10. Within this scriptural frame, *Le Iardin* unfolds an allegorical itinerary of its own that incorporates a series of illustrations. These images, in turn, serve as a point of departure for the meditations: whereas the individual parts of Croix's *Miroir* commence with long quotations, each section of *Le Iardin* begins with an engraving. The illustrations add another hermeneutic level to the text and further complicate the already tangled issues surrounding the representation of gender and the body in religious allegory.

The first meditation of *Le Iardin* begins with the main character, L'Esprit, confessing that in the past, his imagination had been debased (*abaissé*) by sensuality. At present, having gained "une nouvelle vigueur" which allows him to take control of his own fancies, he finds himself "as if transported to a lonely, deserted place" ["comme transporté en un désert solitaire," 10]. This *désert* is both a simile for *la retraite intérieure* and part of a meditative exercise for the reader. A few lines later, the metaphorical/meditative space metamorphosizes into a Biblical "Jardin" where the Soul seeks its Creator. "It is the Garden where the Savior calls his Spouse, saying: 'Come, my Spouse, come into my garden where there are the wells of living waters and the streams of Lebanon'" ["C'est le Iardin où le Sauveur appelle son Espouse, disant Viens mon Espouse viens en mon Iardin où sont les puids des eaux vives & les ruisseaux du Liban," 10; marginal annotation to *Can. 4*]. This quotation, with its reference to the Song of Songs, reveals common imagery with Croix.

At this point, third-person narration gives way to the first person, whose identity has also metamorphosized from Esprit to Ame. At the same time, physical retreat replaces the purely spiritual: the narrator literally interprets the Espoux's call to go out into the fields and vineyards (*Can. 7*) as "go, my soul, far from the noise of cities" ["allez, mon ame, allez loing du bruit des villes," 17]. However, the text continues to vacillate between literal and figurative representations of retreat: while the narrator decries city life and celebrates "the reign of solitude" ["ce regne de la solitude"] of early monasticism (16–17), the Soul is also enjoined by God's Angel to walk "in this Sacred Garden, where you *spiritually entered by the gates of Meditation*" ["dans ce Iardin Sacré, où vous estes *spirituellement entreé par les portes de la Meditation*"; italics added]. This *va et vient* demonstrates the

---

27   The first edition of *L'Hermitage de l'Isle saincte* (Paris: chez Antoine du Brueil et Toussaincts du Bray, 1612) is in the collection of the Bibliothèque de l'Arsenal in Paris. A 1615 edition (Rouen: chez Nicolas Loselet) is at the Folger Library. References to *L'Hermitage* are drawn from the 1615 version, and will be indicated in the text by page number. Quotations reproduce original spelling and punctuation, except that for easier reading I have replaced "v" with "u" when appropriate. The frontispiece bears the comment "C. de Mallory fecit," but I do not know whether the textual illustrations are the work of the same artist.

porousness of the borders separating the allegorical from the real: throughout, the narration rises and falls back from one level to the other, as the Soul rises and falls back from a state of grace.

Whether real or figurative, the solitary life is difficult for the narrator to sustain. He/she confesses: "I softly sigh in the solitary shadows of my home" ["ie souspire doucement dans les ombres solitaires de ma demeure," 39]. Like most of the illustrations, the image accompanying this passage shows a natural scene framed in the foreground by two trees, and in the background by a forest. A small chapel can also be glimpsed among the trees in the back (Fig. 1.1).

In his solitude, the narrator regrets both his/her wasted youth and worldly failure. Discouraged, s/he was led astray by *passions terrestres*: "I left the company of Angels for that of humans" ["je quittais la compagnie des Anges pour celle des humains," 30–31]. In this ongoing struggle, various guides are sent to him/her. S/he sees Christ above "Like a shining star to serve as my lantern, so I can glimpse myself in my darkness" ["côme une éclairãte estoile pour me servir de fanal, à fin que ie me visse en mes obscuritez," 29]. Later, St. Paul and St. Anthony arrive to reveal "some secrets of this solitary vocation" ["quelques secrets de ceste vocation solitaire," 72]. The illustration accompanying this passage shows the two saints standing in front of a hermitage. In a final meditation, the Soul is represented in glory, contemplating the Angels and Archangels, "creatures pures & intellectuelles" (150–51). At this point, all contradictions between the allegorical and the real are resolved: both the *Iardin intérieur* of meditation and the hermitage of physical retreat are revealed as stations on the way to the true Garden of Heaven. But this garden can be entered only after the sufferings of life are over. The narrator tells God: "after resting in these sacred shades, I will contemplate you, and will be transported in your *presence*" ["après … reposant en ces sacrez ombrages, ie vous côtêpleray, & seray ravie en vostre *presence*," 36–7; italics added].

In the preceding paragraph, I have deliberately used the awkward s/he pronoun in order to highlight the ambiguity of the main character's gender. As already noted, the sex of the narrative persona dramatically shifts in mid-narration from a male Esprit to a female Ame seeking her divine *Espoux*. Like Croix, Nervèze draws upon the gendering of the Song of Songs: "*the Spouse's Beloved rose up from the desert*" ["*l'Amie de l'Espoux est montée du desert*," 10–11, marginal annotation *Can. 3*; italics in text]. In the second meditation, again as in Croix's *Miroir*, the female gender is associated with weakness: "So that finding myself completely deformed, pale and languishing, no longer recognizing this ancient work of your hands, you will reject and disavow me as a creature of Heaven, since, having separated myself from your family, I have become a naturalized *daughter of the world*" ["De façon que me trouvant toute difforme, pasle & languissante, ne reconnoissant plus cest antique ouvrage de vos mains, vous me rejetterez & me desadvoüerez pour creature du Ciel, puis que me separant de vostre famille, ie me suis naturalisée *fille du monde*," 24–5; italics added]. However, this feminine marking is unclear or absent in the illustrations, which seem to follow the tradition

Fig. 1.1   Antoine de Nervèze, *Le Iardin Sacré de l'Ame Solitaire*. Paris, Arsenal Library, BnF.

of imagining the soul as an asexual spirit, akin to an angel.[28] In almost all the illustrations, the Soul is drawn as a naked, epicene figure with long hair and delicate features (Fig. 1.2). The arms are often modestly crossed on the chest, or reaching up to heaven; and despite subtle variations in musculature and hair length from engraving to engraving, the body structure appears more male than female.

In the illustrations from the Arsenal library's copy of *Iardin*, any further clues to the Soul's sex have been obliterated by an unknown reader, apparently displeased with the display of frontal nudity. This "veiling" makes our identification of the Soul's gender more difficult; but it also reveals the limits of allegorical representation. Even when the body is clearly meant as an allegory for the soul, it still appears too naked for some readers.[29] In the final illustration (facing p. 246), however, the Soul's form becomes unambiguously feminine: she is shown as a woman with gold ringlets, modestly dressed in embroidered smock, pearls and a tiara (see Fig. 1.3). The Soul's feminine beauty has become unproblematic, not only because "she" is clothed, but because her appearance is now fully in the image of her spiritual essence. She is no longer a diabolically inspired female, "my enemy ... clothed in carnal beauty to reach the eye of my body" ["mon ennemy ... revestu d'une beauté charnelle, pour gaigner l'oeil de mõ corps," 53], but simply a beautiful Soul.

The second of Nervèze's allegorical works, *L'Hermitage de l'Isle saincte*, was published in 1612 with the approbation of the Sorbonne. Like travel narratives from the New World, images of islands and their inhabitants were popular with early modern readers: printed maps and "isolaria" [island books] began appearing in the late fifteenth century.[30] But the island in *L'Hermitage de l'Isle saincte*, like the garden in the previous work studied, is an allegorical rather than a realistic space—a background for the enactment of a spiritual journey. The narrative vector of *L'Hermitage* recalls John Bunyan's better-known allegory, *Pilgrim's Progress*: both works trace the advances and backslidings of the soul as it navigates its way through the world towards holy ground. *L'Hermitage* also displays the same layered structure as *Le Iardin*, containing not only texts and illustrations but allegorical glosses on the illustrations. This structure calls for a reading on several levels. In the most immediate and literal sense, Nervèze enjoins the Christian to escape from the world (*le monde*) into a sacred refuge. Quoting the Gospel according to St. John, Chapter 2, Nervèze characterizes the world as a place of sin, removed

---

[28] Angels are often represented in painting as androgynous figures, like the angelic messenger in Botticelli's *Annunciation*.

[29] The related practices of censorship and iconoclasm seek to police the boundary separating the divine from its earthly and profane form. For other illustrations throughout history, see David Freedberg, *The Power of Images*, Figs 165–76 (pp. 363–8) and 181–2 (pp. 410–11).

[30] On isolaria, see Tom Conley, *The Self-Made Map* (Minneapolis: University of Minneapolis Press, 1996). For the general impact of geographic exploration on early modern French religious discourse, see Papasogli 233.

Fig. 1.2   Antoine de Nervèze, *Le Iardin Sacré de l'Ame Solitaire*. Paris, Arsenal Library, BnF.

Fig. 1.3   Antoine de Nervèze, *Le Iardin Sacré de l'Ame Solitaire*. Paris, Arsenal Library, BnF.

from God and totally given up to carnality: "Love not the world nor the things of the world ... for all that is of the world is the desire of the flesh" ["N'aymez point le monde ny les choses qui sont au monde ... car tout ce qui est au monde est la convoitise de la chair," 129]. In this total divorce between world and God, the former is portrayed almost as a projection of the body, a body described in the negative terms ascetics ascribe to corporeal functions: "this great Babylon of the world is nothing but a quagmire of filth" ["cette grande Babilone du monde n'est qu'un bourbier d'immondices"]. We are trapped in the body with the same fatality as we are trapped in sin: "The body is not more naturally followed by its shadow, than sin by its punishment" ["Le corps n'est pas plus naturellement suivy de son ombre, que le peché l'est de son chastiment," 85]. Thus, whoever remains in the world is determined physically to be lost spiritually. Nervèze prays: "Do not let me lose myself in this labyrinth of the world" ["Ne me laissez pas esgarer dans ce labirinthe du monde," 36]. The textual perspective conflates Babylon and the labyrinth as pagan architectural constructions, both associated with sin and sensuality.[31]

In this gloomy situation, the only hope of escape is to leave society for *le désert*. With military metaphors harking back to the early desert fathers and reiterated by Saint Teresa (Carrión 263), Nervèze describes the desert retreat as a fortress against temptation: "And what are these places? Deserts and solitudes where one constructs trenchs within and without, to close the avenues of approach for the enemy within by the mortification of the will, without by removal from worldly objects" ["Et quels sont ces lieux? Les deserts et les solitudes ou l'on fait les retrenchements dedans et dehors pour fermer les advenuës à l'ennemy dedans par la mortification de la volonté, dehors par l'esloignement des objets mondains"]. At the same time, religious seekers go into the desert for a more positive reason: to find God. Alluding to the Old and New Testament, Nervèze states: "It is in these solitary retreats that God communicates and converses with men: *I knew you in the desert in the land of solitude*" ["C'est en ses retraicts solitaires ou Dieu se communique & converse avec les hommes: *Ie t'ay cogneu au desert en la terre de solitude*," 124; italics in text]. He adds later: "For it is in these dwellings of solitude and silence, that the oracles of Heaven make themselves heard, and not in noisy and populous crowds. ... God only appeared to Moses in the deserts and in the mountains" ["Car c'est en ces demeures de solitude & de silence, ou les oracles du Ciel se font entendre, & non dans les bruits & foules populaires. ... Dieu ne s'est apparu à Moyse, qu'aux deserts, & aux montagnes," 285].

The text and its illustrations combine forest, mountain and island to create a privileged site of natural retreat; yet this *désert* also contains a variety of buildings

---

[31] The comparison of the world to a labyrinth is frequently found in early modern devotional literature: see Johann Amos Comenius, *The Labyrinth of the World and the Paradise of the Heart*. Trans. Howard Louthan and Andrea Sterk (New York: Paulist Press, 1998).

representing various steps along the spiritual journey. The frontispiece shows a traveler crossing a bridge to a rustic island hermitage (Fig. 1.4).

On a metaphorical level, the desert retreat also represents the convent in which, paradoxically, physical imprisonment brings spiritual liberation: "It is true that in this captive condition, we still have the power to earn our liberty, like the beautiful souls who, piously ashamed to live in this earthly captivity, set themselves free within the holy prisons of Jesus Christ" ["Il est vray qu'en ceste condition captive il nous reste toujours le pouvoir de racheter nostre liberté comme font ces belles ames qui devotement honteuses de vivre en ceste captivité terrestre se mettent en franchise dans les sainctes prisons de Iesus Christ," 136]. Both the hermitage and the convent are *isles sainctes* where the soul can take refuge from the world. In the first case, one retreats into a space outside society; in the second, one locks oneself away from society, in a sacred counter-labyrinth which protects against *le labirinthe du monde*.

Moving back and forth across the borders of allegory and fiction, Nervèze will mine the visionary imagery of *Hermitage* in his last *roman dévot*, *La Victoire de l'amour divin sous la description des amours de Polidore & de Virginie* (1608). After sacrificing her love for Polidore, Virginie has a vision of a hermitage in a dream: "It seemed to her that she saw a hermitage on top of a mountain, a Hermit who called her by name; but unable to go there, she walked around the mountain, [and] finding herself closer to this Hermitage, saw a Convent of nuns, where, having entered, an Angel took her by the hand and led her, it seemed to her, into a small chamber looking onto the sea ..." ["Il luy sembla qu'elle voyoit un hermitage au haut d'une montaigne, un Hermite qui l'appeloit par son nom: mais n'y pouvant aller, elle fit le tour de la montaigne, se rencontrant plus pres de cest hermitage, trouva un Couvant de religieuses, où estant entrée un Ange la print par la main & la mena, ce lui sembloit, dans une petite chambre qui regardoit sur la mer ... ," f. 118; Oddo 54]. This dream clearly portrays the convent as a halfway house on the way to the final spiritual goal, perhaps unattainable in life. It also prefigures the conclusion of the novel: Polidore will end his days in a hermitage, Virginie in a convent.[32]

Unlike the hermitage in *La Victoire de l'amour divin*, the soul's destination in *L'Hermitage* is not a real place. As the narrative unfolds, descriptions of physical retreat to desert or convent give way to a purely allegorical movement. The illustrations play an important role in this allegorical transformation: as a faithful disciple of the Counter-Reformation, Nervèze appeals to the senses in an effort to move beyond them, to replace literal sight with spiritual vision. Figure 1.5 depicts the Soul entering with alacrity into a *palais*: a "modern" neo-classical-style

---

[32]   In the *dix-neuvième nouvelle* of Marguerite de Navarre's *Heptaméron*, we also hear of "two lovers who, despairing of ever being married to one another, entered into religion, the man with the Franciscans and the girl with the Poor Clares" ["deux amants qui, par désespoir d'être mariés ensemble, se rendirent en religion, l'homme à saint François et la fille à sainte Claire," 186 in the 1982 edition].

Fig. 1.4   Antoine de Nervèze, *L'Hermitage de l'Isle saincte*. By permission of the Folger Shakespeare Library.

building which looks incongruous in its forest setting. The clouds hovering over the palace divide the picture, like a medieval painting, into levels representing Earth and Heaven. This hierarchical vision is emphasized by the artist's use of space and proportion: more room is given to Heaven than to Earth, and the palace is squeezed into the right corner of the picture by the many crosses scattered on the ground left—crosses which the soul has refused to bear. Finally, Christ and the angel are drawn in a disproportionately large scale, overwhelming the small figure of the Soul pictured below.

In Fig. 1.6, the angel's right arm points upward to Christ on the Cross, the rising path, or Heaven. At the same time, its right wing is projected protectively over the Soul. However, the Soul's posture, arms raised and palms up, seems to resist this protection. According to the gloss, the Soul is looking back at the "vanités du monde" represented by a portrait of a fashionably dressed woman. In the background, we see an austere, fortress-like building (in contrast to both the hermitage and the palace), with a suggestion of a further retreat sketched still higher against the mountains.

The next illustration in the book is a duplicate of Fig. 1.6 with a new gloss— perhaps a printer's economy. The need to kill two emblematic birds with one stone may explain one of the oddities of this figure: the artist could not show the Soul actually looking at the picture, which would make sense in the context of Fig. 1.6, but not if the next illustration is supposed to show the soul reformed. This time the gloss "reads" the repentance of the soul into its closeness to the cross: "The Soul touched by repentance approaches Jesus Christ" ["L'Ame touchee de repentance s'approche de Jesus Christ," 194]. This second gloss further reinterprets the visual allegory by stating that the Cupid figure (*l'amour*) holding the frame is now *l'amour du monde*, and that the image is not a painting, but a mirror: "Cupid wants to show her as in a mirror the human beauties she used to love" ["l'amour … luy veut faire voir comme dans un miroir les beautez humaines qu'elle a jadis aymees," 194].[33] Both the mirror and the female figure within it are representations of *concupiscence*, or attachment to the flesh.[34]

Despite these negative associations, the mirror also has the property, already seen in Croix's work, of showing something other than a literal reflection. As in *Le Iardin Sacré*, the Soul is depicted nude and of uncertain gender; but the mirror image reveals a fashionably clothed woman. The text interprets this dual image as God mirroring back the true image of his creature: "For having been created

---

[33]   The juxtaposition of classical/Renaissance and religious motifs in the illustrations reinforces the opposition between world and retreat, sin and salvation: for example, in Fig. 1.6, a mythological Amour nearly brushes wings with a Christian angel. To distinguish them the artist has illustrated the Angel wearing a robe while the Cupids are represented nude and carrying bows and arrows.

[34]   In several medieval works, the woman's mirror is "converted" into a guide to righteousness. See Ritamary Bradley, "Backgrounds of the Title 'Speculum' in Mediaeval literature." *Speculum* 29.1 (January 1954). 100–115, esp. 104.

Fig. 1.5   Antoine de Nervèze, *L'Hermitage de l'Isle saincte*. By permission of the Folger Shakespeare Library.

Fig. 1.6   Antoine de Nervèze, *L'Hermitage de l'Isle saincte*. By permission
                  of the Folger Shakespeare Library.

from your breath, in your image, and looking at myself in you as in a mirror, I will see this image which was made without art, completely unlike its natural form, and I will recognize that it is the effects of my error and my vice that have changed me thus" ["Car estãt creée de vostre haleine, à vostre semblance, & me regardant en vous comme dans un miroir, ie verray cest image qui fut faict sans art, du tout dissemblable à son naturel, & recognoistray que ce sont des effets de mon erreur & de mon vice, qui m'ont ainsi changée," 27–8]. As stated earlier, the "otherness" of the mirror image, *du tout dissemblable à son naturel*, is also the defining principle of allegory, which shows us the other in the same. In a global sense, then, the whole work holds up a mirror reflecting the true path to God. But this allegorical otherness also resists interpretive closure. Is the naked figure shown in the illustration a woman ("elle" in the text), looking back at (or turning her back on) worldly vanity, reflected in her own form? Alternatively, is the figure that of a man, suffering or overcoming sensual temptation in feminine form?

In the following engraving (Fig. 1.7), the Soul is shown kneeling in front of the cross, indicating her/his further progress towards repentance and salvation. The building in the background now appears closer and more accessible: it is no longer the forbidding fortress of Fig. 1.6, but a small church or chapel with an open door. In front of the structure stands a "good angel" awaiting the Soul's arrival. However, the Soul's trials are not yet over: three cherubs, flitting about like flies, represent the senses which still bind the Soul to "these vain loves of the world" ["ces folles amours du monde"]. In French, the word "amour" has the double meaning of "love" and "cherub/Cupid," further binding the words to the text. The presence of the flies also connotes damnation and the corruption of the body (see below, Chapter 2, 93, 114–15).

Once again, this illustration is intertextually linked to Nervèze's *La victoire de l'Amour divin*. In a meditation, Polidore portrays himself lying at the foot of a tree which he likens to the cross: "Now lying on the spot where stood the foot of your cross, I wish to chant with praises the happy ruin of the love that once made me sigh" ["Ors prosterné au lieu où l'arre de vostre croix fut plantee, je veux chanter avec action de louanges, les ruynes heureuses de cet amour qui me faisoit jadis souspirer," 86]. While in the novelistic *La victoire de l'amour divin*, the love to be conquered is for a specific woman, in *L'Hermitage* it is allegorized into sensuality or *l'amour du monde*.

Fig. 1.8 shows a further progression from the Cross to Christ himself, who has descended from Heaven to lead the Soul by the hand into retreat. The three cherubs of the previous illustration are shown floating in a sea of penitent tears which serves to separate the Soul from the world. This scene marks the closest intersection between illustration and main text: "I offer you an Island that you will create for and within yourself. Your body will be the Earth, and your tears the waters that surround it and flow from a repentant life" ["Je vous propose une Isle que vous formerez pour vous & en vous mesme, vostre corps sera la terre, & vos pleurs les eaux qui l'environneront et couleront d'une vie repentante," 24]. Significantly, there are no buildings in this figure; in contrast to human habitations, the dwelling

Fig. 1.7   Antoine de Nervèze, *L'Hermitage de l'Isle saincte*. By permission
of the Folger Shakespeare Library.

place of God is an open space: "O my God and my Creator ... whom my Angel shows me in a *space* adorned and divinely embellished with your celestial host" ["O mon Dieu et mon Createur ... que mon Ange me montre dans un *espace*, orné & divinement embelly de vos hierarchies celestes," 190; italics added].

To summarize, Nervèze's allegory is both macrocosmic and microcosmic, expanding and contracting in vertiginous fashion like Pascal's infinite universe. On the one hand, the whole earth (*terre*), as distinguished from the world (*monde*), is an *isle saincte*, "a Hermitage for solitary and contemplative spirits" ["un Hermitage aux esprits solitaires et contemplatifs," 444]. On the other hand, the place of sanctuary is localized *within* the human body, which becomes a whole world unto itself. The narrator compares himself to Aeneas who, arriving on an island, nailed his arms to the door. "These arms are the Cross, the door is the heart; being attached to the door with nails of love, they will remain there eternally" ["Ces armes, c'est la Croix, la porte c'est le coeur; ou les cloüant avec des cloux d'amour elles y demeureront eternellement," 445–6]. Within the macrocosmic earth/body, the heart becomes the sanctuary which Christ's arms (the Cross) identify as his own. In addition, the nails that pierce the heart as the crosses are nailed to it reproduce Christ's sufferings when his body was nailed to the cross. Finally, the crosses attached to the door recall the medieval tradition of placing crosses outside the chapel door to indicate the limits of clausura (as was the medieval custom at Fontrevraud). There is no attempt to illustrate this conceit; perhaps the result would have been beyond baroque! In a move that can be conceived of allegorically if not represented visually, the soul takes refuge within the heart, protected by its dedication to Christ, as the religious take refuge behind convent walls. In an earlier *roman dévot, Les chastes et infortunées amours du Baron de l'Espine*, Nervèze's heroine asks her community and readers: "With your prayers, reserve me a *lodging* above for my soul" ["Marquez-moi la hault avec vos prières un *logis* pour mon ame," 112; italics added]. But in the allegorical mode of *Hermitage*, it is the body which, in the end, offers the soul a retreat from the world.

The remaining question to address is: whose body? *L'Hermitage* is dedicated to a woman, Magdalene de Monteclair, who is directly apostrophized as *vous* in the text. In her honor, the narrative contains a meditation on Mary Magdalene who cries an ocean of penitent tears (as illustrated in Fig. 1.8). It may hardly seem flattering for Nervèze to compare his patroness to this personage; in her best-known characterization, Mary Magdalene is a reformed prostitute, a fragile woman *par excellence* who represents human carnality in its most aggravated form. This view of the Magdalene appears in some seventeenth-century fiction; for example *Les Amours de la Magdelene* (1618) describes her as a sensual woman, prey to "folles amours" and "feux profanes" (383). But this popular saint, mentioned 18 times in the New Testament, displays a variety of conflicting identities. In her core persona, she is an early and devout follower of Jesus, who is supposed to have cast seven devils from her. Mary of Magdalene mourned at the foot of the cross and, when visiting Christ's tomb, was the first to bear witness to the resurrection. In the sixth century, Pope Gregory conflated the Magdalene with

Fig. 1.8   Antoine de Nervèze, *L'Hermitage de l'Isle saincte*. By permission
                  of the Folger Shakespeare Library.

two other, very different Biblical Marys: Lazarus's sister who received instruction from Jesus, and a much more dramatic character, the harlot mentioned by Luke who cast herself on the ground in penitence, wiping Jesus' feet with her hair and anointing them with perfumed oil (Cave 23). Peter Paul Rubens painted a sensuous representation of this scene. To this collection of multiple personalities one might add the unnamed adulteress whom Jesus saved from stoning in John 8:1–11, and the third-century recluse Mary the Egyptian, who is always depicted in rags with long unkempt hair falling over her face.

Magdalene was brought to France through a legend which had her sailing from the Holy Land to Marseille, where she preached and taught before retreating into a cave at La Ste. Baume. Magdalene's supposed relics were stolen from Provence in the seventh century and moved to Vézelay, on the pilgrimage route to St. James of Compostela (Duby 33). But the oldest French document celebrating Mary Magdalene's saint's day contains perhaps the most unexpected portrait. Eudes, Bishop of Cluny, writing about 1000 C.E., describes her as a woman of high birth, like his own patroness. Wealthy women, by endowing church buildings, were thus said to be pouring perfume on the Church, as Magdalene perfumed Jesus' feet with precious oil. It was only after twelfth-century Catholic reforms instituted a new sacrament of penance and procedures for atonement that Magdalene was mainly portrayed as a model of the repentant sinner. A contemporary pilgrim's guide speaks of "that glorious Mary who washed with her tears the feet of her Lord" (Duby 20). Although Magdalene was an object of popular devotion among women, members of the so-called weaker sex were denied access to her alleged tomb. However, women of the time were put into convents to prevent them from becoming whores (Duby 38); in Spain, establishments for reformed prostitutes were sometimes called "Magdalene houses."

Like the twelfth century, the Catholic Reform was an era of great devotion to the Magdalene. According to Terence Cave, from the early 1600s "the cult of the Virgin Mary begins to be rivalled by the popularity of Mary Magdalene" (245). The Magdalene is a central devotional figure because she was present at the Crucifixion, a favorite subject for Counter-Reformation meditation. Nervèze alludes to her in this role in *Le Iardin*, when Christ, bleeding from his wounds, appears to the narrator; "when the blessed Magdalene saw him after his triumphant Resurrection" ["lors que la bienheureuse Magdeleine le vid apres sa triomphante Resurrection," 45]. Like the twelfth century, however, the early modern era mainly cast her as a great penitent. Her repentance, and particularly her tears, were extremely popular themes in devotional art of the period. Cesar de Nostredame's meditative poem, *Perles, ou les Larmes de la saincte Magdeleine*, was published in 1606, just six years before *L'Isle*. Both the repentance and the sensuality ascribed to her are evident later in the century in a painting by Carlo Dolci, *The Penitent Magdalene* (circa 1670). Dolci's canvas depicts a beautiful young woman, teary eyes uplifted in prayer, her bare arms only hidden by the long red hair flowing down over her shoulders.[35] However, the early characterization of Mary Magdalene as a respectable Christian woman allows Nervèze, like Bishop Eudes, to make a legitimate connection between this controversial figure and his noble patroness.

Like Mary Magdalene, the soul of the first-person narrator is both female and "a miserable (female) sinner" ["une miserable pecheresse," 101]. But unlike Magdalene de Monteclair, who is addressed formally as *vous*, the Soul is addressed as *tu* and personified as a girl child towards whom the narrator assumes a protective, avuncular attitude: "And I remember that in a sacred Garden where I used to converse with you in solitude, you learned from me several secrets of contemplative life" ["Et me souvient qu'en un Iardin sacré ou ie t'ay autresfois solitairement entretenuë, tu as apprins de moi plusieurs secrets de la vie contemplative," 94]. The *iardin sacré* suggests both a real cloister garden and the *hortus conclusus* of the virgin body. Returning to the Song of Songs typology, the garden also evokes associations with the Mystic Marriage. Unlike Croix, but like conventual writers, Nervèze alludes to the personal union of female Soul and male Savior (34–5). On the point of gender, however, as with *L'Hermitage*, text and illustration are again found to be in disharmony. While the narrator defines the Soul as allegorically (and not just grammatically) female, the drawings depict it as a naked, somewhat epicene, but clearly male being. The only female figure in the illustrations is the woman in the portrait/mirror, who plays the role of temptress and embodiment of concupiscence. The reason for this disparity is unclear; after all, from the Middle Ages on, allegorical illustrations had typically represented spiritual qualities as female (Woshinsky, "Desert Fortress," 151). Perhaps the illustrator of Nervèze's work, which was published under the authority of the Sorbonne, felt reluctant to give the Soul a nude female form.[36]

Whatever the reasons, in *L'Hermitage de l'Isle saincte*, feminine attribution is only allowed to take place in the context of allegorical narrative. Within the strange, shape-shifting, infinitely malleable discourse of allegory, it is possible for the (female) Soul to take refuge within a (male) body (the hermitage, the convent, the Church), which will protect its frailty and seal its purity with the arms of Christ. In Nervèze's particular "construction of femininity," the Soul can retain her femaleness as long as she is disembodied and invisible. But, in the worldly domain of the early modern church, is the body male or female, temple or temptation? Allegory, with its flexibility and slipperiness, may allow one, at least temporarily, to evade such thorny questions. However, as seen in all three

---

[35]   Magdalene-like penitents appear in French fiction throughout the seventeenth and eighteenth centuries. Some examples from the catalogue of the Arsenal Library are: *Floriane, son amour, sa penitence et sa mort* (Paris: 1601); *L'Amante convertie ou l'Eloge d'une illustre Pénitente, présenté à Basiliste par Eusèbe* (The Hague: 1700); *La soeur Adelaide, ses égarements, ses vertus ses faiblesses et son repentir* (Neuchâtel: 1785); see also Works Cited.

[36]   The illustrator of the 1612 edition was a certain Léonard Gaultier. In the 1615 Rouen edition, the name of the illustrator is not given, but the illustrations are identical. See Léonard Gotter, *Livres à figures édités en France de 1601 à 1660* (Paris: J. Duportal, 1914), 156–60.

allegories examined in this chapter, materiality eventually breaks in and breaks down allegorical ramparts. To invert a phrase from Judith Butler's *Bodies that Matter*, "*de*materialization is never quite complete ... bodies never quite comply with the norms by which their *de*materialization is impelled" (quoted in Smith and Watson 367; italics added). In conclusion, these three liminal works from the turn of the seventeenth century reveal how Renaissance neo-Platonism, Counter-Reformation zeal and Catholic Reformation mysticism shaped the early modern concept of sacred space, reinforcing persistent patterns of thought and imagery: the soul's journey, internal and external retreat, the senses as tool and as threat. At the same time, the failure to resolve issues of gender and the body helped set the scene for a contradicted, if not tortured, spirituality. These contradictions will become more glaring in the devotional novels of Jean-Pierre Camus.

Chapter 2
The Body in Early Modern Religious Discourse (2). Living Temples or Vases of Ignominy: Jean-Pierre Camus and the Paradoxes of Female Representation

… with what heat do you imagine his zeal catches fire when sacrilegious men pollute not only sacred vessels, like Balthazar, but his living temples, who are the virgins dedicated to him? (de quelle ardeur pensez vous que son zele s'embrase quand les hommes sacrileges polluent non seulement les vaisseaux sacrez, comme Balthazar, mais ses temples vivans, qui sont les vierges qui luy sont voüées?)

—Jean-Pierre Camus, "L'amant Sacrilege." *Les spectacles d'horreur* (124)

Convert them and they will be converted, and make these vases of ignominy into vessels of honor and temples consecrated to the glory of your divine Spirit (Convertissez les & elles seront converties, & de ces vases d'ignominie faites en des vaissaux d'honneur & des temples consacrez à la gloire de vostre divin Esprit).

—Jean-Pierre Camus, "La femme perduë." *Les spectacles d'horreur* (338)[1]

Representation

The conclusion of the previous chapter highlighted the contradictions present in the representation of women in religious writings from the first decades of the seventeenth century. These contradictions are magnified, one generation later, in the works of the polygraphic bishop Jean-Pierre Camus. Recent criticism has indeed painted Camus as a controversial and paradoxical figure; but the contradictions highlighted thus far have largely lain between his apologetic aims and the fictional genres he practiced.[2] For example, in "Roman historié et histoire romancée:

---

[1] These quotations are drawn from Anne E. Duggan, "The Virgin and the Whore: Images of the Catholic Church and Protestant Heresy in Camus."

[2] The last generation has seen a miniboom in Camus studies, beginning with Vernet's and Robic-de Baecque's work from the 1990s. This current interest may be attributed to several causes: the critical attention newly directed to writing before 1630 in general, and to devotional discourse in particular, both of which had been largely ignored by critics of classicism; Camus's place as the most cogent theoretician of *histoire dévote*; his role in the

Jean-Pierre Camus et Charles Sorel," Christian Jouhaud states: "The paradox resides in the relation of their project (as they sometimes formulate it) and the choice of a form of writing which we identify as novelistic" ["Le paradoxe réside dans le rapport de leur projet (tel qu'il leur arrive de l'expliciter) et du choix d'une écriture que nous identifions comme romanesque," 307]. I situate the Camusian paradox differently: rather than concentrating on the relation between goal and genre, I examine the stresses between text and presumed audience. Camus was by far the best-known and most prolific author of *histoires dévotes*, a genre with an almost exclusively female readership. Some of his novels were reprinted well into the nineteenth century, for a public of convent-educated girls and women. Yet at the same time, Camus's fictional works often exhibit hostility and fear of women. I will seek an explanation for Camus's contradictory stance in his conflicted views of the body. My analysis will mainly concentrate on the two texts most readily available in modern editions: the 1621 novel *Agathonphile* and a collection of short tales, *Divertissement historique* (1632).[3]

According to Robert Birely, "For France in the seventeenth century we can speak of a 'feminization' of religious life, in that for the first time women religious outnumbered men" (37). It is also generally acknowledged that in seventeenth century France, *le sexe dévot*, as Brémond calls them (*Histoire* 1.47, 2.36 ff.), were the principal consumers of both devotional and fictional literature.[4] As we have seen, Nervèze's *L'Isle saincte* was dedicated to a female patron, Magdalene de Monteclair (Chapter 1, 73–6). And the most frequently reprinted book in the seventeenth century after the Bible, François de Sales's 1608 *Introduction à la vie dévote*, was addressed to Philotée (*l'amante de Dieu*), a pseudonym for his devout cousin Louise de Charmoisy. Nancy Oddo considers Sales to be the chief inspiration for a new kind of devout literature addressed to secular, novel-reading women: "One supposes that [devout literature] was encouraged by François de Sales's discourse centered on piety in the world, because it seeks to persuade worldly people, especially the society women who devour quantities of bad novels" ["On suppose (la littérature dévote) encouragée par le discours de François de Sales centré sur la dévotion dans le monde parce qu'elle cherche à séduire des mondains, et surtout des mondaines grandes dévoreuses de mauvais romans," 221].

---

development of realism, explored by Franchetti and Shoemaker; and last but not least, the odd and colorful nature of Camus's personality and style. More re-editions of his works are needed to make this neglected author better known and more accessible (See also Ch. 2, note 9).

[3]   The first part of *Agathonphile* has been republished in an abridged version, edited by Pierre Sage (Geneve: Droz, 1951). In the parenthetical references in the text, the first page number refers to the Sage edition; the second, after the slash, to the original edition of 1621.

[4]   "In most of the great religious enterprises of the seventeenth century, we find a woman's inspiration" ["Dans la plupart des grandes entreprises religieuses du XVIIe siècle, on découvre l'inspiration d'une femme," Brémond 2.36]. Brémond continues rather quaintly: "this fact should not surprise" ["ce fait ne doit pas surprendre"].

But what if an author of devout literature, a feminocentric genre in François de Sales's view, exhibits strong misogynistic tendencies? Such is the case with Jean-Pierre Camus. One of Sales's most ardent male disciples, Camus dedicated part of his enormous energies to writing *histoires dévotes*. In his abridged edition of Camus's *Agathonphile*, Pierre Sage calls Camus "the greatest and almost the single novelist of the episcopacy" ["le plus grand et presque l'unique romancier de l'episcopat," ix]. Certainly, he is the most productive: in his lifetime, Camus published nearly 60 volumes of fiction, including 1000 short stories. He also composed an unbelievable 35 novels in a ten-year period between 1620 and 1630.[5] Born in Paris in 1584, Camus received a secular upbringing, studying law and reportedly making a narrow escape from marriage. (Without drawing ungrounded biographical conclusions, we may note that the motif of men fleeing women certainly appears in Camus's fiction, notably in *Agathonphile*.) Choosing celibacy over marital union, he became a priest and was appointed Bishop of Belley in 1609. Camus's episcopal consecration was performed by François de Sales himself.

In his *Esprit de S. François de Sales*, Camus affirms that the order to write *histoires dévotes* was given him directly by François: "Our blessed Father … assigned me the task as if from God to write devout stories" ["Nostre bienheureux Père … me donna comme de la part de Dieu la commission d'écrire des histoires devotes," ed. Migne, *Oeuvres complètes de Saint François de Sales* (Paris: 1861), II col. 1074]. Camus interpreted this mission as "to discredit novels through Novels themselves" ["décréditer les romans par les Romans mesmes," *Agathonphile*, xiv]. In the preface to *Tapisseries historiques* (1644*)*, Camus defines his project as an "antiroman" (xv), a possible reference to Charles Sorel's *Berger extravagant*, republished in 1633 under the title of *L'anti-Roman, l'Histoire du berger Lysis*. But the two writers use the term differently. Whereas Sorel creates a burlesque of the pastoral form, Camus aims to counteract the pernicious effects of novel reading itself by offering a narrative *contrepoison* (*Tapisseries*, xv). For in Camus's vision, the esthetic notion of *antiroman* overlaps the medical ones of *antidote* and *pharmacos*. In his *Eloge des histoires dévotes*, published as an afterword to *Agathonphile*, he compares the author of religious stories to "That Pharmacist who had discovered the secret of having his patients take bitter drugs as if they were sweets" ["Ce Pharmacien qui avait trouvé le secret de faire prendre ses drogues ameres aux malades comme des confitures," *Eloge* 110/845].[6] And "Les deux Courtisanes," a tale from *Divertissement historique* to which we will return below, begins with a healthy dose of biblical references which the narrator inserts as an *antidotte* to the immorality of the subject matter to follow (182).

---

[5]   Sage, Introduction to *Agathonphile* 139; Shoemaker 1. Marilyn Cox argues that part of Camus's huge production was amassed by copying or "compiling" stories from other sources.

[6]   *Eloge des histoires dévotes*, subsequently referred to as *Eloge*, is printed as a postface to Pierre Sage's abridged edition of *Agathonphile*, as it was in the original edition.

Not all of Camus's contemporary readers accepted his argument that a moral antidote could reverse the pernicious effects of fiction reading: indeed, many times throughout his career, Camus felt impelled to defend his novelistic practice from critics. As Franchetti puts it, "the apologetic river that overflows his works seeks only to establish the licitness of recourse … to a fictitious discourse" ["Ce fleuve apologétique qui déborde de ses ouvrages ne vise qu'à établir la licéité du recours … à un discours fictif," 123]. These attacks upon Camus's fiction mainly focused on what de Baecque calls "une omniprésente thématique amoureuse" (36). Camus's defense fights fire with fire: in *L'Eloge*, he counters the critique that he writes only about love with the Salesian teaching that God is all love, *tout amour*. This divine passion is the prime motor for the creation of the universe: "It is this God who did everything by Love, for Love, and with Love" ["C'est ce Dieu qui a tout faict par Amour pour l'Amour, et d'Amour," 117/862].[7] In opposition to the Jansenist view, Camus and Sales agree with the Jesuits that human passion and love, as part of the divine creation, are not intrinsically evil. Rather, the passions only become evil if they are wrongly directed: "If Love aims for an illicit target, it is worthless; if the bull's eye is truly white with purity and innocence, it is good" ["Si l'Amour tend à un but illicite, elle ne vaut rien; si elle a un blanc qui soit vrayement blanc de pureté et d'innocence, elle est bonne," 116/861].[8] François de Sales's defense of the passions goes even further, arguing that they are not morally neutral but positive; according to Sales, physical pleasure is sent by God to direct our will towards Him: "We are not drawn to God by bonds of iron, like bulls and buffalo … . The proper bond for human will is *sensual enjoyment and pleasure* … . See how the eternal Father draws us: in teaching us *he delights us*" ["Nous ne sommes pas tirés à Dieu par des liens de fer, comme les taureaux et les buffles … . Le propre lien de la volonté humaine, c'est *la volupté et le plaisir* … . Voyez comme le Père éternel nous tire: en nous enseignant *il nous délecte*," *Traité de l'amour de Dieu*, 444; italics added). It is the role of the passions as moral persuaders that enables Sales's and Camus's project of conversion through reading.

The Counter-Reformation argument that serves to rehabilitate the passions extends to the senses and the body as well: "Everything that God has done is not only good but very good, he created the senses of the body as well as the faculties of the soul; whosoever would say that the senses are worthless and arise from an evil source, would fall into the error of the Manicheans" ["Tout ce que Dieu a fait est non-seulement bon, mais trèsbon, il a faict les sens au corps comme les facultez en l'ame; qui diroit que les sens ne valent rien et qu'ils viennent d'un mauvais principe, tomberoit en l'erreur des Manicheans," *Eloge* 126–7/915–16]. This argument reiterates the Ignatian position that the senses, like the passions, are not evil in themselves if applied correctly. At the same time, reflecting Trent's

---

[7]   Camus was one of the earliest seventeenth-century writers to elaborate a theory of the passions. For more on this topic, see Robic-de Baecque 35–6.

[8]   In the original French, Camus plays on the double entendre between *blanc* as white and as the bull's eye of a target.

injunctions against the seductive charm of art, Camus denies that *Agathonphile* displays any untoward sensuality: "Everything exudes a sweet smell; [there is] not the slightest touching, the mildest bad word; everything is [designed] for the Virgin, the chaste woman, the severe Elder" ["Tout n'y respire que baume, non pas mesme le moindre attouchement, non la moindre parole libre, tout y est pour la Vierge, pour la femme chaste, pour le rigide Vieillard," 127/917]. We will see whether these claims are justified.

In the many paratexts accompanying his narratives, Camus lays out not only a justification for the *histoire dévote* but also a rhetoric for its reading. In harmony with his time, he emphasizes the soul's need for retreat and solitude, decrying the lack of opportunities to withdraw from the world and, speaking personally, from the burdens of his own episcopal duties. However, Camus argues, even in our busy modern lives, it is possible to create the "espace de la retraite intérieure" recommended by François de Sales through a correct use of reading (*Introduction à la vie devote*, 2ᵉ partie, Chapter 12). In *Acheminement à la dévotion civile*, written in close intertextuality with *L'Introduction à la vie dévote*, Camus exhorts his audience to spend at least a quarter of an hour a day reading: "Steal away this little *space* from so many calls and visits, so many vanities and frivolous occupations with which the world amuses itself, to give your soul this little spiritual supper; and if you persevere in this exercise for some time, you will come to know how profitable it will be" ["Derobez ce peu *d'espace* à tant de visites actives et passives, et à tant d'inutilités ou d'occupations frivoles, auxquelles le monde s'amuse, pour donner à votre âme ce petit goûter spirituel et si vous perséverez en cet exercise quelque temps, vous connaîtrez combien il vous sera profitable," *Acheminement*, III.14.515; italics added]. Camus's use of *espace* as a temporal rather than a physical referent is consistent with seventeenth-century practice (see above, Introduction); yet the need he describes to carve out a temporal "space" in one's busy schedule also strikes a familiar note for modern readers.

As well as referring to a moment in time, Camus's practice of reading also evokes an inner space of contemplation. According to Robic-de Baecque, "Camusian writing implies ... *reading in an inner space*, which would foster a deepening of one's personal relationship to God" ["Les écrits camusiens impliquent ... *une lecture du for privé*, qui voudrait favoriser un approfondissement personnel de la relation à Dieu," de Baecque, "L'Eloge des histoires dévotes" 32; italics added]. In the passage quoted above, the cozy, domestic tone of "derobez" and "petit goûter spirituel" helps the (female) reader experience a moment of intimacy with God in a *for privé*—an inward space nestled within her heart of hearts. At another point in the *Eloge*, Camus employs the figure of an enormous palace to evoke the interior space explored through reading: "[readers] enjoy being led by the hand, as in superb palaces, through many porticos, passages, long galleries, through a great multiplicity of halls, rooms, closets and contours" ["(les lecteurs) se plaisent d'être conduits par la main, comme aux superbes palais par plusieurs portiques, par divers passages, par de longues galeries, par une grande multiplicité de salles, de chambres, de cabinets et de contours," *Eloge* 2.896]. Camus's meandering syntax, confusing at times, succeeds perfectly here in conveying both the pleasure of reading and the allegorical journey towards a spiritual life which is so integral a part of Catholic Reform tradition.

Camus's images closely emulate Sales's evocations of interior retreat.[9] But Sales, in turn, had retraced the steps of contemporary women mystics, first and foremost Teresa of Avila: according to Brémond, Sales's *Traité de l'amour de Dieu* "follows step by step the example and teachings of St. Teresa" ["suit pas à pas l'exemple et l'enseignement de Ste Thérèse," *Histoire littéraire du sentiment religieux* 2.577]. Teresa's *Interior Castle* [*Castillo interior*], a guide to meditation composed for the nuns under her care, is structured upon the conceit of the soul as a vast castle: "I began to think of the soul as if it were a castle made of a single diamond or of very clear crystal, in which there are many rooms, just as in Heaven there are many mansions" (28). In Teresa's meditation, the soul slowly moves from mansion to mansion as it grows closer to God. This movement is not one of ascension, but of penetration: "the central and midst of them all is the chiefest mansion where the most secret things pass between God and the soul" (29). It is within this secret and intimate space that the "Spiritual Marriage" between God and the nun's soul will take place (*Castle* 207). The interiority of this image is both spiritual and feminine. A lesser-known woman mystic, Marie Tessonnier, also known as Marie de Valence, reported similar architectural visions to her spiritual biographer, Louis de La Rivière. According to La Rivière, in these visions "God gives her a beautiful castle that represents the glorious Virgin Mary" ["Dieu lui donne un beau château qui représente la glorieuse Vierge Marie"]. Another time, she is surrounded by "virtues in the form of young ladies … . And in an admirable way, she felt these amiable virtues enter into her soul, just as doves [enter] into their dovecote and bees into their hive" ["vertus en forme de jeunes dames … . Et d'une manière admirable, elle sentit entrer en son âme ces aimables vertus, ainsi à proportion que des colombes dans leurs colombier et ainsi que des abeilles dans leur ruche"].[10] Hives also figure in the imagery of St. François de Sales; and Sue Monk Kidd has explored the medieval relation of the queen bee to the Virgin in her recent novel, *The Secret Life of Bees*.[11]

Camus differs from mystic visionaries in according his supreme "devotion" to reading and writing. St. Teresa states that she elaborated her interior castle in order to open up a private space for nuns enclosed in cramped convents, whose every movement was constrained by their rule: "and considering how strictly you are cloistered, my sisters, how few opportunities you have of recreation and

---

[9]   The evocation of an inner space was not unique to Sales; as we have seen, before the publication of the *Introduction à la vie devote*, Nervèze and others created similar images.

[10]   R.P.L. de La Rivière, *Histoire de la vie et moeurs de Marie Tessonnière* (Lyon: 1650), quoted in Brémond 2.55.

[11]   New York: Penguin Books, 2003. James F. Gaines analyzed Sales's bee imagery in a paper presented at the 2003 meeting of the North American Society for Seventeenth Century French Literature: "Socio-spiritual Suasion: François de Sales and the Bees."

how insufficient in number are your houses, I think it will be a great consolation for you, in some of your convents, to take your delight in this Interior Castle, for you can enter it and walk about in it at any time without asking leave from your superiors" (234). While Teresa's Castle is an inner refuge for nuns from the inadequacies of their real convents, Camus's retreat is located between the pages of a book: "it is in the book alone that Camus recognizes the virtue of a *space of solitude* carved out of the secular world" ["C'est au livre seul que Camus reconnaît la vertu d'un *espace de solitude* ménagé dans le siècle," de Baecque, "L'Eloge" 40; italics added].

Despite his differences with mystical writers, Camus, like Croix and Sales, relies on allegorical techniques as part of his strategy for convincing the reader. Like children who look at pictures in books without understanding the words, readers "seek only the fact in a Story, a fact that is merely the image of the real thing" ["ne cherchent que le faict en une Histoire faict qui n'est que l'image de la chose," *Eloge des histoires dévotes* 899]. To engage his childlike readers, Camus must first attract them with allegorical images. He also defends his use of allegory in fiction by linking it to religious parable: "Aside from that, I have granted myself a freedom that is not only Christian, but religious and devout, to make parables, so that whatever is not historical is parabolic, and there is nothing in the course of this story that is not true, either in fact or through allegory or moral tale from which one can draw instruction" ["Outre cela je me suis donné cette license non seulement Chrestienne, mais religieuse et devote, de paraboliser de sorte que ce qui n'est pas historique est parabolique, et qu'il n'y a rien en tout le cours de cette oeuvre qui ne soit vray, soit en faict soit en allegorie, ou moralité et dont on ne puisse tirer de l'instruction," *Eloge* 113]. This passage recalls Augustine's instructions for reading Scripture in *De doctrina christiana*: "what is read would be subjected to diligent scrutiny until an interpretation contributing to the reign of charity is produced" (III.xv.23.93). How to tell whether a phrase is literal or figurative? For Augustine, "Whatever there is in the word of God that cannot, when taken literally, be referred either to purity of life or soundness of doctrine, you may set down as figurative" (90). Although some elements may not seem to "contribute to the reign of charity," if they are read "figuratively and prophetically" their spiritual meaning will shine through, because "Scripture enjoins nothing except charity, and condemns nothing but lust" (90–91). By extending Augustine's theory of Biblical exegesis to his own secular works, Camus achieves multiple rhetorical aims: cloaking himself with the mantel and authority of Augustine, he places his novels on a level with holy writ and makes a claim for total veracity in at least one register of meaning. Augustine's assurance that even the least likely elements of Scripture can be read allegorically authorizes Camus to treat his own profane texts similarly, covering entire works with the protective umbrella of what Robic-de Baecque calls "allégorisme" ("Le Salut par l'excès" 283).

Retreat and the Female Threat in Jean-Pierre Camus's *romans dévots*

If Camus's theoretical essays develop the notion of retreat within the allegorical space of reading, his narratives accord it an equally important but different place. Like Nervèze, Camus often sets his novels in hermitages and *déserts*. In *Hermiante*, for example, a series of stories are told in "a hermitage buried in the forest of Senar" ["un hermitage enfoncée dans la forest de Senar"].[12] Camus's novels also feature verses praising the pleasures of the *désert*, *repos* and retreat: again in *Hermiante*, Camus cites St-Amant's poem, "La Solitude" (541–9); and *Elise* contains these verses: "Pleasing deserts, dwelling place for innocence, / Where far from the vanities of magnificence / My rest begins, and my torment ends; / Valleys, rivers, rocks, pleasant solitude / Henceforth be the place of my contentment" ["Agreables deserts, sejour de l'innocence, / Où loing des vanitez de la magnificence / Commence mon repos, et finit mon tourment; / Valons, fleuves, rochers, plaisante solitude, / Soyez-le desormais de mon contentement," 353].

   In addition to these secluded natural settings, Camus's characters also seek refuge within four walls. But his views concerning monasticism are dichotomized along strict gender lines: while Camus's hostility towards male monasteries embroiled the contentious cleric in long debates, he considered strict enclosure in convents as the only acceptable form of religious life for women. Thus, his narratives promote rustic seclusion for men and cloistering for their female counterparts.[13] In the preface or "Dessert" to *La Pieuse Julie, histoire parisienne* (1625), the narrator expresses a dual wish to encourage young women to enter convents, and to castigate all who oppose their religious vocation: "to reveal the just punishment of those who 'try to tear the brides of God from his arms'" ["montrer le juste châtiment de ceux qui essayent 'd'arracher les espouses (de Dieu) d'entre ses bras,'" *La Pieuse Julie*, "Dessert au lecteur" 514–15, quoted in Vernet 54]. The trendy subtitle—*histoire parisienne*—suggests an effort to appeal to young female urban readers of his time. In fact, the mid-century vogue for convent novels and society conversions will lead Mme de Sévigné to comment satirically on "retraite à la mode" (Oddo 48). Camus's pious Julie desires to become a nun, but her family forbids it and marries her off against her will. After her husband's death, she is able to fulfill her initial wish, entering a convent where she sets an edifying example for all. At Julie's own death, her relatives repent their efforts to frustrate her vocation.

---

   [12]   This setting recalls Notre Dame de Serrance, the abbey where the travelers take refuge in Marguerite de Navarre's *Heptameron*.

   [13]   Nervèze also contributed to the genre of the female profession novel: at the end of *Les Chastes et infortunées amours du Baron de l'Espine*, the heroine chooses to enter a convent: "Finally tired of the world, she wants to abandon it; and to leave it she voluntarily enters a monastery called Prouille" ["Enfin lassé du monde, elle le veut delaisser; & pour en sortir elle entre en volonté en un monastère nommé Prouille," quoted in Oddo 47]. Nervèze's gender distinctions are similar to Camus's: when the woman becomes a nun, her lover retreats to a hermitage.

Unlike *Julie*, *Agathonphile ou les amants siciliens*, the second and most popular of Camus's novels, explores religious retreat from a largely masculine point of view. This perspective highlights Camus's apparent difficulty in writing for an overlapping and largely female audience of *dévotes* and/or novel readers.[14] The plot of *Agathonphile* combines elements from the traditional saint's life—solitude, persecution, poverty, martyrdom—with the topoi of romance—shipwrecks and pirates—to bring the novel to an edifying conclusion, while entertaining the reader along the way. Camus is indeed using the novel against (anti) itself. But if *Agathonphile* has a traditional denouement, in other important respects the novel strays beyond orthodox bounds. In saints' tales, male, but more frequently female, virgins must resist pressures to marry or bestow sexual favors, often at the cost of their lives. For example, both St. Agatha and St. Agnes suffered sexual assault and martyrdom when they refused to marry.[15] However, as we will see, *Agathonphile* does not fit neatly into this mold. The 1,000-page work is set at the beginning of the fourth century C.E., during the persecutions of Diocletian. Three Christians—two men and one woman—are imprisoned in Sicily. While awaiting execution, they tell their life stories. The first narrator, Philargyrippe, is loosely based on a real figure, St. Philippe Argyrio. *Agathonphile* is an amalgamation of his name with that of the other male character, Agathon. The title is also allegorical, "agathonphile" signifying "love of the good" in Greek.[16]

Agathonphile is set during the early Christian era, a period of hermitic wandering. While traditional monastic life is not represented, spirituality is linked throughout the novel to the chastity, intactness and enclosure of the body. The imperative of enclosure applies to men as well as women. In part 1, Philargyrippe recounts how as a young man, he had fallen in love with a "genti-fille Romaine," Deucalie, whom he sought to convert to Christianity. Tragically, Deucalie falls sick and dies just after the wedding ceremony. Philargyrippe insists she be given a Christian burial in a tomb rather than being burnt in the pagan manner. After the funeral, instead of deep mourning, "he threw himself into a deep retreat" ["il se jetta en une profonde retraitte," 9]. At this point, the author inserts an excerpt from Psalm LXXII, in Desportes's 1611 translation:

---

[14]   *Agathonphile* was reprinted three times in the seventeenth century: in 1623, 1638 and 1641. An abridged version appeared in 1712 (Sage xxvii–xxviii). Camus's next most-frequently published novel is *Petronille* (1626), which was reprinted twice. Two other titles were reissued in the nineteenth century (Sage 132–6).

[15]   A principal source for saints' tales is the thirteenth-century *Golden Legend* (*Legenda Aurea*).

[16]   The story of Agathon and his beloved, Triphyne, is recounted in part 2 of *Agathonphile*; but the Lesage edition contains only excerpts from part 1, the tale of the priest Philargyrippe. I will concentrate on Philargyrippe's account since the Lesage edition is accessible to readers. To my knowledge, there is only one copy of the complete novel in the United States, in the UCLA library.

A day under your portals is worth more
Than a thousand in magnificent Palaces;
As for me, I will seek
To remain at your door
Rather than lodging in any way
In the pavilions of the wicked.
For God keeps us and enlightens us,
Sun and salutary porch.

Mieux vaut un jour sous tes portiques
Que mille aux Palais magnifiques,
Et pour moy j'iray recherchant
Plustot de rester à ta porte
Que de loger en nulle sorte
Dans les pavillons du meschant.
Car Dieu nous garde et nous esclaire
Soleil et parvis salutaire. (10; 150)

In the context of *Agathonphile*, the psalm represents enclosure [*profonde retraite*] as a kind of open shelter: remaining in retreat [*rester à ta porte* rather than *loger de nulle sorte / Dans les pavillons du meschant*], Philargyrippe is protected from the influences of corrupt society.

In *Agathonphile*, enclosure takes a variety of forms: involuntary as well as voluntary, secular as well as religious. After Deucalie's death, Philargyrippe announces his desire to become a priest; but his parents, who wish to betroth him to his cousin Nerée, refuse their consent to his ordination and lock him up in his room. Philargyrippe welcomes his domestic confinement in these words: "O happy prison! That in the captivity of my body caused me to find the true freedom of my soul" ["O heureuse prison! Qui en la captivité de mon corps me fit trouver la vraye liberté de mon ame," 35]. And even when, after a false accusation of sexual assault, he is thrown into a windowless dungeon, he sees it as a just punishment for his weakness. The oxymoronic images commonly applied to monastic enclosure in religious discourse are a frequent feature of Camus's fiction: in *La Pieuse Julie*, for example, the cloister is called a tomb for the living— "Ce tombeau ou vous m'enteriez toute vive"—from which Julie, phoenix-like, will be reborn: "Oh, but I am content to see a new self reborn from the ashes of this Julie, happily dead to the world" ["O que je suis contente de voir de la cendre de cette Julie heureusement morte au siecle renaistre une autre elle-mesme," 493–4]. Despite the presence of these traditional figures of monastic death and rebirth, I will argue that in *Agathonphile*, the prison/tomb/retreat is mainly seen as a refuge from one's own desire—a means, through enclosure, to negate the body's power.

In Camus's tales and novels, the body is condemned as the domain of sensuality. In contrast to the Salesian tone of his prefaces, Camusian fiction espouses a radical mind/body dualism, according to which the only correct way to live in the body is to suppress its claims. According to Molinié, Christian love for Camus "is essentially a spiritual love which implies scorn for the body" ["est essentiellement

un amour spirituel, qui implique le mépris du corps," "Eros épiscopal," 55].
Yet according to Philargyrippe, "It is more of an angelic than a human form of
existence to live in the flesh without the commerce of the flesh" ["C'est une vie
plus angélique qu'humaine de vivre en la chair sans le commerce de la chair," 15].
Given human weakness, this angelic ideal is rarely achieved: "Outside the sphere
of charity, these carnal palpitations can produce no other sensations than those of
their corporeal nature, which under the circumstances are tormenting" ["Hors de
la sphère de la charité, ces palpitations charnelles ne sauraient produire d'autres
sensations que celles de leur nature corporelle, en l'occurrence torturante," Molinié
55]. The word *commerce* is used in classical French to denote any social relation or
interchange; but the connotation of contaminating commercial exchange—even of
bodies—also makes itself felt. However pure one's original intentions, human love
describes an inexorably descending spiral from the heights of virtue to the abyss of
carnality. As Philargyrippe observes: "One sometimes begins with virtuous love,
but if one is not extremely alert, frivolous love slips in like an impertinent visitor
who crashes the party without being invited; from there, one turns easily to sensual
love; finally, one is thrown into the abyss of carnal love, which is a slough of
impurity and infection" ["On commence quelquefois par l'amour vertueuse mais
si l'on n'est extremement avisé, l'amour frivolle s'y glisse comme une effrontee
qui vient à la feste sans qu'on luy appelle; de là on vient facilement à l'amour
sensuelle; enfin on se precipite en l'abysme de la charnelle, qui est une cloacque
d'impureté et d'infection," *Agathonphile* 55]. In contrast to St. Teresa's spacious
palace of inner spiritual retreat, the domain of the senses in Philargyrippe's spatial
imaginary is a nightmarish, stinking quagmire. An infernal one as well: *cloaque*,
along with *fumee*, *souphre*, *infection*, *fumier* and *voirie*, is among the words
Loyola used for describing Hell (Cave 28). The image of the *abysme* also suggests
female sexuality; and in Camus's pre-classical French, *l'amour*, *cette effrontee*
who causes one to fall into the abyss, is grammatically feminine.

Given all these pitfalls, it seems that the only way to ensure virtuous love
is for the love object to be dead. After Deucalie's decease, Philargyrippe suffers
exquisite pangs of longing for his bride. Speaking to her parents, he compares
true friendship to "a soul in two bodies; and if the conjugal bond makes one flesh
out of two bodies, why could the amiable Deucalie not survive in me, as I am
dying in her?" ["une ame en deux corps, et si le lien conjugal fait que deux corps
n'ont qu'une mesme chair, pourquoi l'aimable Deucalie ne pourra-t-elle survivre
en moy, comme je vais mourant en elle?"].[17] The allegorical conceit continues:
"My soul is so filled with the idea of her perfections, that there is hardly any
room left for myself inside me. As a result, I live only to preserve this living tomb

---

[17]   The depiction of love as one soul in two bodies refers to Plato's *Symposium* as
well as to the "one flesh" of Genesis. While it enjoyed great popularity during the early
modern period, and is often referred to as "Platonic," this image was actually proposed in
the *Symposium* by Aristophanes and rejected by Socrates, who proffered his own definition.
(I owe this remark to Guido Ruggiero.)

for her, where her beautiful image resides so vividly represented" ["Mon ame est si remplie de l'idée de ses perfections, qu'à peine ay-je une petite place en moi pour moy-mesme, de sorte que je n'ayme la vie que pour lui conserver ce vivant tombeau, où reside sa belle image si vivement representée"]. But this internal image of Deucalie, like the medieval *miroir* (see above, Chapter 1), reflects not her outer appearance but her soul: "The representation I am speaking of, moving beyond [the physical], comes to the virtues of this beautiful soul. These virtues are even more elevated above corporeal desires than the fruit surpasses the flower, the solid what is crumbling" ["La représentation dont je parle passant plus outre, va jusques aux vertus de cette belle ame, vertus d'autant plus eslevées sur les dispositions corporelles, que le fruit surpasse la fleur et le solide ce qui est caduque," 14]. In an allegorical inversion, the soul is represented as stronger and more "solid" than the body. It is important to recall that the soul is that of a dead woman, thus now safe for him to allow into his own soul.

Overcoming his parents' strong opposition, Philargyrippe finally succeeds in taking holy orders. But a new misfortune strikes: he is pursued by his cousin Nerée, the very woman whom his parents desired him to wed. While he desires to save her soul, Nerée's designs on him are very different. From this point on, much of part 1 (300 pages in the original edition) is taken up with a highly colored account of the sexual harassment of a priest. This situation gives the narrator the opportunity to vent his bile against women. While Philargyrippe had addressed his dead bride in neo-Platonic and sentimental terms as "Ma chere Deucalie ... ma divine Amante, ma seul Astrée" (28/188), Nerée is the object of repeated and bitter epithets: "this little proud one" ["cette petite orgueilleuse," 17/167]; "this many-colored leaf that hid an asp in its bosom" ["cette feuille diaprée qui cacha dans son sein l'aspic," 17/166]; "this subtle Nerée" ["cette fine Nerée," 18/168]; "this weak spirit, like a light straw" ["cette esprit faible, comme une paille légère," 18/168–9]. As the plot develops, the anti-Nerée epithets become progressively more caustic, moving from "cette rusée" (22/179), "cette fine femelle" (26/186) and "cette Syrene" (repeated twice, 27/186 and 91/395), to the diabolical "enemy full of artifices" ["artificieuse ennemie," 82/357]. This contrast between the descriptions of Deucalie and Nerée rehearses the stereotypic dichotomy between "good" and "bad" women, seen as well in the dual structure of many of Camus's tales. However, there is a consistency in the women's treatment, in that both Deucalie and Nerée are seen most positively once they are dead: finally, "we leave *poor Nerée's* memory in peace" ["nous laissons en paix la memoire de *la pauvre Nerée*," 106/469; italics added].

As a cleric writing an *histoire dévote*, Camus is doubly bound to demonstrate that a priest is impervious to female wiles, however *rusée* or *artificieuse* she may be. Thus Philargyrippe, like l'Espoux in Croix's *Miroir*, stoutly denies that sensual pleasure tempts him: sensuality is "unworthy of man ... whose principal delights are of the soul rather than of the body" ["indigne de l'homme ... dont les principales délices sont plustost en l'ame qu'au corps," 4]. He compares his love letters to his dead fiancée to "ces excrements de mes jeunes erreurs" (82), bodily excretions he has since eliminated. As far as Nerée is concerned, he assures the reader in metonymic language worthy of Pierre Corneille: "I have no eyes for her body, I only regard her soul" ["Je n'ay point d'yeux pour son corps, je ne regarde que son ame," 54]. By directing his mental gaze to her soul, he attempts to efface her body and its effect on him. But again, as in *Le Miroir*, these claims are contradicted by the narrator's own words. To demonstrate this point, I will quote at length from one scene. Having first pretended indifference, Nerée confesses her love to Philargyrippe and bursts out crying. Philargyrippe lyrically describes the effect that Nerée's tears have on him:

> Oh! My resolutions, how they were weakened, especially when I saw how shame turned her face the color of the ruddiest flowers, making her appear so beautiful to me, that I believe her
>> Better than Aurora, who upon her return
>> Spreads out her colors;
>> When she tints the horizon,
>> Opening the gates of day.
> When the dew and the rose exchange kisses, there is nothing so pleasing to the eye, for you will see at the break of Dawn this Queen of the flowers open her beautiful crimson bosom, her purpled eyes, and her satiny leaves, to receive the first drops that fall from the fingers of Aurora, and drink their humid freshness. So did Nerée's face appear to me, when a long string of pearls flowed from the Orient of her eyes onto the intermingled roses and lilies in the flowerbed of her visage.

> O! mes resolutions, que vous fustes esbranlees, principalement quand je vy que la vergoigne luy fit monter au front la couleur des plus vermeilles fleurs, qui me la firent paroistre si belle, que je croy
>> Que mieux en faisant son retour
>> Ses couleurs n'estale l'Aurore
>> Quand l'horizon elle colore
>> Ouvrant les barrieres du jour.
> Quand la rosée et la rose se sont entrebaisées, il n'est rien de si agreable à l'oeil, car vous verriez à la poincte de l'Aube cette Royne des fleurs ouvrir son beau sein incarnat, son oeil empourpré, ses fueilles [sic.] satinées, pour recevoir ces meres-gouttes qui tombent des doigts de l'Aurore, et en boire l'humide fraischeur: telle me parut la face de Nerée, quand une longue file de perles coula de l'Orient de ses yeux sur les roses et les lys entremeslees dans le parterre de son visage. (59)

This passage is dominated by imagery of opening ("ouvrant les barriers du jour ... ouvrir son beau sein ... son oeil empourpré, ses feuilles") and receptivity. Nerée's face embodies all the natural processes described. As dawn, she produces the dew; and like a flower bed, she also receives it "sur les roses et les lys entremeslees dans le parterre de son visage." This purple (or rose) prose, which bursts spontaneously into verse, recalls the Ronsardian style of Pierre de Croix: sensual words like "sein" and "entrebaisées" are camouflaged within the mythological context of "Aurore." In addition, the lyrical phrase "quand une longue file de perles coula de l'Orient" imitates the rhythm of an alexandrine verse and, like Pierre de Croix's metaphors, prefigures Baudelairian Orientalism (see above, Chapter 1, 55). But while Croix attempted (successfully or not) to redeem amorous discourse by sublimating it into allegory, Camus's narrative remains firmly anchored in mimetic desire. Rather than a Soul-Bride, Nerée is a beautiful woman who arouses erotic feelings in a man by lowering all her defenses.

The narrator continues:

> Oh, she seemed so much more pleasing to me, seeing her defeated and humiliated, than when, proud and haughty, she thought she could triumph over my simplicity with her artifices! The pity I felt, seeing her throw at my mercy enough perfections to cause many others to sigh, made me feel as though a flood of flames was pouring into my heart; especially when, with a heart burning with pious love and a face enflamed with shame, folding her half-bared arm over her head, as if to modestly shelter her face, I saw her, lying back lethargically on her pillow, her eyes large and swollen with tears, her breast swollen with sobs, and her silent mouth forming nothing but sighs.

> ô qu'elle me sembla bien plus agréable la voyant vaincue et abaissee, que lors que, superbe et altière, elle pensoit avec ses artifices triompher de ma simplicité! La pitié de voir ranger à ma mercy assez de perfections pour en faire souspirer beaucoup d'autres me pensa verser dans le coeur un deluge de flammes, principalement quand d'un coeur embrasé de dilection et d'un visage allumé de honte, repliant son bras demy descouvert sur sa teste, comme pour ombrager la pudeur de son front, je l'apperceus abbouchee mollement sur son chevet les yeux gros et noyez de larmes, son sein enflé de sanglots et sa bouche muette ne parler point d'autre langage que celuy des souspirs (59–60/297).

While the first part of the passage remained more or less within the bounds of a Renaissance love conceit, this section develops and amplifies in a realistic way the visual eroticism of the scene, dwelling on the image of a recumbent woman, her arm and breast exposed ["bras demy descouvert … sein enfle de sanglots"]. To the opening and expansion of the previous passage it adds troubling new elements. The narrator is struck by the physical beauty and abandon of Nerée, *abbouchee mollement sur son chevet*; but this sight only becomes overpoweringly seductive when he sees himself in a situation of power over her: "elle me sembla bien plus agréable la voyant vaincue et abaissee, que superbe et altière." He feels pity (or some other emotion) at seeing her "ranger à ma mercy assez de perfections pour en faire souspirer beaucoup d'autres me pensa verser dans le coeur un deluge de flammes." The gentle dew of the earlier passage morphs into a flood of fire which, in turn, is a "re-conversion" of the mystical discourse of flames into an erotic register. Philargyrippe's vanity is satisfied at having conquered a woman whom many other men would desire; but the main source of the *deluge de flammes* is her complete submission to him—"rangée à sa mercy," in shame, sobbing, and silenced, she is deprived of the power to speak other than in the "language of sighs." The female subject, in this case a troubled combination of lover and penitent, lacks true subjectivity and autonomy: as Nerée tells Philargyrippe, "Henceforth, you may call yourself the master of my life and death" ["vous pouvez desormais vous dire le maistre de ma vie et de ma mort," 58]. And her total subjection is portrayed and perceived as highly erotic.

At this point, the tables and the imagery are suddenly reversed: no longer a subject viewing a vanquished object, Philargyrippe becomes *subjected* to desire. Despite his earlier protestations to the contrary, Philargyrippe might repeat Tartuffe's famous admission: "though I am religious, I am no less a man" ["pour être dévot je n'en suis pas moins homme" *Tartuffe* 3.3, v. 966]. He confesses: "I wasn't made of marble, nor was I of that frozen age that rendered Socrates as immobile as a statue; rather, I was in a flourishing season, and all the more susceptible to the burning fire that torments so many" ["Je n'estois pas de marbre, ni en cet aage glacé qui rendait un Socrate immobile comme une statue; mais j'estois en une saison florissante et d'autant plus susceptible de ce feu cuisant qui tourmente tant de personnes," 60/297]. Instead of remaining in the dominant male position, Philargyrippe is subject to sex role inversion, or at least confusion, as he becomes the vulnerable party. This reversal of the power dialectic is expressed by a metaphorical transfer: the flower imagery previously associated with Nerée is now applied to Philargyrippe, and the passionate "flood of flames" ["deluge de flames"] now becomes a torturing "feu cuisant" that enters into his body against his will. This penetration of male boundaries perhaps suggests the fear—or the excitement—of sodomitical desire.[18]

Philargyrippe's struggle against sexual subjection is recounted in detail, occupying over six pages in the original edition. With God's help, he is able to resist acting upon the desires the sight of Nerée arouse in him; but he only can do so by flight: "and nonetheless, by a most special divine grace, I *escaped* from this peril, perhaps the greatest I had ever run" ["et neantmoins, par une grace divine toute particulière, *j'eschappay* ce peril peut estre le plus grand que je courus jamais," 60/297; italics added]. Yet temptation follows him into the solitary space of retreat: "I locked myself into my closet, but in that solitary place the devil does not cease, like an importunate fly, to disturb us … [and] incessantly brought back to my imagination this plaintive *idol* who pursued me to extremes" ["Je m'enferme dans mon cabinet, mais dans ce lieu solitaire le diable ne cesse comme une mouche importune de nous inquietter … (et) ramenoit sans cesse à mon imagination cette *idole* plaintive qui me poursuivit à outrance," 61/298; italics added]. This language resembles the railings of St. Anthony and other desert fathers against the female demons who tormented them in the desert. It also recalls Nervèze's comparison of sensual temptation to an importunate fly, carrying the disease of damnation. Philargyrippe further likens Nerée to an "idole"—presumably a heathen one. While in the passage cited earlier, Philargyrippe denied he was a statue, he is now immobilized in retreat; but the idolic Nerée, like the Commander's statue in

---

[18] This argument owes much to the suggestions of Pam Hammons, which I gratefully acknowledge.

Don Juan, can pick herself up and move, pursuing him "à outrance." These images appear to stand in blatant antithesis to the conventual ideal of women's immobility and containment; but in fact, the gynophobia provoked by burgeoning flowers and pursuing idols reinforces the imperative of enclosure: *men* are only secure when women are safely encased in homes or convents.

Philargyrippe's immobility before an "idol" who ceaselessly occupies his thoughts recalls similar obsessive narratives from the tragedies of Racine. For example, Phèdre confesses to Oenone: "Even at the foot of the altars I caused to smoke, / I offered my all to this god I dared not name" ["Même aux pieds des autels que je faisais fumer, / J'offrais tout à ce dieu que je n'osais nommer," *Phèdre* 1.3, 590].[19] From the same play, we may also recall Hippolyte, pursued through the woods by thoughts of Aricie. Even more pointedly, Philargyrippe recalls Racine's Nero in his "appartements" at the beginning of *Britannicus*, obsessed by the image of Junie—a young woman who, like Nerée, is embellished by the tears he himself had caused her to shed. The important difference between the two male characters is that in *Agathonphile*, the excitement felt before the helpless victim metamorphoses into a quasi-erotic penetration of male barriers: Nerée, unlike the passive image of Junie conjured up by Nero, penetrates Philargyrippe's retreat against his will. The point of these comparisons, of course, is not to propose a lesser-known "source" of a canonical text, but rather to question the separation between so-called secular and religious discourses during the early modern period: both are entangled by constructions of femininity and of male desire.

Later scenes in *Agathonphile* go beyond seduction through the gaze to involve the body as well. Nerée, like Phèdre, falls sick from her unfulfilled passion. But unlike Hippolyte, who had the sense to flee his stepmother's presence after her confession of love, Philargyrippe continues to pay ambiguously pastoral visits to Nerée. On one occasion, he even touches her: "As I was taking her arm, to ascertain the state of her health by her pulse, she brought my hand to her mouth, where she impressed on it more urgent and warm kisses than those with which Christians ordinarily honor priestly hands" ["Comme je luy prenais le bras, pour recognoistre l'estat de sa santé par le battement de son pouls, elle porte ma main à sa bouche, où elle imprima des baisers plus pressants et plus chauds que le sont pour l'ordinaire ceux dont les Chrestiens ont de coustume d'honorer les mains sacerdotales," 64/303]. Nor is Philargyrippe immune to these unpriestly caresses. He exhorts the implied reader: "Imagine what shivers I must have felt at this immoderate pressure! Certainly I believe that the bite of a serpent or the sight of a Basilisk would have been less dangerous to me" ["Imaginez-vous quel fremissement devoit donner

---

[19]   In "Eros épiscopal," Georges Molinié quotes another famous line from *Phèdre* (1.3.306) to indicate the Racinian tonality of *Agathonphile*: "for us, [there is] a faultless and strong foreshadowing of *It's Venus clinging to her prey* in this tableau of amorous possession, black and pure" ["pour nous, (il y a) la préfiguration impeccable et forte du *C'est Vénus toute entière à sa proie attachée* dans ce tableau si noir et si pur de la possession amoureuse," 60].

au mien cette empreinte immoderee! Certes je croy que la pointure d'un serpent ou le veuë d'un Basilic m'eust esté moins dangereuse," 64/303]. The exhortation "imaginez-vous" is telling. During this entire episode, the narrator plays upon the reader's imagination—turning up and down the heat, as it were, as he first couches the physical description of Nerée in poetic metaphors, then introduces realistic detail and tone which would not be out of place in an erotic novel. Finally, he increases the distance by inserting Biblical and mythological references to the snake and the basilisk. The snake, of course, harks back to the Garden of Eden and the fault of Eve; while the basilisk, a legendary dragon or serpent of deadly breath and glance, evokes Medusa's snake-like hair and mortal gaze. Unlike the abject imagery of the flower bed earlier associated with Nerée, the phallic images of the snake and the basilisk place the male narrator in a passive position, at risk of *pointure* (bite) or penetration. To summarize this unconventional dialectic, Nerée's traditional feminine submission to Philargyrippe becomes the very cause of his subjection to her. In this situation, the only alternatives are flight and enclosure for the male—conventionally female moves. Thus, Nerée's seductive female power causes the narration to cross the boundaries of the body and of gender in a transgressive way. Although Philargyrippe's lust is not acted upon, he has still committed the sin of desire condemned by Jesus in the Sermon on the Mount: "But I say to you that everyone who looks at a woman lustfully has already committed adultery with her in his heart" (Matthew 5:27–8).

So far, we have seen Nerée portrayed as an evil seductress and Philargyrippe as her helpless and hapless victim: in Molinié's words, the novel relates "a seduction attempt by the beautiful Nerée upon a young Christian, Philargyrippe, who is *completely panicked*" ["une tentative de séduction, par la belle Nereé, sur un jeune chrétien, Philargyrippe, *complètement affolé*," 58; italics added]. But this young Christian is neither so innocent nor so passive as Molinié's characterization suggests. From the beginning of their relationship, Philargyrippe plays a dangerous game. Aware of Nerée's attachment to him, he goes along with it for at least two reasons: to convert her to Christianity and to buy time for himself in the hopes of becoming a priest. He encourages her feelings with affectionate appellations like "my good pupil" ["ma bonne Escoliere"] and "ma chere Novice" (22/179). Philargyrippe recognizes his own deceitfulness ["feinte," "tromperie"] but argues that "My deceit is a good thing because it involved the service of God" ["ma tromperie est bonne puisqu'elle regardoit le service de Dieu," 39/247]. However, Philargyrippe's *feinte* can be seen as largely self-interested, since he pretends an attachment to conserve his own freedom more than to serve God. Nerée, for her part, pretends indifference in order to pique Philargyrippe's vanity and arouse his interest:

> So there we are, Nerée and I, involved in an amusing game. I didn't love her at all, though I pretended to love her with great passion; she loved me passionately, and put on an appearance of such reluctance to seek me out, that you would have mistaken her feelings for real hatred. For my part, I pretended in order to maintain my true freedom in this feigned slavery; for her part, she pretended in order to entangle me in her nets and engage me to her love.

> Nous voyla donc, Nerée et moy, en un plaisant exercise. Je ne l'aymois nullement et je feignois de l'aymer avec beaucoup de passion; elle m'aymoit passionnément et monstroit en apparence un tel mespris de ma recherche, que vous l'eussiez pris pour une hayne veritable; moy je feignois pour conserver une veritable liberté dans ce feint esclavage; et elle feignoit de sa part pour m'enlacer veritablement en ses filets et m'engager à son amour. (44/257)

Refusing marriage in order to become a priest or nun is certainly portrayed in Camus's work, as elsewhere, as a high and holy aim. Still, one wonders whether the definition of "tromperie ... dans le service de Dieu" can legitimately be stretched to include toying with a woman's affections. Furthermore, it is somewhat disconcerting for a would-be priest to characterize flirtation and deception as "plaisant," even in an ironic sense. Philargyrippe shows himself all too much at home in the world of *galanterie*. On a metatextual level, it is interesting to compare the hero's defense of virtuous deception to Camus's own use of rhetorical artifice in the service of religion. In *Eloge*, he declares his intention to "use Eloquence as the Church uses its incense" ["me servir de l'Eloquence comme l'Eglise se sert de ses parfums"] in order to charm the reader's senses and lead her toward God (121/878). Again showing his identification with Counter-Reformation strategies, Camus classifies rhetorical ornaments with church incense as sensual means towards a spiritual end. In Philargyrippe's case, however, the rhetorical ploy goes too far; and Philargyrippe, like Valmont in *Liaisons dangereuses*, is caught in his own trap. Indeed, Philargyrippe later confesses his own strong attraction for Nerée and, despite his imprecations against her, briefly takes some responsibility for his own punishment.

When Philargyrippe finally reveals his true feelings (or lack of feelings) for Nerée, she is understandably furious. She eloquently expresses her anger:

> And you, enemy as proud as you are amiable, will you always mock my simplicity, hiding under a gentle appearance and honeyed words the bitterness of your evil heart? No, only your form is human; too glorious a form, that Heaven seems to have made only for the ruin of my spirit and honor.

> Et toy, autant aymable que fier ennemy, te mocqueras-tu tousjours de ma simplicité, cachant sous un doux semblant et sous des paroles de miel le fiel de ton mauvais courage? Non, tu n'as rien d'humain que la forme, forme trop glorieuse, et que le Ciel semble n'avoir rendüe telle que pour la ruine de mon esprit ou de mon honneur. (67/308)

This is the closest the narrative comes to a physical description of Philargyrippe, seen through Nerée's eyes as a very attractive man ["forme trop glorieuse"]. For his part, Philargyrippe had used almost the same words to describe Nerée: "She thought with her artifices she could triumph over my simplicity" ["Elle pensoit avec ses artifices triompher de ma simplicité," 59–60/296–7]. Quoting Nerée's own words allows the reader, for at least one moment, to see her side of the story; but this opportunity for female expressiveness, or at least even-handedness, is not pursued. Instead of acknowledging that Nerée's desire for vengeance, however immoral, has provocation, the narrator falls back on the bitter consolations of misogyny. Confronted by Nerée and her servant, Philargyrippe recounts: "I remain[ed] motionless as a statue, more amazed by the *effrontery of these girls* than my own misfortune" ["Je demeure immobile comme une statuë, admirant plustot *l'effronterie de ces filles* que mon Malheur," 79; italics added]. Once again, misogynistic language masks the passivity of Philargyrippe, "immobile comme une statuë."

Even knowledge of his deception and indifference does not stop Nerée from pursuing Philargyrippe. Her persistence is not so surprising, given the passionate nature ascribed to her in the novel. What *is* surprising is that Philargyrippe keeps coming back to see Nerée. After he has renounced trying to convert her, even after she literally tries to seduce him, he still returns in order to keep up appearances, and for "commune civilité" (76). The character/narrator seems unaware that the lameness of these excuses may hide other motives for wanting to see his "chère ennemie" (63/302). By continuing to send ambiguous signals to a woman maddened by passion, he is playing a risky game not only with her, but with himself. While Philargyrippe appears blind to these dangers, they are clearly visible to the reader.

After this ambiguous but fascinating interlude, the plot seems to resume a more conventional pattern, both as *histoire dévote* and as romance. Through prayer, Philargyrippe finally cures himself of his passion for Nerée. But he is then forced to undergo another series of trials reminiscent of saints' tales. Nerée, outraged by his coldness, entraps him and causes him to be accused of assault. On her testimony and faked circumstantial evidence, everyone turns against him, including the church, his family and even his best friend. Philargyrippe is imprisoned, defrocked and exiled to Sardinia. When he first arrives there, he finds work as a gardener; but in a mini-reprise of the Nerée saga, he must leave this position because his employer's daughter falls in love with him. He then lives miserably for several years by begging, until Nerée's deathbed confession leads to his vindication and return to Rome. Reinstated as a priest, he regains the respect of both sexes: "Girls honored me, Priests venerated me" ["Les filles m'ont en honneur, les Prestres en veneration," 105/468]. All goes well until during a missionary expedition, his vessel is attacked by pirates, then shipwrecked on the coast of Sicily. Captured by persecutors of Christians, he is imprisoned with Agathon and Tryphine and finally dies a martyr's death. However, this religiously correct ending does not erase the ambiguous portrait of sexuality which occupies such a large part of the plot. While the uncovering of the characters' blind spots and unconscious drives works to undermine *Agathonphile*'s mission as a religious novel, these shadowy revelations certainly heighten its interest as a novel. Camus always refused to apply the sinful word *roman* to his fictional works, preferring to call them *histoire dévotes*. But in his bibliography of early fiction, Gustave Reynier places religious novels along with "mondain, pastoral et mythologique" under the general rubric of "Roman Sentimental" (Reynier 384 ff.).[20] Perhaps Reynier has it right.

Policing Conventual Enclosure in Camus's *Histoires tragiques*

After 1630, Camus abandoned his ten-year experiment in novel writing and turned entirely to composing collections of *histoires tragiques*, bearing titles like *L'Amphithéâtre sanglant* and *Les Spectacles d'horreur*. Aside from their historical authority and topical appeal to the reader, these allegedly true contemporary accounts license the author to indulge his penchant for lurid, violent and misogynistic stories, while absolving him of the artistic and moral responsibility for their invention.[21] *Divertissement historique* (1632?), the first of these collections, contains several tales praising convents and the religious life for women. Theodosia, the heroine of "L'Accordée," is twice betrothed (*accordée*) but never married. She is first engaged to a young man who immediately goes abroad. When his absence becomes protracted, Theodosia's parents arrange a match with a second suitor, with whom she falls in love. But her first fiancé returns and, outraged, kills her new betrothed in a duel. However, according to the narrator, Theodosia experiences "the happiest ending for a girl in love" ["la fin plus heureuse d'une fille amante"] because after the death of her betrothed, she enters a convent (88).

"La Fille forte," another tale from *Divertissement historique*, also centers on women's cloistering. This is the longest piece in the collection, which seems to confirm Camus's interest in the topic of female enclosure. In the introduction to the story, Camus states: "Religious vocation is one of the richest graces that Heaven can bestow upon a soul during the course of this mortal life" ["La vocation Religieuse est des plus riches graces que le Ciel puisse verser dans une ame durant le cours de cette mortelle vie," 210]. The plot concerns a poor widow, Anastasia, left with three daughters in her care. The oldest girl, Cleriane, though plain, wishes to marry; but her mother forces her instead to enter a convent. The second daughter, Engevine or "la fille forte," epitomizes the opposite case. Despite a strong religious vocation, her mother wishes her to marry; for unlike the plain Cleriane, Engevine's beauty will bring her a good match. Engevine displays a long and stubborn resistance to wedlock; but Anastasia, through a combination of persuasion and deceit, finds "some kind of miserable Cleric" ["je ne sçai quel miserable Ecclesiastique," 228] who is willing to perform a marriage ceremony without Engevine's consent.

---

[20]   Other titles listed by Reynier under this mixed category include *Les Amants de Sienes* (Fr. De Louvencourt 1598); *Amours de la chaste nymphe Pegase* (J. Corbin 1600); *Les Religieuses Amours de Florigene et de Meleagre* (Nervèze 1601 [?]); *L'Enfer d'Amour* (J.B. du Pont 1603); and *Les Douze Livres de l'Astrée*, 1re partie (d'Urfé 1607).

[21]   Peter Shoemaker points to an Italian origin for these violent tales in Boccaccio and Mateo Bandello. The popular French adaptation of one of Bandello's stories is often cited as the source for *Hamlet* (Shoemaker 549).

The narrator intervenes spontaneously at this point to condemn the mother's action: "It can't be helped, this word must escape me for the justification of children against the unjust abuses of fathers and mothers" ["Il n'y a point de remede, il faut que ce mot m'échape pour la justification des enfans contre les injustes violences des peres & meres," 222]. Camus asks why, if it is illegal for children to marry without their parents' consent, the opposite is sanctioned:

> I don't know why public laws, that have declared null and void the marriages of minors when they are contracted without the consent of their parents, did not also arrange to protect children from the subjection of parents who call themselves masters of their will. For if it is forbidden for [minors] to marry against the will of those who brought them into the world, what law allows parents to marry off their children without the consent of the very children who are being married?

> Je ne sçai pourquoi les loix publiques, qui ont declaré nuls les mariages des mineurs quand ils sont contractez sans le consentement de leur parents, n'ont aussi pourveu à garantir les enfans de la contrainte de ceux qui se disent maistres de leur volontez. Car s'il est deffendu à ceux-là de se marier outre la volonté de ceux qui les ont mis au monde, quelle loi permet aux parens de marier leurs enfans sans le consentement de ces enfans mesmes que l'on marie? (222)

In his introduction to "La Fille forte," Venesoen argues that Camus favors individual freedom only when it is a question of choosing the religious life. In the light of the previous quotation, this judgment seems one-sided; in fact, the narrator condemns equally the use of parental constraint in the case of marriage and of religious profession. Without advocating the free choice of marriage partners, Camus insists on the need for the consent of both parties to the match: "the single knot that forms this sacred bond is the reciprocal will and mutual consent of both parties" ["le seul noeud qui compose ce sacré lien, c'est la reciproque volonté & le mutuel consentement des parties," 222]. He harangues the girls' mother: "why did you not direct Engevine in accordance with her religious plans? And why do you want to force Cleriane to carry a cross too heavy for her shoulders?" ["que ne destinez-vous Engevine conformement à son dessein Religieux? Et pourquoi voulez-vous contraindre Cleriane à porter une Croix trop lourde pour ses espaules?" 215].

Camus's position on religious profession seems similarly balanced. He realistically accepts the practice of placing surplus daughters in convents so they can amass a dowry sufficient for one sister to marry: "This practice is so common in society, that to ignore it is to be unaware of what is going on in the world, and to hide it is a kind of betrayal" ["Cette pratique est si commune dans le monde, que l'ignorer c'est ne sçavoir ce qui s'y passe, & la dissimuler c'est une espece de trahison," 215]. At the same time, he holds a religious vocation to be indispensable for monastic profession: "[placement in convents] is still acceptable, provided that the will is not thwarted; and without frustrating the vocations made by the spirit of God, which sends some souls into the desert and the solitude of Cloisters, one does not replace them with vocations proposed by flesh and blood" ["Encore cela est suportable, pourveu que l'on ne violente point les volontez, & que sans suffoquer les vocations de l'esprit de Dieu, qui pousse quelques ames au desert & à la solitude des Cloistres, on ne mette point en leur place des vocations suggerées par la chair & le sang," 215]. This is consistent with the Council of Trent's condemnation of forced monachization. Camus presents an interesting supporting argument at this point: the space God has reserved for those he has called to the convent should not be taken up by unwilling residents for whom the convent is truly "the tomb of the living" ["le tombeau des personnes vivantes," 216].

Nor does the narrator totally condemn marriage, as Venesoen asserts (210). Camus's support of marriage is orthodox, though falling short of François de Sales's exceptionally positive and frank attitude (Bernos 126): he presents marriage as a sacrament ordered by God, "which is called great and honorable" ["qui est appellé grand & honorable," 222]. But compared to the religious life, wedlock is a miserable fate indeed. In flowery neo-Platonic language, the narrator condemns those parents who, ignoring their children's religious vocation, tear them from the foot of the altar and force them "like bastard eaglets, to lower their eyes to the ground and to abandon spiritual nuptials, more pure than the Sun's rays, in order to embrace a carnal union formed only of blood and matter"[22] ["comme des Aiglons bastards de ravaler leur prunelles vers la terre, & de quitter les nopces spirituelles, plus pures que les rayons du Soleil, pour embrasser les charnelles, qui ne sont que de sang & de matiere," 222–3].

After her forced wedding, Engevine continues to resist her husband Artemon's advances and refuses to consummate the union. Artemon hesitates to use force: "This man conceived some kind of secret horror at possessing a body whose spirit would be removed from him" ["Cet homme conceut je ne sçai quelle secrete horreur de posseder un corps dont l'esprit seroit esloignée de lui"]. A stalemate results: "Ten days passed in this [state of] obsession without possession" ["Dix jours se passerent dans cette obsession sans possession," 228]. Finally, Artemon is convinced by Anastasia, and his own desires, to tie Engevine up and claim his marital rights by force. But there is no real suspense here; the strongly "pro-convent" narrative perspective assures the reader in advance that the *fille forte* will come out with her virtue and her vocation intact. At the last moment, a servant takes pity on the girl and exchanges clothing with her, allowing Engevine to run away to a relative's house. This pious relation, scandalized by the mother's actions, has the marriage annulled and Engevine is finally able to fulfill her wish to enter a "strictly reformed Monastery" ["Monastere fort reformé," 223].

The fate of Engevine's sister Cleriane is less "happy" from Camus's perspective. At first, Cleriane's situation is presented with a certain degree of sympathy: in her eyes, we are told, a convent is worse than a prison—it is a sepulcher (216). But his narrative empathy ends when Cleriane, led astray by a man who promises marriage,

---

[22]   This image refers to the belief that young eagles gazed fixedly at the sun; the "aiglon bastard," in contrast, looks down at the ground (*Divertissement* n. 402, pp. 222–3).

seeks to break her holy vows. Camus condemns this project as a "shameful goal" ["honteuse poursuite," 232]. We do not learn Cleriane's actual fate; because Camus claims that the story is confidential, and also because he needs to end a *divertissement* which threatens to grow into a novel, the denouement is left open.[23] But the narrator does relate at length, and with a rich mixture of metaphors, the misfortunes that await Cleriane in this world and the next if she breaks her vows. This diatribe has the air of a sermon:

> Certainly if Cleriane succeeds in achieving her shameful goal, she will commit two evils at the same time, and strike two bad blows with the same stone: for she will abandon the source of living waters to build herself a broken cistern that cannot hold water; and when she has arrived on the open seas of the tribulations of the flesh and the world … in vain will she cry that the storm engulfs her, in vain will she raise her eyes towards Heaven, where she has lost sight of the North Star. God withholds his help from those who lack faith in him, and when death comes to them, when after this life they descend into the afflictions of Hell, the Almighty will mock them, shake his head at them, and laugh at their destruction.

> Certes si Cleriane vient à bout de son dessein de sa honteuse poursuitte, elle fera deux maux à la fois, & d'une mesme Pierre deux mauvais coups: car elle quittera la source de l'eau vive pour se bastir une citerne cassée, qui ne peut garder des eaux, & lors qu'elle sera arrivée en la haute mer des tribulations de la chair & du monde … elle aura beau crier que la tempeste l'engloutit, beau lever les yeux vers le Ciel, dont elle aura perdu la tramontane [étoile du Nord], Dieu manquera de secours à qui lui manque de foy, & quand la mort viendra sur eux, & quand ils descendront en un enfer d'afflictions dès cette vie, le Tout-Puissant se moquera d'eux, hochera la teste sur eux, se rira de leur perte. (232)

This passage paints a deliberately frightening picture of a merciless, even sadistic God laughing at the sufferings of the damned. Clearly, breaking one's religious vows is the one unforgivable sin. While it is possible in certain cases to annul a secular marriage, the nun's union with Christ, even if performed under duress, appears indissoluble.

On an allegorical level, the unbreakable connection between nun and convent is linked to images of female hollowness, porousness and fragility. Camus compares Cleriane to a broken vessel, "une citerne cassée" which can no longer hold water. While Cleriane's body is a useless, shattered container, Engevine's is a sacred temple which can only be entered through the "front door" of marriage: "Her modesty, as it were the general commander of her virtues, made known to the most intemperate that they could only gain access to this Temple of honor through the door of marriage" ["Sa modestie, qui estoit comme la gouvernante generale de ses vertus, faisoit bien cognoistre aux plus intemperans qu'on ne pouvoit avoir d'accez à ce Temple d'honneur que par la porte d'hymen"]. The narrator reiterates

---

[23] "Je passerois les bornes de la brieveté que je me prescrits en ce Divertissement …" (224).

this point more explicitly a few lines later: "there was no other way to enter her than through the door of the Church, nor to possess her than through legitimate nuptials" ["il n'y avoit point moyen d'entrer chez elle que par la porte de l'Eglise, ny de la posseder que par des nopses legitimes," 221]. Women are temples, churches or, in a bivalent metaphor, vases: "vases sacrés" if, like Engevine, they remain intact (230); "vases d'ignominie" when, like Cleriane, they do not (187). All these images come from traditional religious discourse; but Camus renews their force through development, accumulation and repetition. Moreover, Camus's insistence upon entering by the front door of the Church contains implied sexual suggestion.

These metaphorical meanings aside, "La Fille forte" explicitly endorses the Tridentine edict of strict perpetual enclosure. Not only must nuns remain "for their whole lives in the Houses consecrated to His service" ["tout le temps de leur vie dans les Maisons consacrées à son service," 211], but the convent must be a reformed one. Somewhat ironically, while the narrator criticizes Anastasia for forcing Cleriane into religion, he is even more outraged by the fact that, unlike Engevine's reformed convent, the establishment Cleriane's mother has chosen for her is lax. The narrator fumes:

> Finally, her mother finds her a Religion made according to her fashion. I mean one of these houses that possess only the name and habit [of a convent], with nothing of its observances and customs; without enclosure, without subjection; to say more, without piety, without rule, poverty without community, chastity without retreat, obedience without submission, a veil made to receive the wind of vanity rather than to hide the face … let us say no more, for fear that people might take truth for calumny, and just blame for a tract full of enmity.

> En fin sa mere lui trouve une Religion faite à sa mode, je veux dire une de ces maisons qui n'en ont que le nom & l'habit, nullement l'observance & les habitudes, sans closture, sans sujetion; disons plus, sans pieté, sans regle, une pauvreté sans communauté, une chasteté sans retraicte, une obeyssance sans soumission, un voile à recevoir le vent de la vanité plutost qu'à cacher le visage … n'en disons pas davantage, de peur que l'on ne prist la verité pour médisance, & une juste reprehension pour un tract de malignité.[24] (216)

In its lack of discipline, Cleriane's convent is not even Christian: "She made her profession within this troop of daughters of Baal, that is without yoke and without observance" ["Elle fit profession dans cette troupe de filles de Baal, c'est à dire sans joug & sans observance," 217]. Worst of all, Cleriane's downfall—the meeting with the man who seduces her—is enabled by the convent's laxness. The narrator sardonically comments: "This blind child [Cupid] did not pass through the grills, for this, may I say, Religious or irreligious House was ignorant of their use" ["Ce ne fut point au-travers des grilles que passe cet enfant aveugle (Amour) … car cette, dirais-je Religieuse ou irreligieuse Maison en ignoroit l'usage," 217]. Worst of all, the abbess, who should set the example of chastity, exercises no control over

---

[24]   In this passage, Camus plays on the double meanings of *voile* ("veil" and "sail").

her charges because she herself is corrupt. The narrative intervention ends with a sarcastic harangue: "Go on, parents! To get rid of your daughters and burden your families with shame and opprobrium, dedicate your daughters to Molor [sic], not to the true God, in libertine and dissolute locales, and recall that you will drink, for their follies, a part of the chalice of repentance which accompanies them" ["Allez maintenant, ô parens! & pour vous décharger de vos filles & recharger vos familles de honte & d'opprobre, consacrez vos filles à Molor (sic), non au vray Dieu, en des lieux libertins & deréglez, & souvenez-vous que vous boirez, pour leur sotizes, une partie du calice du repentir qui les accompagne," 219].

"Les Deux Courtisanes," another tale from *Divertissement historique*, shows in more detail what can happen to women who break their religious vows. As in "La Fille forte," renouncing one's vows is represented as the one unforgivable sin; far worse than mere human adultery, it violates the marriage bond with God.[25] When one of the female characters, Gildarde, is seduced by her employer, the narrator first treats her with a certain sympathy, calling her "cette pauvrette" (183). Made aware of her sins by "devout persons," Gildarde enters the Repentirs convent, an establishment for "girls of immoral life" ["filles de mauvaise vie," 184]. But once Gildarde leaves the Repentirs and goes back to her lover, she loses all claim on the narrator's mercy: "Concerning Gildarde, as her backsliding was infamous, so her fate was wretched" ["Quant à Gildarde, comme sa recheute fut infame, sa fortune aussi fut miserable," 186]. Pregnant, she is arrested, thrown into prison for immorality and dies there of a miscarriage. Shockingly, the narrator applauds her fate as an act of providence: "adorable change from the hand of him who creates and honors vases of ignominy" ["Changement adorable de la main de celui qui fait & met en honneur des vases d'ignominie," 187].

Degrees of Conventual Enclosure in Seventeenth-Century France

To what degree do Camus's imprecations against lax convents and broken vows reflect the historical situation in the early seventeenth century, when strict enclosure

---

25   "Les Deux Courtisanes," like "La Fille forte," displays a double parallel structure. Gildarde and Caliope, two girls from impoverished noble families, are sent to the city to earn their keep as servants. Both are seduced by male members of their households: Gildarde by her master, Caliope by her employer's son, Clodulphe. Gildarde seeks refuge in the Repentirs; but Clodulphe, however, still enamored of her, leaves his wife and goes to live alone in his country house. On his return, he asks Caliope to visit her friend in the convent and convince Gildarde to run away. This mission is successful: Gildarde leaves the convent and resumes her liaison with Clodulphe, scandalously taking up residence in Clodulphe's town house so that his wife is forced to retreat in turn to the country. In a further musical chairs-like move, Caliope regrets her role in Gildarde's departure and enters the Repentirs in her place: "Caliope withdrew from the arms of Julian [her lover], taking the place of the one she had torn away from the foot of the Altar" ["Caliope se retira d'entre les bras de Julian, prenant la place de celle qu'elle avoit arrachée du pied de l'Autel," 186].

was not yet universally enforced? Did many women's religious communities actually resemble the "maisons qui n'en ont que le nom & l'habit ... sans closture, sans sujetion" that Camus decries? Or is the author merely expressing a cleric's biased perception of these problems? This question is a complex one, and probably impossible to answer definitively. On the one hand, the late sixteenth and early seventeenth centuries were a time of "devotional fever" for women, many of whom sought out reformed orders or worked to reform them from the inside. Along with St. John of the Cross, Teresa of Avila imposed reform on the Carmelite order, which became one of the most respected in France (see below, Chapter 3, 119–21). And as already noted, Mother Agnès unilaterally reformed Port-Royal in 1609, long before strict enclosure of women was generally enforced.

On the other hand, as we have seen, Church policies of the time concerning the enclosure of nuns were not completely clear-cut. The decrees of the Council of Trent only applied to religious communities whose members had taken formal vows of poverty, obedience and stability. In the bull *Circa Pastoralis* (1566), Pope Pius V had tried to close up loopholes for women in so-called tertiary communities who, since they had not taken complete vows, were not covered by the 25th session of Trent; but his actual power to enforce enclosure depended on the attitude and cooperation of local bishops. These tertiary groups showed "une diversité déconcertante," ranging from béguines to canonesses (Lemoine 266). At the same time, the Counter-Reformation fervor of the early seventeenth century led not only to a "fantastic conventual invasion" by women (Bardet 1.90, translated in Rapley, *Les Dévotes* 19), but to the invention of new ways for them to be together in religious community. This somewhat free-wheeling moment recalls in some ways the early history of Christianity: before either church edifices or institutions were too solidly constructed, there was still a broad spectrum of what might be called "sacralized secular spaces." Often, the sacred/secular space was also a domestic one: for religious women, choosing to cloister themselves within their homes was a frequent and recommended practice (see Suzanna Elm) among other monastic practices. Counter-Reformation spirituality, with its emphasis on both literal and figurative interiority, absorbed this house-as-convent metaphor: for example, in *Les Amours de la Magdelene* (1618), the narrator observes: "Votre maison est un petit couvent" frequented by the faithful (206).

The number of women living in non-traditional, "open" religious communities was especially great at the beginning of the century. According to Linda Timmermans, a "multitude of daughters of Charity and ladies doing good works" ["multitude des filles de la Charité et des dames d'oeuvres"] felt called to go out and minister to the poor, gaining social and clerical acceptance by their sheer numbers (404). While Camus's use of the phrase "couvent reformé" evokes a traditional convent placed under stricter rule, his description of the heinous "anti-convents" as "sans grille" more closely resembles these newer congregations, which deliberately avoided the presence of grills and other traditional architectural elements in order not to be confused with "real" convents and criticized for failing to maintain clausura. Camus's own patron François de Sales, along with Jeanne de Chantal, created the Order of the Visitation for women of delicate health whose constitutions could not withstand the "extreme harshness" ["grande âpreté"] of traditional convent discipline (Brémond 566). Jeanne, a widow, was Sales's friend, penitent, chief patroness, and the first abbess of the convent of the Visitation, which was founded in Annency in 1609, shortly before the publication of the *Introduction à la vie dévote*. The Visitation's first Constitution of 1613 afforded the nuns unusual contact with the world. Widows were allowed to deal with their children's business affairs; and before the practice was forbidden, the sisters of the Visitation left their convent to visit the sick, "offering a good part to external works of charity and the best part to the inwardness of contemplation" ["donnant une bonne partie aux oeuvres extérieures de charité et la meilleure partie à l'intérieur de la contemplation," Sales, quoted in Brémond 2.570]. This relaxed rule, accepted in its Swiss homeland, was not long tolerated in France; as early as 1616, the Bishop of Lyon ordered the Visitation to become a closed congregation. This episode will be discussed further in Chapter 3. However, the enclosure debate did not always present a clear-cut lineup of bishops against founders. This more complex reality is apparent in the history of the Ursulines.

The Ursuline congregation was founded in Italy in 1535 by Angela Merisi, with a mission of educating girls. After a first French house was established in Avignon in 1592, the order quickly spread throughout the south of France: by 1630, a total of 80 Ursuline establishments had been created. It would go on to become the most important teaching order in Old Regime France: when Mme de Maintenon's school at St-Cyr was reformed, instruction was taken over by Ursuline nuns. The original Italian Urusuline community had remained uncloistered, even after they were congregated by Charles Borromeo, Bishop of Milan. The members of the first French Urusuline congregation in Avignon initially lived at home, then in an open community; but the Ursulines soon found themselves in a contested situation in France. Unlike their Swiss and Italian neighbors, French Catholics, having just emerged from a long and bitter religious war and viewing innovation with suspicion, often took a narrow and conservative view of *clausura*. And as we have seen, in addition to the hostility of religious authorities, the absence of formal vows could also raise legal issues for families (cf. Introduction, n12). Finally, the post-Trent era was marked by a "hardening in attitude toward female sexuality" (Rapley 4) on the part of some clergy and a general increase in misogyny and open hostility toward women. When the Ursulines of Dijon left their convent to perform their teaching duties, they were harassed by crowds: "Whenever they passed in the streets, they were looked on with scorn; the little children shouted after them and threw mud at them" [Mère de Pommereu, ursuline, *Chroniques de l'ordre des Ursulines*, in Rapley 56]. Rather than be treated as "women of the street," the Ursulines, like the Visitandines, fell into line; the last Ursuline convent became a regular monastery in 1658.[26]

---

[26]   Strictly speaking, church vocabulary distinguishes between *couvents*, which are not necessarily subject to formal rule, and *monastères*, or regular religious houses for men or

Yet pressure for the closing of the Avignon convent did not come from the outside community alone. Lierheimer identifies a kind of "generation gap" among the Ursulines themselves, with the older sisters wanting to remain free to work in the community, and the younger ones embracing with fervor the contemplative ideal of Teresa of Avila and others. In fact, the original impulse behind enclosure came from a woman, Madame de Sainte-Beuve, who endowed the Paris Ursuline convent as a closed monastic community (Lierheimer 214). Divisions over the issue of enclosure were so strong that "many communities were literally torn apart by the process." The case of the Dijon Ursulines is particularly illuminating. In 1606, another rich Parisian widow offered their community a sizable endowment on the condition that they become a regular closed convent. The Dijon community did not split apart, but the sisters debated for a year before deciding that enclosure would not hinder their teaching mission.

After 1660, due in part to the success of the Ursulines and other teaching orders, the first wave of religious enthusiasm among French women began to die down, or at least to take a different form.[27] Convents became more involved with the outside world; new orders, like that of St. Vincent de Paul, found ways to get around the imperative of enclosure by restricting the scope of the nun's vows. Real or perceived abuses provoked pro-enclosure tracts by male clerics, the most insistent of whom may be Jean-Baptiste Thiers. This curious figure is the author of several tracts, the best known being the *Traité des Superstitions* (Paris 1697–1704). His religious conservatism led him to write a treatise on *L'Histoire des Perruques*, criticizing ecclesiastical wig-wearing. In his *Traité de la clôture des religieuses* (1681), the Abbé Thiers cites at exhaustive and boring length all Catholic precedents for female enclosure, from the fourth century through Boniface's twelfth-century *Pericoloso*, the Council of Trent and the Ordonnance of Blois of 1629, repeating in each instance "it was forbidden to leave their Cloister" ["il estoit défendu de sortir de leur Clôture"]. Despite the weight of all these precedents, Thiers complains that "There is hardly today any point of Discipline more neglected or ignored" than clausura ["Il n'y a gueres aujourd'hui de point de Discipline ou plus negligé ou plus ignoré," preface, no page number]. He gives no evidence for this assertion, merely remarking on the (excessive) number of women religious to be seen wandering about in Paris: "how many of them does one see every day, and *how likely* is it that they are all there in conformity with the Rules of the Church?" ["combien y en rencontre-t-on tous les jours, & *quelle apparence* y-a-t-il qu'elles y soient toutes conformement aux Regles de l'Eglise?" 121; italics added].

The next part of Thiers's treatise, dealing with passive enclosure, lists the reasons for which the Church has forbidden nuns to leave their cloisters— reasons combining religious notions of female chastity with social constraints

---

women. In this book, I generally use the word *couvent* in a looser and more modern sense of a religious house for women.

[27] On the openness of late seventeenth-century convents see also Bluche, *La vie quotidienne au temps de Louis XIV* (Paris: Hachette, 1984); see also Chapter 4, "Parlors."

on women. Quoting the jurisconsult Philippus Probus, he states: "clausura is the faithful guardian of Virginity: a woman ought to have either a husband, or a wall" ["la clôture est la fidele gardienne de la Virginité *aut virum, aut murum oportet mulierum habere*," 245]. It is a truism that the choice for early modern women was marriage or the convent; but the version of this prescription cited by Thiers puts the alternative in brutally metonymic terms. Moreover, nuns seen exiting the convent constitute a sin against modesty and propriety, and a cause of scandal for the church. Acceptable excuses for exiting the convent are few: nuns can *rompre leur clôture* in case of fire (providing the conflagration is severe enough) or if the convent buildings are falling into ruin around them; but not merely because of bad air, which might serve as a useful "mortification." Above all, even if they are ill, they must not be allowed to walk in public parks where people might see them.

The last part of the treatise lays down in detail the rules for active and passive enclosure. As a strict principle, strangers, whether female or male, are not to be allowed into the convent. However, Thiers makes exceptions for married women who are mad or who fear "the rage of their husbands" ["la fureur de leurs maris"], and for young girls whose engagements are in dispute (Chapter 37). Doctors are to be admitted with precautions, and only when "dangerous and extraordinary disease" prevents the patient from being carried to the grill (407). Finally, Thiers suggests an architectural modification for teaching orders whose students must enter the cloistered space. The girls should come in through a special room, locked on both ends: "a space between the street and the classroom, off limits to Nuns" ["un espace entre la porte de la rue et la classe defendue aux Religieuses," 447–8]. This threshold space, which serves as a kind of isolation chamber protecting the nuns from the infection of the outside world, was indeed created in many teaching convents.

If we are to credit J-B Thiers, some convent reforms were deemed necessary by the late seventeenth century. Yet it is hard to understand why Jean-Pierre Camus was so exercised about abuses of enclosure in the early part of the century. As seen in the case of the Ursulines, the pressures to enclose came not just from public opinion or the male church hierarchy, but from within the female faith community itself; such women hardly needed a Jean-Pierre Camus to spur them on to stricter observance. Nor was Camus's attitude towards strict enclosure shared by all his fellow churchmen. The members of François de Sales's own Order of the Visitation enjoyed unusual freedoms before its enclosure. Ironically, the Dijon Ursulines' original hesitation to accept clausura was influenced by the opinions of Camus's master, who considered "the vocation of an Ursuline was incompatible with cloister" (Lierheimer 215). In sum, the reform movements of the Early Modern period, a time of deep religious change, created at least a temporary "opening" for women to expand their traditional roles and express their spirituality in differing ways. Thus, Camus's advocacy of strict conventual enclosure in the early seventeenth century may reflect not only a post-Trent indignation at the laxness of still-unreformed houses but also an anxiety regarding the important presence of women in the Catholic Reformation, and their freedom to explore multiple forms of religious life.

Misogyny and Sexuality in Camusian Fiction

Camus's advocacy of enclosure is congruent with the gynophobic attitudes expressed in his narratives. The Salesian spirituality and vocabulary of *retraite intérieure*, so central to Camus's theory of reading, hardly carry over into his fictional practice. Gone is the cozy tête-à-tête between writer and female disciple within a private shaded reading alcove. Unlike the kindly paternalism of Nervèze and Sales, or the allegorical exaltation of the female in Marie de Valence's visions, Camus's narrative representations of the body and of women are mainly negative. We have already seen these attitudes expressed in *Agathonphile*. But Camus's novels, more likely to be addressed to a female audience, are less openly violent and critical of women than his *histoires tragiques*.[28] These tales, allegedly "fondés sur les faits réels" (*Divertissement historique* 27) rather than fiction, may have attracted a less exclusively female readership than the novels. For whatever reason, a misogynistic tone prevails in the *histoires tragiques*. Misogynistic traits range from unquestioned stereotypes, such as the description of women's wiles in "La Fille forte"—"causing tears to flow from her eyes (that women always hold in reserve to deliver when they please) she tried to persuade by this language" ["faisant couler de ses yeux des larmes (que les femmes ont tousjours en reserve pour les debiter quand il leur plaist) elle tascha de persuader par ce langage," 221]—to graphic descriptions of physical abuse.

Camus's tales often apply a stereotyped, brutal logic to women: since they are "pretty and arouse desire" ["jolies et inspirent le désir," 19] they also fatally inspire suspicion, jealousy and violence. Thus, the three convent stories in *Divertissement* are balanced by a trio of tales concerning jealous husbands. In all three instances, marital jealousy leads to murder. The first and second jealous husbands kill their wives; in "Le Troisième Jaloux," the wife dies as well, but her husband, though responsible, does not do the deed himself. However, the actual description of the murder is horrific. The husband, Similian, orders a servant to strangle her while he watches; he then places her body in quicklime to dissolve it. While condemning this horrible crime, the narrator cites extreme provocation in Similian's defense: the wife had loved another man, though the passion was never consummated. "And of course, it is to be believed that this woman's outrages pushed Similian so far beyond the bounds of reason and patience that, carried away by rage and in hot blood, he did what he would never have done in a cooler and more restrained state" ["Et certes, il est à croire que les outrages de cette femme mirent tellement hors des gonds la raison & la patience de Similian, qu'il fit, transporté de fureur &

---

[28]   There is no direct evidence as to Camus's readership, but his own stated desire to entice female readers away from corrupt love novels, and the general readership for the novel during this (and all) periods, imply a largely female audience.

à la chaude, ce que jamais il n'eust prastiqué d'un sang plus froid & retenu," 208]. It is hard to accept the spontaneous "sang chaud" defense when Similian does not commit the murder himself, but asks a servant to do it. In comparison, no such tolerance is shown the wife, even though her "outrages" were of intent rather than of act. Again, it is the fault of Eve.

In one of the misogynistic low points of *Divertissement*,[29] the narrator apparently cannot resist making a pun about the death of Similian's wife. He claims that she died of an obstruction of the uterus: "those blockages and obstructions common to women, that are called suffocations of the womb" ["ces estouffements & opilations communes aux femmes, que l'on appelle suffocations de l'amari (matrice)," 208]. The narrator comments: "but one could say without feigning and with some truth, that she was dead from suffocation of the husband" ["mais on pourrait dire sans feinte & avecque verité, qu'elle estoit morte de la suffocation du mari," 208]. We have already noted on more than one occasion how puns and plays on words form part of Camus's style. But as is often the case with jokes, this one is revelatory. In linking the wife's death both to her husband's "suffocation" by jealousy and to a "common" female complaint, the play on words reveals the extent to which Camus embraces the received opinion that women are at the mercy of, and defined by, their internal female organs. Similarly, in "L'Accordée," after her first promised husband had been gone for several years, the abandoned fiancée "caught that pale malady which attacks nubile girls" ["(a) pris cette pasle maladie qui attaque les filles nubiles," 89]. Camus's acceptance of the medical myth of hysteria is consistent with his distaste for the body, and especially the female body. In describing Camus's disparagement of women, Venesoen aptly comments: "It is the unavoidable law of an epoch and its *visceral* misogyny" ["C'est la loi incontournable d'une époque et de sa misogynie *viscérale*," 203; italics added]. The viscera involved here, however, are not the man's but the woman's, contained in their bodily *vases d'ignominie* ("Les deux Courtisanes" 187).

Venesoen accounts for the misogyny endemic throughout *Divertissement* by placing it in the context of early modern tradition: "The numerous treatises and opuscules that militated in the sixteenth and seventeenth centuries against female nature and denounced its diabolical origins establish that it is 'above all woman's unremitting propensity for sensual desire that makes her the privileged chosen one of Satan and the enemy of humankind'" ["Les nombreux traités ou opuscules qui militent au XVIᵉ et XVIIᵉ siècles contre la nature féminine et en dénoncent les origines diaboliques établissent que c'est 'par-dessus tout l'irrémissible propension de la femme à la concupiscence qui en a fait l'élue privilégiée de Satan et l'ennemie du genre humain," Venesoen 302–3].[30] This broad statement somewhat simplifies the complex situation prevailing in early modern France. Virulent hostility towards women certainly existed, but women also were making

---

[29] See also the misogynistic gems collected by Bernos in *Femmes et gens d'églises dans la France classique*, Annexe 1, 347 ff.

[30] See Venesoen 22–3, 33, 180; and Bernos, *Femmes et gens d'église*.

their voices heard through the *précieux* movement, the salons and the development of the modern novel. In the field of religion, women were important leaders of the monastic movement; married women were also expected to play a major role in creating a Christian home and instructing their children. Moreover, as we have seen, not all clerics were prone to *misogynie viscérale*; François de Sales had to defend himself against other churchmen for his close relationships to women, but he is not a singular exception (Timmermans 402). Camus's narrators, on the other hand, seem to experience a kind of male "hysteria" in face of the suffocating female womb: "les suffocations de l'amari" attack them as well. Franchetti identifies this repugnance with the author himself, reading as quasi-autobiographical the hero's statement in *Alexis* that he had been raised "with a bunch of girls" ["parmy un tas de filles"], and "It is this prolonged rearing with the female sex that formed in me an aversion to them, as if with [mother's] milk" ["C'est cette longue nourriture avec ce sexe, qui m'en a comme avec le laict imprimé *l'aversion*," *Alexis*, Ve partie, 20–21; quoted in Franchetti 142n52; italics added].

If, for Camus, the daughters of Eve are irredeemably weak and sensual, how then can he create positive heroines with whom a woman reader can identify? The answer is: with difficulty. His overt rhetorical strategy is to contrast "good" and "bad" women, often in a parallel tale structure. But Camus's actual descriptions often subvert this strategy. In "La Fille forte," the narrator castigates Engevine's mother for forcing her to marry because of her beauty, which seems to deny the importance of outward appearance; but at the same time, he calls attention to the older sister's ugliness: Cleriane "was intended by [Anastasie] for the Cloister, so that with a veil hiding her from the eyes of those who might observe her, she would spend her days in darkness, among those dead to the World" ["fut destinée par (Anastasie) au Cloistre, afin qu'un voile la dérobant aux yeux de ceux qui la pouvoient considerer, elle passast ses jours entre les obscuritez, parmi les morts du Siecle," 214]. It seems almost as though Cleriane's enclosure in the convent is a punishment for her ugliness. The narrator brutally mocks Cleriane's desire to remain in the world: "the ugly one wanting to appear in the light of day, and to show herself, *like monkeys* [in a menagerie]: the more she would be looked at, the more ridiculous and worthy of scorn [she would appear] ["la laide voulant paroistre à la lumiere du jour; & se monstrer, *comme des singes*, d'autant plus ridicule & digne de mépris qu'elle seroit plus regardée," 215; italics added]. In this passage, clerical condemnation of *les filles d'Eve* makes an odd alliance with common or garden sexism. The narrator's comments undermine his early defense of freedom in religious vocation and the sanctity of the cloister: instead of a holy space reserved for those with a religious bent, it becomes a prison where ugly girls should go to hide their faces from the world.

In speaking of Engevine, the narrator does take some distance from misogynist received opinion, calling it "*this common belief* in the natural weakness of the sex" ["*cette commune creance* de la naturelle foiblesse du sexe," 226; italics added]. But the *fille forte* who defends her virtue through all trials derives her superhuman (or superfemale) strength from direct divine intervention: "since the Son of God through his languishing fortified our weaknesses ... girls, who by nature are merely leaves shaken by the least wind, become courageous, not only above their own sex and condition but more than men ..." ["depuis que le Fils de Dieu par ses langueurs a fortifié nos foiblesses ... les filles qui de leur nature ne sont que des feuilles, agitées des moindres vents, deviennent courageuses, non seulement au dessus de leur sexe & de leur condition mais plus que des hommes," 213]. This superiority of women can only be explained through divine intervention; only the grace of God can transform natural "vases d'ignominie" into "Vases sacrés" ("Fille forte" 230).

What moral can a female reader draw from these tales of "la naturelle foiblesse du sexe?" And what pleasure will gild the pill of this lesson, allowing it to be swallowed? The obvious moral is a cautionary one: rather than waiting for external punishment—even a miserable death—it is better that a woman voluntarily choose *self*-denial and mortification. In this view, the female pleasure of the text would be of a pretty masochistic kind, not usually associated with light reading. A second interpretation, not excluding the first, is that a female reader might enjoy a vicarious sense of power and excitement in identifying with negative characters like Nerée or Clériane—a more sadistic pleasure, transgressing the devotional novel's supposed aim. But what if these narratives are addressed, deliberately or unconsciously, to a male audience? Given this premise, the power dialectic described above takes on a certain logic—a logic that also explains Camus's objection to monasticism for men and his championing of it for women. While in "La Fille forte," his positions on marriage and religious profession fall within the Catholic mainstream of his time, the length and virulence of his diatribes against errant nuns and unfaithful wives far outweigh his criticisms of forced marriage and monachization. If sexual subjection of the female inevitably leads to subjection of the male, the solution is not the man's flight, but the woman's enclosure in a "Monastere fort reformé"— a strictly reformed convent ("Fille forte" 223).

In conclusion, where other critics have situated the Camusian paradox in the opposition between his apologetic project and the novelistic genre, in my view the main conflicts involve women and repressed sexuality. Whereas the writings of Camus's mentor François de Sales, and even Camus's own prefaces, exhibit a positive attitude toward women, Camus's fiction represents them as lost and dangerous beings. Camus's problematic depictions of women are connected to his conflicting views of the body as enclosed and enclosure. While his theoretical works affirm the value of love and the body, Camusian narratives radiate a profound distaste for the corporeal and the material, both of which are concentrated in the female sex.[31] However, the same narratives that condemn the body are permeated with corporality. As we saw in Chapter 1, part of the Catholic Reformation's mission,

---

[31]   Similarly, in "Robert Herrick's Gift Trouble: Male Subjects 'Trans-shifting' into Objects," Pamela Hammons observes that Robert Herrick's love lyrics exhibit a "general distrust of materiality itself," and that this distrust is related to the early modern association of matter with woman.

through the centrality of the Incarnation, is to "incorporate" religion. According to Terence Cave, this corporality determines the "high degree of physical urgency one finds in devotional poetry" (Cave 303). A similar physical urgency makes itself felt in prose writers like Nervèze and Camus: Peter Shoemaker has pointed out the extreme physicality of Camus's writing, where "violence is presented as physiological and physical ... rather than psychological and moral" (555). Camus denies that his stories contain any sensual "impurities" (*Eloge* 127/917); yet for anyone who has read *Agathonphile*, this disclaimer is unconvincing. At best, Camus's argument, like a legal rape defense, is based on technicalities. There is no profane or explicit language in *Agathonphile*, and passion remains unconsummated; but the novel contains plenty of suggestive material, near nudity and a close approximation of "attouchements." Further, Camus's treatment of passion is even more graphic in the story of Agathon, presented in Part II of the novel. In one episode, Agathon's stepmother falls in love with her stepson, tries to seduce him and then accuses him of assaulting her. In describing this scene, Molinié cites "the exacerbated eroticism of the talk about love ... we are spared nothing, in the passages not quoted, not a single detail of Irene's physical behavior" ["l'erotisme exacerbé des propos d'amour ... on ne nous épargne rien, dans les passages non cités, aucun détail du comportement physique d'Irène," 58]. In the genre of post-Tridentine adaptations of love stories to pious ends, Camus's work might fall in the category that Terence Cave wittily calls "forced conversion" (261).

Despite all its excesses, *Agathonphile* was apparently read and approved by François de Sales, perhaps because its legendary structure hides a multitude of sins. The long subtitle carefully establishes the novel's resemblance to a traditional saint's tale: "Agathonphile, or the Sicilian martyrs, Agathon, Philargyrippe, Triphyne and their companions; devotional Story where one discovers the Art of loving well, as an antidote to dishonorable affections; and where through admirable outcomes, the Holy Love of the Martyr triumphs over the Martyrdom of evil Love" ["Agathonphile, ou les martyres siciliens, Agathon, Philargyrippe Triphyne et leurs associés: Histoire dévote où se descouvre l'Art de bien aymer, pour antidote aux deshonnestes affections: et où par des succez admirables, la Saincte Amour du Martyre triomphe du Martyre de la mauvaise Amour," *Agathonphile*, first ed., title page]. Camus also reiterates in *Eloge*: "and in the end, all these holy and pure loves terminate in glorious Deaths" ["et enfin toutes ces amours sainctes et pures se terminent en de glorieuses Morts," 127–8/917]. Even if the martyrdoms related in *Agathonphile* never really took place,[32] the pious "happy ending" gives Camus license to venture outside orthodox lines in the earlier course of the narration. This licensed wandering, so prevalent in Camus's work, is in keeping

---

[32]   Despite Camus's claims to historical accuracy, "St. Philip Argyrio in any case did not live at the time of Diocletian, no more than the problematic Agathon and Tryphine did, and never was venerated as a martyr" ["saint Philippe Argyrio en tout cas n'a pas vécu sous Dioclétien pas plus que les problématiques Agathon et Tryphine, et n'a jamais été vénéré comme martyre," Sage xxxiii].

with Counter-Reformation apologetic strategy: one must first attract the reader through the senses and passions before attempting to sublimate those passions. This process is also somewhat analogous to Camus's own sublimated "passion" for writing devotional fiction. He states in so many words: "Certainly for a long time I have *desired with an extreme passion* to see spirits intoxicated and as if enchanted by fictional or secular Stories" ["Certes il y a long temps *que je desirois avec une extreme passion* de voir ces esprits enyvrez et comme ensorcelez de ces Histoires ou fabuleuses ou profanes," 110/846; italics added].

This discussion leads to a related point. The potentially explosive nature of Camus's material requires a "difficile procédé de contrôle de lire" [de Baecque 41]: a delicate control over the way the text will be read. Christian Jouhaud puts it clearly: "Fictional techniques must be turned against the novel of simple pleasure; edification should break down the narcissistic identification of the reader to the hero or heroine" ["Les procédures romanesques doivent être tournées contre le roman de simple plaisir: l'édification doit faire succomber l'identification narcissique du lecteur au héros, ou à l'héroïne," 308]. The aim is to distance the reader from the text, thereby turning identification into conversion. As we have seen, techniques of reading control are frequent and varied in Camus's works, ranging from allegory to narrative commentary and harangue to exemplary plot endings.[33] But another kind of control is even more problematic for him: *contrôle d'écrire*, or control over one's own writing. Perhaps because of the haste with which Camus wrote, or for other, less straightforward reasons, he does not always appear in command of his tone or subject matter. His descriptions often verge on the lurid; his style ranges from the oratorical to the mundane to the frivolous to the near licentious; his metaphors contain unconscious puns that would have intrigued Freud; his tales threaten to expand into novels; and his *romans dévots* turn into *romans tout courts*: simply, novels.

However, the desired sublimation of the sensual remains incomplete for both reader and author. The overall allegorical architecture does not annul the effect of the passages we have examined, in which "license" grows into licentiousness. A number of similar examples could be cited. Yet I would not go so far as Molinié, who states categorically that in Camus's fiction "Eros remains separated from any spirituality" ["Eros reste hors de toute spiritualité," 60]. Such a separation would simplify the case too much. Rather, I see Camus's writing as displaying an ambivalent, even trivalent, attitude toward sensual pleasure: condemning it on the one hand, using it rhetorically on the other, but in the end displaying a troubling penchant towards it. As Camus himself is aware, this trivalence requires a delicate balancing act. Paraphrasing the Psalms, Camus states in *Divertissement*: "I say to you, rejoice in him, in such a manner, however, that you do not cross the boundaries of modesty" ["Je vous dy, rejouissez-vous en lui, de maniere toutefois que vous ne franchissiez point les bornes de la modestie," *Divertissement* 30].

---

[33] For further discussion of distancing techniques in Camus, see Franchetti 112–13.

Clearly, these boundaries are neither defined nor maintained easily. Like Philargyrippe, Camus plays a dangerous game, or as Robic-de Baecque puts it, makes a scandalous bet ["pari scandaleux," 33]: in trying to entice and entrap the reader with love stories written in the service of God, he crosses over the line between sacred and profane.

Perhaps sensing his own vulnerability, Camus offers multiple back-up arguments. He argues that in order to counteract the spell worked by secular fiction, any and all narrative means are justified: "I mix here the Comic with the Tragic, the serious with the ridiculous, the bitter herb with the sweet, oil with vinegar, to make you a salad, Reader, that will stimulate your appetite" ["J'entremesle icy le Comique avec le Tragique, le serieux avec le ridicule, l'herbe amere avec la douce, l'huile avec le vinaigre, pour te faire une salade, Lecteur, qui te reveille l'appetit," *Avertissement* to *Divertissement historique* 32]. Or else, comparing a devotional writer to a doctor, he exclaims: "Oh, he who could successfully disguise antidotes to sin or protections against contagion of the soul by *historic or oratory inventions* should be even more respected" ["O! que celuy-là seroit bien plus à estimer qui pourroit si bien desguiser par des *inventions ou historiques ou oratoires*, les antidotes du peché et les preservatifs de la contagion de l'ame," *Eloge* 110/845; italics added]. Failing that, Camus wishes to see his readers "disabused or *at least diverted* by devotional Stories" ["desabusez ou *pour le moins divertis* par des Histoires devotes," 100/846; italics added].

Yet in the end, after all these interpretations and justifications have been offered, a certain narrative surplus remains unaccounted for. While Camusian contradictions partly arise from the complex ideological and social context in which he worked, much of the explanation also seems to be personal and individual. The writer himself appears "diverted" by his own act of composition, which goes off in unexpected directions: is it really necessary for him to show holy men pursued by beautiful women *quite* so often? Can this priestly fantasy be related to the erotic excitement of gender role reversal and implied male penetration? Oddo's description of devotional fiction, quoted in the epigraph to this chapter, calls it "délicieusement retorse"—an oxymoron evoking not only Baroque style, but also a kind of perverse delight, or delight in perversity. All of these meanings are applicable to Camus. In his works, *diverti*, or turned, metamorphoses into something *retorse*, or twisted. Franchetti quotes a particularly illuminating passage in this regard:

> Certainly, at worst, one can only accuse Writers of a certain mental itch, or incurable craving to scratch paper [with a pen]. Should one be surprised if someone scratches himself, who feels a mite attack him between the skin and the flesh, in an even sharper and more burning way than a fly [....] If in scratching he scrapes himself, who can he accuse other than himself? If blood flows, it is his own blood he is spilling, if he feels the smarting, he is the only one to suffer from it.

Certes au pis on ne peut accuser les Escrivains que d'un certain prurit d'esprit, ou demangeaison incurable qu'ils ont de gratter du papier, et se faut-il estonner si celuy qui sent des cirons se gratte, cela le presse entre cuir et chair, d'une façon plus poignante et cuisante que ne font les mouches … . Si celuy qui se gratte s'écorche à qui faict-il tort qu'à soy, si le sang en vient, c'est le sien qu'il répand, si la cuisson se fait sentir, c'est luy seul qui en a la peine.

In this revealing passage, Camus compares the "itch" to write with the painful pleasure of scratching an insect bite until it bleeds. He specifies that the bite is from a mite (*ciron*) which lodges itself between flesh and skin (*chair et cuir*); but the expression "entre cuir et chair," as in "wounded to the quick," emphasizes the intimacy of the experience. Scratching, like masturbation, is a solitary act which hurts no one else: "si la cuisson se fait sentir, c'est luy seul qui en a la peine."

Camus goes on to compare the masochistic and guilty pleasure of writing to childbirth and, almost explicitly, to ejaculation:

> Do you not see that he who writes resembles a pregnant woman; if you ask her why she gives birth, why she does not keep her fruit contained in her womb, she will answer that it is in spite of herself […] that she can no longer keep the child within her […] the writer, in the same way, his violent mind pregnant with his imaginings, wishes like the silkworm to project his seed onto leaves.

> Ne vois-tu pas que celuy qui escrit ressemble à la femme enceinte, demandez à celle-ci pourquoi elle accouche, et pourquoi elle ne retient son fruit dans son sein, elle repondra que c'est malgré elle […] qu'elle ne peut plus retenir dans son flanc l'enfant […] l'autre [i.e. l'écrivain] de meme, la vehemence de son esprit gros des ses imaginations, veut comme les vers à soye, jetter sa semence sur des feuilles (*Alcime, Issue aux Censeurs* 567, quoted in Franchetti 125–6).

While most comparisons between writing and childbirth focus on the creative process, Camus's parallel instead emphasizes their physical and involuntary nature: "c'est malgré elle … elle ne peut plus retenir dans son flanc l'enfant." He connects the self-pleasuring of composition first to women, and then, through a transparent comparison with the silkworm, to masturbation: like the worm, the writer, "gros de ses imaginations … veut … jetter sa semence sur des feuilles." Clearly, then, Camus's fiction pushes devout proselytism to its limits and beyond.[34] In his tales as in his novels, Camus's difficulty in maintaining *contrôle de lire* and *d'écrire* in the face of sexuality risks arousing the wrong emotions. This risk imperatively leads to the narrative enclosure of women, alleged sources of temptation, in convents—or in tombs.

---

[34] "… [les histoires de Camus] poussent à ses limites le prosélytisme dévot," de Baecque 32.

Chapter 3
Thresholds:
Crossing the Boundaries
of Conventual Space

> ... those who see a nun in the world, occupied with business affairs, will be
> scandalized ... furthermore, Protestants and libertines will be able to criticize
> clausura in our Monasteries, since by the device of "congregations," we are
> simply bypassing it, and proving that there was no enclosure in the early church.
> —François de Sales, *Oeuvres* 25: 319–20, translated in Rapley, *The Dévotes* 38

In these terms, Denis Simon de Marquemont, Archbishop of Lyon, refused
permission in 1616 to François de Sales's Filles de la Visitation to leave their
religious houses for any reason. The Visitandines took as their inspiration the
Virgin Mary's visit to her kinswoman Elizabeth at the time they were both pregnant
(Luke 1: 39–40). The Visitandines sought the same freedom to go about exercising
charity through good works: "to advance the active life to which they now laid
claim, they endowed the Virgin with a new identity: she became a 'vagabond,'
hurrying across the hills of Judah to serve her neighbor" (Rapley 194). When their
claim for freedom was denied, Sales submitted to episcopal authority and Visitation
convents were reformed as regular monasteries under the rule of St. Augustine. This
decision, made not by the church in Rome but by a Gallican archbishop, underscores
the anxieties aroused in Counter-Reformation France when women attempted to
cross the threshold between sacred and secular space. Such anxieties manifested
themselves in a long and heated debate concerning uncloistered women's orders,
or orders whose missions directed them to leave their cloisters on some occasions.
How the boundaries of conventual space are determined, and, more significant,
who makes that determination, are questions of utmost import for the history of
women's monasticism. This chapter will examine the convent "threshold" and
the varied ways it was crossed, both literally and discursively, in the seventeenth
century. It will also crisscross the labile frontiers between history, memoirs and
fiction: from the Parisian couvent du Grand Carmel to the imagined communities
of Mme de Montpensier and Margaret Cavendish, to the solitary retreat of the
Princesse de Clèves.

Gérard Genette defines the threshold or *seuil* as "that uncertain zone between
the inside and the outside" ["ce zone indécise entre le dedans et le dehors," 8].
The ambiguity of this formulation suits my purposes; for as we saw in Chapter 1,
the boundaries between the sacred and secular are as solid, or as porous, as those
between allegory and literality—or, for that matter, between the convent and the
world, or between "truth" and "fiction." A main premise of this study is that *clôture*,

belonging to the symbolic realm, need not entail a material barrier (see Foreword). Our examination of the varied markers used throughout the centuries to set off the limits of *clôture*—crosses, grills, even glass doors—has pointed to this symbolic function. In a similar way, I consider the convent threshold not as a material object but as a discursive one: a spatial metonymy that marks both a barrier and a place of passage. Both these meanings are central to an understanding of conventual spaces and other spaces of female retreat. In simple terms, the conventual threshold is whatever defines and delimits the nun's spatial (and special) realm. Yet the dictum "walls do not a prison make, nor iron bars a cage" can work both ways: the convent is far from impermeable, and its permeability is concentrated at the threshold, a place of passage and encounter with the world. As shown in Chapter 2, this permeability, and its associations with female vulnerability, imposed itself in devotional writing, but clerical authors like Jean-Pierre Camus could not seal the convent barriers against innovation.

In fact, the closure of the convent grill was not so absolute as the history of orders like the Visitandines makes it appear; for in conventual as in other social settings, status often trumps gender. While "rank and file" nuns were subject to strict enclosure, the threshold between convent and world remained porous for the high nobility, who were able to move in and out of the conventual space with relative ease.[1] A good example is Marie-Eléanore de Rohan, Abbess of the Trinité convent in Caen known as the Abbaye aux Dames, and later of the Abbaye de Malnoue in Brie. As a member of the upper aristocracy—daughter of the Duke de

---

[1]   In addition, the mid-century movement of *les filles séculières* allowed lower- and middle-class women to live a religious life outside the traditional convent. Leaders like Vincent de Paul found a loophole in the requirement for women to be enclosed: as long as his *filles de la charité* took only "simple" vows, they could remain uncloistered, because the Council of Trent edict only applied to formal vows. Curiously, in order to go out on the street without causing scandal, the women were warned to divest themselves of all exterior signs of the religious life, such as robes and veils; and their convents could not have grills, for fear that clausura might appear to be violated. The *filles séculières* were still sometimes harassed, but these negative injunctions *not* to resemble a religious order freed them to circulate and do their work. This work fulfilled many essential social needs: by serving the poor, caring for the sick and teaching girls, they were a main charitable force throughout the Old Régime and again in the nineteenth and much of the twentieth centuries. Girls and women from the upper middle class and aristocracy, however, did not become *filles séculières*; in fact, the stabilization of regular orders through strict enclosure increased their membership, because respectable families were more comfortable placing their girls in traditional convents. The *filles séculières* will not be examined further in this book, because girls of humble origins and occupation were infrequently represented in Old Régime literature. For more on the topic, see Rapley, *Les Dévotes* and *A Social History of the Convent*. There is also a recent study by Michel Fiévet, *L'Invention de l'école des filles: Des amazones de Dieu aux 17ème et 18ème siècles* (Paris: Imago, 2006). On literary representations, see P.L.-M. Fein, "The Convent School as Depicted through the Characters of Certain French Eighteenth-Century Novels." *Studies on Voltaire and the Eighteenth Century* 264 (1989): 737–41.

Monbazon and of Marie de Bretagne—Rohan was able to leave her cloister and frequent the Paris salons of Scudéry, Sablé and "la Grande Mademoiselle," the Duchesse de Montpensier. Rohan's literary production was equally of a crossover nature: she wrote in both sacred and salon genres, producing Biblical paraphrases, portraits, letters, rhymes and riddles. In "Between Salon and Convent: Madame de Rohan, a Precious Abbess," Mary Rowan also points out the stylistic porosity of the Abbess's writing: both her devotional and salon works exhibit *précieux* characteristics. A *grande dame* removed from court and raised in a convent from the early age of seven, Rohan seemed to feel ambivalence toward society—an ambivalence which took the form of what Rowan calls a "fort und da" [back and forth] between the poles of convent and salon. The Abbess herself ascribes her retreat more to what she calls "disgust for the world" ["dégoût du monde"] than to a positive religious calling (Rowan 317); on the other hand, her disgust with convent politics and pressures propels her back into the world, in a repeated cycle.

This *fort und da* also took place from the other side of the convent threshold: uncloistered high nobility and members of the royal family had *entrée* to the most secluded convents, where they attended mass or spent retreats. Louis XIV's cousin Mademoiselle de Montpensier accompanied Queen Anne d'Autriche on what Vincent Pitts calls "an endless round of convent visits" (Pitts 123–31). The destination of these royal pilgrimages was often the Couvent du Carmel de l'Annonciation, or "Grand Carmel," on the rue St-Jacques. This first Carmelite convent in France was established in 1602[2] under the leadership of Madame Acarie, a gentlewoman whose *salon dévot* attracted famous names of the time: St. Francois de Sales and Pierre de Berulle, the Queen's confessor and later a cardinal, were among her circle. In addition to the support of these religious leaders, the Carmelite project received the patronage of the Duchesse de Longueville and her cousin Henri IV, and of Queens Marie de Médicis and Anne d'Autriche. After the failure of the Fronde, Longueville would divide her time between the Carmelite convent and a house of her own near Port-Royal, setting a precedent for the Princesse de Clèves's "threshold" retreat (DeJean, *Tender Geographies* 233n40).

Despite this impressive array of patrons, the establishment of a new convent was not easy. The church hierarchy was opposed to what they saw as a "Spanish invasion" and a possible loss of jurisdiction over religious congregations in France. On the other hand, as Lemoine ironically points out, the "invaders" themselves did not want to come: "The Spanish nuns felt a great reluctance to expatriate; France was described to them as a 'country in a state of mission,' half heretic, still shaken by the disorders of the Wars of Religion" ["Les religieuses (espagnoles) eurent une grande répugnance à s'expatrier: on leur dépeignait la France comme un 'pays en état de mission,' à demi-hérétique, encore secoué par les désordres de la Ligue," 280]. Last but not least was the space issue: the multiplication of new religious orders, combined with a chronic shortage of real estate in Paris, made sites for

---

[2]   The date of 1602 is given by Brémond (2.284); Lemoine dates its founding to 1604 (Lemoine 279).

new convents scarce and sought after. However, the influence of the Carmel's aristocratic patrons and the power of Rome overcame all these obstacles. The Pope promulgated a special bull, placing the Carmelites under the direction of French clerics; and a location was found for the new convent, in the priory of Notre Dame des Champs (see above, Fig. I.1, 23). This eleventh-century house belonged to the Religieux de Marmoutier, of whom only three or four remained in residence in 1600. In 1602, the last religious brothers were removed, and the Carmelites moved in. Once established, the Carmel de Paris quickly became the mother house for 63 other convents established in France between 1615 and 1618 alone.

When the Carmelites took over the old priory, its buildings were "in a state of extreme dilapidation" ["dans un état de délabrement extrême," Biver 256]. Fig. I.1 shows that one wing of the building has apparently collapsed. The Spanish nuns lived in these broken-down buildings during the period of reconstruction; the first French postulants were housed in the mansion of M. Acarie (Brémond 323). By the middle of the seventeenth century, however, the Grand Carmel had been transformed into a sanctuary worthy of the high nobility who patronized it. The church interior was repaired and richly, almost overwhelmingly, decorated in the Baroque style. The church was destroyed during the Revolution, but an English visitor, the Reverend Cole, has left a detailed evocation of it:

> The inside of the church is so painted, gilded and decorated in every way that it is impossible to determine its style of construction. The entire surface, including the smallest corners of the pillars and the vault, is painted and gilded with the greatest sumptuousness. The vault is remarkable for its curious trompe l'oeil paintings, particularly a crucifix depicted in the middle of the nave so as to appear upright if you look in the right place.

> L'intérieur de l'église est tellement peint, doré et décoré de toute façon qu'on n'arrive pas à juger dans quel ordre il a été construit. Toute la surface et jusqu'au plus petit coin des piliers et de la voûte est peint et doré avec la plus grande somptuosité. La voûte est remarquable par ses belles peintures et ses curieux trompe l'oeil, particulièrement un crucifix, figuré au milieu de la nef pour paraître tout droit, si on regarde à l'endroit qu'il faut. (Cole, quoted in Biver 263.)

Other paintings, arrayed under each window of the church, included works by the well-known artists Charles le Brun and Laurent de la Hire, as well as six canvasses by the important painter Philippe de Champaigne. Many of these pictures were lost or destroyed at the time of the Revolution (Brice 3.104–19; Biver 264). The sacristy walls were decorated with more paintings by Champaigne, gifts of Marie de Médicis, as well as with the Carmelites' exquisite needlework, incorporating gold and pearls the postulants had brought with them as part of their dowries. One wonders what an English cleric thought of this Baroque extravagance.

Following the architectural pattern set down by St. Teresa, the main church altar was raised high above the level of the nave, to symbolize the climbing of Mont Carmel by the prophet Elijah. This high altar was reached from the nave by climbing a stairway of over 20 marble steps. The stairway was bounded by marble balustrades with copper railings "that create the most handsome effect upon entering the Church" ["qui font le plus bel effet quand on entre dans l'Eglise," Brice, quoted in Biver 262]. The nun's choir [*choeur des religieuses*] was located behind and above the sacristy, on a level with the main altar. The front of the choir was closed off by a monumental grill of decorated ironwork, 12 feet high by 11 feet wide, flanked by pilasters and surmounted by three windows lighted by the church. In contemplating the grill separating the altar from the choir, Bossuet exclaimed: "How rigorous is this enclosure! How inaccessible its grills, and how they strangely threaten all who approach!" ["Que cette clôture est rigoureuse! Que ces grilles sont inaccessibles et qu'elles menacent étrangement tous ceux qui en approchent!" *Oration for the Profession of Mlle de la Vallière*, quoted in Biver 266].

However, the Carmelite's cloister was not so rigorous, nor its grill so menacing, as to exclude royal visitors and patrons. As Lemoine states: "Despite the strictness of their enclosure and the authenticity of their contemplative life … . Royal visits were impossible to prevent, even in clausura, especially for the monasteries close to Paris; princes would come with a large following" ["Malgré la sévérité de leur clôture et l'authenticité de leur vie contemplative … . Les visites royales étaient impossibles à empêcher, même en clôture, surtout pour les monastères proches de Paris, les princes venaient avec une suite nombreuse," 284]. To accommodate these powerful visitors, the church design was modified to incorporate a threshold space: a second *petit choeur* located in the sanctuary itself, within a large tribune to the west side of the main altar. From within this threshold cloistered space, the nuns (with veils lowered) and sometimes the Queen "accompagnée de quelques dames," could hear the sermons being preached—including Bossuet's famous oration on the occasion of Mlle de la Vallière's entering the Carmelite order in 1674, quoted above. The grill shutting off the *petit choeur* from the nave, like that of the main choir, was of ornate ironwork. Further ornamentation was supplied by four sea-green marble pillars topped with gilded bronze capitals (Biver 261). To enable her to go into retreat at the convent, Marie de Médicis also had a private apartment ["le pavillon de la Reine"] built at the southwest corner of the facade, facing the garden. The "popularity," if one may use that word, of St. Teresa's austere order among the royal family and high aristocracy of France, and the openings made in the convent space to receive them, are surely one of the ironies of Counter-Reformation religiosity in France. For royalty, a red carpet was truly laid across the convent threshold.

Secularized Sacrality

At the same time that debates over the boundaries of sacred space exercised the religious community, lay people experimented with what might be called "secularized sacrality." According to Orest Ranum and others, all this activity formed part of the general construction of the private realm during the late

Renaissance and early modern period, with a concomitant development of the concept of "private space." The dangers and uncertainties of religious and civil strife in the late sixteenth century had stimulated reflections on personal retreat. Montaigne resigned his post as Mayor of Bordeaux to withdraw to his ancestral home and dedicate himself to writing and contemplation. In "De la Solitude" (*Essais* 1.39), however, Montaigne points out the inadequacy of physical retreat alone as a means of escaping our problems and ourselves: "Ambition, avarice, irresolution, fear, and lust do not leave us when we change our country. *Behind the horseman sits black care*. They often follow us even into the cloisters and the schools of philosophy. Neither deserts, nor rocky caves, nor hair shirts, nor fastings will free us of them ..." ["L'ambition, l'avarice, la peur et les concupiscences ne nous abandonnent point pour changer de contrée. *Et post equitem sedet atra cura*. Elles nous suivent souvent jusques dans les cloistres et dans les escoles de philosophie. Ni les dessers, ny les rochez creusez, ny la here, ny les jeunes nous ne nous en démeslent ...," Montaigne 269; trans. Frame 213].[3] Far better to retreat into one's own inner refuge, "onto one's inner lands" ["sur les terres intérieures," Duport 97]. As Montaigne writes in a oft-quoted passage, "We should always keep a little back shop, entirely our own and uninhabited, where we can experience the true liberty of solitude" ["Il se faut reserver une arriere boutique toute nostre, toute franche, en laquelle nous establissons nostre vraye liberté et principale retraicte et solitude," Montaigne 271, trans. Frame 215].

Montaigne's metonymic musings reflect the interiorization of space we have already identified as one characteristic of seventeenth-century thought. On a more concrete level, the *cabinet*, an aristocratic cousin of Montaigne's *boutique*, exerted a strong hold on both the architectural and the literary imagination during the classical age. *Cabinets* became *de rigueur* in Paris mansions, where they either occupied a transitional position between public and private rooms or served as private retreats for solitude, study, reading or meditation (Beugnot 177). One of Motteville's letters to Montpensier concerning their ideal community lists the *cabinet* as an essential part of the simple dwellings that should be built there, and reveals some of its manifold functions and associations—reading, writing, spiritual retreat:

> I would like there to be, in all these little houses, rooms paneled with wood whose only ornament would be symmetry, and that each of us would have a study, which, according to your orders, beautiful Amelinte, would be filled with good books. There, learned men would produce works worthy of immortalizing our rural Republic, and we shepherdesses would learn through reading how to perfect our life and our morals and to enjoy the repose that we would prefer to the turbulent agitation of the court and society. (De Jean, *Against Marriage* 38–9)

---

[3]   *Montaigne's Essays and Selected Writings: A Bilingual Edition.* Trans. and Ed. Donald M. Frame (New York: St. Martin's Press, 1963).

Je voudrais que dans toutes ces petites maisons il y eût des chambres lambrissées de bois tout uni dont le seul ornement serait la netteté, chacun de nous eût un cabinet qui, selon vos ordres, belle Amelinte, fût rempli de livres, et dans lesquels les hommes savans produiroient des ouvrages dignes d'éterniser notre champêtre république, et où nous autres, bergers, nos apprendrions du moins à perfectionner notre vie et nos moeurs, et à jouir de ce repos que nous aurions préféré aux turbulentes agitations de la cour et du monde." (*Lettres de Mademoiselle de Montpensier* 20–21)[4]

While Montaigne's vision of the private sanctuary finds its origins in the Neostoic currents of the late Renaissance,[5] comments like Motteville's indicate that secular metonymies of retreat in the seventeenth century also retain a close connection to their religious counterparts. Along these lines, in Mlle de Scudéry's *Conversations* the *cabinet* is described as a "hermitage," or as leading to a library containing devout reading (Beugnot 178). And Matthew's scriptural "closet" appears in contemporary guise in Bossuet's *Cabinet du coeur*. As Beugnot points out, "If seventeenth century literature borrows so easily … from the images and vocabulary of the moralists, it is not only to legitimize itself by offering instruction, but also because the spiritual dimension is not foreign to it" ["Si enfin la littérature au XVIIe siècle emprunte si aisément … les images et le vocabulaire des moralistes, ce n'est pas seulement pour se légitimer par le *docere*, mais aussi parce que la dimension spirituelle ne lui est pas étrangère," 192]. The lasting attraction that images of inner refuge exerted on the classical age is demonstrated by their reincarnation, over a century later, in St-Simon's "arrière-cabinet" which combines Montaigne's and Scudéry's metonymic visions (*Mémoires* 4.244). Moreover, as the previous discussion indicates, these visions of retreat will take on a strong feminine cast.

---

[4] Most of the surviving correspondence between the two is published in *Lettres de Mademoiselle de Montpensier*, ed. Collin, listed in the Works Cited. The manuscript letters are located at the Arsenal Library, Conrart in fol+xi, fol. 63ff. These letters are not in the original hands, and it is not known who copied them or what changes may have been made. Finally, a recently discovered portion of the correspondence is contained in the manuscript collection of the Bibliothèque Nationale, bound with *Histoire de la Princesse Adamize*: MS Fr. 25670. Correspondance Montpensier-Motteville 1660–61. This last manuscript is the source for Joan DeJean's translation (Montpensier, *Against Marriage*. Ed. and Trans. Joan DeJean. [Chicago: University of Chicago Press, 2002]). I use this translation in most instances. In this passage, DeJean appropriately translates *cabinet* as "study." One of Richelet's definitions of *cabinet* as "A kind of apartment in a house where books and papers are kept, to which one withdraws for study" ["Espece d'apartement dans une maison où sont les livres avec les papiers, où l'on se retire pour étudier"] is congruent with Motteville's description. In other contexts, where privacy is emphasized over reading and study, a more correct translation might be "closet." For further discussion of the *cabinet*, see below, 121–3, 143–6.

[5] "The exercise of self-knowledge is continually demanded in order to achieve wisdom" ["Continuellement, c'est l'exercice de la connaissance de soi qui est revendiqué pour accéder à la sagesse," Duport 92].

Feminutopias

In some women's writing of the period, metonymies of retreat evolve into fully-imagined feminine communities. These authors create "a worldy utopia that negates the misogynist views of most male utopians" ["une utopie mondaine, une utopie féminine renversant les positions misogynes de la plupart des utopistes masculins," Timmermans 337]. In other words, a feminutopia. Feminutopic discourse was European in scale, involving Spain and England as well as France. As Rebecca d'Monté states in *Female Communities 1600–1800*, women throughout the early modern period "explore the restraints of gender in their respective societies, and the possibilities of circumventing those constraints by creating distinct alternatives for women, namely female communities" (2).[6] This emphasis on community, though central to religious rules and practice, is largely passed over in male representations of women's life. Yet the idea of community is already present in the sixteenth century, in the works of writers like Louise Labé and Anne de Marquets, the latter a nun at the Convent of Poissy who defends her writing through her attachment to her religious congregation.[7] D'Monté also points out there was no firm line between fictional and actual utopian thinking; rather a fruitful discursive "dialogue" existed between literary visions on the one hand, and proposed or actual arrangements, such as Protestant convents and female academies, on the other. These real or imagined spaces are feminotopic, because they represent an alternative place for women; yet at the same time, they are also feminutopic, because they suggest alternate forms of community, often in opposition to dominant social views.

Some representations of female retreat also stake out a "threshold" position between the sacred and the secular. Thus, the women's community Mary Astell describes in 1694 in *A Serious Proposal to the Ladies* has three essential features: service to God, women's education and an absence of vows. But perhaps the best-known English feminutopia of the period, Margaret Cavendish's *The Convent of Pleasure* (1668), is self-consciously, even aggressively, secular. Margaret Cavendish, Duchess of Newcastle, was a flamboyant personality and a prolific writer. A contemporary of Mme de Lafayette and the Princesse de Montpensier, she belonged to the same small circle of international nobility: Cavendish was a member of the court of Queen Henrietta-Maria, known in France as Henriette de France, and visited France during the Queen's exile there. Lafayette's connection with this royal family was long and close: before her marriage, she was a friend and protégée of Mère Angélique de Lafayette, Superior of the convent of Chaillot where Henrietta-Maria and her daughter Henriette d'Angleterre both lived in exile

---

[6]   Cf. also Nina Auerbach's *Communities of Women: An Idea in Fiction* (Cambridge: Harvard University Press, 1978), which deals with a later time period.

[7]   See Read, Kirk Dorrance. *French Renaissance Women Writers in Search of Community: Literary Constructions of Female Companionship in City, Family and Convent* (Ph.D. Dissertation, Princeton, 1991, DAI 9115071).

during the English Civil War. Mlle de la Vergne married Angelique's brother, Conte François de Lafayette, in 1655, and later became lady-in-waiting to "Madame" Henriette d'Angleterre, the first wife of Philippe d'Orléans. Lafayette's *Histoire d'Henriette d'Angleterre* was not published until 1722, long after the death of all the principals. As we will see later, Mademoiselle de Montpensier twice refused the hand of Charles, her first cousin and Henrietta-Maria's son. While *The Convent of Pleasure* was not published in France, these noble ladies formed part of a closely-knit group who shared common acquaintances and common ideas across the Channel (or Manche).

One constant thread running through the writings of these women was the need to offer an alternative to what Carolyn Heilbrun and others have called "the marriage plot" (51). The word "plot" obviously has a double meaning here: it connotes both a neat, "happy" way to close a story and the social closure marriage imposed on real women's life stories. The marriage plot lies at the heart of *The Convent of Pleasure*. Its heroine, Lady Happy, eschews wedlock, but does not wish to renounce all human pleasures by "incloistering herself" in a regular Monastery. She argues, "What profit or pleasure can it be to the gods to have Men or Women wear coarse Linen or rough Woolen, or to flea their skin with hair-cloth, or to eat and saw through their flesh with Cords ...?" (9). Instead, she decides to found a secular "convent" under the rule of Nature: "I mean to live incloister'd with all the delights and pleasures that are allowable and lawful; My Cloister shall not be a Cloister of restraint, but a place for freedom, not to vex the Senses but to please them" (11). The only missing element will be men, which is all to the good: "Men are the only trouble of Women for they only cross and oppose their sweet delights, and peaceable life; they cause their pains, but not their pleasures ... but I will not be so inslaved, but will live retired from their Company." Lady Happy understands the true happiness of her lot: as an upper-class woman in control of her own fortune, she has the ability to escape marriage and create her own life: "Wherefore those Women that are poor, and have not means to buy delights, and maintain pleasures, are only fit for Men, for having not means to please themselves, they must serve only to please others" (11).

Act 2 gives an interesting perspective on the new convent from the male viewpoint. The unsavory characters Monsieur Take-pleasure and his servant Dick arrive at Lady Happy's estate, set on wooing her; but they learn to their chagrin that she has "incloister'd her self, with twenty ladies more." Since her cloistering is voluntary and freely chosen, she "will suffer no grates" locking women in. Men, on the other hand, are locked out. The functions they usually perform in women's convents, such as doctor, surgeon or confessor, are all fulfilled by Lady Happy and the other ladies, "so as there is no occasion for men" (14). The males grouped outside her walls recognize the grave and subversive nature of Lady Happy's project. As one of them states: "Her Heretical Opinions ought not to be suffer'd, nor her Doctrine allow'd; and she ought to be examined by a Masculine Synod, and punish'd with a severe Husband, or tortured with a deboist [debauched] husband" (14).

Within the Convent, in keeping with the rule of Nature, the ladies enjoy luxuries appointed to each season. Lady Happy explains that in the spring, their chambers will be hung with silk-damask; in the winter, their beds will be of velvet, lined with satin. The Ladies exclaim in response: "None in this world can be happier" (16). To entertain the ladies and to make them further appreciate their own good fortune in contrast with that of the majority of womankind, Lady Happy has a play within a play performed which details, in a series of short vignettes, the many afflictions marriage brings to women of all ages and classes: unfaithful and negligent husbands, domestic tyranny, the appropriation of wives' fortunes and property, the sickness of "breeding" and the pain of labor, even death in childbirth. As one character sums up in epilogue: "Marriage is a Curse we find, / Especially to Women kind: / From the Cobbler's wife we see, / To Ladies, they unhappy be" (25).

At this point, even the gentlemen agree that "There is no hopes of dissolving this Convent of Pleasure" from the outside, because it is founded on the wealth and power of aristocratic women, "ennobled with the company of great Princesses, and glorified with a great Fame." The men fear that following this model, "all the rich Heirs will make Convents, and all the Young Beauties associate themselves in such Convents." Their only hope is "to get Wives before they are Incloister'd" (25).

However, ensuing events show that the Convent is not immune to attack from either outside or inside. In a variation on an age-old convent joke, a prince gains entry to the Convent disguised as a woman, and wins Lady Happy's love. Lady Happy is at first very *un*happy when she thinks she has fallen in love with a woman, or, for that matter, fallen in love at all. But in the end the couple will marry, Happy will leave her estate to follow her husband, and the Convent of Pleasure will be converted into a home for "old decrepit and bed-rid Matrons" (37). The play thus falls back into the traditional marriage plot, ending, like so many of Molière's comedies, with a wedding. This comic dénoument, while it does not totally erase the problematic issues brought up earlier, pushes them into the background.

Cavendish's sudden reversion to the conventional marriage plot is disconcerting, not to say disappointing. It is easy to understand its use by Molière: as a playwright/ director, he was continually operating under the practical constraints of audience and censorship. In contrast, Cavendish's plays were never staged, and did not rely on the approval of readers or censors; yet she was dependent on her husband for the publication of her works. It would be difficult for a wife in this situation to write a play totally condemning marriage! In addition, the denouement reminds us that Lady Happy's establishment is a convent in the air, a fragile construction that, like any utopia, can crumble at its point of apparent triumph. Finally, Cavendish, like Molière and other contemporaries, seems to take a naturalist view of the passions: neither wealth, nor rank, nor rational convictions of the evils of marriage are proof against the force of Nature which Lady Happy ostensibly worships, yet tries to tame by bringing it within her convent walls.

As already intimated, in France at about the same time, another "feminutopic" alternative to woman's conventional place was imagined by the Duchesse de

Montpensier, known as "la Grande Mademoiselle."[8] According to Mademoiselle's memoirs, this idea first originated during a trip she made with the court to St-Jean-de-Luz in 1658, to celebrate the marriage of Louis XIV and Marie-Thérèse. Montpensier's memoirs relate: "[Mme de Motteville and I] began talking about solitude, the wilderness, and what a happy life we could live there, the difficulties and weariness of the court … . I wished that in this deserted place, both flirting and marriage would be banned" ["Mme de Motteville et moi] nous nous mîmes à causer sur la solitude, le désert, et combien on y pouvoit mener une vie heureuse, l'embarras et la fatigue de celle de la cour … . Je ne voulois point que dans ce désert on y eût ni galanterie ni même que l'on s'y mariât," *Mémoires* 3.452–3].[9]

In this passage, Mademoiselle describes not only the nature of her wilderness retreat but its elaboration as a triple-layered discursive space: first conceived of in conversation, then developed in an exchange of letters, and finally alluded to in the memoirs, which relate how her initial conversation with Motteville and a subsequent solitary walk along the seashore fired Mademoiselle's enthusiasm for writing: "I ran back to my lodging; I took up pen and ink and wrote a letter of two or three pages to madame de Motteville that I had copied and sent to her by a stranger. She guessed it was I who had written. She answered me" ["Je m'en allai toujours courant chez moi; je pris une plume et de l'encre et j'écrivis une lettre de deux ou trois feuilles de papier à madame de Motteville, que je fis copier et que je lui envoyai par un inconnu. Elle devina que c'étoit moi qui lui avois écrit. Elle me fit réponse," 453]. The correspondence continued for over a year.

It is interesting to note, despite the enthusiasm with which Montpensier runs back to write down her ideas, what pains she takes to envelop her writing in a veil of privacy. She has her first letter to Motteville copied in a different hand and sent anonymously, presumably because many would be eager to exploit or copy writings under a famous name. Her concerns are validated when some of the correspondence is purloined and published without her consent in *Recueil de pieces nouvelles et galantes* (Cologne: 1667, 2.21–46). Mademoiselle reports in her *Mémoires* that she was incensed by this exposure and mutilation of her private letters, which she terms "maimed" ["estropiées"]. On the other hand, the anonymity of the letters is a game as well, played between intimates: the first letter ends with the playful line, "Guess if you can, and answer if you dare" ["Devine si tu peux, et réponds si tu l'oses," DeJean 35, Collin 14]. The reader can sense Mademoiselle's satisfaction that Motteville penetrated the veil of anonymity and "divined" the author, because she recognized and sympathized with Mademoiselle's views.

---

8   Juliette Cherbuliez has pointed out that the appellation "Mademoiselle" was sometimes applied pejoratively to Montpensier in the seventeenth century and beyond. However, it was also simply used as a personal title, like Madame. And since Montpensier referred to herself as Mademoiselle, I will do so as well.

9   French quotations from Montpensier's *Mémoires* are taken from the Cheruel edition (see Works Cited).

Like Cavendish's *Convent of Pleasure*, the retreat described in the Montpensier/ Motteville correspondence affords all the comforts of an aristocratically intellectual lifestyle in a pastoral setting: plenty of reading and writing materials, conversation, music, good food, combined with walks by the river, picnics on the grass and the tending of sheep (*Lettres* 6–11).[10] However, Mademoiselle does not share Cavendish's glorification of the rule of Nature: "This would not be a pagan utopia but a Christian community" (Pitts 153). Significantly, Mademoiselle again turns to the Carmelites as an example of piety and austerity.[11] She would endow a Carmelite convent in the woods near her community, where the nuns, following the strict rule of St. Teresa, would live a hermitical existence. Mademoiselle continues: "Their hermit's life would keep us from having much contact with them, but the more distanced from the business of the world they would be, the more we would admire them. It would be in their church that we would pray to God" ["La vie d'hermite nous empêcheroit d'avoir un commerce trop fréquent avec elles. Mais plus elles seroient retirées du commerce du monde, plus nous aurions de vénération pour elles. Ce seroit dans leur église qu'on iroit prier Dieu," DeJean 33, Collin 13]. Maintaining a strict hierarchical segregation, Mademoiselle would also build a parish church for the villagers, "staffed by secular priests" ["servie par des prêtres séculiers," DeJean 34, Collin 14]. Mademoiselle's imagined community thus remains firmly *other*: although it is physically adjacent to, even inspired by, aspects of the conventual space and ideal, she wishes neither to inhabit nor to imitate that space. In her response to this letter, Motteville expresses some reservations about the sheep-tending, but agrees that this existence should "bring together the wisdom of the philosophers and Christian piety, as well as the politeness of the marvelous shepherds of Lignon" ["joindre à la piété chrétienne la sagesse des philosophes et la politesse des fabuleux bergers de Lignon," DeJean 37, Collin 16].[12] The correspondence between Mademoiselle and Motteville underscores the close connection in seventeenth-century feminist discourse, already noted in Cavendish's comedy, between retreat and refusal of marriage. Mademoiselle's own attitude toward marriage, like her position in the court world, was shifting

---

[10] For more on the relation between Mademoiselle's utopia and the feminine-dominated pastoral society of D'Urfé's *Astrée* (1607–27), see Timmermans 257–8.

[11] A close friend of her youth, Mlle d'Epernon, joined the Carmelites after the death of her fiancé, and Mademoiselle briefly considered doing so as well; but here, the two realms are clearly separated. (I owe this information to Juliette Cherbuliez.)

[12] Lignon is the imaginary realm described in D'Urfé's *Astrée* (see above, n10). Montpensier's polite and idealized vision of pastoral life contrasts with the female sanctuary/ convent stories included in Margerite de Navarre's *Heptaméron*, who was also Mademoiselle's great-grandmother. In conte 22, for example, a nun is "sollicitée de son honneur" (176) by a prior who attacks and rapes her. This tale also falls into the category of anticlerical erotic satire to be examined in Chapter 4: "Therefore he feasted so well that from a very thin monk he turned into a very fat one" ["Parquoy si bien se festoya que, d'un moyne bien meigre, il en feyt ung bien gras," 176]. More important in the book's context, the story ends to the glory of the young nun: her reputation is rehabilitated and the monk loses the right to visit the convent.

and complex. Given her exceptional status as the only child of Gaston d'Orléans and the heiress, on her mother's side, of the vast Montpensier fortune, one would not expect her to be under the same pressure to find a mate as most women of her time. However, Montpensier's personal fortune alone could not win her an established position within French court society. "Had she married, she would have had an 'establishment,' a definite place in the social order, which situates women with respect to men" (Cholakian 5). As a young woman, she expected to marry brilliantly, even royally; but Mademoiselle's "establishment" did not take place as expected. Her Montpensier mother, who died at her birth, was not present to help arrange a suitable marriage for her daughter; her Bourbon father had no interest in promoting a mere girl's position; and the head of the male Bourbon line, Louis XIV, was not at first eager to set up a rival power establishment, with the Montpensier fortune behind it, by marrying off his cousin.

Perhaps because of these obstacles, Mademoiselle's early positive attitude toward matrimony underwent a reversal as she matured. As Pitts observes, "Her exchange with Madame de Motteville at the time of the king's marriage [in 1658] indicates that as she entered her thirties, Mademoiselle adopted the views of some *Précieuses* that marriage, with its permanent subjugation of wife to husband, was not a desirable state" (245). He puts it even more strongly, and I think accurately, in another passage: "While at St-Jean-de Luz her feelings hardened into an outright hostility to the married state" (155) which she saw as the main cause of women's subjection. This "hostility to the married state" is central to the construction of Mademoiselle's feminutopic retreat. The negative relation between marriage and retreat may be expressed in the following "syllogism": marriage destroys women's freedom; if women are to be free, they must remain unmarried; therefore, in order to escape marriage, they must withdraw from society. In other words, only retreat can afford women escape from marriage. Although Mademoiselle's ideal community, unlike Cavendish's exclusively female domain, would admit "people of the highest rank of both sexes" ["de fort honnêtes gens de tout sexe," DeJean 29, Collin 4], the company would exclude married couples and restrict membership to widows and widowers and to those who had resolved not to marry: "I would rather there were no married people and that everyone would either be widowed, or have renounced this sacrament, for it is said to be an unfortunate undertaking. You know how lucky we are to be out of it" ["J'opinerois assez qu'il n'y eût pas de gens mariés, et que ce fût toutes personnes veuves, ou qui eussent renoncé à ce sacrement; car on dit que c'est un embarquement fâcheux, vous savez si l'on est heureuse d'en être dehors," DeJean 29, Collin 5–6]. Moreover, while witty conversation between the sexes would be an essential part of the community, love (*galanterie*) would not be permitted: "I would like us sometimes … to imitate what we have read in *L'Astrée* though without amorous pursuit, for that does not please me in any guise" ["Je voudrois qu'on … imitât quelquefois ce qu'on a lu dans l'Astrée, sans toutefois faire l'amour, car cela ne me plaît point en quelque habit que ce soit," DeJean 33, Collin 11].

Motteville fully agrees, from her own personal experience, that marriage is indeed an *embarquement fâcheux* and a menace to women's freedom: "I was subjected to this bond that so displeases you for only two years of my life; when my freedom was restored to me, I was at an age that seemed to invite me to imitate honorable human weaknesses. However, liberty always seemed preferable to me to all the other possessions valued by those of our station …" ["Je n'ai été soumise à ce lien qui vous déplaît si fort que deux seules années de ma vie, quand la liberté me fut rendue j'étais dans cet âge qui semblait me convier à suivre les honnêtes faiblesses des humains, mais cette liberté m'a toujours semblée préférable à tous les autres biens que l'on estime dans le monde … ," DeJean 48–9].[13] As role models for the single life, she looks to the aristocratic "widows of Randan," a well-known mother and daughter who lived a quiet, virtuous life in the country after the deaths of their respective spouses. Motteville even elevates "these illustrious widows" to the level of living heroines: "because of the glory of their widowhood [they] are heroines I have always deemed worthy of being the glory of all other women" ["par la gloire de leur veuvage, (elles) sont des héroïnes que j'ai toujours estimées dignes d'être la gloire de toutes les autres femmes," my translation from Collin 56–7]. Yet Motteville objects to Mademoiselle's proscription on love and marriage— not because it is undesirable, but, rather, because it is unenforceable. Motteville writes in a half-joking, half-serious manner: "But I fear, my Princess, that this very wise and necessary law will be but poorly observed" ["Mais j'ai grande peur, ma princesse, que cette loi si sage et si nécessaire ne fût mal observée"], especially if the members of the company are allowed to write verses (DeJean 39; Collin 22). Combining naturalistic common sense with Christian orthodoxy, Motteville suggests that in the end, Mademoiselle would be forced to allow "that error so common that time-honored custom has made it legitimate, known as marriage" ["cette erreur si commune qu'une vieille coutume a rendue légitime, et qui s'appelle mariage," my translation from Collin 22–3]. Mademoiselle, however, holds firm in her opposition, choosing to expel from her community anyone who enters into matrimony. She concludes her attack on marriage in these stirringly feminist, as well as feminutopic, terms:

> … marriage is that which has given men the upper hand … this dependence to which custom subjects us, often against our will and because of family obligations of which we have been the victims, is what has caused us to be named the weaker sex. Let us at last deliver ourselves from this slavery, let there be a corner of the world in which it can be said that women are their own mistresses, and do not have all the faults that are attributed to them; and let us celebrate ourselves for the centuries to come for a way of life that will immortalize us.

---

[13]   In this passage, I follow the French version in DeJean's edition, which is different from Collin's, in order to keep closer to her translation. For the next two quotations I have chosen to translate Collin's text because it includes elements the DeJean source does not.

... ce qui a donné la supériorité aux hommes a été le mariage, et ... ce qui nous a
fait nommer le sexe fragile, a été cette dépendance où le sexe nous a assujetties,
souvent contre notre volonté, et par des raisons de famille, dont nous avons été
les victimes. Enfin, tirons-nous de l'esclavage, qu'il y ait un coin du monde où
l'on puisse dire que les femmes sont maîtresses d'elles-mêmes, et qu'elles n'ont
pas tous les défauts qu'on leur attribue, et célébrons-nous dans les siècles à venir
par une vie qui nous fasse vivre éternellement. (DeJean 47–9; Collin 35)

In commenting on this passage, Pitts observes that Mademoiselle's ideas "suggest
a new sensibility at work as well as the influence of the literary circles surrounding
her" (245). But in the context of this study, it is equally important to note that the
words Mademoiselle chooses to castigate marriage, as a state of "slavery" where
women are thrust "souvent contre notre volonté, et par des raisons de famille, dont
nous avons été les victimes," are almost the same terms (male) writers will use to
criticize the conventual enclosure of women.

While it never took the ideal form outlined in this correspondence,
Mademoiselle indeed tried to establish a private retreat for herself and a select
company of friends at her country estates. One of her favorite pastimes was to buy
and renovate property—a predilection she was able to indulge freely, due to her
independent wealth. During her first exile at St-Fargeau, appalled by the condition
of this medieval château-fort, she immediately undertook extensive renovations.
As an interesting indicator of the post-Fronde political climate, Montpensier
considered the château's most positive feature to be its security from a possible
attack by the king's forces: designed as a military fortress, St-Fargeau had very
thick walls and a number of useful exits, including a hidden *échappée* leading
into the orchard (*Mémoires* 2.228–9). The first round of construction culminated
in 1653 in a new set of personal apartments, with which she expressed herself
"delighted" (*Mémoires* 2.284). For a second and more ambitious renovation phase,
she hired a fashionable architect who added an elegant contemporary facade to the
courtyard, creating a new set of apartments within its walls (Mayer 59). In 1660,
Mademoiselle bought the vast domain of Eu in Normandy from the impoverished
Guise family, and undertook an ambitious program of restoration and construction
there as well. Her residences were also centers of creativity: the tradition of private
concerts and ballets begun at Gaston d'Orléan's Paris mansion in the 1620s was
continued by his daughter during her post-Fronde exile at St-Fargeau.

Most important, according to Jean Garapon, Mademoiselle "discovered"
writing at St-Fargeau, where she first began her memoirs (37).[14] Taking this
point further, Cholakian remarks that the first part of the *Mémoires* ends with
an unfinished sentence, marking Mademoiselle's return from St-Fargeau to
court. Seventeen years later, while staying at Eu, "she completed the unfinished

---

[14]   Mademoiselle is one of the first women to write her memoirs, which up until then
had been an exclusively male genre. If, as Fumaroli states, the genre itself is located on the
"crossroads" or the "margins" of literature—what I call its "threshold"—Mademoiselle's
act of writing crosses simultaneous thresholds of genre and gender (cf. Cholakian 4).

sentence" and began part 2 (Cholakian 9).[15] Thus, Cholakian sees Mademoiselle's memorial project as "writing the story of her house" (4) in both the dynastic and the architectural sense.

Whatever their power as producers of memorial discourse, Mademoiselle's sojourns on her land were not always utopic. Despite her high rank and wealth, she owed the same absolute submission to the king as did his other subjects. And if this submission was not complete enough in his view, Louis had the power to transform locations of autonomous retreat into sites of exile and confinement. Thus in 1652, Mademoiselle, along with other members of the nobility, was exiled from court for five years for her active opposition to Louis XIV during the Fronde. During this period, however, she was not completely confined to her lands, and was able to travel about the Loire Valley while renovations on St-Fargeau were being completed.

Mademoiselle's owed submission to Louis as royal "father" also included his right to choose her a husband. As mentioned above, she repeatedly spurned the advances of her exiled cousin Charles Stuart, later Charles II of England. While there was some question of a match with Charles de Lorraine, it did not take place either.[16] She also openly defied Louis XIV's express wishes by refusing to marry the cruel and unattractive King of Portugal, Alfonso VI, stating "it is very pleasant to be Mademoiselle in France with five hundred thousand livres of income, bestowing honor on the Court, not asking anything from it, respected for myself as well as my rank. When one is in such a position, one remains there. If one wearies of the Court, one can go to the country, to one's houses, where one has a Court. One builds there; one amuses oneself" ["Il fait bon être Mademoiselle en France avec cinq cents mille livres de rente, faisant honneur à la Cour, ne lui rien demander, honorée par ma personne comme par ma qualité. Quand l'on est ainsi, on y demeure. Si l'on s'ennuie à la Cour, l'on ira à la campagne, à ses maisons, où l'on a une cour. On y fait bâtir; on s'y divertit," *Mémoires* 3.537]. It is not irrelevant that this praise of country retreat was reported in the memoirs as a bravado response to Turenne's arguments in favor of her marriage.

This time, Mademoiselle's defiance was not tolerated by Louis: she was threatened by the king's emissary with "exile, house arrest, or confinement to a convent" (Pitts 167), and when these threats did not win her compliance, she was again exiled to St-Fargeau in 1662. In some ways, the consequences of opposing the royal choice of a husband were more severe than they had been for her earlier blatant political opposition. Mademoiselle's second exile was shorter than the first, lasting only two years; but while she had had some freedom to travel during her first removal from court, this time a strict exile was imposed, almost amounting to

---

[15]   Gabrielle Verdier asserts that the composition of all three parts of the Memoirs was associated with the houses Mademoiselle inherited from her mother (see Cholakian 8).

[16]   Additional letters in De Jean's edition reveal Montpensier's discomfort at going back on her principles when she was considering marrying Charles de Lorraine, and her relief when the marriage did not materialize (DeJean 60–66).

house arrest. Only after complaining to her royal cousin of the ill health brought on by her confinement at St-Fargeau was Mademoiselle granted permission to relocate to her larger property at Eu. She was not allowed to return to court until 1664, when Louis had apparently given up on the marriage plan.

The hostility to marriage Mademoiselle expressed so eloquently in her early thirties underwent a sea change when, at the age of 43, she became acquainted with the love of her life, the Comte de Lauzun. Although a favorite of Louis XIV, Lauzun was a totally unsuitable match for Mademoiselle: six years her junior, he was far inferior to her in rank, being a younger scion of a noble, but not princely, Gascon family. Despite his glaring ineligibility, Mademoiselle decided to marry Lauzun and convinced Louis XIV to go along with the match, as recorded in Mme de Sévigné's famous letter of December 15, 1670: "I'm going to write you about the most amazing, surprising, marvelous, miraculous … unheard-of thing …" ["Je m'en vais vous mander la chose la plus étonnante, la plus surprenante, la plus merveilleuse, la plus miraculeuse … la plus inouïe"]. In her anticipated happiness, Mademoiselle resembles "Madame, soeur du roi," as rather ironically described by "la reine dauphine" in *La Princesse de Clèves*: "Never had a person of the age of this princesse felt such an unalloyed joy at being married" ["Jamais personne de l'âge de cette princesse n'a eu une joie si entière de se marier," 307]. The vociferous opposition of Mademoiselle's relatives on both sides of the family made Louis cancel the wedding at the last moment. However, it is now considered likely that, with the approval of the King, Lauzun and Mademoiselle were married secretly, either in 1670 ["as most modern biographers agree," Pitts 208] or some years later.

In 1671, Lauzun was arrested by Louis XIV without charge, and imprisoned for 10 years in the same Italian dungeon where Nicolas Fouquet later ended his days. After long and tortuous negotiations with the King and his mistress Mme de Montespan, Mademoiselle ceded much of her estate—including Eu—to ransom Lauzun. She kept a life interest in the property; at her death, it would go to Montespan's and Louis's illegitimate son, the duc du Maine. The outcome of this sacrifice was not happy: when Lauzun was finally freed in 1681, he returned an embittered man. He rewarded Mademoiselle's generosity with ingratitude, infidelity, and contempt; worst of all, he attempted to take control of her finances. (If nothing else, this "husbandly" behavior indicates that the two probably were married, either in 1670 or on Lauzun's return from prison.) Not tolerating such tyranny, Mademoiselle broke off the relationship in 1684.

This unhappy, even humiliating passion seemingly contradicted Mademoiselle's strongly-expressed opposition to love and marriage—while, ironically, it also confirmed her beliefs about matrimony's disastrous consequences. As those wise women, Cavendish and Motteville, both suggested, however *fâcheux* marriage may be, the power of Nature over the human heart cannot be overcome. Yet at the same time, by choosing Lauzun, Mademoiselle in a sense remained true to herself. In an unprecedented example of gender reversal, she made the advances to him, and endowed him with her rank, wealth and name, insisting that he be called "M. de Montpensier." This sort of misalliance was unthinkable at court, as it would have been for Mademoiselle herself at an earlier age (Pitts 244). But it allowed her to remain in control. Beyond that, as Cholakian astutely suggests, "Mademoiselle's 'take-over' of Lauzun is in fact her attempt to found through Lauzun the house of Montpensier. She was trying to establish him in the same way that men establish women" (13), or, in the case of the celibate Cardinal Mazarin, by insisting that his niece's husband take the Mazarin name. It is impossible to know Lauzun's real feelings, if any, for Mademoiselle; but if there had been any initial attachment, it is unlikely it could have survived her intrepid assault on his male prerogatives.

Therefore, Cholakian argues that "When [Mademoiselle] took up her pen in 1677, to continue her memoirs … she was telling of yet another unsuccessful attempt to prevent her mother's fortune from being absorbed by the paternal line" (13). But if her project was inevitably unsuccessful on a dynastic level, Mademoiselle maintained to the end her personal autonomy: she steadfastly refused any man the right to govern her affairs and finally showed Lauzun the door. As Pitts suggests, Mademoiselle's ability to end the relationship was partially due to the special circumstances of a secret marriage and of Lauzun's disfavor with the king (246). But it also stemmed from the unique characteristics of Mademoiselle herself: her exceptional rank and her unshakable belief in her own autonomy and entitlement.

Mademoiselle had always been a devout Catholic. In addition to accompanying Anne d'Autriche on her frequent retreats to the Carmelites, Mademoiselle had also visited the Solitaires of Port-Royal on her own in 1657 (*Mémoires* 3.67–73). In her letters to Motteville, she makes a point of placing a convent in, or at least adjacent to, her utopic retreat. Towards the end of her life, her religiosity grew more manifest. The writings of Teresa of Avila were among Montpensier's favorite reading, and she wrote several pious books of her own. She endowed hospitals and religious communities at St-Fargeau, Trévoux, Blanzy and Criel, as well as at Eu, which became her principal residence from 1680 until her death (Mayer 70; *Mémoires* 3.576). Unlike the inhabitants of Cavendish's *Convent of Pleasure* or of real female communities, Mademoiselle ended her life in solitude. Like the Princesse de Clèves, la Grande Mademoiselle left other women "an inimitable example."

Tropes of Place in *La Princesse de Clèves*[17]

Until recently, the settings in the *Princesse de Clèves* received slight attention from critics. One traditionally assumed that physical location played little or no part in

---

[17]   In Lafayette's 1678 historical novel, Mlle de Chartres, a young heiress, is brought to the court of Henri II in 1558 to make a suitable marriage. A match is arranged with the Prince de Clèves, an acceptable candidate whom Mlle de Chartres accepts "with less repugnance than another." But she soon meets and falls in love with the charismatic duc de Nemours, who pursues her discreetly but relentlessly. In a desperate attempt to protect

the abstract and universal world of French classical esthetics; in anthologies of seventeenth-century literature, references to natural settings were limited to a few lines from Sévigné or Molière, such as Cléante's "The countryside is not much in flower yet" ["La campagne à présent n'est pas beaucoup fleurie," *Tartuffe* I.4.225]. Similarly, Lafayette's *nouvelles historiques* were seen as "modern" and "realistic" in their attention to time, but not to place. However, the broadening of critical scrutiny beyond a narrowly defined classical canon has revealed in seventeenth-century writing a lively sensibility to setting and architecture: the correspondence and memoirs of Montpensier, examined above, clearly reveal this bent. Recent studies have also concentrated on the function of space and setting in Lafayette's work.[18] Although my interpretation differs somewhat from these, I argue that in Lafayette's narrative, tropes of place is of essential importance. Place is the novel is not restricted to a static backdrop. The plot describes a fluid and complex movement through space, following a dynamic of "out" to "in," and returning, after some fluctuations, to a final "out." Within this general flow, one also observes a dilation and contraction of spaces—a kind of *fort und da*. This double movement is conveyed narratively by zooming in from a non-placed introduction through a series of progressively more intimate settings: *cour, maison, cabinet, pavillon* and, finally, *couvent* and *chez soi*. I will now examine these locations in order to reveal their verbal and emotional resonances.

Confirming neo-classical impressions, the opening of the novel offers little in terms of concrete setting. Conversations seemingly take place no place, in a kind of discursive void. For instance, the account of Nemours's projected marriage with Queen Elizabeth features a long speech Nemours makes to the king. This speech also constitutes the first instance of direct quotation in the novel: "At any rate, Sire, if I undertake a fantastic enterprise under the advice and in behalf of your Majesty, I beg of you to keep it secret ..." ["Au moins Sire, lui dit-il, si je m'embarque dans une enterprise chimérique par le conseil et pour le service de Votre Majesté, je la supplie de me garder le secret ..." 258, Lyons 7].[19] While the quotation goes on for another three lincs, no location is given for the exchange, beyond a vague "the king remained on the frontier" on the preceding page. Another non-placed speech takes place shortly after Mlle de Chartres's engagement. M. de Clèves has already realized that his fiancée does not really love him: "It gave him much pain to see that what Mademoiselle de Chartres felt for him was only esteem and gratitude. ... Hardly a day passed when he did not complain to her of this. 'Is it possible,' he said, 'that I may not be happy in my marriage?'" ["Il voyait avec beaucoup de peine que les sentiments de Mlle de Chartres ne passaient pas ceux

---

her virtue, the Princesse confesses her infatuation to her husband, who dies of jealousy. Stricken with guilt, but also convinced that marriage to Nemours could not produce lasting happiness, the young widow refuses him and retreats permanently from court.

[18]   See in particular Michael Donahy and Eva Pósfay in the Works Cited.

[19]   Translations of *La Princesse de Clèves* are taken from *The Princess of Clèves*. Edited and with a revised translation by John D. Lyons (New York: W.W. Norton & Company, 1994).

de l'estime et de la reconnaissance. … Il ne se passait guère de jour qu'il ne lui en fit ses plaintes:—Est-il possible, lui disait-il, que je puis n'être pas heureux en vous épousant?" 270–71, Lyons 15]. Although these "plaintes" are introduced in the imperfect tense, indicating repeated, almost daily, action, they seem to take place nowhere.[20]

Two explanations have generally been offered for Lafayette's apparent indifference to setting. The first, a familiar reference to "so-called classical restraint," ["(la) retenue dite classique," Pósfay 118], is a circular argument, akin to explaining the non-classical characteristics of early seventeenth-century literature by citing the "structure of Baroque thought." I will allude later to other reasons for this alleged *retenue*. A second, more modern argument is made by Donahy and Pósfay. In the wake of Claudine Herrmann, both these critics emphasize the "male dominance" or "genderizing" of social spaces in fiction in general and in *La Princesse de Clèves* in particular. According to Pósfay, the court setting is left undescribed because it is male-dominated, and Lafayette does not choose to dwell on purely "masculine" spaces. I would certainly agree that court society, like most societies, is intrinsically patriarchal; but gender relations in the *Princesse de Clèves* are somewhat more nuanced in my view. Lafayette, precisely because she is a "feminocentric" (if not feminist) writer,[21] takes pains to emphasize the real power women hold at court, through the potent combination of rank and sexuality—a power that leads to the exile, even the death, of men. A prime example of this scenario is the Princesse de Clèves's uncle, the vidame de Chartres, who enters into a dangerous intimacy with Queen Catherine de Médicis. In exchange for her confidence, she demands complete fidelity and control over him: "… I choose you for the recipient of my confidence. Remember that I wish yours without reserve, that I want you to have no friend, man or woman, except such as shall be agreeable to me, and that you will give up every aim except pleasing me" ["… je vous choisis pour vous donner toute ma confiance. Souvenez-vous que je veux la vôtre toute entière, que je veux que vous n'ayez ni ami, ni amie, que ceux qui me seront agréables, et que vous abandonnerez tout autre soin que celui de me plaire," 334, Lyons 55]. This personal subjection is greater than that required of courtiers by the king. The vidame realizes the dangers involved in entering into this bargain: he tells Nemours that the Queen is "the woman from whom I have most to fear" ["la personne du monde que je dois le plus craindre," 337, Lyons 57]. The vidame knows that in breaking the rules she has set out, "I bring upon myself an implacable hatred, which will certainly cost me my fortune, and may cost me something more" ["je m'attire une haine implacable, qui me coûtera ma fortune et peut-être quelque chose du plus," 330, Lyons 53]. However, the vidame continues to play a dangerous game of multiple gallantry, and in the end, his fears are realized. As the narrator relates: "Their intimacy was at an end, and

---

[20]   I have changed the end of Lyons's English translation: it reads "Within a few days he complained to her …," which appears to be incorrect.

[21]   Pósfay uses the phrase "l'architecture féminocentrique" in relation to the novel (123).

she accomplished his ruin afterwards at the time of the conspiracy of Amboise, in which he was implicated" ["Leur liaison se rompit, et elle le perdit ensuite à la conjuration d'Amboise où il se trouva embarrassé," 346, Lyons 63]. According to Brantôme, Lafayette's main source, the historical vidame was indeed imprisoned for conspiracy, dying shortly after in 1662. In an inexorable chain, personal leads to political *embarras* which then leads to imprisonment and death. Thus, while ruled by an absolute king, the court is not entirely a masculinized social space. "L'architecture féminocentrique" must be regarded within a larger public/private context: as a site where rules—and the infringement of rules—control the lives of both sexes.

In contrast, my account of setting (or the lack of it) in the *Princesse de Clèves* centers more on "place" than on "gendered space." As seen in the Introduction, instances of "place" [*endroit, place, lieu*] in classical dictionaries are far richer and more frequent than of "space" [*espace*]. This lexical generalization is borne out in Lafayette's novel: according to Jean de Bazin de Bezons's *Vocabulaire de 'La Princesse de Clèves'*, the word *lieu* appears 59 times in the novel, but *espace* not once.[22] Furthermore, place at Henri II's court, as for Richard Sorabji, is "a measure of positioning" (see above, Introduction, 12).While court position can be shifting and uncertain, it is still fixed to some degree by birth and hierarchy. To use an aristocratic if anachronistic comparison, the relative positioning of the courtiers calls to mind one of those slotted cardboard mats that Edwardian ladies or their housekeepers used to plan the arrangement of guests around the dinner table. By indicating the location of scenes and characters, Lafayette is laying out place cards on the court table; and so one could argue that if places are basically "place settings," there is often no *need* to describe them.[23] This argument is supported by the related point that *La Princesse de Clèves* is a quintessential "insider" novel. As readers, we are assumed to be familiar with the aristocratic names and places mentioned and their importance; and if we are not, Lafayette supplies a long, often-criticized historical introduction designed to make us all *cognoscenti*. This

---

[22] Paris: Nizet, 1967. Although Bazin's is the only lexicon for the *Princesse de Clèves* that I know of, its accuracy cannot be vouched for since it leaves out many words, including *pavillon* and *couvent*.

[23] Cognizant of her public's obsession with precedence, Lafayette does describe with precision the seating arrangements for the wedding banquet of Madame, soeur du roi and the duc d'Albe, with details taken from contemporary chronicles: "The king, the queens, the princes, and princesses ate at the marble table in the great hall of the palace, the Duke of Alva being seated near the new Queen of Spain. Below the steps [from] the marble table, on the king's right hand, was a table for the ambassadors, the archbishops, and the knights of the order, and on the other side a table for the members of parliament" ["Le roi, les reines, les princes et princesses mangèrent sur la table de marbre dans la grande salle du palais, le duc d'Albe assis auprès de la nouvelle reine d'Espagne. Au-dessus des degrés de la table de marble, et à la main droite du roi, étoit une table pour les ambassadeurs, les archevêques et les chevaliers de l'ordre et, de l'autre côté, une table pour MM. du parlement," 372, Lyons 80–81].

narrative strategy of placing the reader in an insider position is one of the main reasons why the novel's impact is so intimate, and yet so powerful. At the same time, it is also the reason the narrative texture is so elusive—or allusive. Jean Cocteau describes Lafayette's descriptive talent in an elegant phrase: "this facility of depicting without describing" ["cette facilité de peindre sans dépeindre," Pósfay 118]. To gloss Cocteau's formulation, Lafayette "paints" what is private or unknown, and merely alludes to what is public and known. Thus, the court setting can be simultaneously all-important and invisible, or invisible because it is all-important. On the other hand, as we will see, the novel does contain repetitively-used words of location. These terms, ranging from the general (*chez*) to the concrete and particular (*pavillon de la forêt*) are visual cues meant to enlist the imagination of the seventeenth-century reader. By perusing old dictionaries and illustrations, modern day readers can recover a sense of these settings, and a closer imaginative connection to the work.

Both the allusiveness of setting in the novel, and the close ties between social and spatial localization, are brought out by the words Lafayette uses to place her characters and action. By far the most frequent place word in the novel is not a noun, but a preposition: "chez." To give but a few among numerous examples: "[le prince de Clèves] alla le soir chez Madame, soeur du roi" (261); "Il [Nemours] alla ensuite chez les reines" (274); "Mme de Clèves revint chez elle" (275); "elle le vit chez la reine dauphine" (276); "La reine dauphine s'en alla chez elle" (284); "elle revint chez sa mere" (290). Lacking an English equivalent, *chez* is translated in various ways: "That evening [the Prince de Clèves] called on Madame, the king's sister" (Lyons 9); "[Nemours] went next to pay his respects to the queens" (Lyons 17); "Madame de Clèves went home … she met him at the drawing room of the dauphiness" (Lyons 18); "the crown princess went to her own apartment" (Lyons 22); and "she went back to her mother" (Lyons 27). Though idiomatic and expressive, these equivalents cannot convey the distinctive spatial nature of the French "chez."

The purpose of "chez" is often to place characters in initial contact with one another, in a common location: in the first examples above, the Princesse de Clèves and Nemours. As we will see, more concrete place words, such as *cabinet* or *antichambre*, are introduced if further development of the scene is desired. Occasionally, *chez* morphs into *chez soi*, a private enclosure recalling its etymological origins (Latin *casa*): "Monsieur de Nemours locked himself up *in his own room*, being unable to contain his joy at having in his possession a portrait of Madame de Clèves" ["M de Nemours alla se renfermer *chez lui*, ne pouvant soutenir en public la joie d'avoir un portrait de Mme de Clèves," 318, Lyons 45; italics added; in this instance, the translation is more place-oriented than the original]. On the whole, however, *chez*, as a content-free preposition of location, perfectly performs the function of alluding and "placing" without describing.

On the threshold between location (*chez*) and concrete place (*cabinet, pavillon*) stands *la cour*. The court setting is a *sine qua non* for the novel's action, indeed for its very existence; and the word itself is rich in both literal and figurative denotations.

The word *cour* still retains some of its original architectural meaning of an enclosed domestic space: "courtyard" in English. Furetière defines it as "an unroofed piece of ground enclosed by walls that forms part of a dwelling" ["Terrain enfermée de murs & à découvert qui fait partie d'une habitation, " Furetière, *Dictionnaire universel*]. He also notes that in certain regions of France, the word *cour* was used metonymically for residence, somewhat in the manner of *chez*: "it was said, I'm going to so and so's *court*, meaning to his house, his castle" ["on disoit, Je m'en vais à la *court* d'un tel, pour dire en sa maison, en son chasteau"]. *Cour* with a capital "C" also shows a place-like quality in another of Furetière's entries: "Place where a King or Sovereign Prince lives" ["Lieu où habite un Roy ou un Prince Souverain"].

With increasing levels of abstraction, the following entries refer to the royal court as a social and political hierarchy rather than a physical place: "[court] also denotes the King and his Council, or his Ministers … all the Prince's officers and following" ["(cour) signifie aussi le Roy & son Conseil, ou ses Ministres … tous les officiers & la suite du Prince"]. Yet *cour* never quite becomes a dead metonymy; it retains a kernel of locality. This combination of social and physical place is illustrated in the anonymous drawing of the court featured in the Robert edition of Furetière's *Dictionnaire universel* (Fig. 3.1). This engraving, with its serried ranks of courtiers arranged in hierarchical order, resembles any group photograph taken at a college or company gathering. But the walls and draperies also evoke an enclosed, courtlike setting—a setting created simultaneously by the place and its inhabitants.

The word *cour* is used in this double sense to describe Mlle de Chartres' arrival: "At that moment there appeared at court a beauty to whom all eyes were turned …" ["Il parut alors une beauté à la cour, qui attira les yeux de tout le monde," 259, Lyons 7]. Her arrival enhances the gallery of portraits already present; but the eyes in the portraits look back at her.

The Furetière definition of *cour* closest to Lafayette's meaning is "way of living at *Court*. That man knows the *court* well, knows how to pay *court* …" ["manière de vivre à la *Cour*. Cet homme sçait bien la *cour* sçait faire la *cour* …"]. In a letter to Lescheraine praising her own (anonymous) novel, Lafayette writes in almost the same words, "it is a perfect imitation of the world of the court and the way people live there" ["c'est une parfaite imitation du monde de la cour et de la manière dont on y vit," *Correspondance* 2.181]. This *manière de vivre* resembles what Certeau terms *l'art de faire*: a social practice cutting across fictional and non-fictional discourses. Lafayette's representation of *la manière de vivre à la cour* emphasizes the absolute and central necessity of presence. Again paralleling Furetière's definition, the chief *manière de vivre à la cour* is *faire la cour*. Thus, after a stay in the country following his mother-in-law's death, "Monsieur de Clèves went to Paris to pay his respects at court" ["M. de Clèves vint à Paris pour faire sa cour," 292, Lyons 29]. His wife must soon follow him: "As it was some time since her mother's death, Madame de Clèves had to appear again in society and to resume her visits at court" ["Comme il y avait déjà assez longtemps de la mort de sa mère, il fallait qu'elle commençât à paraître dans le monde et à

Fig. 3.1 Balthazar, *La cour du roi Louis* [1665]. Paris, BnF.

faire sa cour comme elle avait accoûtumé," 313, Lyons 42]. Mme de Clèves is not forced to return by a tyrannical husband (Danahy 116), but rather because attendance at court is a necessity of life for the nobility: the narrator's "il fallait" is echoed by Furetière's "A Courtier must always be at *Court*, or often go to *Court*" ["Un Courtisan doit estre toûjours à la *Cour*, ou aller souvent à la *Cour*"]. Whatever their personal circumstances, this constraining law of presence weighs equally, though differently, on both men and women. Just after the Princesse has confessed to her husband, a messenger arrives to tell him he must return to court immediately by the order of the king. "Monsieur de Clèves was *obliged* to leave at once, and he could say to his wife nothing except that he begged her to return the next day ..." ["M. de Clèves fut *contraint* de s'en aller, et il ne put rien dire à sa femme, sinon qu'il la suppliait de venir le lendemain ... ," 353, Lyons 68; italics added].

These obligations grew out of the family connections that bind courtier to courtier and to the king. When Mlle de Chartres first appeared at court, we were told she was of the same family as the Vidame de Chartres; but the French original specifies *maison*, or house: "elle était de la même *maison* que le vidame de Chartres, et une des plus grandes héritières de France" (260; Lyons 7). According to Furetière, *maison* can be a dynastic metonymy: "*house* is also said of a noble family, of a succession of illustrious people coming from the same stock, who are distinguished for their bravery, their occupations, or the great honors they have received by birth" ["*maison* se dit aussi d'une race noble, d'une suite de gens illustres venus de la même souche, qui se sont signalez par leur valeur, ou par leurs emplois, ou par les grandes dignitez qu'ils ont eu par leur naissance"]. As in Corneille's dramas, *maison* is akin to *sang* as a metonymy for noble birth; Lafayette includes both *maison* and *sang* in the same sentence, while adding her own distinctively ironic touch: "The Vidame of Chartres, descended from the old *house* of Vendôme, a name not despised by princes of the blood, had won *equal triumphs in war and gallantry*" ["Le vidame de Chartres, descendu de cette ancienne *maison* de Vendôme, dont les princes du sang n'ont point dédaigné de porter le nom, *était également distingué dans la guerre et dans la galanterie*," 255, Lyons 4; italics added]. No such irony is directed, however, towards his niece: in her wealth and connections, Mlle de Chartres is almost comparable to Mademoiselle de Montpensier. Yet again, like the Grande Mademoiselle, Mlle de Chartres requires marriage to turn her "house" into an "establishment." While Montpensier, to her misfortune, lost her mother at her birth and had no one to promote her marriage, Mlle de Chartres's mother is alive, active and "extremely proud" (Lyons 8). She wishes to see her daughter "established" in a high position worthy of her family, fortune, beauty, and virtue; and to accomplish this goal, she must enter Mlle de Chartres into the court marriage market.

Mlle de Chartres's first appearance in the novel takes place not in the court setting, but in the *maison* of a rich Italian jeweler. This unexpected venue has provoked numerous commentaries. For Pósfay, it indicates the heroine's antisocial and "revolutionary" nature (131). In her discussion of the scene, Peggy Kamuf compares Mlle de Chartres to a jewel seeking its "match" (133). Changing this comparison slightly, I would liken her to a precious stone needing to be "set," and thereby set off, in an appropriately rich fashion. According to social law for women, only matrimony can furnish this setting. Most significantly, this first meeting, which will lead to Mlle de Chartres's "setting up" a household with M. de Clèves, occurs in a place of commercial exchange. It is necessary to the dignity of Mlle de Chartres and his other noble clients that the bourgeois, mercantile status of the Italian jewelry merchant be camouflaged to some degree. Hence, in describing this establishment, the narrator does not use the words *boutique* or *magasin*, but *maison*: "his *house* seemed that of some great nobleman rather than of a merchant" ["Sa *maison* paraissait plutôt celle d'un grand seigneur que d'un marchand," 261, Lyons 8]. Nonetheless, Lafayette does not seek to erase the commercial reality of the setting; on the contrary, she emphasizes it with words like "trafiquant," "trafic" and "marchand." Just as the glory of the dynastic *maisons* ennobles the exchanges taking place in the court marriage market, the elegant appearance of the Italian's house ["paraissait celle d'un grand seigneur"] gentrifies, but does not fully conceal, the financial (and matrimonial) deals taking place there.

With the above discussion, we have moved across the threshold from the metonymic into the "real" house. In the *Princesse de Clèves*, aristocratic mansions, like the jeweler's establishment, can sometimes function to show off one's wealth and enhance one's social status: "The Marshal of St-André, who was always on the look-out for opportunities to display his magnificence, made a pretext of desiring to *show his house*, which had just been finished ..." ["Le maréchal de Saint-André, qui cherchait toutes les occasions de faire voir sa magnificence, supplia le roi ... de *lui montrer sa maison*, qui ne venait que d'être achevée ... ," 283, Lyons 23; italics added]. But the primary function of *maison*, according to Furetière's first entry for the word, is to provide shelter and seclusion: "Lodging, place where one can withdraw and protect oneself and one's belongings from bad weather" ["Logis, lieu où on se peut retirer & remettre à couvert son bien et sa personne des injures du temps"]. In keeping with this need for retreat, the ideal house or apartment contains a series of rooms arranged in an ascending order of privacy and exclusivity: according to Richelet, "un bel appartement doit avoir *antichambre*, *chambre*, *cabinet*." Furetière gives an identical enumeration.

While rooms themselves in *La Princesse de Clèves* are often left undescribed, the control of, or access to, personal space implied by their disposition, and the hierarchical implications of such access, are carefully noted by Lafayette: "the dauphin, whose health was delicate, had been ailing and had seen no one ... toward evening, he received all the persons of quality who were in his *ante-chamber*" ["le roi dauphin, dont la santé était assez mauvaise, s'était trouvé mal et n'avait vu personne ... sur le soir, il fit entrer toutes les personnes de qualité qui étaient dans son *antichambre*," 284, Lyons 23; italics added]. The number of these *personnes de qualité* waiting in the *antichambre* is a sign of his or her status: "[Nemours] used to stay in the ante-chamber of Madame de Chartres, *where were assembled many persons of quality*" ["(Nemours) demeurait dans l'antichambre de Mme de

Chartres *où il y avait toujours plusieurs personnes de qualité*," 290, Lyons 27; italics added]. According to Furetière, the *antichambre* serves as a waiting room for both visitors and their *domestiques*; Lafayette does not mention the latter, who play no role in her story.

If one privilege of high rank is to keep people waiting in the *antichambre*, higher rank can also sanction entry. In one incident commented on by Donahy, the Reine Dauphine retires *chez elle* with her female favorites, telling her attendants she will not receive anyone ["fit dire qu'on ne la voyait point"; note the additional distance created by the indirect *fit dire*].[24] Nevertheless, the prince de Condé is allowed in because "his rank gave him free admission everywhere" ["sa qualité lui rendait toutes les entrées libres," 284, trans. Lyons 23]. While Donahy sees this observation as an example of overweening male privilege at court (104), I interpret it somewhat differently. Lafayette defends the prerogatives of the Reine Dauphine and is careful to explain why, on a rare occasion, her exclusive circle was broken into. The gender imbalance of entries in the novel (more men enter women's apartments than vice versa) can also be interpreted in differing ways: as a sign of men's aggression, a symbol of women's "inner spaces," or—as I argue—a representation of literal "feminotopias:" not utopic but real female spaces.

Continuing our penetration into the aristocratic dwelling, one of the striking differences between early modern and modern domestic spaces is the function of the *chambre*. Where we think of the bedroom as the most private part of the house (except for the bathroom, a *commodité* even gentlefolk mostly did without in the seventeenth century), the early modern *chambre* was an amalgam: part bedroom, part *salle de réception*. According to Furetière, "It is ordinarily the place where people sleep and receive visitors" ["C'est ordinairement le lieu où on couche, & où on reçoit compagnie"]. In keeping with this usage, M. de Clèves recounts how he paid a visit to his sister rather early in the morning and "trouvai Mme de Touron au chevet de son lit [at her bedside]" (296). Since this locution would be misinterpreted by modern readers, the English translation merely states: "I found Madame de Tournon *there*" (Lyons 31; italics added). In this instance, differences in both linguistic construction and social behavior make the English rendering of the novel even more abstract than the original. Mme de Clèves also receives guests "sur son lit"; this common practice acquires an erotic charge when Nemours arrives at the end of visiting hours to find her alone, or employs her husband's authority to gain entry into her room early in the morning (308, 340, Lyons 38, 59).

The semi-public nature of the seventeenth-century *chambre* may help explain the vogue of the *cabinet*, already mentioned above. Although we have described the French *cabinet* in an architectural context, its original meaning was closer to English usage: a piece of furniture that can contain fragile or valuable objects (cf. "china cabinet"). For Furetière, "a *cabinet* is also a buffet with many doors

---

[24] Lyons's translation seems to give a false impression: "[the crown princess] sent word [to the Queen] she could not come" (Lyons 23).

and drawers for locking up very precious things, or simply to act as an ornament in a bedroom or gallery" ["*cabinet* est aussi un buffet où il y a plusieurs volets & tiroirs pour y enfermer les choses les plus precieuses, ou pour servir simplement d'ornement dans une chambre, dans une galerie"]. In the context of the *Princesse de Clèves*, it is interesting to note that *cabinet* can also refer to a jewelry case. Both Estienne and Nicot detail the contents of the *cabinet d'une femme* in these terms: "all the different kinds of ornaments, jewels and trinkets that she keeps to dress up and deck herself out with" ["toutes les sortes d'ornemens, joyaulx & affiquets qu'elle ha pour s'accoutrer et attifer"]. Cotgrave's *French-English Dictionary* (1673) contains both meanings: "A cabinet, or casket for jewels, & also, a closet, little chamber, or wardrobe, wherein one keeps his best, or most esteemed, substance." The "closet" in which one keeps one's "best ... substance," is also an early English equivalent of the *cabinet*, into which one can retreat to preserve one's intimate, underlying "substance."

We have already seen how Mademoiselle de Montpensier's house renovations reveal the demand among fashionable people for small, enclosed spaces where they can withdraw in comfort and privacy. In addition to a "rather pretty" bedroom, Montpensier's apartments at St-Fargeau include "a *cabinet* at the end and a wardrobe, as well as a small *cabinet where there is only enough room for me*" ["un cabinet au bout et une garde-robe, et un petit cabinet *où il n'y a place que pour moi*," *Mémoires* 2.284; italics added]. Associations of the cabinet with "modern" style and comfort are also frequent in period dictionaries: for example, "well-appointed *cabinet*" ["cabinet bien accommodé," Richelet] or "this *cabinet* is quite comfortable" ["ce cabinet est bien aisé," *Académie française*]. Montpensier's memoirs are again an excellent source in this regard. While visiting Champigny en Poitou, another of the dilapidated châteaux belonging to the Montpensier side of her family, she writes: "I went up to my room, that I did not find to be as ugly as I expected; for it was a place where my grandfather Montpensier's pages slept. I found a spot to make myself a *cabinet*; I settled in *comfortably* for the time I had to stay there" ["Je montai à ma chambre que je ne trouvai pas si laide que je croyais; car c'était un logement où logeoient les pages de mon grand-père de Montpensier. Je trouvai une place à me faire faire un *cabinet*; je m'y établis pour être *commodément* le temps que j'avais à y demeurer," *Mémoires* 3.173–4; italics added]. Thus, while the examples cited earlier in this chapter highlighted the religious and studious functions of the *cabinet*, later seventeenth-century writing emphasizes its associations with luxury, personal comfort and retreat. In one *Académie française* entry, *cabinet* and privacy are almost synonymous: "to have retreated into one's *cabinet*, into one's private [space]" ["estre retiré dans son cabinet, en son particulier"].

Yet even after it has expanded from a storage cabinet into a personal living place, the *cabinet* continues to keep its earlier meaning as a depository for precious objects. The *cabinet* is often used to display private collections of valuables: "Place in a house where valuable paintings are kept" ["Lieu dans une maison où sont les tableaux de prix," Richelet]. The *Dictionnaire de l'Académie française*'s "her *cabinet* is full of trinkets … he has a *cabinet* completely full of jewels" ["son cabinet est rempli de babioles … il a un cabinet tout plein de bijoux"] simply becomes in Richelet: " his *cabinet* is a jewel" ["son cabinet est un bijou"]. The word "bijou," still used in real estate parlance, signifies high elegance, luxury and comfort condensed into a small living space. While such descriptions are not exclusively associated with a woman's refuge, they display many traditional feminine connotations. As Montpensier says of St-Fargeau, "I decorated the *cabinet* with numerous pictures and mirrors; in the end, I was delighted and thought I had created the most beautiful thing in the world" ["J'ajustai le cabinet avec force tableaux et miroirs; enfin, j'étais ravie et croyais avoir fait la plus belle chose du monde," *Mémoires* 2.284].

Combining all these layered meanings, the *cabinet* in the *Princesse de Clèves* is an inmost retreat where one seeks protection for what is most precious and fragile: one's private feelings, hidden from others and sometimes even from oneself. The *cabinet* appears in this light in several scenes. For example, after Mme de Chartres deliberately relates gossip about Nemours and the Reine Dauphine to her daughter:

> Madame de Clèves went home and *locked herself up in her room.* It is impossible to express her grief when her mother's words opened her eyes to the interest she took in Monsieur de Nemours; she had never dared to acknowledge it to herself. Then she saw that her feelings for him were what Monsieur de Clèves had so often supplicated …

> Mme de Clèves s'en alla chez elle et *s'enferma dans son cabinet.* L'on ne peut exprimer la douleur qu'elle sentit de connaître, par ce que lui venait de dire sa mère, l'intérêt qu'elle prenait à M. de Nemours; elle n'avait encore osé se l'avouer à elle-même. Elle vit alors que les sentiments qu'elle avait pour lui étaient ceux que M. de Clèves lui avait tant demandés … . (289, Lyons 26)

Alone in her *cabinet* like a penitent in the confessional, the feelings and insights the Princesse had suppressed in public come to her conscious awareness [*elle sentit … elle vit*]. A similar *cabinet* scene takes place late in the novel, after Mme de Clèves has learned that her secret confession to her husband is known, and worse, has been revealed by Nemours: "She shut herself up alone in her room. What most distressed her was to have grounds for complaint against Monsieur de Nemours, with no chance of excusing him" ["Elle s'enferma seule dans son cabinet. De tous ses maux, celui qui se présentait à elle avec le plus de violence, était d'avoir sujet de se plaindre de M. de Nemours et de ne trouver aucun moyen de le justifier," 369, Lyons 78]. Once the *cabinet* door has been locked, the narration automatically shifts into an inside view of the Princesse's feelings. There is no need for transitions because the *cabinet* code is clear to the implied reader. In harmony with the spiritual figures of interiority encountered in Sales and Camus, it is tempting to go further and see the *cabinet* as a metonymic figure for the inner self.

In tension with its private, introverted role, the court *cabinet* is also appropriated as a social space, albeit one that offers greater intimacy than the *chambre*. This is particularly true of royal apartments: "Madame de Clèves called on the dauphiness after dinner, and found her in her room with two or three ladies *with whom she was on intimate terms*" ["Mme de Clèves ne laissa pas d'aller l'après-dînée chez Mme la Dauphine: elle était dans son cabinet avec deux ou trois dames *qui étaient le plus avant dans sa familiarité*," 289, Lyons 26–7; italics added]. On another occasion, also in the *reine dauphine*'s apartment, "the king came out of a room where he had been" ["le Roi sortit d'un cabinet où il était"] to come speak to Mme de Clèves (323, Lyons 48). Finally, the first—and last—frank private conversation between Nemours and the Princesse takes place in a *cabinet* at the Vidame de Chartres's house: "Mme de Clèves came; the Vidame went to receive her, and led her into a *small room* at the end of his apartment. Shortly after, Monsieur de Nemours came in, as if by chance" ["Mme de Clèves vint; le vidame l'alla recevoir et la conduisit dans *un grand cabinet*, au bout de son appartement. Quelque temps après, M. de Nemours entra, comme si le hasard l'eût conduit," 403, Lyons 100].[25] The word "room" cannot convey the special public-private quality of the *cabinet*.

This encroachment upon the last personal refuge at court underscores the necessity for analogous spaces in the country. Outdoor constructions, whether *pavillon*, *cabinet de jardin*, summerhouse or folly, claimed a place in the country estates of Europe as long as landholding families were able to maintain their aristocratic lifestyle. Louis XV was a "devoted pavilion-builder" (DeLorme 9); Thomas Jefferson, inspired by European architectural models, built a garden pavilion at his Monticello estate for reading and writing, after his retirement from active political life in 1809 (Rogers 270). This small, elegant structure, made almost entirely of glass, still looks out over the Virginia fields and hills. While varied in design, such buildings share an open, temporary, sometimes rustic quality, opposed to the permanence of formal architecture. According to Thomas Corneille, "what is properly called a *Cabinet de jardin* is a small isolated building in the form of a pavilion. It should be open on all sides, and one retires there to enjoy the fresh air" ["ce qu'on appelle proprement Cabinet de jardin est un petit bâtiment isolé en forme de pavillon. Il doit être ouvert de tous costez, & c'est là où l'on se retire pour prendre le frais"].

---

[25]   The involvement of the *cabinet* in the love intrigue is a constant in Lafayette's narration: in *La Comtesse de Tende*, we read: "she informed her servants she would see no one, and locked herself in her *cabinet*, lying on a day bed and given up to all the cruelest feelings that remorse, love and jealousy can provoke. While she was in this state, she heard a hidden door of her *cabinet* open and saw the chevalier de Navarre, adorned and with a grace beyond what she had ever seen in him" ["elle fit dire qu'on ne la voyait pas et s'enferma dans son *cabinet*, couchée sur un lit de repos et abandonnée à tout ce que les remords, l'amour et la jalousie peuvent faire sentir de plus cruel. Comme elle était dans cet état, elle entendit ouvrir une porte dérobée de son *cabinet* et vit paraître le chevalier de Navarre, paré et d'une grâce au-dessus de ce qu'elle ne l'avait jamais vu," 422].

"Adelayde Comtesse de Roussillon, ou l'Amour constant," a tale from the collection *Nouvelles françaises*, formerly attributed to Segrais but likely authored by Montpensier and her friends, contains a description of a splendid outdoor *cabinet*. Set on a terrace which is built into a hill, the *cabinet* appears almost suspended in air: "open on all sides and enclosed only by large windows, which, on each side, afford all the most beautiful views you could wish for" ["ouvert de tous les côtés et n'est fermé que de grandes vitres, qui de chaque côté, ont toutes les plus belles vues qu'on puisse souhaiter," Segrais 1.315]. This *cabinet de jardin* resembles one Mademoiselle erected at St-Fargeau.

Other *cabinets de jardin* were more simple and rustic. While Cotgrave defines the structure succinctly as "an arbor in a garden," Richelet's description gives insight into the *cabinet*'s actual construction: a "little retreat in the form of a round chamber, ordinarily made of long sticks tied together with wicker" ["petit réduit en forme de chambre ronde, fait ordinairement de perches liées avec des osiers"]. During the strange interlude between M. de Clèves's death and his widow's definitive retreat, the Princesse comes upon Nemours in such an outdoor *cabinet*, dreaming of his love:

> After passing through a little thicket, she saw at the end of the path, *in the most retired part of the garden, a sort of summer-house open on all sides*, and she turned in that direction. When she had got near it, she saw a man lying on the benches who seemed sunk in deep thought, and she recognized Monsieur de Nemours.

> Après avoir traversé un petit bois, [Mme de Clèves] aperçut, *dans l'endroit le plus reculé du jardin, une manière de cabinet ouvert de tous côtés*, où elle adressa ses pas. Comme elle en fut proche, elle vit un homme couché sur des bancs, qui paraissait enseveli dans une rêverie profonde, et elle reconnut que c'était M. de Nemours. (400, Lyons 98; italics added)

An illustration from Marivaux's *Vie de Marianne*, entitled *Rupture dans un cabinet de verdure*, shows a structure similar to that in the *Princesse de Clèves* (Fig. 3.2). We will return to this scene later on; but in this context, it is significant, if unsurprising, that both the Princesse and Nemours are drawn to settings that are isolated, without walls, and open to nature.

The country retreat most amply described in the novel, and most commented upon by critics, is of course the *pavillon* at Coulommiers. The *pavillon* design combines a rustic setting with a "modern" desire for elegance. In a rare practical aside, Mme de Clèves remarks that the *pavillon* at Coulommiers is of recent construction—"c'est un lieu achevé depuis peu" (371). In fact, as Niderst notes, the construction of the real Coulommiers was not begun until 1613, almost 45 years after the events narrated in the novel (459n149). This date reaffirms the modernity of the *pavillon* and the ideal of natural yet civilized seclusion

Fig. 3.2   *Rupture dans un cabinet de verdure*. Engraving J. van der Schley. Marivaux, *La Vie de Marianne*. Paris 1873. III. 136–7. Paris, BnF.

it represents.[26] The *pavillon*, like the *cabinet de jardin*, is a garden structure whose main characteristics are small size, isolation, and proximity to the outside; but it is generally of sturdier constuction: "[pavilion] also refers to a single structure, like a small separate building that one has built in a garden to take advantage of the beautiful view" ["(pavillon) se dit aussi d'un corps de logis seul, comme d'un petit bastiment separé, qu'on fait faire dans un jardin, pour y joüir de la belle veuë," Corneille].[27] Furetière underlines the isolation of the structure: "Pavilions are also built at the edge of a garden" ["On bastit aussi des *pavillons* aux extremitez d'un jardin"]. But in contrast to the *cabinet*, whose origins are in domestic furniture, the *pavillon* comes out of the military camp. Its name comes from the square shape and domed or raised roof which cause it to resemble the campaign tents of the time. The *Dictionnaire de l'Académie française* describes it in this way: "a kind of portable lodging … . A square building, given this name because of its resemblance to army pavilions" ["espèce de logement portatif … . Un corps de bastiment carré, appelé ainsi à cause de la ressemblance de sa figure avec celle des pavillons d'armée"]. As DeLorme points out, "In its simplest form a pavilion is nothing more than a tent which meets a ceremonial social or military need" (13).[28] The expression "sous le pavillon," used twice in the *Princesse de Clèves*, affirms its connection to an outdoor, tent-like shelter (349, 384).

In addition to the above meanings, *pavillon* also signifies a canopy, a bed hanging—or a flag: "in general, it is said of flags, standards, signs, banners, etc." ["en general, se dit des drapeaux, estendarts, enseignes, bannieres, &c.," Furetière]. Indeed, most classical dictionaries focus more on this meaning than on the architectural one. Both are relevant to the novel. A place of retreat, the *pavillon* is also the setting for important skirmishes in the amorous "war" waged between

---

[26] Choisy, Montpensier's last, and arguably most successful, architectural project, includes a "belvédère" on the banks of the Seine. This structure, called "le Pavillon de l'Aurore," "was enclosed by glass panels or doors that opened from the top to the bottom. The interior was finished with paneling and upholstery; it was decorated by Coypel fils, Monsieur's principal painter" ["était clos de chassis de verre ou porte-croisées qui s'ouvraient depuis le haut jusqu'en bas. L'intérieur en était orné de menuiseries et d'étoffes; il était decoré par M. Coypel fils, premier peintre de Monsieur," Blondel 2.14, quoted in Mayer 69]. This "cabinet with a view" resembles the *pavillon* at Coulommiers. Construction at Choisy was begun in 1680, two years after the publication of the *Princesse de Clèves*.

[27] It should be added that the word *pavilion* is also often used to describe a separate wing attached to a building, with a distinctive peaked roof. Pavilions are found in many famous buildings of the classical age, including the Louvre and the Luxembourg Palace—the latter designed by Salomon de Brosse, architect of Coulommiers. Brosse's design for Coulommiers includes two such pavilions (Ward 1.235).

[28] A striking example of this military tent-style pavilion stands in the grounds of the Drottningholm palace in Sweden. The pavilion and gardens were commissioned by the dowager Queen Hedvig Eleonora in 1681. While designed by a German landscape architect and called a "Turkish Tent," the pavilion nevertheless shows the influence of French models (Rogers 209).

Nemours and the Princesse. Nemours overhears Mme de Clèves's confession to her husband while hidden in the *pavillon*, and his reaction combines the aggressiveness of the battlefield with the pleasure of that aristocratic substitute for war, the hunting field: "He felt, nevertheless, great pleasure in having brought her to this extremity" ["Il sentit pourtant un plaisir sensible de l'avoir réduite à cette extrémité," 354, Lyons 69]. It is to be recalled that Nemours had first come upon this *pavillon de la forêt* after getting lost while out hunting. As DeLorme observes, "[pavilions] were always associated with members of the privileged classes and often with hunting, which was a royal ritual and patrician sport" (13). When Nemours returns at night, his entry into the Clèves property is described like a military attack on a castle. To reach the garden, Nemours must first pass through a tall barrier: "The palings were very high, and there were some beyond to bar the way, so that it was not easy to get in; nevertheless, monsieur de Nemours succeeded" ["Les palissades étaient fort hautes, et il y en avait encore derrière, pour empêcher qu'on ne pût entrer, en sorte qu'il était assez difficile de se faire passage. M. de Nemours en vint à bout néamoins," 385–6, Lyons 89]. He then comes upon a lighted *cabinet*, with all its glass doors open, where he sees Mme de Clèves contemplating a painting of the siege of Metz that contains his portrait (386, Lyons 89). No siege is necessary; but the Princesse never lowers the flag [*met pavillon bas*] in surrender. On the contrary, Nemours is defeated by his own emotional conflicts, which prevent him from acting with his usual grace:

> All his courage abandoned him, and more than once he was on the point of deciding that he would go back without seeing her. But he was so anxious to speak to her, and so encouraged by what he had seen, that he pushed on a few steps, though in such agitation that his scarf caught on the window and made a noise.

> Tout son courage l'abandonna, et il fut prêt plusieurs fois à prendre la résolution de s'en retourner sans se faire voir. Poussé néanmoins par le désir de lui parler, et rassuré par les espérances que lui donnait tout ce qu'il avait vu, il avança quelques pas, mais avec tant de trouble, qu'une écharpe qu'il avait, *s'embarassa* dans la fenêtre, en sorte qu'il fît du bruit. (387, Lyons 90; italics added)

His emotional trouble manifests itself in a physical awkwardness unusual for the adroit Nemours. As a result, his scarf catches in the window. In the original, *s'embarrassa* also conveys emotional complications.[29]

Mme de Clèves, alarmed at the sound, seeks refuge in the adjoining room where her attendants are assembled. This detail draws additional attention to the pavilion's architecture. Commentaries on this scene usually pass over the fact that the building is not a single room, but an extended structure with

---

[29] For another interpretation of the Coulommiers scene, see Kurt Weinberg, "The Lady and the Unicorn, or M. de Nemours à Coulommiers," in Lyons ed. *La Princesse de Clèves* (190–205).

several interior spaces, including two *cabinets*. Large, elaborate garden pavilions were frequently built at the country estates of royalty and wealthy landowners in the seventeenth century: Louis XIV's retreat at Marly comprises an imposing central structure and a double row of smaller guest houses in the same style for the visiting courtiers, connected by *treillage* passageways. All these buildings, including the central structure, are called *pavillons*. And like the pavilion at Coulommiers, they are all two-story structures (Rogers 177). We see these design features of the Coulommiers pavilion through Nemours's eyes, on his first visit to the estate: "These paths led to a summer-house, which consisted of a large room with two small side-rooms, one opening on a flower-garden separated from the forest by a fence, and the other opening on one of the walks of the park" ["Il trouva au bout de ces routes un pavillon, dont le dessous était un grand salon accompagné de deux cabinets, dont l'un était ouvert sur un jardin de fleurs, qui n'était séparé de la forêt que par des palissades, et le second donnait sur une grande allée du parc," 348, Lyons 65]. The labyrinthine syntax of this sentence, with its imbricated prepositional phrases (*dont ... dont*) evokes the hierarchical, concentric intentionality of the *bel appartement* leading into an inner core of retreat. Within this *pavillon*, "[Madame de Clèves] had sought absolute solitude, spending her evenings in the garden unaccompanied by her servants" ["Cette princesse avait même cherché le moyen d'être dans une solitude entière et de passer les soirs dans les jardins sans être accompagnée de ses domestiques," 383–4, Lyons 126]. Yet even there, Mme de Clèves's isolation is always relative: "she used to go into the summer-house where Monsieur de Nemours had overheard her talking with her husband, and enter the little room which opened on the garden. Her women and the servants would stay in the main room or in the other wing, coming to her only when they were called" ["Elle entrait dans le cabinet qui était ouvert sur le jardin. Ses femmes et ses domestiques demeuraient dans l'autre cabinet, ou sous le pavillon, et ne venaient point à elle qu'elle ne les appelât," 384, Lyons 89]. Thus, the symbolic architecture of the *pavillon* combines the military with the domestic, the wild with the civilized, the public with the private, representing in microcosm all the contradictions of noble life.

Retreat

The trope of retreat retraces and sums up much of what has already been said concerning the dynamics of space in the *Princesse de Clèves*. *Retraite* is both a place (*une retraite*) and an action (*la retraite*, *se retirer*). Mme de Clèves's abortive retreats at court, and her retirement into the Parisian countryside on the margins of *le monde* or society, are rehearsals for, and prefigurations of, her final withdrawal *hors du monde*.[30] But before arriving at that final threshold, it is necessary to revisit the themes of presence and absence raised at the beginning of this discussion—

---

[30] For an analysis of these stages in Mme de Clèves's retreat, see Woshinsky, *La Princesse de Clèves* 98–100, 118.

no longer, as before, as a social imperative, but as a passionate one. Throughout the work, Nemours and Mme de Clèves perform a dance of presence and absence choreographed by the author. In fact, the Princesse and Nemours are first brought into one another's presence at a ball (Lyons 17). This is one of the few fully enacted scenes in the *Princesse de Clèves*; the description even includes one of the only two items of furniture mentioned in the novel—a chair Nemours leaps over to reach the dancers. (The other is a bed.)

In this choreography of love, absence can be as expressive as presence. Early in the novel, Mme de Clèves decides not to attend the maréchal de St-André's ball because Nemours will be away on an official trip. Feigning illness, "Madame de Clèves gladly consented to stay at home for a few days, in order not to meet Monsieur de Nemours, who left without having the pleasure of knowing that she was not going to the ball" ["Mme de Clèves consentit volontiers à passer quelques jours chez elle pour ne point aller dans un lieu où M. de Nemours ne devrait pas être, et il partit sans avoir le plaisir de savoir qu'elle n'irait pas," 286, Lyons 25]. Her chosen absence from that place (*lieu*), matching Nemours's obligatory absence, is a negative sign of her interest in him. Absence is also a sign of respect and apology from Nemours: after he has revealed her secret to the vidame, "he considered ... that the best thing he could do would be to show his profound respect, and by silence and evident distress to make it clear that he did not dare to meet her ..." ["il pensa ... que le mieux qu'il pût faire était de lui témoigner un profond respect par son affliction et par son silence, de lui faire voir même qu'il n'osait se présenter devant elle ..." 371, Lyons 80].

However, Nemours's nearness is far more powerful than his absence: for the Princesse, "the mere presence of this prince would excuse him and overthrow all her plans" ["la seule présence de ce prince le justifiait à ses yeux et détruisait toutes ses résolutions," 375, Lyons 82]. His power of presence is especially palpable during the episode of the vidame's letter, when the Princesse is drawn for the first and last time into court intrigue. She spends hours in private with him, working, even conspiring together, in a vain attempt to save her uncle's reputation and to protect him from the queen's anger. The closeness of the loved object exerts an almost irresistible force on her; but this effect lasts only until their meetings end: "as soon as she was deprived of the presence of the man she loved, she seemed to awaken from a dream" ["sitôt qu'elle ne fut plus soutenue par cette joie que donne la présence de ce que l'on aime, elle revint comme d'un songe," 346, trans. Lyons 63]. She realizes that if she succumbs to the power of Nemours's seductive presence, she will forfeit the exalted position so carefully cultivated by her mother and "fall like other women" ["tomber comme les autres femmes," 291, trans. Lyons 28], finding herself on the same level with them for the first time. The whole "construction" of the Princesse—by both her mother and her creator—rests on her *distance*—her unreachability. Her mother had aimed to make her daughter "une personne où l'on ne pouvait *atteindre*,"[31] even when "*exposed* to all the temptations of the court" ["*exposée* au milieu de la cour," 273, Lyons 16; italics added]. She therefore resolves: "I must tear myself away from the society of Monsieur de Nemours; I must go to the country" ["Il faut m'arracher de la présence de M de Nemours; il faut m'en aller à la campagne," 347, Lyons 64].

The tension between attraction and resistance, *proximité* and *éloignement*, produces a kind of ballet of avoidance, following the physical law that two bodies, at least those of the princesse de Clèves and the duc de Nemours, cannot be in the same place at the same time. A variation on this dance, which brings a melancholy pleasure to both characters and reader, occurs when one lover retraces the other's footsteps and enters into locations previously occupied by the other. On Nemours's first visit to the Coulommiers estate, "he entered the summer-house … He entered the room near the flower-garden …" ["Il entra dans le pavillon … il entra dans le cabinet qui donnait sur le jardin des fleurs," 348–9, Lyons 65]. From that vantage point, he overhears Mme de Clèves's confession to her husband. Nemours's steps are retraced, first unknowingly then knowingly, by the Princesse herself in her nightly quest for solitude. These moves are described by the narrator in almost the same words applied to Nemours. In a passage already cited, "She used to go into the summerhouse where Monsieur de Nemours had overheard her talking with her husband, and enter the little room which opened on the garden" ["Elle venait dans ce pavillon où M. de Nemours l'avait écoutée, elle entrait dans le cabinet qui était ouvert sur le jardin," 384, Lyons 88]. These repetitions lend the narrative an obsessive, almost Marguerite Duras-like quality.

A final example of successive occupation takes place near the end of the novel, in a suburban garden [*jardin des faubourgs*] where Mme de Clèves has gone after catching sight of Nemours watching her house from an opposite window. As already related above, she discovers Nemours lying in a *cabinet de jardin*: "She … sat down in the place which Monsieur de Nemours had just left, and there she remained, completely overwhelmed. … At last, after spending two hours there, she returned home …" ["Elle s'alla asseoir dans le même endroit d'où venait de sortir M. de Nemours. … Enfin après avoir demeuré deux heures dans le lieu ou elle était, elle s'en revint chez elle," 401, Lyons 99]. This lingering choreography of proximity and avoidance conveys the poignancy of longing and unfulfilled love. Symbolically, it also suggests that there is no place where Nemours and the Princesse can happily be together at the same time.

The sole possible solution, then, is retreat. Mme de Clèves's definitive withdrawal from court has been interpreted in almost as many ways as the word "retreat" has meaning. Taken in a military sense, the novel's denouement is sometimes seen as a defeat, or failure of nerve, on the part of the main character. Peggy Kamuf implicitly supports this view by arguing that in refusing Nemours and leaving the court, Mme de Clèves is merely acting out a scenario her mother had programmed

---

[31]   Lyons's English translation misses out on this sense of distance: "a woman to be sighed for in vain."

for her. It is true that Mme de Chartres set her daughter a strong model by spending many years away from court. In this sense, Mme de Chartres's withdrawal is a replay of her mother's retired widowhood, spent raising her daughter in seclusion. Despite this parallel, I do not consider Mme de Clèves's retreat as a passive or defeatist enactment of her mother's will. Rather, it arises from her own rational assessment of court life, marriage and the possibilities for happiness there, arrived at through her own tragic personal experience. It is well established that Lafayette frequented feminine court circles and salons where critiques of marriage and alternate life styles were discussed. Given the prevalent hostility towards marriage in such *milieux*, one might wonder why Lafayette has Mme de Chartres emphasize the importance of *loving* one's husband—an unconventional notion for the time. One can speculate, as I have in the past (Woshinsky, *La Princesse de Clèves* 113), that Mme de Chartres's teachings are influenced by *précieuse* notions of *amitié tendre*, or close, sincere friendship between men and women. In salon writings and conversations, however, such notions usually applied to relationships outside of marriage, and for cause; applying them to marriage appears to be a utopic and risky move.

On a more pragmatic level, Mme de Chartres's exorting her daughter to love and be faithful to her husband may also be seen as a rational strategy: if marriage is unavoidable, attachment to one's spouse is perhaps the only way to make it bearable. Enlisting Mlle de Chartres's virtue and self-esteem [*mérite*] as reinforcements in the defense of her honor, Mme de Chartres hopes to safeguard her daughter's position and happiness in a place so full of political and emotional dangers. In this light, the author's attribution of such ideas to Mme de Chartres may be considered an attempt to defend and support her character and mitigate her apparent ambition. Mme de Chartres accepts the Prince de Clèves's offer, "not fearing that her daughter would find Monsieur de Clèves a husband she would not be able to love" ["elle ne craignit point de donner à sa fille un mari qu'elle ne pût aimer en lui donnant le prince de Clèves," 270, Lyons 14]. I believe this statement should be taken without irony: as a mother, she did the best she could for her daughter under uncertain circumstances. However, the conclusion reached by the Princesse de Clèves is very different from her mother's advice, and more in keeping with *précieuse* views. She refuses Nemours's hand partly out of guilt at her husband's death, couched as "duty" (*devoir*), but mainly because she is convinced marriage cannot bring women a happy, or even stable, emotional life (*repos*). Certainly Mme de Chartres would not have anticipated, or desired, the situation her daughter finds herself in at the age of 18; we may even speculate that she might have combated Mme de Clèves's refusal as "singular" (*particulière*), as she did her decision to stay home from the maréchal de St-André's ball. But as in the earlier situation, one feels the Princesse would have remained stubborn (*opiniâtre*).

A final explanation of Mme de Clèves's retreat, which brings us back to some central concerns of this book, places it in a religious context. Again, Mme de Chartres had set a strong example by refusing all further human contact, even with her daughter, before her death: "she turned away and bade her daughter call her women, without hearing or saying more. Madame de Clèves left her mother's room in a state that may be imagined, and Madame de Chartres thought of nothing but preparing herself for death" ["Elle se tourna de l'autre côté en achevant ces paroles et commanda à sa fille d'appeler ses femmes, sans vouloir l'écouter, ni parler davantage. Mme de Clèves sortit de la chambre de sa mère en l'état que l'on peut s'imaginer, et Mme de Chartres ne songea plus qu'à se préparer à la mort," 291–2, Lyons 28]. In keeping with seventeenth-century spiritual views of "l'usage de la maladie," at the end of the novel Mme de Clèves will "use" her sickness to help detach her from worldly ties. The interpenetration of religious and secular vocabulary and ideas is apparent at other moments in the tale: for example, when Mme de Clèves is beset by jealousy during the vidame's letter episode, she bitterly regrets "that she had not *withdrawn from the world*" ["de ne s'être pas opiniâtré *à se séparer du commerce du monde*," 327, Lyons 51; italics added]. In addition, the word *austère*, often associated with a religious lifestyle, is used to describe the Princesse's and other women's behavior within a secular context. After her husband's death, Mme de Tournon lives, or pretends to live, *dans une retraite austère* (295); and the Princesse follows a *conduite austère* in avoiding Nemours (358).

Perhaps on account of these linguistic ambiguities, as well as a general modern tendency to conflate religious retreat with institutional enclosure, some otherwise excellent studies have confused the Princesse's final retreat with formal entry into a convent. Erica Harth states for example: "Free at last to marry Nemours, who presses her insistently to do so, she chooses instead to enter a convent, where she ends her days" ["An Official 'Nouvelle'" in Lafayette, *Princesse de Clèves*, ed. Lyons 231]. The end of the Princesse's life is certainly nun-like in its isolation and austerity; but taking vows is never mentioned as an option for her.[32] Instead, "part of each year she spent in this religious house, and the other part at home, but in retirement, busied with severer tasks than those of the austerest convents. Her life, which was not long, furnished inimitable examples of virtue" ["Elle passait une partie de l'année dans cette maison religieuse et l'autre chez elle, mais dans une retraite et dans des occupations plus saintes que celles des couvents les plus austères, et sa vie, qui fut assez courte, laissa des exemples de vertu inimitables," 416, Lyons 108]. Her retreat compares "favorably" to the austerity of a convent—but she still remains *chez elle*. At this point, it is illuminating to return to the example of the Duchesse de Montpensier, who likewise spent the end of her life in retreat on her own lands. We are not told from whom Mme de Clèves holds her own property,

---

[32] Fitting this pattern more closely are the *novellas* of María de Zayas, where women characters, learning of men's inconstancy, refuse marriage and retreat to a convent. On de Zayas, see Margaret Greer, *María de Zayas tells Baroque Tales of Love and the Cruelty of Men* (University Park, PA: Pennyslvania State University Press, 2000). Mme de Clèves instead chooses a "threshold" position, as will Henriette-Sylvie de Molière in Villedieu's memoir-novel of that name (see below, Chapter 4).

but can assume that it is also a maternal legacy, since it is described as "some large estates that she owned in the Pyrénées" ["De grandes terres qu'elle avait dans les Pyrénées," 413, Lyons 107], rather than land coming from her husband's family.[33] In the end, she has indeed returned to the feminine space of "motherland." As Niderst points out in his edition of *La Princesse de Clèves*, the choice of this location on the borders of the kingdom also suggests "an immense distance between the Princesse and the court" ["une immense distance entre la princesse et la cour," 462n193], a distance sought by the Princesse.[34] The haunting, oxymoronic final phrase of the book, "laissa des exemples de vertu inimitables," reconfirms the essential quality of the Princesse as "une personne où l'on ne pouvait atteindre" (273);[35] but it takes on a new meaning if we recall Montpensier's description of the Carmelites in her letters to Motteville: the more secluded they are, the more they are to be revered. But to revere is not to imitate; Montpensier, like the Princesse, declines to enter a convent formally, because she does not need to. Both follow the aristocratic practice of the time by crossing the convent threshold for shorter or longer stays.[36] At the end of the novel, the fictional Clèves, like the real Montpensier, exchanges the tensions of court life for a "conventual" existence, lived not under monastic rule but on her own land and on her own terms.

Thus, the beauty who *parut à la cour*, and was constrained to *paraître* at royal functions against her will, gains her highest distinction by disappearing without trace. This vanishing from dynastic history both resembles, and differs from, the fate of the only woman referred to in the novel as actually entering a convent: an anonymous *dame de Piémont*, mother of one of the King's illegitimate daughters, "who entered a convent after the birth of her child" ["qui se fit religieuse aussitôt qu'elle fut accouchée," 257, Lyons 5]. Unlike the *dame du Piémont*, Mme de Clèves has committed no misdeed meriting conventual enclosure in the eyes of society; but she judges herself with equal severity. Another difference between them is that while the daughter of the *dame de Piémont* is integrated into court history, even marrying a nobleman, Mme de Clèves disappears without issue. One wonders what will happen to her property after her death—whether it will be appropriated by others, as was the case with Montpensier's—but that is not at "issue" for the Princesse, who, valuing personal repose above dynastic considerations, precisely

---

[33]   On the question of Mme de Clèves's property, see also DeJean 122–3, 251n59.

[34]   The words *distance* and *éloignement* appear recurrently in the novel, in both literal and figurative senses. *Eloignement* is used especially often at the moment of the king's death, when the general disorder and dispersal of the court allow Mme de Clèves to distance herself without her absence being remarked—see 293 and 378 (three occurrences).

[35]   I draw from Peggy Kamuf the idea of "reading" the word "atteindre" in a spatial sense. See Kamuf, "A Mother's Will" in Lyons ed. *Princesse de Clèves* (214).

[36]   A similar example is offered by the duchesse de Longueville, sister of the Prince de Condé and a founding, active member of the *parti des princes* that opposed Mazarin during the Fronde. After their defeat, she retired to a house she had built near the convent of Port-Royal. Longueville divided her time between stays on her own property and retreats to Port-Royal.

dies without issue.[37] Perhaps the most interesting difference between the two women is the anonymity of the unfortunate *dame*, maintained to protect her reputation. In her narration of the history of Diane de Poitiers, Mme de Chartres mentions in passing another anonymous lady, a kind of proto-Princesse:

> The Duke of Orléans … loved one of the most beautiful women of the court, and was beloved by her. I shall not tell you who it was, because her life since that time has been most decorous; and she has tried so hard to have her affection for the prince forgotten that she deserves to have her reputation left untarnished. It so happened that she heard of her husband's death on the same day that she heard of that of Monsieur d'Orléans; consequently she was able to conceal her real grief without an effort.

> M. le duc d'Orléans … aimait une des plus belles femmes de la cour et en était aimé. Je ne vous la nommerai pas, parce qu'elle a vécu depuis avec tant de sagesse et qu'elle a même caché avec tant de soin la passion qu'elle avait pour ce prince, qu'elle a mérité que l'on conserve sa réputation. Le hasard fit qu'elle reçut la nouvelle de la mort de son mari le même jour qu'elle apprit celle de M. d'Orléans, de sorte qu'elle eut ce prétexte pour cacher sa véritable affliction, sans avoir la peine de se contraindre. (280–81, Lyons 21)

This anecdote, imbedded in court history as part of the narration of the life of Diane de Poitiers, offers a microcosmic model that fits Mme de Clèves's fate more closely than can her mother's teaching and example. The Princesse is not anonymous; but once she exits the domain of public space, she leaves no trace other than what is contained in the narrative itself. Yet the movements taking her from appearance to disappearance argue for the importance of space and setting in classical fiction, and the gains to be made from trying to discern their subtle, elusive, yet essential presence.

---

[37] As DeJean observes, Mme de Clèves's *repos* "is seen (logically) as possible for a noblewoman only if she refuses marriage and a place in the landed order" (122)—which also means refusing to "hold" a place for her family.

Chapter 4
Parlors:
The Implicated Convent

PARLOIR: Place where people speak. It is now only said of places where Nuns come to speak with outside visitors through a grill. There are Convents where you need to reserve the *Parlors* early.

PARLOIR: Lieu où on parle. Il ne se dit plus que des lieux ou les Religieuses viennent parler aux gens de dehors à travers d'une grille. Il y a des Couvents où il faut retenir de bonne heure les *Parloirs*.

—Furetière, *Dictionnaire universel*

The preceding chapter has shown how seventeenth-century women—and their writing—began to cross, recross and redefine the thresholds of conventual space. This chapter will explore how, as the century advanced, the outside world encroached on the cloister itself: rather than a separate alternative to secular life, it increasingly became part of a larger social and political network, fully implicated in the twistings and turnings of real and novelistic plots.[1] Instead of seeking or remaining in static retreat, women on the move flee to friendly convents or are carried off to hostile ones. These moves are represented in the women's self-writing which flourished in the latter half of the century: personal memoirs like those of Hortense and Marie Mancini, as well as fictional accounts like Mme de Villedieu's *Mémoires de la vie de Henriette-Sylvie de Molière* and the Comtesse de Murat's *Mémoires de la Comtesse de M****. These works also served as long-unrecognized prototypes for canonical eighteenth-century memoir novels, notably Marivaux's *La Vie de Marianne*.[2] In the development of women's self-writing, truth and fiction are inextricably blended. Not only does Marie Mancini's account read like a romance novel; in 1676, two years before Marie's own memoirs were published, an apocryphal version of them

---

[1]   In addition to the bibliographies found in Ponton and Mourão, titles of classical convent novels can be culled from Maurice Lever, *La Fiction narrative en prose au XVIIe siècle* (Paris: CNRS, 1976); Gustave Reynier, *Le Roman sentimental avant l'Astrée* (Paris: 1908; Geneva: Slatkine, 1969); Ralph C. Williams, *Bibliography of the Seventeenth-Century Novel in France* (New York: The Century Co., 1931); Ralph W. Baldner, *Bibliography of Seventeenth-Century Prose Fiction* (New York: Columbia University Press, 1967); and the manuscript catalogues of the Arsenal Library in Paris. See also the Works Cited at the end of this volume.

[2]   René Démoris has given official recognition to this parentage: see Démoris, "Écriture féminine en je et subversion des savoirs chez Mme de Villedieu (*Les Mémoires d'Henriette-Sylvie de Molière*)" in *Femmes savantes, savoirs des femmes* (Geneva: Droz, 1999) 208; and also *Romans à la première personne* 398.

appeared.[3] And four years before Hortense Mancini published her own life story in 1675, it was alluded to by Catherine de Villedieu in her *Mémoires de Henriette-Sylvie de Molière*, which is also dedicated to Hortense.[4] Villedieu's novel, published between 1671 and 1674, is the first French work of fiction to bear the title *Mémoires*.[5] Thus, written memoirs, letters, even the gossip of the time served as models for the new memoir novels, and influences were both reciprocal and simultaneous. As Claire Carlin points out, "Both [Mancini] sisters present themselves as exceptional in their misfortune, as heroines in an adventure novel despite themselves" (1). The beginning of Hortense's account confirms this characterization: "And if the events that I have to recount to you *seem like something out of a novel*, blame it on my unhappy fate rather than my inclination" ["*Que si les choses, que j'ai à vous raconter, vous semblent beaucoup tenir du roman*, accusez-en ma mauvaise destinée plutôt que mon inclination," trans. Nelson 27, ed. Doscot 32; italics added].[6]

---

[3]   [anon.] *** *Les Mémoires de M.L.P.M. M. Colonna, G. Connétable du royaume de Naples*. (Cologne: P. Marteau, 1676). That Marie's memoirs were issued in response to this apocryphal work is clear from their original title: *La Vérité dans son jour*. The title of Brémond's revised edition also reflects this work of refutation: *Apologie, ou les Véritables mémoires de Mme Marie Mancini, connétable de Colonna, écrits par elle-même*.

[4]   After centuries of neglect, *Les Mémoires de Henriette-Sylvie de Molière* were republished in a modern edition in 1974, edited by Micheline Cuénin. In 2003, René Démoris produced a more readily accessible edition, based on the same original text as Cuénin's. French quotations in this chapter are taken from the Cuénin edition; English quotations are from Donna Kuizenga's edition and translation in the "Other Voices" series (Chicago: University of Chicago Press, 2004). In the last quarter-century, Villedieu has also been the subject of an increasing number of excellent critical studies by Kuizenga and others. *A Labor of Love* (2000), ed. Roxanne Decker Lalande, contains a good selection of this criticism. Also see Works Cited.

[5]   See Démoris 16. The precise genre definition of the *Mémoires de Henriette-Sylvie* is still a matter for discussion. Margaret Wise and Adrienne Zuerner refer to the six parts of the novel as "letters" (Wise 132, Zuerner 100). Nicole Boursier calls the work "mémoires/roman épistolaire" ["Le corps de Henriette-Sylvie" 274]. Donna Kuizenga remarks: "Villedieu's *Mémoires* are a complex creation. Neither autobiography, nor novel, nor memoirs, nor epistolary novel, the text is rather one that has something of all these genres" ("The Play of Pleasure and the Pleasure of Play" 147). In the introduction to her translation, she refers to the work as "pseudo-autobiographical" (8). The *Mémoires*, like an epistolary novel, have a single explicit addressee, and Parts 3 through 6 end with an epistolary conclusion: "I remain your very humble and obedient servant" ["et avec tant de respect, très humble, et très soumise servante"]. In my view, however, they display no other distinguishing markers of the epistolary genre. Sylvie never says that she is writing letters or that Son Altesse is reading them; she twice refers to the text as "a very long reading" ["une si longue lecture"], never as "une si longue lettre" (179). In contrast, a self-referential remark at the beginning of part 3 emphasizes the "novelhood" of the work: "nous allâmes commencer une troisième partie de *roman*" (Démoris 111; italics added).

[6]   French quotations from Hortense's *Mémoires* are taken from Gérard Doscot ed., *Mémoires d'Hortense et de Marie Mancini* (Paris: Mercure de France 1965, 1987). English

It is my contention that through the mingling of these genres, the role of convents in women's social networks (implicitly accepted at the time as a fact of everyday life) came into fictional representation. This chapter will explore some of the ways in which convents were implicated in the negotiations of social life for women, and how these implications are represented discursively in the Mancini sisters' memoirs, *Les Mémoires de Henriette-Sylvie de Molière* and *La Vie de Marianne*. I will begin with an overview of the social trends linking the convent to the outside world.

Social Integration of the Convent

Our view of convents tends to be a polarized one: we think either of mystics spending their days in ecstatic contemplation or, more likely, of unfortunate victims locked up against their will. Readers who have followed the argument thus far will realize that the reality was more complex than this opposition. The seventeenth-century convent was no longer an island unto itself (if, indeed, it had ever been). Rather, it formed part of a larger spatial and social landscape: women were placed in convents, or retreated to them voluntarily, for mixed reasons, often having little to do with devotion. These convent stays could be temporary or permanent: the residents' status ranged from *retraitante* to boarder to lay sister to choir nun— to prisoner. For the stereotype of convent-as-jail is not without historical foundation. The issue of forced vocations for nuns was made notorious by Diderot's *La Religieuse*, but it is less widely known that convents in the Old Regime were also used to confine lay women, with little or no legal process in the modern sense. For example, upon issue of a *lettre de cachet*, wives accused of adultery by their husbands could be taken away and incarcerated in convents. The consequences were occasionally severe: in one notorious case involving high-profile court nobility, Mme de Stainville, sister-in-law of the Duc de Choiseul,[7] was arrested for adultery on a *lettre de cachet* requested by her husband, and sequestered in the convent of the Filles de Sainte-Marie in Nancy for the remainder of her life.

Although life imprisonment without trial for alleged adultery may have been exceptional, the practice of women's conventual incarceration was legal and difficult to reverse. In addition, convents were pressured to take in as involuntary pensioners "madwomen who posed little danger" ["des folles peu dangereuses"], "committed" by their families (Reynes 223). The abbé Thiers, a great champion of strict enclosure, objected to this secular appropriation of sacred space; but abbesses

---

quotations from both of the Mancini sisters' memoirs are from a new translation by Sarah Nelson: Hortense Mancini and Marie Mancini, *Memoirs* (Chicago: University of Chicago Press, 2008). For more on the memoirs' publication history, see below, n20.

[7]   Choiseul, maréchal de France under Louis XIV, was renowned for his participation in the siege of La Rochelle and other military campaigns. For more on the imprisonment of allegedly adulterous wives in monasteries, see DeJean 258n29. On *lettres de cachet* see also Rapley, *Social History* 250–52.

often had no choice in the matter.[8] Because of a lack of facilities in the seventeenth century for confining women—especially women of good family—the use of convents as houses of detention was one that "the monarchy particularly wanted to encourage" ["le pouvoir royal souhait[ait] particulièrement encourager," Reynes 222]. Convents were employed ever more broadly throughout the century to imprison not only social deviants, but women considered to be political or religious dissenters—and for Louis XIV, this was a distinction without a difference. After the revocation of the Edict of Nantes in 1696, some convents were required by the regime to incarcerate Huguenot women and children.[9]

The co-opting of the convent as a container for individual transgressors or undesirables forms an integral part of a developing social practice in seventeenth-century France. This practice, explicitly called *renfermement* ["imprisonment"] at the time, entailed "the involuntary incarceration of groups considered marginal or potentially dangerous" (Chill 403). As part of the scheme of social controls imposed by the monarchy, *renfermement* meant locking away not only political or religious dissidents but the poor. As early as 1611 there was a move to incarcerate the beggars of Paris. As Rapley observes, this threat alone had the desired effect "of clearing the streets, as those beggars mostly preferred to leave town" (91). By mid-century, however, the situation had deteriorated: due to a rampant rise in unemployment in the cities, the number of wandering poor had increased dramatically (Chilcoat 7). In post-Fronde Paris, the percentage of vagrants had grown to one-tenth of the entire urban population. To cope with this problem, in 1656 mendacity was banned by royal edict, as was the age-old tradition of distributing alms. Beginning the following year, beggars were rounded up by paid "enforcers" and taken to state/ religious institutions: principally the Hôpital général for men and the Salpétrière for women. At the Salpétrière, located in a former gunpowder factory, new construction was ordered by Anne d'Autriche and Mazarin. Renovations were designed by Le Vaux, one of the main architects of Versailles; construction according to Le Vaux's plans continued during the eighteenth century. According to Matt Senior, Le Vaux's architectural design for the Salpétrière basically implemented St Vincent de Paul's division of the poor into "good" and "bad."[10] Among the former class were

---

8   In relation to cloistering women against their will on the orders of their families, Elizabeth Rapley observes: "Too often, it seems, the nuns cooperated with the families in such discreditable behaviour. But in their defense it should be pointed out that their communities were always highly dependent on public support and had little leverage against the powerful families of their neighborhood." Rapley even cites one example where family members threatened to break into the monastery and create havoc if the nuns refused to take a girl as a postulant (*Social History* 179).

9   On this topic, see Probes and also Rapley, *Social History* 249–50.

10   On the design of La Salpétrière, see Matt Senior, "Confining Humans, Confining Animals: The Salpétrière and the Ménagerie" (Conference paper, SE 17, Society for Interdisciplinary French Studies, 28–30 October 2004, College of William and Mary, Williamsburg, Virginia). See also Maximilien Vessier, *La Piété-Salpétrière: quatre siècles d'histoire et d'histoires* (Paris: Hôpital de la Piété-Salpétrière, 1999).

women who could work—single mothers, orphans, and the old. The latter included women arrested on *lettres de cachet* or convicted by a tribunal, prostitutes, and the mentally ill. These social categories were segregated in separate quarters: women confined by *lettre de cachet* were housed in La Force, prostitutes in Le Commun, and the insane, who received the worst treatment of all, in the Basses Loges. Since they could not work, the mentally ill were considered useless burdens on society; moreover, as Foucault points out, having lost their reason, they were viewed as animals, and treated as such—or worse. The descriptions of the insane held in La Salpétrière parallel the horrifying depictions of nuns considered mad or possessed in Diderot's *Religieuse*.

Renfermement of the poor was in keeping with other practices, such as the creation of hospitals, asylums and prisons, which Michel Foucault outlines in *Histoire de la folie* and *Surveiller et punir*. These confining practices and institutions served to police the boundaries of society by defining acceptable and unacceptable behaviors and removing violators from sight.[11] As Rapley points out, the policies and attitudes toward the indigent in mid-century France resembled those of Protestant England more than of Catholic Italy or Spain, where beggars and gypsies were enclosed much later, if at all. However, according to Foucault and others, *renfermement* was less a matter of religious leanings than of political control and economic policy. Incarcerating vagabonds and forcing them to perform a "useful" social role was seen to serve the purposes of early capitalism: one of the early and enthusiastic sponsors of the workhouse system was Louis XIV's minister Colbert.[12]

Convents and religious congregations were directly implicated in this disciplinary action since, in most cases, they were the only institutions coping with the needs of the poor. Reactions of religious leaders to *renfermement* were mixed. While he saw the necessity of lodging the indigent and homeless, Vincent de Paul objected on principle to charitable institutions taking involuntary residents, and argued that entry be kept voluntary. This counsel was ignored, and in the end some of the Filles de la Charité did participate. Members of other religious orders also served in semi-carceral institutions. The Jansenist Antoine Arnaud even saw incarceration as having a positive social value; he states in eerily pre-Foucaultian terms: "The greatest benefit of incarcerating the poor is the good education of the children. This is best achieved by watching over them ceaselessly, and, by this constant *surveillance*, cutting them

---

[11]   See *Histoire de la Folie* (Paris: Gallimard, 1972), 60–75, 163–5; *Surveiller et punir* (Paris: Gallimard, 1975), 120; and a special issue of *L'Esprit créateur* (XXXVII.3 [Fall, 1998]). The social policy of incarcerating, or keeping under surveillance, members of groups that are considered marginal or threatening still prevails in modern, supposedly democratic societies: in the United States, for example, in 2003 one out of every three young African-American men was in prison, on probation or on parole (Leonard Pitts, Jr, "Wedding Bell Blues. *The Miami Herald*, May 19, 2003. B1).

[12]   This imperative of usefulness to the state accounts for Colbert's hostility to monastic institutions. As will be discussed in Chapter 6, Colbert's attitude prefigures that of the "liberal" *philosophes* of the eighteenth century.

off from evildoing."[13] In any case, the approval or disapproval of religious authority was irrelevant in the face of a sweeping social trend.

However, this bleak picture has a more positive side. Despite families' desire to protect their honor, and the state's power to control unwanted members, some women still managed to negotiate the conventual system in ways beneficial to themselves—ways having more to do with survival than with spirituality. For example, convents served as a kind of genteel "rest home" or halfway house for women who were going through physical or mental crises. A little-noted fictional example appears in the *Princesse de Clèves*. After the death of her husband, the heroine is removed in a totally distraught state to the shelter of a convent: "Madame de Clèves was almost crazed by the intensity of her grief. The queen at once came to see her, and carried her to a convent without her knowing whither she was going" ["Mme de Clèves demeura dans une affliction si violente, qu'elle perdit quasi l'usage de la raison. La reine la vint voir avec soin et la mena dans un couvent sans qu'elle sût qu'on la conduisait," 397, Lyons 96]. Aside from showing the extraordinary favor Mme de Clèves enjoys from the queen, this incident portrays women helping women to find refuge in a time of need; that the refuge chosen is a convent needs no contemporary explanation.

The conventual system also served women who, for one reason or another, needed to "put a little distance between themselves and their family" by retreating to a friendly cloister for a period of time ["prendre quelque distance avec leur famille," Reynes 227]. In this way, convents functioned as refuges for daughters who refused the husbands chosen for them by their families; for married women separating from their husbands; and even, as a counter-example to the sad case of Mme de Stainville cited above, for wives accused of adultery. This contrast between "good" and "bad" convents features prominently in *Les Mémoires de Henriette-Sylvie* as well as in Marivaux's *La Vie de Marianne*. Finally, the convent afforded a respectable refuge for widows and other single women who, without taking vows, could rent apartments or rooms belonging to the order, sometimes within the conventual space, sometimes nearby. While not inexpensive, room and board were affordable for the upper middle class. Convent boarding was even a useful option for those noblewomen who lacked property and wealth of their own; in the convent, they could live relatively comfortable lives independent from their families' control. Taking in adult boarders became a more widespread practice in the eighteenth century, given the poor financial condition of many women's convents, although some nuns objected to the effect secular women might have on the religious community (Rapley, *Social History* 253–4). Certain period memoirs

---

[13]   René Taveneaux, *Le catholicisme dans la France classique* (Paris: Hachette 1973) 1.220, trans. Rapley, *The Dévotes*, 91; italics added. For more on the institutionalization of charitable works in the seventeenth century, and the sometimes-reluctant involvement of women's orders in that process, see Rapley 89–92; see also Coliny Jones, *The Charitable Imperative: Hospitals and Nursing in Ancien Régime and Revolutionary France* (NY: Routledge, 1989).

paint a pleasant picture of the convent boarder's existence. Mme de Genlis says of the months she spent in the convent of Origny during her husband's absence in the army: "I cried a lot when I separated from M. de Genlis and afterwards I had a wonderful time at Origny" ["Je pleurai beaucoup, en me séparant de M. de Genlis et ensuite je m'amusai infiniment à Origny," Reynes 230].[14] Prison, asylum, *pension*, women's shelter, community: all form part of the complex role convents played in the lives of early modern women.

The penetration of worldly residents and attitudes into religious buildings at the end of the Old Regime finds an interesting architectural expression in the renovation plans for the Abbaye Royal de Panthemont (or Pentemont), presented by Diderot in his architecture supplement to the *Encyclopédie*. This convent stood on the rue de Grenelle, almost adjoining the Grand Carmel (Biver, plate 55).[15] The plans Diderot discusses, proposed by the royal architect Franque, were never executed; the renovations and additions to Panthemont actually completed were the work of Constant d'Ivry. But Diderot admires Franque's plans for their qualities of "grandeur" and "simplicité" (8).[16] In the description and illustrations for the Abbey project (Diderot, *L'Encyclopédie*, s.v. "architecture," plates 16–21), grandeur is much more apparent than simplicity. Baroque and court esthetics placed great emphasis on the front and rear facades of buildings. (Diderot also uses Perrault's West façade for the Louvre as an example of architectural grandeur.) This preoccupation with the facade extends to religious architecture: both the street and garden elevations of Franque's Panthemont project are impressive and ornate, even though the nuns would not see the street facade; and the elegance of the garden facade, within the cloistered space, does not evoke a modest life in religion. As at the Grand Carmel, the nun's choir is located behind the altar and opens onto a gallery and monumental staircase, leading to the back garden and the rooms and dormitories above. There is no main cloister in the strict sense. Instead, the building contains two courtyards; a public *cour d'entrée* opening onto the rue de Grenelle and a small *cour intérieure* within the cloistered space.

The plans for Panthemont also show a large number of "thresholds" and intermediate spaces providing links with the outside world. Some of these spaces

---

[14]　See also Sophie Hasquenoph, "Faire retraite au couvent dans le Paris des Lumières." *Revue Historique* 598 (1966) 353–65.

[15]　After a somewhat checkered history as the Prieuré des religieuses du Verbe Incarnée, the convent property was handed over to the Abbaye de Pentemont in 1672. This house had been founded in 1217 by Philippe de Dreux, Bishop of Beauvais, under the name of Pentemont, because of its location at the foot of the Montagne de St-Symphorien. For financial and geographical reasons, the abbess Hélène de Tourville moved the convent to Paris. The third Paris abbess, Mme de Béthisy de Mézières, spent the rest of her life, and a great deal of money, refurbishing and expanding the convent. Work at Pentemont was still incomplete at the time of the Revolution.

[16]　According to Amédée Boinet, the Constant façade, "built at an angle, has a rather unattractive effect" ["construite en biais, est d'un effet assez disgracieux," Boinet II, 272–3; Biver 456].

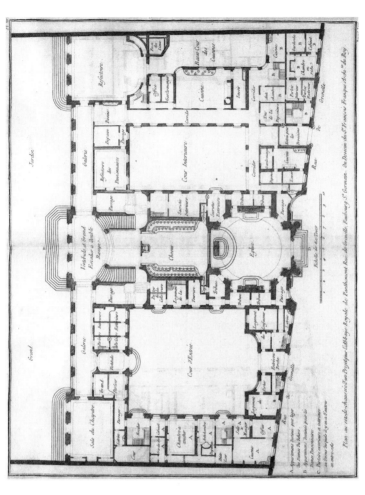

Fig. 4.1   *Plan du Rez de chaussée d'un projet pour l'Abbaye royale de Panthemont.*
Diderot, *Encyclopédie. Recueil des planches*, op. cit., vol. 1, plate XVI.
Minneapolis, University of Minnesota, Special Collections and Rare
Books.

are discernable in Fig. 4.1. First, two confessionals on the level of the nun's choir open onto *sacristies extérieures*. The resident confessor would reach the sacristy from a hallway leading to his lodgings, located directly off the archway leading to the *cour d'entrée*. The *Tourière*'s room also opens onto the large, public *cour d'entrée*. A smaller street entrance leads to the service areas and the turnstile of the convent *dépositaire* who received deliveries. Finally, the plans show a quantity of large and small parlors, each of which is divided into *parloir extérieur* and *intérieur*. The downstairs *parloirs intérieurs* are accessible to the nuns through the gallery, which replaces the traditional cloister as the main passageway through the convent. There are also a number of upstairs parlors, whose means of access is hard to deduce from the plan. The worldly character of this convent is also indicated by the fact that some of the nun's "chambres" (in contrast to his practice in *La Religieuse*, Diderot uses this word instead of "cellule") possess *antichambres*, *gardes-robes* and *cabinets*, like suites in a palace or wealthy mansion. These rooms, presumably for boarders, faced on the rue de Grenelle; the "chambres des religieuses" faced the back garden. The "chambres des novices" occupied the most protected position: their rooms faced a small inner courtyard, separated from the outside by another courtyard and a corridor. The *soeurs converses* were assigned to smaller rooms on the third floor.

This complex structure, with its multiple openings and concentric spaces, reflects Panthemont's status in the late eighteenth century as a "couvent à la mode." The young girls who boarded there paid high fees for the privilege of associating with the "best" aristocratic families. Adult lay women also frequented the convent for other reasons: Alexandre-Françoise de Beauharnais took refuge at Panthemont while in the process of obtaining a separation from her first husband. The future wife of Napoleon "will make her entry there into elegant society" ["y fera ses débuts dans la vie élégante," Rousseau 34]. Like Mme de Genlis, Beauharnais remembered her convent stay with affection. Towards the end of the Old Regime, some convent inmates enjoyed themselves a bit too much: according to a police report of 1768 concerning the abbaye de Longchamp, young men "gathered quite often in the parlors and put on plays, to the great contentment of the young nuns and boarders" ["s'assemblaient assez souvent dans les parloirs et y jouaient des comédies, au grand contentement des jeunes religieuses et des pensionnaires," Reynes 231–2].[17] Since this account comes from a book entitled *Notes secrètes sur l'abbaye de Longchamp en 1768*, published in the "Bibliothèque galante" series in 1870, it is difficult to gauge its accuracy; but it is certainly representative of a certain view of convent parlors at the end of the Old Regime. In any case, it is pleasant for us to picture young boarders and nuns enjoying themselves in this relatively harmless way.

---

[17]   Mme de Genlis, *Mémoires inédits* (Paris: Ladvocat, 1825, 2e edition, I), 199–205; *Notes secrètes sur l'abbaïe de Longchamp en 1768* (Paris: F. Henry, 1870). Both are quoted in Geneviève Reynes, *Couvents de femmes*. Reynes does not give an exact page source for either of these quotations, and I have been unable to locate the original sources.

Conventual Exposure in Hortense and Marie Mancini's Memoirs

Instances of both "good" and "bad" convent experiences abound in the Memoirs composed by Cardinal Mazarin's nieces, Hortense and Marie Mancini. They each relate their voluntary and involuntary stays in convents, as each tried to separate from a tyrannical husband.[18] Reputedly the first love of Louis XIV, Marie is perhaps better known than her sister Hortense. (The fact that Louis had already been the lover of Marie's older sister Olympe, as well as of other women, casts his liaison with Marie in a less romantic light.)[19] In any case, at the end of the affair Marie did not disappear into a convent like Louise de La Vallière. Instead, she and her sister both married, left their husbands, led nomadic lives in several European countries, had various lovers or admirers—and wrote their memoirs. Though six years younger than her sister (Marie was born in 1639, Hortense in 1645), Hortense's memoirs were the first to appear, in 1675. Hortense begins her account by bemoaning her "mauvaise destinée." Her destiny was certainly unfortunate as far as marriage was concerned. She was wed at the age of 15 to the fanatically devout Armand de la Meilleraye; as part of the marriage contract, Meilleraye took the name of the Duc de Mazarin. He was also given control of Hortense's rich dowry, an unusual provision which caused her grief throughout her life. Hortense endured the lies, jealous rages and possessiveness of a man whom Doscot calls "this terrible husband" ["ce terrible époux," 19]; but after he had wasted much of her large fortune and even taken her personal jewels, she decided to leave him. For some months, Hortense lived with friends and relatives while attempting to negotiate the return of her jewels. Matters came to a head when the duc de Mazarin had to leave for Alsace. Since it was scandalous, as well as illegal, for a married woman to live independently, especially in her husband's absence, Mazarin offered her two options, neither satisfactory to her: "Monsieur Mazarin gave me the choice of staying at the hotel de Conti or at the abbey of Chelles, the two places in the world which he knew I most hated, and for the best of reasons" ["M. Mazarin me donna le choix de demeurer à l'hôtel de Conti ou l'abbaye de Chelles, les deux lieux du monde qu'il savait que je haïssais le plus et pour les plus justes raisons," trans. Nelson 48, ed. Doscot 52]. Hortense chooses Chelles as the lesser of two evils, even though her husband's aunt is the abbess there.

---

[18]   As noted in Chapter 3, women's memoirs were both a novelty and a rarity well into the seventeenth century. Hortense's, published in 1675, and Marie's a year later in 1676, were the first to appear since 1628, the year of the inaugural publication of the memoirs of Mlle de Montpensier's grandmother, Marguerite de Valois, which served as an inspiration for Montpensier. Both sets of Mancini memoirs precede the publication, though not the composition, of Montpensier's work, begun in 1652. Unlike Valois's and the Mancini's, Montpensier's memoirs were not published at all in her lifetime, and afterwards only in an abridged and censored edition.

[19]   According to Doscot's introduction to his edition of the Mancini memoirs, "the king made Olympe his mistress, and loved Marie" ["le roi fit d'Olympe sa maîtresse, et aima Marie," 25].

The marital situation did not improve upon Mazarin's return six months later; in fact the duc de Mazarin, seeing that his wife was being treated well at Chelles, forced her to move to a different convent. But she is, finally, allowed to seek a legal separation. As we have seen, the practice of living in a convent while separating from one's husband was not an uncommon one; but in this case, the convents were not of her choice. After three months, Hortense and her servant are allowed to return to Chelles, "where I knew that we would be treated more reasonably, although we could not have as many visitors there" ["où je savais que nous serions traitées plus raisonnablement, quoique nous ne puissions y avoir tant de visites," trans. Nelson 51, ed. Doscot 55]. However, the story of Hortense at Chelles is not over: a few days later, Hortense's husband arrives "with sixty horses and permission from Monsieur [the archbishop] of Paris to enter the convent and to take me away by force" ["avec soixante chevaux, et permission de M. de Paris, pour entrer dans le couvent et m'enlever de force," trans. Nelson 51, ed. Doscot 55]. The Abbess defies episcopal authority and foils Mazarin's abduction plans. Although she is Mazarin's aunt, her defense of the abbey's prerogatives comes first. Legal deliberations surrounding the proposed separation were long and tortuous. At one point, the *parlement* decreed a *séparation des biens* [division of marital property between the spouses], but the case was referred to a higher court, the *grande chambre*, which refused to grant Hortense a *séparation des corps* [the right to live separately from her husband] and ordered her to move back into Mazarin's house. Realizing that the judges have been won over to her husband's position, in 1668 Hortense takes the risky step of fleeing to her sister Marie in Milan, accompanied by only one maid, both dressed in men's clothes (Goldsmith 35). Some years later, as Marie also recounts, they both escaped back to France. Hortense's memoirs end while she is enjoying a temporary asylum in Chambéry.

Marie Mancini's memoirs, like the whole new memoir genre, are an inextricable mixture of truth, fiction and manipulation. Marie first published her story in Spain in 1677, under the title *La Vérité dans son jour, où les véritables mémoires de M. Mancini, Connétable Colonne*. As its title indicates, even before the memoirs' publication, an apocryphal volume had appeared, trading on the notoriety of Hortense's life. This fictional version is entitled *Les Mémoires de M.L.P.M.M. Colonna, G. Connétable du royaume de Naples* (Cologne 1676).[20]

---

[20] This edition never attained wide circulation. Another version, extensively revised and altered by Gabriel Brémond, appeared in Holland the following year, under the title *Apologie, ou les Véritables mémoires de Mme Marie Mancini, connétable de Colonna*. Brémond's revision is generally wordier and less lively than the original; nevertheless, it remained the standard text of Marie's *Mémoires* for more than three centuries. The authentic original version was finally reissued in 1998 under its original title, *La Vérité dans son jour* (Patricia Cholakian and Elizabeth Goldsmith eds., Delmar, NY: Scholars' Facsimiles and Reprints, 1998). Nelson bases her translation of Marie's memoirs on *La Vérité*, and French references to Marie's memoirs are taken from this text. The most generally available French edition, however, is still Gérard Doscot's, which reproduces Brémond's revision (Paris: Mercure de France, 1965, 1987, 2003). For more on the publication history of Marie's

Marie states that she decided to write *La Vérité dans son jour* to counteract the lies and distortions published in the false *Apologie*. While declaring that her version of her life is the "true" one, Marie's memoirs read more like an adventure novel than does Lafayette's soberly historical *La Princesse de Clèves* which appeared in the same year, 1678. Marie's memoirs run the gamut of convent experiences. She recounts how, as a child, she was placed in a convent by her mother, who preferred her sister Hortense, in the hope that Marie would become a nun. However, Marie is not actually forced to profess. At the age of 14, she travels to France with Hortense who has been sent for by her uncle. There she is again placed in a convent—but this time for more benevolent reasons. In addition to hoping that convent life "would fatten [her] up a bit" (Nelson 87), Cardinal Mazarin wished Marie to be educated and "polished" by the elite teaching sisters of the Visitation. Her sister Hortense joins her there a few months later. Marie's review of her "polishing" is positive: "So there we both were in a convent, under the supervision of Sister Marie-Elisabeth de Lamoignon, sister of the *premier président* of the Parlement of Paris, who had the task of instructing us and teaching us the language and everything that she judged necessary for girls of our age and our station, a task which she carried out extremely well" ["Nous voilà donc toutes deux dans un monastère, sous la conduite de la Soeur Marie Elisabeth de Lamoignon, soeur du premier Président de Paris, qui avait le soin de nous instruire, et de nous enseigner la langue et tout ce qu'elle jugeait nécessaire à des filles de notre âge, et de notre rang, dont elle s'acquittait le mieux du monde," trans. Nelson 87–8, Cholakian 35–6]. Thus, the Couvent de la Visitation plays the role of an elite "finishing school" where Marie and Hortense enjoy the privilege of being tutored by a noblewoman with important connections.

The convent continues to play mixed roles in Marie's life after she marries Prince Colonna, a member of the Roman nobility. She agrees to this marriage "on the rebound" after Louis XIV weds the Spanish Infanta. Louis then proposes other possible suitors; but piqued by these helpful suggestions coming from her former lover, she insists on pursuing the match with Colonna. Her insistence is expressed in an ironic reversal of the conventional threat to lock a girl up if she refuses to marry the partner chosen for her: "since I was already committed, as much out of spite as out of honor I replied to His Majesty's kind offers that I would enter a convent for the rest of my days if the constable refused me" ["comme j'étais déjà engagée, autant par dépit que par honneur je répondis aux obligeantes offres de Sa

---

memoirs, see Goldsmith 36–7 and Nelson's translation, 10–12. An English version, *The Apology, or the Genuine Memoires of Madame Maria Mancini*, appeared in 1679 (London: J. Magnes and R. Bentley; available through Early English Books Online). This rapid translation into English indicates both the international notoriety of the Mancinis and the popularity of women's memoirs at the time. Mancini was a well-known name in England as well as France: Hortense lived in London for 20 years, where she presided over a prestigious literary salon. The fact that she is still best known as the mistress of Charles II betrays the tendency to look upon the Mancini sisters in a sexually stereotyped way: Doscot in his edition refers to them with coy diminutives as "Mazarinettes" and even "Mancinettes" (23).

Majesté, que j'entrerais dans un couvent pour le reste de mes jours, si Monsieur le Connétable me refusait," trans. Nelson 101, Cholakian 44]. After some years of apparent happiness, their marriage turns sour. To escape Colonna's oppressive behavior, she escapes to France with her sister Hortense, who had already fled in the other direction for a similar reason. Under Colonna's orders, Marie is later held captive in various convents in Turin and Madrid—even spending four months imprisoned under arduous conditions in the Alcázar in Segovia. Marie's response to these incarcerations was one of defiance. Carlin speculates that Colonna might have agreed to some of his wife's demands and set her free, "had she not … left so many convents where she was supposed to be cloistered abruptly and without permission just to prove she could do so" (14n15). And according to Goldsmith, "in her account she takes pains to describe precisely how she had made her exits from within the convent walls, and to assert that her sojourns there were freely chosen" (38).

Rather than attempting to dig her way out, as the apocryphal memoirs claim, Marie leaves her second convent boldly, in daylight, with the help and support of her women friends:

> … I went out of the convent in broad daylight, and not as I had the first time, but through the gate, in plain sight of all the porteresses; I climbed into a coach with a lady friend of mine, who was waiting for me for that purpose, and I went straight to the home of the marquise de Mortare … who … treated me very obligingly, although she was very surprised to see me, and my visit was the last thing in the world that she had expected.

> … je sortis du couvent en plein jour, et non pas comme la première fois, mais par la porte et à la vue de toutes les portières, et étant montée en carrosse avec une dame de mes amies, qui m'attendait pour cet effet, je fus droit chez la marquise de Mortare … qui … me traita d'une manière très obligeante, quoiqu'elle fût fort surprise de me voir, et que ma visite fût la chose du monde à laquelle elle s'attendait le moins. (trans. Nelson 168, Cholakian 193–4)

On the other hand, Marie had at one point negotiated with her husband to enter a convent in France of her own choosing—again suggesting that it was not conventual enclosure itself that was objectionable to her so much as enclosure in convents selected by her husband against her wishes. However, retreat into a convent only appeared a viable alternative for Marie while her husband was alive. At Colonna's death in 1689, she gained her freedom and sufficient wealth to live as she wished, moving from country to country until her own death in 1715.[21]

---

[21] This version of Marie's story, as outlined by Carlin, Goldsmith and other modern scholars, stands in contrast to Doscot's romanticized view: "She died at seventy-five, the same year as the king she had loved, we don't even know where, some say in Pisa, an eternal wanderer, incapable of settling anywhere, of forgetting the one dream of a short season of her adolescence" ["Elle mourut à soixante-quinze ans, la même année que ce roi qu'elle avait aimé, on ne sait même pas où, à Pise disent certains, éternelle errante, n'ayant pu se fixer, n'ayant su oublier le rêve unique d'une saison de son adolescence," 26].

Flight and Enclosure in Villedieu's *Mémoires de la vie de Henriette-Sylvie de Molière*[22]

Hortense Mancini's memoirs have another "prequel," this one more overtly fictional: before Hortense Mancini wrote her own life story, it is explicitly referred to by Catherine de Villedieu in the *Mémoires de Henriette-Sylvie de Molière*, which is also dedicated to Hortense. Villedieu's novel, published in 1671–72, is the first work of fiction to bear the title *Mémoires* (see Démoris's introduction to the 2003 edition of Villedieu's *Mémoires*, 16). In addition to the dedication and explicit mentions of Hortense, the textual resemblances of Villedieu's novel to both sisters' memoirs are striking—including their escapes into and out of convents.[23]

Like the Mancini sisters, Sylvie is an *aventurière*—a largely pejorative term applied in the late seventeenth century to women who lived by their wits and their pens, often without husbands, money or family support.[24] But the label *aventurière* is deliberately attached by Villedieu to her heroine: she calls Sylvie a "nouvelle Aventuriére" (ed. Cuénin 83). This word, with its scandalous aura, provokes fascination, excitement, perhaps even envy of a mobile lifestyle then unavailable to most women. Etymologically, an "adventurer" is one who takes what comes—*adventus*—moving freely through life's events from place to place, moment to moment. This nomadic energy is felt from the beginning of the *Mémoires de Henriette-Sylvie de Molière*. In a liminal "fragment de lettre," seemingly addressed to a friend and publishing agent in Paris, Villedieu (or Sylvie) writes: "I'm bringing with me a lovely lady whom you know, and who threatens to make me take an even longer journey. She has this strange desire to see Paris again, but I doubt that she will be able to convince me to go there, and not only because my own business calls me back to Toulouse" ["J'amène avec moi une belle Dame que vous connaissez, & qui me menace de me faire aller bien plus loin. Elle a une

---

[22]   An orphan of unknown parentage, the beautiful and spirited Sylvie is raised by a *financier*, M. de Molière. Partly in revenge for his wife's dalliance with a neighbor, the Marquis de Birague, Molière starts showering attentions on his young ward. Unfortunately, his attraction to her gets out of hand, leading to attempted rape. Sylvie, who prefers riding and hunting to more "feminine" occupations, takes out a pistol and shoots him. This act of self-defense leads to a long pursuit. While taking refuge in a neighboring chateau, Sylvie gains the affection of the chatelain's son; this forbidden relationship gives her an added need to flee. After many adventures, the couple meet and marry, but their union quickly sours, as does Sylvie's attitude toward marriage. The last part of the novel explores alternate life choices for women in convents.

[23]   On these resemblances see Cuénin's edition 121, 332; also Démoris's edition 266n5.

[24]   "Les autoresses, assez nombreuses, de la deuxième moitié du XVIIe siècle, Mme de Villedieu, Mme d'Aulnoy, Mme de Murat, Mlle de la Force, etc., étaient presque toutes des aventurières … ." Wetsel and Canovas, *Les Femmes au Grand Siècle*, 12. It is clear from this quotation how the word *aventurière* was traditionally used to discredit "autoresses" and their works. Mme de Lafayette escaped this condemnation—and remained in print—because she was seen as respectable and, ironically, published her work anonymously.

étrange démangeaison de se revoir à Paris, mais je doute qu'elle puisse obtenir sur moi de me faire faire ce pas-là, outre que mes affaires me rappelleront bientôt à Toulouse," trans. Kuizenga 25, ed. Cuénin 42]. She does not even have time to stop for lunch with her correspondent. Like her creator, Sylvie moves constantly and hurriedly from place to place; but at the same time, the basic motivation of her wanderings is to find a "lieu de seureté" ["some place where I will be safe," ed. Cuénin 18, trans. Kuizenga 31]. Young, attractive, of unknown parentage, lacking social position and family background (*maison*), she suffers constant attacks on her reputation and her person. Thus, she is constantly in need of hiding places: in Cuénin's useful lexical index to the novel, the words "cacher" and "se cacher" appear 21 times. We will see how these seemingly contradictory impulses work themselves out in the novel, and the role the convent plays in them.

Like Hortense Mancini, Henriette-Sylvie de Molière tells her patron and reader that her main purpose in writing her memoirs is to defend herself against all the calumnies spread about her:[25] "It is no small comfort to me, Madame, in the midst of all the evil stories by which my reputation is slandered everywhere, to see that Your Highness wishes me to justify myself" ["Ce n'est pas une legere consolation, Madame, au milieu de tant de médisances qui déchirent ma reputation par tout, que Vôtre Altesse desire que je me justifie," ed. Cuénin 5, trans. Kuizenga 26].[26] In distinction to Hortense, however, Sylvie continues: "I will willingly obey your command to entertain you with a faithful account of my innocent mistakes" ["j'obéirai volontiers au commandement qu'elle me fait de la divertir, par un récit fidèle de mes erreurs innocentes"]. Hortense's exposition and defense of her own "innocent errors" are also entertaining to the reader, but she never states that *divertissement* is a specific aim of her memoirs. Sylvie, in contrast, does so repeatedly: "Here I promise more adventures. Your Highness will have pity for me, and may also laugh while having pity" ["C'est ici que je promets des aventures, & que vôtre Altesse me va plaindre, & qu'elle rira peut-être aussi en me plaignant," ed. Cuénin 141, trans. Kuizenga 84]. She also exhorts herself at one point: "But that's enough of my defense of myself. Let us return to the story" ["laissons l'Apologie, & revenons au récit," ed. Cuénin 78, trans. Kuizenga 57]. In this quotation, the implied author not only maintains the twin goals of self-justification and entertainment, *apologie* and *récit*, but gives a higher priority to the latter. It is in part this imperative to keep the story moving, that gives the novel its kinetic urgency. Sylvie, like the Mancinis—and Villedieu herself—crisscrosses the map

---

[25]   Unlike Hortense's, Sylvie's interlocutor is a woman. In the introduction to her edition of the *Mémoires*, Cuénin suggests that the Altesse is Marie d'Orléans de Longueville, duchesse de Nemours, wife of Henri de Savoie and a friend of Villedieu (Cuénin iv).

[26]   Compare with Hortense's memoirs, which she addresses to the duc de Savoie "in gratitude, and to defend myself against slander, at least with those who have done us great favors" ["en reconnaissance … et pour se defendre contre la medisance, du moins auprès de ceux qui nous ont rendu de grands services," 31]. In addition, a prefatory dedication to "Son Altesse sérénissime … le duc de Zell, Brunswick et Lunebourg" (91) was added by Brémond (see Goldsmith 40).

of Europe, moving from France to Lorraine to Holland, back to France, and then to Brussels … . And this is far from a complete list. The longest respite in this frenzied itinerary comes at the end of part 1, when Sylvie spends two years in Brussels with her benefactress the marquise de Séville, but this time of "repos" is not described. In part 2, she continues the pattern of fleeing to and from the various châteaux, houses and, particularly, religious houses, where she is either being held prisoner or has sought refuge. It is only at the end of the novel that the possibility of a stable life is held out—within a convent.

The diverse roles convents played in the lives of early modern women—prison, asylum, boarding house, women's shelter, community—are all represented in *Les Mémoires de Henriette-Sylvie de Molière*. Convents seem to dot Villedieu's fictional landscape at close and convenient intervals: both "good" and "bad" *abbayes de filles* are located close to Sylvie's childhood home; and later in the novel, an erring Marquise dashes across her garden into a neighboring cloister, to escape her jealous husband (see below, 176). The important place that convents occupy in the novel is also attested to by lexical evidence: the word *abbaye* occurs at least nine times, *cloître* six times—and *couvent* 24 times.[27] The role of the conventual space evolves through the six volumes of the *Mémoires* from a surface plot element to a location for important encounters to, finally, a serious life option. A social outsider, Sylvie spends much of her time running to and from various prisons and refuges—some religious, others secular. In the process, she meets the women who will shelter and befriend her. It is noteworthy that of the five important women's friendships featured in the novel, two are with abbesses and a third with a woman residing in a convent.[28] After shooting her guardian, M. de Molière, in self-defense at the beginning of the *Mémoires*, Sylvie flees to the nearby Château de Sersac. This is not the best choice, since Sersac is the property of the Marquis de Birague, who is carrying on an affair with Mme de Molière. Worse, Birague in turn tries to seduce Sylvie. When she becomes aware of his intentions, however, she decides it is better to manipulate him to her advantage rather than to "commit a second murder" ["faire un second meurtre," ed. Cuénin 22, trans. Kuizenga 33].

Shortly after, Sylvie takes refuge in a nearby convent: "going to hide myself in a convent about a league from there" ["je m'allaye jeter dans une Abbaye de filles à une lieuë de-là," ed. Cuénin 25, trans. Kuizenga 34]. In this "Abbaye de filles," Sylvie becomes friendly with the superior, a worldly, "badine"[29] woman who shares laughs with Sylvie over Birague's love letters. After his wife finds out about the intrigue, however, Birague transfers Sylvie to the estate of the Comtesse d'Englesac: "He hid me only half a league from the convent, in a fortified

---

[27]   According to Cuénin's thematic index; my informal count is higher.

[28]   The two lay women are the marquise de Séville, whose legacy finally gives Sylvie financial independence, and Angélique, Sylvie's faithful companion in part 5. She also acquires the enmity of jealous women, but in my view this is overshadowed by her positive relationships.

[29]   On the various senses of *badine* ["lively," "playful," "wanton"], see Chapter 5, 241–2.

house that belonged to the Countess of Englesac, sister of *my friend* the abbess" ["Il m'alla cacher dans une maison forte de madame la Comtesse d'Englesac, soeur de *mon* Abbesse, qui n'étoit éloignée du couvent que d'une petite demi-lieuë," ed. Cuénin 27, trans. Kuizenga 35; italics added]. Thus, far from being an independent and separate sphere, *un monde à part*, the convent is linked by close extramural family connections to the larger world—a very important factor in this novel as in early modern Catholic society.

All goes well at the Chateau d'Englesac until the Comtesse's son falls in love with Sylvie and fights a duel over her. In reaction, Sylvie reports, d'Englesac's mother "had me shut up in a cloister the very next day" ["me fit dés le lendemain enlever dans un Cloître"], and orders her to be kept there without seeing anyone until she agrees to take vows. This strictly reformed convent is at the opposite pole from the first: "What I found even more upsetting about this was that it wasn't even the same convent where her sister was the abbess and where I could at least have hoped for some company. It was a convent—good God what a convent!—that was more like a horrible *prison* than anything else" ["Ce que j'y trouvai encore d'affligeant, fut que ce n'étoit pas le même lieu dont sa soeur était Abbesse, où j'eusse pû du moins espérer quelque société. C'étoit un couvent, bon Dieu: quel couvent! qui sembloit plutôt une affreuse *prison* que tout autre chose," ed. Cuénin 38, trans. Kuizenga 39; italics added]. The contrast between the "good" convent, where the comtesse's sister is abbess, and the "affreuse prison" seems borrowed from Hortense Mancini's memoirs (see above, 168–9).

However, Sylvie is again befriended by a nun. This time, it is a young woman who had been placed there against her will by her father, in order to keep the family fortune intact for her brother: "She was the daughter of the deceased Baron of Fontaine, who had followed the principle of the majority of the nobility and sacrificed his daughter to the convent in order to make his son richer" ["Elle éstoit fille du défunt baron de Fontaine, qui suivant la maxime de la plus grande partie de la noblesse en avait fait un sacrifice au Couvent pour rendre son fils plus riche," ed. Cuénin 43, trans. Kuizenga 42]. In a clearly parodic scene, Sylvie escapes by climbing over the garden walls with "*ma* religieuse" (ed. Cuénin 65; italics added) and her lover Fouquet—only to fall once again into the hands of her old pursuer Birague. And all these changes of venue take place within the first pages of a six-volume novel! At one point, Sylvie moves three times in the course of one page. This movement betokens the freedom of her life choices, the openness of the story and, finally, the porousness and negotiability of the convent—features that will be further developed as the novel unfolds.

One of the ways Villedieu keeps her heroine—and her story—on the move is by extending, twisting and, in the end, completely rejecting the conventional marriage plot.[30] The first two volumes of the novel, despite the multiplicity of episodes they contain, follow a fairly traditional pattern: two lovers are first separated by a series of obstacles, then seem set on a fair course for matrimony.

---

[30] On this point, see also Kuizenga, "Play of Pleasure" 148.

These obstacles include the opposition of d'Englesac's mother, whom Sylvie calls "une terrible dame" (ed. Cuénin 125); Sylvie's judicial pursuit for the death of her guardian; her fatal attraction for other men, including her evil genius Birague ["ce demon de Birague," ed. Cuénin 188] as well as new suitors; and the acquisition of a husband, the old, twice-married marquis de Menéze. At one point, when Menéze plans to carry her away and lock her up in one of his houses, Sylvie, like Hortense Mancini, escapes the country with her servant, both disguised as men.

Last but not least among the obstacles to a happy resolution of the plot, Sylvie's reckless and adventurous spirit keeps getting her into gratuitous trouble. One episode affords a rich example of many of these elements and their conventual implications. While Sylvie is hiding in Paris, her friend the abbesse d'Englesac reappears: "An important matter, which had to be pleaded at court, had temporarily brought her out of her cloister" ["Une affaire importante qu'il falloit solliciter à la Cour, l'avoit tirée pour un temps de son Cloître," ed. Cuénin 87, trans. Kuizenga 61]. The abbess "offered me the chance of retiring again to her abbey until I was able to work things out with my husband" ["elle m'offrit de me donner encore une retraite dans son Abbaye, jusqu'à ce que j'eusse fait mon accommodement avec mon mari," ed. Cuénin 91, trans. Kuizenga 62]. Again, the convent is identified as a temporary retreat for women undergoing marital difficulties. But Sylvie refuses this offer. Believing she will find "meilleur azile" in men's clothes than in a women's convent, Sylvie continues to impersonate a real German nobleman, the Prince de Salmes, even frequenting the court under Salmes's name, contrary to her friends' advice.

Predictably, this "comédie" leads to a "terrible dénouement" (100): a marquise falls in love with the false Salmes and demands concrete proof of "his" affection. The comte d'Anglesac obligingly agrees to satisfy the Marquise's desires, doubly disguised as Sylvie playing the false Salmes. This stratagem works well until one day, the marquise demands to see "Salmes" when d'Anglesac is not available, so Sylvie has to take his place. At this point, the marquis unexpectedly arrives to catch his wife in the act. The marquise escapes into a convent conveniently located across the garden; but Sylvie, still dressed in men's clothes, is caught on the scene by the marquis. He orders the unfortunate lover stripped, with the implied intent of emasculating "him": "The order was unusual; people can think what they like. A husband who does not kill right away sometimes takes strange forms of revenge" ["L'ordre étoit bizarre, chacun en peut penser ce qu'il voudra. Un mari qui ne tuë point d'abord, se vange quelquefois d'une étrange sorte," ed. Cuénin 109, trans. Kuizenga 71]. Before things can reach that point, Sylvie's masculine "cover" is removed, with the result that she must flee once more. Her undressing is literally her "undoing," an act through which she loses the metonymic shelter of male garb and identity she had believed would provide a more potent protection than convent walls. As a woman, she cannot be castrated; but she is symbolically "unmanned" and humiliated for taking on male identity.

Here as elsewhere, Villedieu introduces plot material that subverts traditional gender roles; but the subversion is kept within careful limits. Sexual farce functions as a safety valve, deflecting the possibility (or threat) of the homorerotic implications raised. Indeed, it is difficult to tease out the various strands of comedy, satire and picaresque entwined in this episode; nor is it the aim of the present study to do so.[31] Where conventual representation is concerned, however, two connected points can be made. First, the walls of the convent are effectively porous in two directions: both to the abbess who exits to do business and to the erring marquise who enters when running away from her husband.[32] Entangled in this very earth[l]y plot, the nuns act as go-betweens for the marquis and his wife when the marquise refuses (on good grounds) to believe that her lover is really a woman: "The oaths by which the marquis sought to persuade the nuns that he was telling the truth seemed to her to be so many traps he was setting" ["Les serments avec lesquels le Marquis tâchoit de persuader aux Religieuses qu'il disoit la vérité, lui sembloient autant de pièges qu'il lui tendoit," Cuénin 110–11, trans. Kuizenga 71]. Second, Sylvie, like the marquise, sees the convent as a possible *azile* on the same level as, and no different from, other means of refuge, whether they be houses, châteaux or the adoption of male clothing and identity.[33] Implicitly acknowledging the superior power of men, Sylvie had first chosen, or fallen under, male protection; but by this point in the story, both reader and narrator have begun to realize that shelter either within masculine walls (the château of the marquis de Birague) or dress (as the Prince de Salmes) does not provide the *lieu de seureté* she seeks; this will only be found at the very end of the novel, within an exclusively female space.[34]

---

[31]   On Henriette-Sylvie as *picara*, see Démoris's edition, 26; and Francis Assaf, "Henriette-Sylvie, objet du désir," *French Review* 73.3 (Feb. 2001): 518–26.

[32]   In "The Play of Pleasure," Donna Kuizenga amusingly lists all the disguises Sylvie uses to escape from the convent (149); but it is a place to run *to* as well as from.

[33]   The way in which Sylvie weaves the convent into her own escape plot is evident in part 5, when she spreads the rumor she will be entering the abbaye de St-Pierre in order to throw her pursuers off the track (Démoris 194).

[34]   The situation is somewhat more complex than this phrase indicates: after the fiasco with the Marquise, Sylvie has become too hot for a French convent to hold. D'Englesac places her instead with the duc de Guise: "the Count d'Englesac, having decided that I could not be safe in any cloister, had preferred entrusting me to the duke's magnanimity" ["Le Comte d'Englesac n'ayant pas jugé que je pûsse être assez en seureté en aucun Cloître, avoit mieux aimé me confier à la générosité du Duc," ed. Cuénin 112–13, trans. Kuizenga 72]. However, as Sylvie repeatedly experiences to her chagrin, the protection offered by the "magnanimity" of a strong male is precarious: male protection soon turns into *quid pro quo* demands. In another example from the end of the novel, Dom Pèdre, inviting Sylvie to his château, assures her that "I was as safe in this house as in the convent in Cologne. The abbess was not persuaded of this. She could not resign herself to abandoning me to the desires of a man who was in love with me and had absolute power over me" ["j'étois en aussi grande sureté dans cette maison que dans un Couvent de Cologne. C'étoit dequoi l'Abbesse n'étoit pas bien persuadée, elle ne pouvoit se resoudre de m'abandonner ainsi aux desirs d'un homme amoureux & absolu," ed. Cuénin 349–50, trans. Kuizenga 170]. Instead of being "protected," Sylvie is being held under house arrest by Dom Pèdre's own guards, "comme si j'eusse été prisonniere." As will be seen, true "seureté" is only afforded her by the double barriers of the German frontier and convent walls.

At this juncture in the plot, however, things seem to be looking up for Sylvie's marriage plans. By the end of part 2, after many more adventures, escapes and rescues, she learns of the fortunate death of her husband, the marquis de Menéze. And her friend (possibly her real mother), the marquise de Séville, gives Sylvie "a large portion of her wealth" ["une grande partie de ses biens"] to encourage the Count's family to accept the marriage (ed. Cuénin 116, trans. Kuizenga 74). The story appears set for a happy ending at this point; in fact, the first edition of 1671 was marked FIN at the end of part 2. But there are still four parts to go; and at the beginning of part 3, Sylvie promises the "Altesse" to whom her memoirs are addressed that Englesac will have "a number of adventures worthy of my own" ["Elle vouloit qu'il meritât d'estre mon Heros par une infinité d'autres traverses," ed. Cuénin 119, trans. Kuizenga 73] before resolution is achieved.[35] In an effort to keep her reader entertained, Villedieu continually ups the ante on bizarre and shocking adventures: if part 2 features gender-bending women dressed as men, fighting duels and entering male monasteries, part 3 moves on to scenes of sorcery and black magic which Sylvie herself terms "ridicule" (ed. Cuénin 151–3).[36] More important, the marriage plot is further parodied and subverted. By this point, Sylvie's life of flight and pursuit has been going on for six years, and the reader's remaining hopes that a marriage will soon take place are once again frustrated. However, Sylvie promises at the end of part 3: "I will recount to Your Highness all the things we had to endure before this marriage could be happily accomplished" ["Je rendray compte à vôtre Altesse, dans une quatriéme, de tout ce qu'il nous fallut encore essuyer avant que ce mariage fût accomply heureusement," ed. Cuénin 178, trans. Kuizenga 98].

The marriage does in fact take place in part 4; but at the beginning, rather than, as one might expect, as an "heureuse" conclusion to the volume. After all the waiting and buildup, the wedding is performed quickly, in secret; and the account itself, occupying less then three lines of text, is hidden away at the end of a long sentence: "... with the help of some friends whom we had to let in on the secret, we were married without the knowledge of the Countess of Englesac and with no ceremony" ["... par les soins de quelques amis, qu'il fallut mettre du secret, nous épousâmes à l'insceu de la Comtesse d'Englesac, & sans aucune ceremonie," 179, trans. Kuizenga 99]. In fact, one must read and reread the first few pages of part 4 just to find where the so-called happy event is recorded. Furthermore, the author's promise—and the generic premise—of a traditional happy ending are not fulfilled. As the brief account of the wedding seems to predict, the marriage begins to fall apart almost as soon as it is celebrated. Her mother-in-law the countess, still furious, plots to have the marriage annulled and to put Sylvie back in a convent. D'Englesac had already shown himself a suspicious and somewhat fickle lover

---

[35]   On the relationships between narrator, reader and dedicatee see Kuizinga, "La Lecture d'une si ennuyeuse histoire."

[36]   Catherine Hoffmann reports in *Society of Pleasures* that in 1685 a woman dressed in men's clothes killed a man who had jilted her—an interesting parallel to Sylvie's account.

before the marriage; at one point, in a fit of jealous pique, he had left Sylvie to join the army and had even been reported dead (195). Resurrected for the wedding, he fails to come up to conjugal expectations: Sylvie complains that d'Englesac "was married to no purpose" ["se trouva marié inutilement," ed. Cuénin 180, trans. Kuizenga 99].[37] And soon after the marriage, Sylvie reports that d'Englesac "became tired of me, as is usual" among married men ["(il) se dégouta comme c'est la coûtume," ed. Cuénin 195, trans. Kuizenga 105–6].

Tired of his coldness, suspicion and "scornful glances" ["regards méprisants," ed. Cuénin 211], Sylvie finally falls out of love with the Comte, musing: "There is no heart so constant that it cannot in the end be put off by persistent disdain, and to hide nothing from Your Highness, I was becoming quite indifferent to the Count of Englesac" ["il n'y a point de coeur si constant, qu'un mépris opiniâtre ne puisse à la fin rebuter; & pour ne rien celer à Vôtre Altesse, le Comte d'Englesac me devenoit fort indifferent," ed. Cuénin 219, trans. Kuizenga 117]. At the beginning of part 5, d'Englesac goes off to war again, this time dying for real. His widow is left to deal with the "persecutions" of her mother-in-law and the aspiring heirs to d'Englesac's estate—hardly the romantic denouement one would wish for. The lame ending to their drawn-out relationship has the effect of minimizing the importance of marriage in Sylvie's life, and, by extension, in women's lives in general. This anti-marriage strategy had already been self-consciously revealed by the narrator much earlier, in a passing allusion to Louis XIV's marriage to Maria Teresa of Austria. Although la marquise de Séville had attended the wedding ceremony at the Spanish border, near the town where Sylvie was staying, a meeting between her and Sylvie did not take place: "The marriage of the king *was not the end of a novel* in which all the heroic characters find themselves reunited. On the contrary, it was the reason why she did not think of coming back to look for me in Toulouse …" ["Le mariage du Roi *n'étoit pas une conclusion de Roman*, où tous les personnages héroïques se dussent retrouver; & au contraire cela fut cause qu'elle ne put point s'aviser de me venir chercher à Thoulouze … ," ed. Cuénin 56, trans. Kuizenga 48; italics added]. Rather than a resolution to Sylvie's and the novel's problems, the royal marriage merely constitutes another obstacle.

After Sylvie's story moves beyond the "marriage plot," the "convent plot" begins to take on a central position. The convent had already been implicated in the novelistic structure as more than a simple refuge/prison alternative. For example, in a subplot of part 3, a monastery is used as a "bank" where money or documents left Sylvie by the duc de Candale are held in escrow for her:[38] "the duke himself

---

[37] A "charm" has supposedly been laid upon d'Englesac, rendering him impotent: see *Mémoires* 180, 193–4 (ed. Cuénin).

[38] This use of a monastery as a safety deposit recurs in Tencin's *Mémoires du Comte de Comminges*: papers establishing the comte's father's rights to a disputed family legacy are kept in the archives of an abbey (17). In the case of the *Mémoires of the Life of Henriette-Sylvie de Molière*, the narrative leaves ambiguous whether the deposit consists of money or papers. While the *l'* in the quotation from page 127 appears to refer to *l'argent*, we read

had put it into the hands of a monk belonging to the Chartreuse de Villeneuve who had been at that time the procurator of the monastery and … this Carthusian monk had promised to give it to me if it happened that my father the financier did not make the best use of it" ["le Duc, lui-même, l'avait mis en dépost entre les mains d'un Religieux de la Chartreuse de Villeneuve, pour lors Procureur[39] de la Maison; & que ce Chartreux avait promis de me le donner, s'il arrivoit que mon pere le Financier[40] n'en usât pas bien," ed. Cuénin 127, trans. Kuizenga 78]. As the novel progresses, the convent is transformed from a depository or a refuge into an important setting: in its parlors, encounters take place which are essential to the plot. Even the austere, prison-like couvent d'Avignon is not free from social involvement. While Sylvie is living there, a visit from the king and court temporarily transforms the convent parlor into an extension of the political and social world: "This meant that all the gallant men of the court spread out through the area, and that the inhabitants of the convents found their parlors inundated with a large share of these courtiers" ["Cela fit que tous les galants de la Cour se répandirent de côté et d'autre, et que les parloirs des dames religieuses eurent part à cette inondation de courtesans," ed. Cuénin 38, trans. Kuizenga 40]. The metaphors *se répandirent* and *inondation* express how male secular power flows over the convent walls, flooding the feminine religious space.

Interestingly, the relaxation of the rules restricting parlor visits is a tribute to the visit of the most powerful representative of secular society, Louis XIV: "The moments of freedom that the nuns had allowed themselves to take in the parlor since the king's entrance into the city were, as I have already said, contrary to the rules of the order—an extraordinary gesture intended to honor this monarch" ["les momens de liberté qu'on se dispensoit de prendre aux Parloirs contre la regle, depuis l'entrée du Roi; & c'éstoit, comme j'ai déjà dit, pour honorer ce Monarque par quelque chose d'extraordinaire," ed. Cuénin 43, trans. Kuizenga 42]. These "momens de liberté" create an unforgettable interlude in the residents' dreary lives, especially for the young women: "I will always remember this stay of the court in Avignon. It gave so much joy to the youngest of these poor nuns" ["Je me souviendrai même toûjours de ce passage de la Cour à Avignon, qui donna tant de joïe à ces pauvres Recluses," ed. Cuénin 39, trans. Kuizenga 40]. These moments of exhilarating freedom also lead to more serious infractions of convent rules. Among the "assailants de nos parloirs" (ed. Cuénin 40; Kuizenga does not translate this literally) who take advantage of the unusual circumstances is a

---

shortly after: "I left the next day to go to the Chartreuse to get *my document*. It was indeed there, and they gave it to me; I then went and gave it to the people in the court, to begin the first steps in the lawsuit" ["je partis le jour suivant pour aller à la Chartreuse demander *mon papier*, que j'y trouvai, qui me fut rendu, & que je revins donner aux gens du Palais, pour en faire les premières poursuites," ed. Cuénin 131, trans. Kuizenga 80; italics added].

[39]   The monk responsible for the temporal affairs of the monastery ["le religieux chargé des intérêts temporels de la maison," ed. Cuénin 127].

[40]   *Financier*: i.e., Sylvie's foster father, M. de Molière.

certain Fouquet, who convinces the baron de Fontaine's daughter to run away with him—hence, as we have seen, enabling Sylvie's escape as well.

This romanticized episode is not the only one where the world intrudes into the convent parlor: during a stay at the Abbey where d'Englesac's aunt is the superior, Sylvie encounters not only her lover's mother, the comtesse d'Englesac, who is, after all, sister to the abbess, but also the girl whom the comtesse wishes her son to marry instead. According to Sylvie, this unwelcome parlor encounter with her rival was one of the most uncomfortable moments in a life full of difficult scenes. Not a word was spoken: "We took turns looking each other over disdainfully from head to foot, so much had our reciprocal anger (at finding in the other someone to fear) silenced us and made us jealous" ["nous ne faisions que nous examiner dédaigneusement, & tour à tour, depuis la teste jusqu'aux pieds; tant la colere reciproque de nous trouver toutes deux à craindre, nous avoit renduës interdites & jalouses," ed. Cuénin 132, trans. Kuizenga 80]. As Sylvie rather maliciously reports, her rival contracts smallpox shortly after this visit and dies, not from the disease itself, but from the shock of losing her beauty (133).[41]

A final set of convent intrusions takes place late in the novel. Sylvie has gone to visit a friend who is a boarder at the Abbaye de S. Pierre in Lyon. Although she does not reside in the convent, Sylvie spends most of her time there, consoling herself for her problems by abusing the male sex in conversation with her friend: "She had hardly any more reason to praise men that [*sic*] I did, and we spent whole days strengthening the hatred we had for them" ["Elle n'avoit guère plus de suiet de se louër des hommes, que moy, & nous passions les iournées entières à nous fortifier dans la haine que nous leur devions," ed. Cuénin 242, trans. Kuizenga 126]. But the parlor also receives male guests. When an acquaintance of a resident nun calls, the portress sends him in while Sylvie is visiting. The account of this event is more evocative of a worldly *salon* than of a convent parlor: "One day we were talking like this when the Count of Tavanes, who was in Lyon and who knew the nun of whom I speak, came and asked to see her. A *tourière* sent him to the parlor where we were. …" ["Nous nous entretenions un jour de cette sorte, quand le Comte de Tavanes, qui étoit à Lyon, et qui connaissoit fort la Religieuse dont je parle, vint demander à la voir. Une Tourriere l'envoya au Parloir, où nous étions … ," ed. Cuénin 242, trans. Kuizenga 126]. We later learn that the nun in question is his "ancienne amie" who engages in a plot to win Sylvie for Tavannes. In her present mood, Sylvie is almost as impatient of male intrusions into the convent parlor as a strict Mother Superior would be: "The next day I told my friend that if her parlor became open to everyone in this way, she would rarely see me there" ["Je mandai

---

[41]   Cuénin suggests that the disfigurement of Sylvie's rival is a kind of literary wish-fulfillment on the part of Villedieu, who herself was marked by smallpox; but the light tone and implausibility of this episode make it difficult to take it seriously. Villedieu did not die (or kill herself) as a result of smallpox, but lived on to playfully use her life material in her fiction.

le lendemain à mon amie, que si son parloir devenoit ainsi commun à tout le monde, elle ne m'y verroit plus guère," ed. Cuénin 243, trans. Kuizenga 126].

Another male acquaintance, the chevalier de la Mothe, pursues Sylvie with his unwelcome advances into sacred territory: "He followed me to every church. He was constantly on my route to the abbey" ["(il) me suivoit à toutes les Eglises; il étoit incessamment sur le chemin de ma maison à l'Abbaye," ed. Cuénin 253, trans. Kuizenga 130]. When she ignores him, he becomes bolder, breaking all rules of religious propriety:

> ... one day when I was at the abbey for the investiture of a nun, which I had to attend, he found a way to have a seat near mine. Without any respect for the holiness of the place, he talked to me of love. ... I looked at him with a proud air and told him imperiously that he should find someone else to address his gallantries to, which he did not dare continue. He remained embarrassed and left before the end of the ceremony.

> ... un jour que j'étois à l'Abbaye à la Vesture d'une fille, où je n'avois pû me dispenser d'aller, il trouva moyen d'avoir une chaîne [i.e. chaise] auprés de la mienne, & sans respect pour la sainteté du Lieu, il me parla de son amour. ... Je le regardai d'un air si fier, & lui dis si imperieusement qu'il cherchât une autre pour ses galanteries, qu'il n'osa les pousser plus loin; & demeurant tout confus, il sortit avant la fin de la Ceremonie. (ed. Cuénin 254, trans. Kuizenga 131)

In part, the preceding incidents demonstrate that Sylvie's attractions will fatally draw lovers to her no matter where she goes: "it is undoubtedly written in the stars that, despite what I wish, suitors will make problems for me all my life" ["il est sans doute écrit dans le Ciel, que malgré moi les Amans me feront toute ma vie des affaires," ed. Cuénin 272, trans. Kuizenga 138]. But they also point to a final important aspect of the convent: the female relationships that Sylvie develops and maintains there. From the beginning, she uses the possessive pronoun "my" [*mon abbesse, ma religieuse*] to refer to the friendly nuns who help her along her way. This unconscious appropriation of a cloistered individual, supposedly living a life apart from the world, emphasizes the extent to which the convent is imbricated into the social life of the latter seventeenth century—an imbrication so great that it is unstated and requires no explanation for contemporary readers, many of whom have cousins, sisters or aunts living a cloistered life. The first of Sylvie's friendly nuns is the abbesse d'Englesac, the Superior of the Abbaye de Filles, where Sylvie stays early in the novel. Almost immediately, Sylvie reports: "I had struck up a close friendship with the abbess of this convent" ["Madame l'Abbesse, avec qui j'avois contracté une étroite amitié," ed. Cuénin 25, trans. Kuizenga 34]. As already noted, this character reappears twice in the story.

Her return is not unusual: the recirculation of characters is a main structural feature of the novel, providing continuity through myriad changes of setting. However, the convent governed by the abbesse d'Englesac is practically the only *place* that recurs often. After her initial stay there in part 1, Sylvie returns to the Abbaye in part 2 for a longer period, not to seek asylum but to visit her friend. She underlines the close, reciprocal intimacy she shares with the abbess: "I was so fortunate to find her still of good will towards me, and to have in her someone to whom I could talk sometimes about my unhappy love, for *she was my confidante and I was hers*" ["J'étois trop heureuse de la retrouver toûjours bien intentionnée pour moi, & d'avoir en elle, avec qui parler quelquefois du malheur de mes Amours; *car elle étoit ma confidente & j'étois la sienne*," ed. Cuénin 131, trans. Kuizenga 80; italics added]. This friendship threatens to take on an erotic note when the abbesse d'Englesac becomes attracted to the cross-dressed Sylvie; but again, the narrator pulls back from this path in time, asserting that the abbess's *galanterie* is verbal rather than actual.

Sylvie's encounter with the abbesse de Cologne at the end of part 5 ushers in a focus on convent voices that will dominate the end of the novel. The interchanges between Sylvie and the abbesse de Cologne provide our best chance to hear women reflecting on the advantages of the cloister vis-à-vis the outside world. Sylvie meets the abbess at Spa, where she is presumably taking the waters with "two very pretty nuns" ["deux religieuses très bien faites," ed. Cuénin 294, trans. Kuizenga 148]. This phrase aside, the depiction of the abbesse de Cologne lacks the playfully satiric tone with which Sylvie describes most other characters, even nuns: the abbess is "a reasonable and charming person" ["une raisonnable et engageante personne"] whom she wishes "Son Altesse" could meet one day (ed. Cuénin 297, trans. Kuizenga 149). In an exalted style reminiscent of Mme de Chartres's speeches to her daughter in *La Princesse de Clèves*, the abbess exhorts Sylvie to seek the protection of the cloister for her own safety and peace of mind: "You will see that a misfortune will occur that will reduce you to despair. Do not wait for this extremity. Retire with me to my solitude, and shelter yourself from the storms that threaten you" ["vous verrez qu'il surviendra quelque nouveau malheur qui vous fera sentir tous les autres, & qui vous reduira au désespoir; n'attendez pas cette extremité, retirez-vous avec moi dans ma solitude, & venez vous y mettre à couvert de tous les orages qui pourroient vous arriver," ed. Cuénin 301, trans. Kuizenga 151].

In her response, Sylvie expresses for the first time religious or moral scruples about entering a convent for expediency alone: "It seemed to me shameful to leave the world because I was unhappy in it. I wanted my retreat to be a choice dictated by my heart and not by necessity" ["il me sembloit qu'il étoit honteux de quitter le monde, parce que j'y étois malheureuse, & j'aurois voulu que ma retraite eût été un choix de mon coeur, & non pas une necessité"]. This statement shows a very different attitude from the lighthearted convent-hopping she and other women characters engage in repeatedly throughout the novel. In a striking reversal of expectations, it is the abbess who puts personal happiness rather than religious vocation at the center of the choice of a religious life: "She criticized my reasoning and told me it was a false pretext for continuing to run around the world. She said that one would hardly leave the world if one could live happily in it" ["Elle se mocquoit de ma delicatesse, & me disoit que c'étoit un faux pretexte pour demeurer encore dans le monde: qu'on ne quittoit guere quand on pouvoit y vivre heureuse"]. Whether happy or not, Sylvie is still reluctant to leave the outside world at this point; she states frankly, "I would have preferred the inheritance Mme de Seville left me to life in retreat" ["j'aurois mieux aimé le bien que Madame de Seville m'avoit laissé, qu'une retraite"]. But she agrees to accompany the abbess to Cologne because the convent offers her "a present resource" ["une ressource presente"] in an uncertain situation. Thus, Sylvie falls back upon convent residence as a temporary and reversible expedient: "I accepted it, therefore, with the intention of leaving if Fortune became more favorable to me" ["c'étoit à faire à la quitter, si la fortune me devenoit plus favorable"].[42]

Sylvie's insistence on an easy exit from the Cologne convent reflects a "claustrophobic" fear, based on her real experience in Avignon, of being locked up behind monastery walls. She explains in a key passage:

> I still looked at the necessity of retiring to a convent as a misfortune. It was not that I did not really love my abbess, and that in any place other than a cloister I would not have considered myself happy to spend my days with her, but the word *cloister* frightened me. I still remembered the sorrows I had had in my old convent, and I imagined I would have as many in all the other convents where I might find myself.

> … je regardois encore comme un nouveau malheur, la necessité de me retirer au Couvent où je m'allois. Ce n'étoit pas que je n'aimasse veritablement mon Abbesse, … mais ce mot de Cloître me faisoit peur. Je me souvenois encor des chagrins que j'avois eus dans mon ancien Couvent; & je m'imaginois toûjours que j'en aurois autant dans tous les Convens où je serois. (Ed. Cuénin 305, trans. Kuizenga 152; italics in translation.)

In retrospect, however, she characterizes her imaginings as "weakness." In a foreshadowing of the ending, she remarks: "I was mad to imagine these things … and I admit that I never did a better thing than to follow the abbess's advice" ["J'étois pourtant une folle d'avoir ces imaginations … & j'avouë que je ne fis jamais mieux que de suivre les conseils de l'Abbesse"].

Unsurprisingly, however, given the previous structure of the novel, Sylvie's journey and tale do not reach their conventual closing by the most direct route. As she puts it, "We did not take the shortest route" ["Nous ne prîmes pas le chemin le plus court"] to reach Cologne, but stopped on the way to visit friends of the abbess at a Collège de Chanoinesses in nearby Maubeuge (ed. Cuénin 302, trans. Kuizenga 151). This episode, which occupies most of part 6, gives Villedieu the opportunity to explore an alternative mode of religious life for women. Like the better-known Béguinages, the Collèges were informal women's religious communities whose members were not bound by vows of stability to remain within a convent enclosure.[43] Béguinages and Collèges were most prevalent in

---

[42]   All quotations in this paragraph are drawn from Cuénin 301–2, trans. Kuizenga 151.

[43]   Rapley, *Les Dévotes* 95. There is abundant literature on béguinages and other alternate religious communities for women. See for example Brenda Bolton, "Mulieres

northern France, Germany and the Low Countries—Bolton counts at least 298 béguinages founded in the Netherlands before 1566 (48)—but they also existed in Provence. There were even male communities of Beghards or Béguins, but the great majority were female. The origin of the Béguines was popular and informal. They had no real founder; but like other thirteenth-century religious women who were rejected by the regular orders, they formed groups around leaders or spiritual guides. One such leader was Jacques de Vitry, protector of a group of Béguines in the diocese of Liège in present-day Belgium. Unlike many clerics, Jacques de Vitry interested himself in the situation of religious women, and even traveled to Italy to visit the *humiliati* (a similar group living in Milan), and the Poor Clares in Umbria. He did not consider these women heretical, and was impressed by their dedication to poverty and prayer. The Béguines whom he sponsored in Liège were members of what we now might call a "grass-roots" urban movement. Unlike the regular convent orders, the Béguine population was socially and economically diverse;[44] while women of more affluent classes bought their own houses to share, others lived in a room in a Béguine community or "court" (Simons 100–101). Many Béguines supported themselves by their own labor in the new textile crafts, and helped meet the needs of the new urban populations they served. Other male clerics, like Bishop Fulk of Toulouse, admired the Béguines and protected them to some degree. The risks of the Hundred Years' War in Northern France caused some Béguines to flee their communities and take refuge in regular houses (Labarge 120). Béguines did not come under the control of the edicts of Trent which dealt only with *moniales* (nuns taking solemn vows). The bull *Circa Pastoralis*, issued in 1566 by Pope Pius V, tried to tighten up this loophole by ordering all women religious to take solemn rather than simple vows and to submit to enclosure. While the Béguine courts died out in France in the seventeenth century, women's communities whose members worked outside found a more favorable environment in the North; some béguinages continued to function in Germany and the Low Countries up to recent times. Among the best-known and most beautiful are the béguinages of Bruges, Ghent and Anvers, which can still be visited. Bruges became a Benedictine convent in 1937, but a small number of Béguines still live in Saint-Amandsberg, near Ghent.

Chanoinesses or canonesses, like Béguines, are women who live together in religious community without taking formal vows; but the higher social level of the canonesses may explain Villedieu's choice of a Collège de Chanoines over

sanctae," in Susan Mosher Stuard ed. *Women in Medieval Society* (Philadelphia: University of Pennsylvania Press, 1976), 125–40; Margaret Wade Labarge, *A Small Sound of the Trumpet: Women in Medieval Life* (Boston: Beacon Press, 1986); Walter Simons, *Cities of Ladies: Beguine Communities in the Medieval Low Countries, 1200–1565* (Philadelphia: University of Pennsylvania Press, 2001). The second half of the seventeenth century also saw the creation of numerous uncloistered *congrégations actives* in France, but most of these were teaching orders which play no role in Villedieu's novel.

[44] "Virtually all these [traditional] orders accepted only noble ladies and women of patrician families; commoners did not have a place there, except as lay sisters" (Simons 110).

a Béguinage for Sylvie's visit. Whatever the real level of religious commitment among canonesses might have been, Sylvie's representation of the Collège de Maubeuge is completely secularized. Since canonesses, unlike regular nuns, take no vows "contre le mariage," they are free to receive male suitors, chaperoned only by one "sociable" female companion. These visits are legitimized because they are supposed to lead to marriage ["en vûë d'un marriage," ed. Cuénin 307]; but as Sylvie shrewdly points out, not every courtship ends in matrimony, and the line between legitimate courting and simple flirtation can easily be crossed.

This flirtation with secularity is a constant theme in the life stories recounted by the women at Maubeuge. Their reasons for ending up in a convent are varied and colorful: while one, like Sylvie, is on the run from threatened imprisonment, most fall into the category of "ill-starred lovers" ["amantes infortunées"] whose love affairs had gone awry. The first story concerns a flirtatious canoness who has resided in the Collège for a long time. Her lover is a soldier, and her father did not allow her to marry him before he went off to war in Spain. The canoness, again like Sylvie, receives false news of her betrothed's death in battle. Before learning that he indeed is alive but in prison, she begins receiving other suitors, which is hardly the behavior of an inconsolable fiancée. The lover naturally returns, and the resulting imbroglio is still going on when Sylvie leaves Maubeuge.

A second *amante infortunée* is the Abbess of Cologne herself, whose story we now hear for the first time. The abbess, who belongs to an aristocratic German family, was engaged to a man she loved, but was tricked by her uncle and mother into marrying someone else. Upon discovering this subterfuge, she refuses to consummate the marriage; in Villedieu's playfully allusive style, "our new bride … was not, however a wife" ["notre nouvelle mariée … n'était point pourtant la femme de son mari," ed. Cuénin 327, trans. Kuizenga 161]. After two months of this situation, her repentant husband himself escorts her to the convent of Cologne where her aunt is abbess. The young woman's former fiancé also renounces the marriage planned for him, although he does not become a monk. His beloved, however, holds firm to her intention of taking the veil and eventually becomes the new Abbess of Cologne, succeeding her aunt.

The abbess's story again highlights the importance of family power on both sides of the convent walls. The abbess stands out among the *Mémoires'* other, all-too-human characters as a kind of "beau idéal" of the virtuous woman. As her former fiancé says, "by a privilege that Heaven has given you, you are a wife, a lover, and a nun, without failing in any of your duties" ["par un privilège que le ciel n'a jamais donné qu'à vous, vous vous trouvez femme, amante, et Religieuse, sans manquer à aucun de vos devoirs," ed. Cuénin 329, trans. Kuizenga 162]. It is significant that in this view, the *devoirs* of *femme* and *amante* are not annulled or superseded by the state of *religieuse*. In fact, when the abbess learns that her lover has been injured during the siege of Cologne, she is eager to come to his aid: "She was all the more impatient to do so since her wounded friend was still very ill, and it seemed to her that if she went in person to contribute to his recovery she would see his health restored all the sooner" ["Elle en avoit d'autant plus d'impatience, que son Ami blessé étoit toûjours fort malade, & qu'il lui sembloit que si elle alloit en personne faire travailler à sa guerison, elle verroit sa santé plutôt rétablie," ed. Cuénin 347–8, trans. Kuizenga 169]. In case readers find a nun rushing to her lover's side implausible, the narrator cites the story's resemblance to that of "une fameuse Abbesse de France" whose identity, if authentic, no one has yet discovered.

In contrast, the third Maubeuge story falls back into the familiar "in-out" pattern of Villedieu's narrative. It is told by Sylvie's friend, whom she had visited earlier at the Abbaye de St-Pierre in Lyon. Jilted by her lover, she had retreated into a convent with the intent of remaining there permanently. Sylvie encourages her in this aim: "For even though I do not like convents, I find them very happy places for those who like them, and I willingly advocate convents to those who can stay in them without great displeasure" ["Car encore que je n'aime pas les Convens, je les trouve très-heureux pour qui les aime, & je les conseille volontiers aux personnes qui peuvent y demeurer sans grande repugnance," ed. Cuénin 334, trans. Kuizenga 164]. These words reveal a very pragmatic, non-ideological attitude toward convent life. It is a very individual matter, depending both on the nature of the religious house and the disposition of the inhabitant. In any case, the young woman's plan is abandoned when the former fiancé arrives and effects a reconciliation. She begins meeting him in town "on the pretext of business" ["sur quelques pretextes d'affaires," ed. Cuénin 335, trans. Kuizenga 164]. When her parents find out, they plan to abduct her and shut her up "entre quatre murailles" (ed. Cuénin 336), presumably in a strictly enclosed convent; but she escapes and makes her way to Flanders. While there, she pays a visit to the Collège de Maubeuge where she is reunited with Sylvie.

What is most striking about conventual representation in these three tales, as well as in the novel as a whole, is the degree to which clausura is treated as irrelevant. In reality, the Council of Trent's edict on strict enclosure of women had led to serious conventual reforms in France in the early seventeenth century. Clausura was imposed on existing convents, and many new, stricter orders were created or imported. Some of these reforms were initiated by religious women themselves before the French church hierarchy even demanded them: for example, on the famous Journée des Guichets in 1609, Angélique Arnauld, the sixteen-year-old Superior of Port Royal, refused entry to members of her own family. As we have seen, by 1650, the first wave of Catholic Reformation fervor had diminished and the number of alternative forms of women's religious community had grown. Nevertheless, for both satirical and ideological reasons, Villedieu probably exaggerates the freedom enjoyed in seventeenth-century convents. This combination of satire and social message requires a careful balancing act. On the one hand, glimpses of convent goings-on are a sure source of entertainment for her readers. On the other hand, the satire always stops at the edge of sexual taboos, perhaps because of an intent to portray the convent in a mainly favorable light, as a sometimes viable, and not overly restrictive, place for women.

Thus, of the three ladies whose stories are told in part 6, the first leads a full life within a very loosely structured religious community, and the two who are supposedly cloistered do not remain in their convents, but move about with apparent ease. We are never told why the abbesse de Cologne went to Spa with her three attractive companions—presumably to take the waters, but afterwards she seems free to prolong her absence from her convent indefinitely. She first visits Sylvie on the rather flimsy excuse that she is waiting for her coach, then stops at the Collège de Maubeuge to see friends. When she is kept out of Cologne by a prolonged siege, the abbess finally becomes impatient to return, but not because she fears reprisals for her absence; when Sylvie tries to persuade her that "one should always stretch out one's reasons for traveling as long as possible, she answered that she had much business at home" ["il faut alonger autant qu'on peut les permissions de voyager, elle me répondit qu'elle avoit des affaires chez elle," ed. Cuénin 306, trans. Kuizenga 153].

Finally, Sylvie's friend from L'Abbaye de S. Pierre is on the run from possible detention, but seems under no immediate danger while at the Collège de Maubeuge. However, her arrival in Maubeuge serves to put the plot and Sylvie in motion again; Sylvie's true identity is revealed, and it is time for "mon Abbesse et moi" (ed. Cuénin 339) to leave. Yet the Collège de Maubeuge is more than a respite between adventures. While much has been written about the *Mémoires* as Sylvie's apprenticeship in love and independence, critics have generally passed over her *apprentissage du couvent*.[45] The protracted episode at the Collège de Maubeuge affords an opportunity for Sylvie to learn about the lives and feelings of women choosing a cloistered life, a fate she had long feared. In this way, the episode psychologically prepares the denouement of the novel.

After a last series of adventures, Sylvie arrives at the Abbaye de Cologne to await the delivery of a long-disputed inheritance from the marquise de Séville. Significantly, the fortune establishing her independence comes not from her legitimate husbands, but from a woman friend. A Flemish marquis, who had helped her gain her rights, would have escorted her anywhere, but Sylvie persists in visiting the Abbaye de Cologne to prove that the abbess's faith in her had been justified: "I wanted to see our abbess again and make her understand by the rectitude of my conduct that she had not been wrong in having such a favorable opinion of me" ["je voulois revoir nôtre Abbesse, et lui faire connôitre par l'honnêteté de mes procedez, qu'elle ne s'étoit pas trompée, quand elle avoit fait de moi un jugement si favorable," ed. Cuénin 368, trans. Kuizenga 178]. The legacy gives her the long-desired freedom to live

---

[45]   The only article I have found on this subject is Nicole Boursier's "La retraite au couvent dans les *Mémoires de Henriette-Sylvie de Molière* et *La Princesse de Clèves*," in *Topiques du dénouement romanesque du XIIe au XVIIe siècle*, ed. Colette Piau Gillot. Boursier identifies four basic conventual *topoi*: *couvent-débarras*, *cloître-prison*, *couvent-asile* and *maison religieuse-hôtel*. All four of these functions are present in the *Mémoires*, but the last two are more prominent, which again distinguishes Villedieu from most (male) authors of convent fiction.

comfortably as she wishes: "I find myself able to lead a quiet and rather comfortable life in whatever circumstances I might choose" ["je me trouve en état de mener une vie tranquille & assez aisée, dans quelque condition que je vëuille choisir," ed. Cuénin 375, trans. Kuizenga 181]. Unlike the explicitly religious reflections surrounding Mme de Clèves's retreat, the "vie tranquille" sought by Sylvie does not appear to entail anything beyond financial security and freedom from judicial and amorous pursuit.[46] Yet rather than returning to the world, as she predicted she would do if she had the means, Sylvie opts to stay on in the Abbaye de Cologne. A statement by Adrienne Zuerner, referring to crossdressing in the *Mémoires*, also perfectly describes the evolution and denouement of the convent plot: "what begins as an act motivated by necessity becomes one of agency and conscious choice" (105). Earlier, Sylvie had expressed her reluctance to enter a convent out of "necessité" (Cuénin 302–3). In the end, she stays of her own free will.

The abbess had not expected this decision either: she had remarked to Sylvie "that if by some event that she could not predict I could settle my affairs, I would have only less desire to retire to a convent" ["que si par quelque revers qu'elle (l'Abbesse) ne prévoyoit pas, je pouvois venir à bout de mes affaires, je n'en aurois que moins d'envie de me retirer dans un couvent," ed. Cuénin 302, trans. Kuizenga 151]. But Sylvie's fears concerning the cloistered life have not been realized: "I find it sweet. The convent no longer seems what it had appeared to be from a distance" ["Je la trouve douce, le Couvent ne me paroît plus ce qu'il m'avoit paru dans une vûë éloignée," ed. Cuénin 375–6, trans. Kuizenga 181]. Since her choice is a free one, her status in the cloister, as well as the actual length of her stay, remain indeterminate. The telescoped ending of the novel affords no description of Sylvie's life there; but words that would indicate a formal and final commitment to a religious community, such as "becoming a nun," "taking the veil" or "taking vows," are conspicuously absent from the narrative. On the contrary, Sylvie's "vow of instability" contains the proviso "should I remain in my present state of mind" ["si je continüe dans l'humeur où je suis," ed. Cuénin 375, trans. Kuizenga 181]. Although in her "present state of mind" she finds convent life "sweet," her options and the convent door are left open. If Sylvie's "humeur" should change again as it had in the past, Sylvie might walk out that door—and add a sequel to her memoirs.

Thus, while it is chronologically true, as Micheline Cuénin states, that Sylvie "retires into a convent after the death of her lover" ["se retire dans un couvent après la mort de son ami," v], this rather conventional phrase leaves a doubly false impression. Sylvie does not retire from the world in order to mourn her dead love. On the contrary, her experiences have left her completely disillusioned with men: "since in the mood I was in I hated lovers in the form of husbands just as much as in any other form" ["car de l'humeur dont j'étois, je haïssais autant les Amants sous la forme d'un mari, que sous une autre," ed. Cuénin 330, trans. Kuizenga 162]. Instead, as we have already seen, at the end of the novel Sylvie reserves

---

[46]   For a different view, see Assaf 325.

her "tendresse" for other women.[47] The romantic "amante infortunée" scenario developed in the convent tales in part 6 does not apply to her; in fact, the narrator seems to introduce this scenario only to dramatize her own divergence from it. Nor does Sylvie convert to piety and take the veil. Her reasons for choosing the convent, like those of the nuns whose stories she has heard, have little to do with religion and everything to do with the life options available to women in the seventeenth century.[48] For these women, as for most women throughout the ages, life centers on love, marriage and family ties; and as Villedieu shows, these ties are attenuated, but not destroyed, upon passing through the convent gate. The abbesse de Cologne had asserted that "one would hardly leave the world if one could live happily in it" (Kuizenga 151); but by choosing a religious house where they have relatives or close friends, women may hope, on balance, to live more happily inside the cloister than their worldly circumstances would allow them to live outside it.

In conclusion, the *Mémoires de la vie de Henriette-Sylvie de Molière* paint convent life with both the satiric verve and the hardheaded realism of a picaresque novel. Yes, Villedieu mildly flirts with the *topos* of lascivious nuns; yes, the threat of the prison/cloister sometimes looms for girls who marry, or refuse to marry, against their family's wishes. Yet most of Sylvie's stories go beyond these *topoi*, in order to highlight the everyday ways women use convents to "parley" their individual positions, to negotiate as much space as possible for themselves amid the familial and legal restrictions surrounding them. Throughout, the accent is on freedom of movement and of choice. Mediated by memoirs, doubly freed from the constraints placed upon real nuns' narratives and the fictional stereotypes

---

[47]   The last flirtation mentioned in the book carries another strong hint of homoeroticism. As has already happened more than once, a girl falls in love with Sylvie while she is dressed as a man; but this time, Sylvie actively encourages her infatuation and seems to take pleasure in the relationship: "I took pleasure in seeing how her young heart became inflamed little by little. It could have let itself be led quite a distance had I been of such nature as to make it go that route" ["je prenois plaisir à voir comme son jeune coeur s'échauffoit petit à petit, se seroit laissé mener bien loin, si j'avois été propre à lui faire ce chemin-là," ed. Cuénin 372, trans. Kuizenga 179]. However, the narrator again pulls back from further explorations, instead shifting to a sentimental comparison between the girl's feelings for Sylvie and the beginnings of her own love for d'Englesac. For more on cross-dressing and female desire, see Zuerner, "Disclosing Female Desire: Transvestite Heroines in Villedieu's *Mémoires de la Vie d'Henriette-Sylvie de Molière*" in Zuerner, *(Re)constructing Gender: Cross-Dressing in Seventeenth-Century French Literature*, 98–135.

[48]   In "Villedieu's Transvestite Text: The Literary Economy of Genre and Gender in *Les Mémoires de la vie de Henriette-Sylvie de Molière*," Margaret Wise states that "... in removing herself from the world, Sylvie refuses to participate in an economy that trades in women" (142). It may be true that Sylvie abstracts herself from the social exchange of women, but in economic terms she cannot remove herself from the world because the world is not removed from the convent. Though she is invited to Cologne as the abbess's guest, one assumes that Sylvie would eventually need to pay board to stay on there; women without funds could enter convents, but only as lay sisters who performed menial tasks. These economic realities of convent life will be explored further in Marivaux's *Vie de Marianne*.

imposed by male novelists like Guilleragues or Diderot, these women's voices make themselves heard for one of the rare occasions during the Old Regime.

Marianne in the Convent Parlor: Marivaux's *La Vie de Marianne*

After centuries of neglect, the importance of Villedieu's writings for the eighteenth century has now been recognized. The fact that a complete edition of her works was published in 1720 attests to their continuing popularity; and her influence on the burgeoning memoir-novel is no longer occulted. This influence is particularly apparent in the works of Pierre Carlet de Chamblain de Marivaux. Among canonical writers of the eighteenth century, Marivaux is arguably the most sympathetic to women.[49] Annie Rivara even asserts: "Marivaux is perhaps the most feminist of eighteenth-century writers" ["Marivaux est peut-être le plus féministe des écrivains du XVIIIᵉ siècle," 66]. As a young man, he frequented the salon of the marquise de Lambert, which had retained some of the ambiance of the aristocratic *précieuses* circles of the previous century, such as Catherine de Rambouillet's famous *chambre bleue*. "Indeed," as Aurora Wolfgang remarks in *Gender and Voice in the French Novel*, "Marivaux places the writing of [Marianne] in the late seventeenth century … which was a period of significant publication by French women novelists" (68). Marivaux also knew and was influenced by Villedieu's work: the heroine of *La Vie de Marianne* (1731–42), a spirited, attractive girl of unknown parentage who runs from peril to peril but triumphs through her eloquence, could be a younger sister to Henriette-Sylvie, and many plot elements are similar in the two novels.[50]

---

[49] As a sign of Marivaux's interest in women's issues, in 1729 he wrote a three-act comedy, *La Nouvelle Colonie ou la Ligue des Femmes*, which explores the possible role of women in the creation of a new government. The play was revised and performed in a one-act version in 1750.

[50] French references to the *Vie de Marianne* are taken from the Garnier edition (ed. Frédéric Deloffre. Paris: 1963, 1990). The only English version I have seen is an eighteenth-century translation by Mary Mitchell Collyer, *The Virtuous Orphan or, the life of Marianne Countess of ****. Ed. William H. McBurney and Michael F. Shugrue (Carbondale and Edwardsville: Southern Illinois University Press, 1965). The text shows differences from the modern edition. In his 1963 edition, Deloffre mentions Villedieu in relation to forced vocations of nuns (xlii); but in his discussion of the sources of *Marianne*, he gives no credit to women memoir-writers, citing instead Challes and Courtiz de Sandras. The only women writers he mentions, the canonical Scudéry and Lafayette, are dismissed as possible sources (xx). However, René Démoris has recognized Villedieu's influence (see n2). Marianne's father and mother had been killed by robbers while traveling. Left an orphan at the age of two, she is raised by a country priest and his sister. After the priest's death, the sister brings Marianne to Paris to claim an inheritance; but she dies in turn without being able to succeed in her suit, leaving Marianne alone in an inn. The sister's confessor introduces her to M. de Climal, who he believes to be a pious man. Climal places her in lodgings with a washerwoman, but then pressures her to move into a private house where she would be free to accept his attentions.

In the introduction to the first installment of *La Vie de Marianne*, Marivaux claims that the manuscript was found by a friend in a cupboard of a country house which he was having renovated. The writing was "in a woman's hand" ["d'une écriture de femme"] and the date at the end indicated it was approximately 40 years old, placing it in the 1690s, the period of the *aventurières* who took up Villedieu's model.[51] The narrator emphasizes the identification with feminine memoirs and Villedieu by repeating: "it is a women recounting her life; she is speaking to one of her friends," like Sylvie to "Son Altesse" ["c'est une femme qui raconte sa vie; elle parle à une de ses amies," Deloffre 7–8].

What is more, Marianne's flights and confinements follow the convent route laid out by Villedieu and other seventeenth-century women writers. And Marivaux carries the religious setting still further: Marianne spends much of her childhood in a priest's home, and is escorted to Paris by his sister. Moreover, most of the action takes place while Marianne is a convent boarder. This fact may not be immediately apparent to the reader, because many important scenes take place outside the convent walls; but each time Marianne goes out, she must obtain permission from the superior. For example, when her lover Valville comes to take her to see his dying uncle, M. de Climal, Valville observes that upon hearing of the seriousness of Climal's illness, "my mother immediately wrote to your abbess asking permission for you to go out" ["ma mere aussitôt a écrit à votre abbesse de vous permettre de sortir," Deloffre 243].[52]

Marianne's convent stay begins through the actions of this same M. de Climal. Left friendless in Paris, she meets Climal and is offered his protection; but under the cloak of false piety, he attempts to seduce Marianne: ironically, he asks her to tell her landlady that she is going to enter a convent as a pretext for going away with him. Marianne refuses to acquiesce in this ruse; but she cannot afford to stay where she is. In this quandary, she goes to see the priest who had originally introduced her to Climal. Kindly but weak, the priest refuses to believe such horrors of the pious M. de Climal. Marianne finally exclaims: "let them put me in a convent, so I'll never see or meet him again" ["qu'on me mette dans un couvent, afin que je ne le voie ni ne le rencontre jamais," Deloffre 143]. While agreeing in principle, the priest has no practical help to offer. But her rhetorical conventual retreat actually materializes. On the way back to her lodgings, a providential traffic jam ["quelque embarras dans la rue"] causes Marianne to stop outside a women's convent. The convent location is urban, and, as in the *Vie de Henriette-Sylvie de Molière*, conveniently at hand. Finding the chapel door open, she enters and kneels in an empty confessional. Her sighs and lamentations attract the attention of a lady

---

[51]   For more on the female adventure novels of the late seventeenth century, see Démoris, *Le Roman à la première personne* 280–86, and DeJean, Chapter 4.

[52]   One of the few critics to discern the pervasiveness of religion in Marivaux is Paul Pelckmans. In "Dieu soit béni que je vous aime …" Pelckmans points out the "Christian turns of phrase" in Marivaux's novels (23).

who takes pity on her; when Marianne asks to speak to the prioress,[53] she finds the same lady again in a convent parlor.

This, the first of many parlor scenes in the novel, introduces Marivaux's nuanced portrayal of convent life. At first, the prioress receives her warmly, even cloyingly; but when she learns that Marianne has neither money nor family, she refuses to take her in, claiming the impoverishment of the house as justification: "our only support comes from our boarders, whose numbers have greatly decreased of late. So we are in debt, and so ill provided for that the other day I had the mortification of refusing a very promising young lady who wished to be a lay sister" ["nous ne subsistons que par nos pensionnaires, dont le nombre est fort diminué depuis quelque temps. Aussi sommes-nous endettés, et si mal à notre aise, que j'eus l'autre jour le chagrin de refuser une jeune fille, un fort bon sujet, qui se présentait pour être converse," Deloffre 153]. Her cry of poverty is less than convincing, since the narrator has already described the comfortable plumpness of the prioress, explaining in a parenthetical essay how ecclesiastical *embonpoint* differs from ordinary fat. Nevertheless, the prioress accurately paints the economic straits of women's convents in the eighteenth century (see below, Chapter 7, 284). The depiction of nuns as *douceureuses*, displaying excessive sweetness and flattery in order to attract new postulants, which will become something of a cliché in eighteenth-century fiction, may be tied to this financial pressure.

Marianne is offended by the prioress's suggestion that she might become a lay sister, and incensed by her condescending offer to take up a collection for her. The unknown lady in the parlor, however, comes to the rescue and offers to pay Marianne's expenses as a boarder. She moves in that very day and resides there through the end of the unfinished novel, over 400 pages later. Yet in the many studies of *La Vie de Marianne*, which concentrate on its love plot or psychological analysis, the convent setting is almost entirely ignored.

Marianne is disconcerted by her sudden entry into a religious space: "it seemed to me ... that under God's protection I was entering a foreign country, without having had the time to get my bearings. It was if I had been abducted" ["il me sembla ... que j'allais, à la garde de Dieu, dans un pays étranger, sans avoir le temps de me reconnaître. J'étais comme enlevée," Deloffre 150]. Though her entry is voluntary, indeed serendipitous, it still resembles an abduction in its suddenness and strangeness. When Valville leaves her there after a visit, these feelings of alienation are particularly strong:

Leaving is an action that distracts, but nothing distracts those who stay; it is the ones you leave, who see you go, who regard themselves as abandoned, especially in a convent, which is a place where everything that happens is so foreign to what is in the heart, where love is out of place.

S'en aller, c'est un mouvement qui dissipe, et rien ne distrait les personnes qui demeurent; c'est elles que vous quittez, qui vous voient partir, et qui se regardent

---

[53] *Prieure*: the assistant to the abbess, often also director of novices.

comme délaissées, surtout dans un couvent, qui est un lieu où tout ce qui se
passe est si étranger à ce que vous avez dans le coeur, un lieu où l'amour est
dépaysé. ... (Deloffre 231)

Interestingly, the narrator does not say that love is actually forbidden in the convent;
rather, it finds itself exiled in a country foreign to ordinary needs and feelings.
However, as we will learn, love quickly becomes naturalized in this strange land.

Marivaux explores this foreign country more deeply than any writer we have yet
encountered; and paradoxically, this exploration confirms that in many ways convent
society resembles the larger world outside. Marianne states: "I met a lot of women
there; I was loved by some, and disliked by others" ["j'y connus bien des personnes;
j'y fus aimée de quelques-unes, et dédaignée de quelques autres," Deloffre 159],
a normal circumstance in social life. On the whole, she is well liked by the nuns,
partly because she makes it her business to be liked: "my sweet and engaging
ways had earned me everyone's good will" ["mes façons douces et avenantes
m'avaient attiré la bienveillance de tout le monde," Deloffre 235]. However, in a
closed community where gossip is rampant, everyone soon learns of her penniless
situation. Tactfully, the nuns do not reveal their knowledge, but they treat her with
an extreme kindness that imperfectly masks a subtle condescension. "You see how
clever they were! If they had said to me: 'Poor little orphan, how pitiable you are
to be reduced to living on charity!' they could not have expressed themselves more
clearly" ["Voyez, que cela était adroit! Quand elles m'auraient dit: Pauvre petite
orpheline, que vous êtes à plaindre d'être réduite à la charité des autres! Elles ne
se seraient pas expliquées plus clairement," Deloffre 233]. The only resident who
expresses open disdain for her is another boarder; but one of the nuns, "qui était
mon amie," speaks in her defense. While criticizing the pettiness and hypocrisy of
the nuns, the narrator's account does not markedly differ from what might happen
to a "charity pupil" in a lay institution, such as a girl's boarding school.[54]

Unlike earlier writers, Marivaux also gives a role to the lay sisters or *soeurs
converses*. We see them serving and clearing away meals or arranging clothes,
maintaining the class distinctions dominant within the convent and society as a
whole. But they also speak out and give advice in their own right. When Marianne
asks a lay sister for paper and pen to write her will, the sister exclaims: "Oh! Jesus
and Mary! What are you thinking of, miss?" ["Eh! Jésus Maria! À quoi est-ce
que vous allez rêver, mademoiselle?" Deloffre 360]. And when she is recovering
from a fever, another lay sister, described as "naturellement gaie" (385), suggests
a change of air: "'Go on, go on,' she said to me, 'you're almost as ruddy as a rose,

---

[54]   The eighteenth century sees the first works of fiction set in convent schools; Colette
and Willy's Claudine novels, which recount the goings-on in a village girl's school, will
perpetuate this genre in a flirty variation 150 years later. For the classical origins of the
literature of erotic education, see James Turner, *Schooling Sex*. On girls' convent schools,
see Chapter 4, n2, and also P.-M. Fein, "The Convent School as Depicted through the
Characters of Certain Eighteenth-Century Novels." *Studies on Voltaire and the Eighteenth
Century* 264 (1989), 734–41.

our sickness is all gone, it doesn't show any more. Won't you take a little stroll in the garden after supper?" ["Allons, allons, me dit-elle; vous voilà déjà presque aussi vermeille qu'une rose; notre maladie est bien loin, il n'y paraît plus; ne ferez-vous pas un petit tour de jardin après souper?" Deloffre 385]. These free-speaking lay sisters resemble the servant and peasant characters from comic novels and theater. While their characterization does not go very deep, their presence and colloquial language add a refreshing variety to the text. In addition, they deepen the subtle secularization of the convent from within operated by Marivaux.

This secularization is dramatized by the use the author makes of the convent parlor, where a number of important and dramatic scenes take place. The day after Marianne enters the convent, she is visited by her new benefactress, Mme de Miran, accompanied by a woman friend, Mme Dorsin. During this long scene (19 pages in the Deloffre edition), she learns that Mme de Miran's son is in love with an unsuitable girl, who of course turns out to be Marianne herself. And not only is Mme de Miran the mother of Valville, Marianne's lover; she is also the sister of her pursuer, M. de Climal. The implausibility of this situation is heightened by the fact that the two women talk about Mme de Miran's private affairs, especially her son's love for a "petite fille," in front of a young, unknown girl. But after all, they are in a parlor, a place where people will talk. In the kind of dramatic reversal at which Marianne excels, she spontaneously confesses her identity to Mme de Miran and renounces Valville. His mother is completely won over. Both agree she will break with Valville; and to make the argument stronger, Mme de Miran suggests she feign a desire to become a nun (Deloffre 184).

The next day, the convent parlor witnesses another key scene, this time involving Marianne, Mme de Miran and Valville. Following Mme de Miran's suggestion, Marianne expresses her intention to become a nun; but a clear allusion to Tartuffe reveals that her statement is indeed a feint: "Nevertheless, I had said I would take the veil, and was going to repeat it *out of an excess of zeal*" ["J'avais pourtant dit que j'allais être religieuse, et je pensais le répéter *par excès de zèle*," Deloffre 200; italics added].[55] However, events do not go according to plan; converted by Marianne's dangerous charm, Mme de Miran agrees at least to consider a marriage between her and Valville.

This parlor scene, according to Deloffre, is considered the first example of "sentimental" literature in the eighteenth century. Its appeal is confirmed by the fact that the scene was one of those chosen to illustrate in the first edition of the novel (Fig. 4.2). In this engraving, we see Mme de Miran seated in front of an imposing parlor grill reaching from floor to ceiling. On her left, Valville is bending forward to kiss his mother's hand. At the same time he is also embracing the hand of Marianne, extended through the grill behind which she is demurely sitting. Doors and archways fade into the background, evoking the forbidden convent space. This double hand-kissing scene is accurately reproduced from the novel,

---

[55]   While Tartuffe is attempting to seduce his patron's wife, she complains that he is squeezing her hand too hard. Tartuffe replies: "It is through excessive zeal."

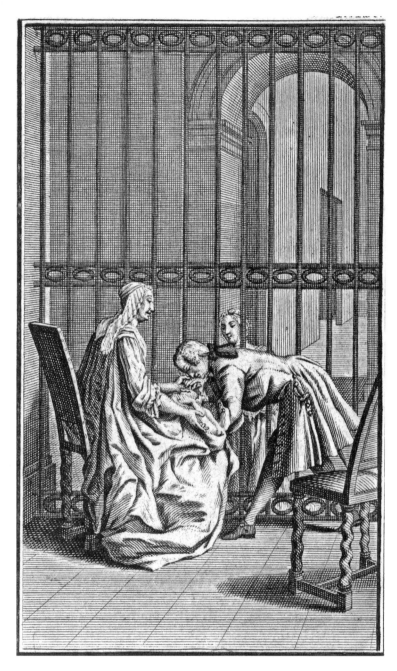

Fig. 4.2   *Valville et Mme de Miran au parloir*. Engraving J. van der Schley.
Marivaux, *La Vie de Marianne*, op. cit. I. 288–9. Paris, BnF.

but it actually comes from the next parlor conversation, in which Mme de Miran announces she will do her best to foster a match between Marianne and Valville. But she warns, in a foreshadowing of future events, that they will have serious opposition. Hearing this news, Marianne recounts: "I threw myself at her feet, and slid part of my hand through the grill to grasp Mme de Miran's, which was reaching for mine; and Valville, overwhelmed with joy and almost beside himself, threw himself upon both our hands and kissed them in turn" ["je m'étais jetée à genoux, et j'avais passé une moitié de ma main par la grille pour avoir celle de Mme de Miran, qui en effet approcha la mienne; et Valville, éperdu de joie et comme hors de lui, se jeta sur nos deux mains, qu'il baisait alternativement," Deloffre 206].

As a successful playwright, Marivaux knows how to exploit the grill "prop" for dramatic and pathetic effect. Rather than a religious image, it is a social one, indicating the barriers placed between Marianne and a happy life in the world. When Marianne first takes leave of Mme de Miran to enter the convent, she recounts: "I came back, I thanked her through the convent grill; she left and I became a boarder" ["J'entrai, je revins la remercier à travers les grilles du parloir, elle partit, et me voilà pensionnaire," Deloffre 159]. Notes are passed through the parlor grill; and hand-holding and -kissing through the grill recur repeatedly in the novel—as many as three times in one scene. During her visit with Mme Dorsin described above, Mme de Miran extends her hand through the grill to take Marianne's, "only three or four fingers of which could pass through" ["dont je ne pus lui passer que trois ou quatre doigts"]. Immediately after, the process is reversed. As Marianne describes it: "Her answer touched me, my eyes filled with tears; I tried to kiss her hand; in turn she could only extend a few fingers" ["Cette réponse m'attendrit, mes yeux se mouillèrent: je tâchai de lui baiser la main, dont elle ne put à son tour m'abandonner que quelques doigts," Deloffre 173]. At the end of the scene, Marianne takes Mme de Miran's hand for the third and final time, "the best I could" ["du mieux que je pus"], and kisses it in gratitude "a thousand times, on my knees" ["mille fois à genoux," Deloffre 181]. Finally, in a later scene, Marianne "throws herself like a madwoman" on Mme de Miran's hand which is resting on the grill ["me jettant comme une folle sur une main dont, par hasard, elle tenait alors un des barreaux de la grille," Deloffre 285]. As in a prison setting, the narrowness of the bars accentuates the pathetic effect of this tearful exchange, much to the taste of Marivaux's readers. In this situation, it is easy to forget that Marianne is only a boarder who can eventually leave the convent, not a prisoner in jail or a nun committed by eternal vows.

The play of parlor grill and curtain is again used to dramatic effect later in the novel. After Valville has broken off their engagement, Marianne enters the parlor, expecting to find his mother, Mme de Miran. "A curtain, drawn on my side over the parlor grill, still hid the person with whom I was going to speak. ... Ah, my dear mother, is it you? I cried, walking towards the grill with the intention of pulling the curtain open." But as in a *coup de théâtre*, the closed curtain parts, unexpectedly revealing her unfaithful lover ["Un rideau, tiré de mon côté sur la grille du parloir, me cachait encore la personne à qui j'allais parler; mais prévenue que c'était Mme de Miran: Ah! ma chère mère, est-ce donc vous? m'écriai-je en avançant vers cette grille, dont je pensai arracher le rideau, et qui, au lieu de Mme de Miran, me présenta Valville"]. In true dramatic fashion, Marianne cries out: "Ah! mon Dieu!" (Deloffre 395).

In addition to the parlor grill, the choir grill [*grille de choeur* or *grande grille*], separating the cloistered area from the public space of the church, plays a dramatic role in the novel, as it will in Diderot's *La Religieuse* (see below, Chapter 6, 259).[56] Both novels stage profession ceremonies: Mme de Miran and her son attend such a ceremony at Marianne's convent with Marianne watching from "backstage," as it were, while in *La Religieuse* it is the heroine herself who is expected to take vows. The real ritual was theatrical enough, as Lusseau's description of eighteenth-century profession ceremonies at Fontevraud attests. First, "All the bells ring and the organ plays as for high holy days" ["Toutes les cloches sonnent et l'orgue joue comme aux fêtes de première classe," Lusseau 100]. Then the sub-deacon and priest process in, carrying the sacrament and the relics of St John and St Benedict. During the chanting and prayers, the dignitaries face the open grill, behind which are seated the abbess and her nuns, hierarchical order determining their closeness to the opening. In other words, this is a ceremony in which the world and the convent come into close visual contact, if not into dialogue. As Lusseau puts it, "Thus, this ceremony is performed publicly, with the window in the grill open, the sisters inside and the brothers outside, as is the family" ["Cette cérémonie est donc faite publiquement, la fenêtre de la grille ouverte, les soeurs étant dedans et les frères au dehors, ainsi que la famille," Lusseau 107].

In *La vie de Marianne*, this solemn ceremony is seen entirely from the secular and amorous point of view of the heroine; eschewing hierarchy, she is seated in her usual place "quite close to the grill" ["fort près de cette grille"] and therefore as close as possible to the worldly space. Since she does not know that Mme de Miran and her son will be attending, "It was a pleasant surprise for me to see her walking across the church and seating herself near our grill" ["ce fut pour moi une agréable surprise lorsque je la vis qui traversait pour venir se placer près de notre grille," Deloffre 202]. Subtle communication takes place between them through body language. Valville is the first to notice her: "he greeted me with an indescribable air of gaiety and confidence that seemed to bode well for our affairs" ["(il) me salua avec je ne sais quel air de gaîté et de confiance qui était de bon augure pour nos affaires," Deloffre 203]. When Mme de Miran catches sight of her, a whole mute exchange takes place: "A deep curtsy on my part drew from her demonstrations of friendship, expressed by waving her hand, meaning: 'Hello, dear child, so there you are'" ["Ce furent aussitôt de profondes révérences de ma part, qui m'attirèrent de la sienne de ces demonstrations, qui se font avec la main, et qui signifiaient: Ah! Bonjour, ma chère enfant, te voilà"]. It is a less agreeable surprise for Marianne to see they are accompanied by M. de Climal,

---

[56]   The choir grill in the Paris Carmelite convent is described above in Chapter 3, 121.

Mme de Miran's brother and Marianne's would-be seducer. M. de Climal catches sight of her while taking a breviary out of his pocket (faithfully playing the role of Tartuffe). He turns red and fails to greet her; nor does Marianne acknowledge him. This dumb show completely occupies Marianne's attention during the profession ceremony, which Marianne does not describe except to say that the sermon is too "beau" to be morally instructive (Deloffre 204)—an ironic criticism coming from Marianne, herself a master of virtuous eloquence.

After the ceremony, Mme de Miran tells Marianne that in a month she will move her to a different convent so no one will know her whereabouts. But before that can happen, Marianne is abducted under the orders of one of Valville's influential relatives and placed in yet a different convent. Recalling an episode from Villedieu's *Mémoires de Henriette-Sylvie*, Marianne is to be kept enclosed and secluded until she agrees either to marry someone else or to take the veil. However, in contrast to the description of the "bad" convent in the *Mémoires de Henriette-Sylvie*, this new house is portrayed positively by the narrator; in fact, all the nuns are on Marianne's side and rejoice when she later wins out over the relatives blocking the marriage. Yet they are powerless to help her. The abbess remarks: "I would gladly have offered to inform Mme de Miran of your presence; but, however pleased I would be to oblige, I am not allowed to do you this favor. I have been ordered not to interfere; I even gave my word, which makes me very sad" ["Je vous aurais volontiers offert d'envoyer avertir Mme de Miran que vous êtes ici; mais, quelque plaisir que je me fisse de vous obliger, c'est un service qu'il ne m'est pas permis de vous rendre. On a exigé que je ne me mêlerais de rien; j'en ai moi-même donné parole, et j'en suis très fâchée," Deloffre 303]. This episode again illustrates the extent to which the convent in the *ancien régime* was implicated in the political and familial control of women (see above, 161–3). Yet in Marianne's case, the nuns are not merely passive onlookers in the drama; on the contrary, it is through the convent doorkeeper's description of the livery of the carriage that had taken Marianne away that Mme de Miran is able to find her (Deloffre 323). These events also dramatize the identification of the heroine with "her" convent. Like Sylvie, Marianne uses the possessive pronoun "mon" to refer to the house where she had been boarding (Deloffre 295, 323); Mme de Miran calls it "ton" or "son couvent" (Deloffre 413). Whether this identification by possession is copied from Villedieu or, more likely, a current usage of the time, it confirms the close intertwining of the conventual and worldly lives of women.

After winning out over family opposition, Marianne loses Valville to his own fickleness. There are early signs, unnoticed by Marianne until later, that he is losing interest; and while visiting Marianne in "her" convent, Valville sees and falls in love with an English girl, Mlle Varthon [Wharton?] who is also a boarder there (Deloffre 348). Nevertheless, the convent remains a refuge for her: after Valville breaks off their engagement, Marianne asks to be taken back there so she will not have to see him. Mme Dorsin agrees: "She is right, this event is still too recent, and I agree with her. Let's return her to *her* convent" ["Elle a raison, cette aventure-ci est encore trop fraîche, et je pense comme elle: remettons-la dans *son* couvent,"

Deloffre 413; italics added]. In her grief, Marianne even considers leaving the world. She is consoled for the loss of her lover by her friend the nun, who indicates that a similar misfortune had befallen her. The nun repeats the words of consolation she had heard from her own friend, enlarging the circle of women supporting women. Marianne is grateful for her advice and sympathy. She adds: "I even put a friendly arm around her, meaning: 'Thank you, it is very sweet to be in your hands'" ["je laissai même tomber amicablement mon bras sur elle, d'un air qui signifiait: Je vous remercie, il est bien doux d'être entre vos mains," Deloffre 384]. This physical expression of affection between women recalls Mme de Villedieu: according to Nicole Boursier, "Healthy and sincere affection is expressed freely and openly by bodily contact" ["L'affection saine et sincère s'exprime et coule librement par le contact corporel"] without the erotic overtones sometimes present in such scenes ("Le corps de Henriette-Sylvie," 277).

Shortly after these events, a new visitor appears in the parlor: an older gentleman who has heard of Marianne's plight and offers her marriage based on reason and esteem. He gives her a week to consider; and "her" nun promises to tell her own story so Marianne can carefully reflect before making an irrevocable decision whether to enter the convent permanently. This nun's tale is truly Marianne's "shaggy dog story," repeatedly announced and put off through four volumes of the novel. We first hear of the nun's tale at the end of part 4: "I had promised you in my third volume to tell you something about my convent; I was not able to do it here, and it's put off again. I will even reveal to you that a nun's story will take up almost all of my fifth volume" ["J'avais promis dans ma troisième de vous conter quelque chose de mon couvent; je n'ai pu le faire ici, et c'est encore partie remise. Je vous annonce même l'histoire d'une religieuse qui fera presque tout le sujet de mon cinquième livre," Deloffre 216]. The convent milieu is indeed described in part 5, but no nun's story appears. Instead, Marianne states: "I promised you the story of a nun, but this is not yet the place for it. What I am going to tell you will lead up to it" ["Je vous ai promis l'histoire d'une religieuse, mais ce n'est pas encore ici sa place et ce que je vais raconter l'amènera," Deloffre 237]. At the end of part 5, she reiterates: "I haven't forgotten, by the way, that I announced a nun's story, and this is its proper place; part 6 will begin with it" ["Je n'ai pas oublié, au reste, que je vous ai annoncé l'histoire d'une religieuse, et voici sa place; c'est par où commencera la sixième partie," Deloffre 268].

The same protestation is repeated, almost jokingly by this time, at the end of part 6: "[part 7] will begin, I promise, with the nun's story; I did not think it would be so long in coming when I began this sixth part" ["(la septième partie) débutera, je le promets, par l'histoire de la religieuse, que je ne croyais pas encore si loin quand j'ai commencé cette sixième partie-ci," Deloffre 318]. Marianne finally gives the stage over to the nun at the end of the eighth volume; it takes up much of part 9, published three years later in 1742, and all of the last two parts of the novel. According to Deloffre, these last three parts constitute an independent episode, almost like *Manon Lescault* in relation to the *Mémoires d'un homme de qualité* (xli).[57] At the end of part 11, the nun's story is still left unfinished, as is Marianne's own—and the novel itself. These repeated procrastinations lend an air of parody to what is, after all, a well-worn topos; but at the same time, the repeated announcements suggest that nun's stories are still a popular theme, expected to entice readers to buy successive volumes of the novel in hopes of finding the long-delayed adventures.

By the time the nun's story begins, "une religieuse" of part 4 has become "ma religieuse," a close friend to Marianne who plays an important role in the main plot. Her immediate function is to dissuade Marianne from becoming a nun herself, following her disappointment in love. The nun, whose secular name was Mlle de Tervire, owes her misfortune to her father's imprudent marriage to a noble but penniless girl. After her father's death and her mother's remarriage to an important nobleman, Mlle de Tervire becomes a virtual orphan, leading a Cinderella-like existence under the "care" of a concierge. A neighbor takes pity on her and raises her in his home. The poor but beautiful Mlle de Tervire is then taken up by a pious widow, Mme de Sainte Hermières. At the instigation of her mother, this lady tries to convince Tervire to take the veil. As well as serving her mother's ends, Tervire's profession would also enhance the widow's reputation among her circle of self-styled *dévotes*: "[Mme de Sainte Hermières] multiplies her caresses and expressions of friendship for me; it is true that a girl of my age, with a rather pretty face (as people said I had), would not have added little to her prestige if I buried myself in a convent after leaving her care" ["Elle redouble de caresses et d'amitié pour moi; et il est vrai qu'une fille de mon âge, et d'une aussi jolie figure qu'on disait que je l'étais, ne lui aurait pas fait peu d'honneur de s'aller jeter dans un couvent au sortir de ses mains," Deloffre 453]. Mme de Sainte-Hermières takes Tervire to a neighboring *couvent de filles* where she is treated "with all the monastic cunning" ["avec toute l'adresse monacale," Deloffre 454] already deployed during the attempt to entice Marianne to enter the convent, before the prioress learned she was penniless.

Tervire interrupts her narrative with a commentary emphasizing the power that a nun's friendship can have over the mind and heart of an impressionable young girl:

> It is hard to believe how attractive a nun's friendship can be, how it can engage a young girl who has seen nothing and has no experience of love. One loves a nun differently from how one might love a friend in the outside world; the innocent attachment one forms to her is a kind of passion; and it is certain that the habit that we, and only we, wear, and the peaceful physiognomy it lends us, contribute to that [passion,] as does the air of peace that seems to permeate our convents, and makes one imagine them to be a sweet and tranquil asylum … .

> On ne saurait croire combien l'amitié d'une religieuse est attrayante, combien elle engage une fille qui n'a rien vu, et qui n'a nulle expérience. On aime alors

---

[57]   For a list of other novels with a forced vocation theme, see Deloffre xli–xliv.

cette religieuse autrement qu'on n'aimerait une amie du monde; c'est une espèce
de passion que l'attachement innocent qu'on prend pour elle; et il est sûr que
l'habit que nous portons, et qu'on ne voit qu'à nous, que la physionomie reposée
qu'il nous donne, contribuent à cela, aussi bien que cet air de paix qui semble
répandu dans nos maisons, et qui les fait imaginer comme un asile doux et
tranquille ... . (Deloffre 455)

But the verbs she uses—*semble, imaginer*—indicate that the peace and tranquility
are as superficial as the habits the nuns wear.

Mme de Sainte-Hermière's scheme might well have succeeded if Tervire,
during her convent visits, had not made the acquaintance of an unhappy young
nun who warns her off by recounting her own experience. This episode is a *mise
en abyme* of Tervire's own warning to Marianne:

> "You want to become a nun?" She then said to me. "And our sisters' caresses,
> the welcome they extend to you, the speeches they make ... Mme de Saint-
> Hermières's insinuations ... all this carries you along, and you are about to
> commit yourself to our state on the belief in a vocation you think you have, and
> that you might not have without all that. Take care!"

> Vous voulez vous faire religieuse? Me dit-elle alors, et les caresses de nos soeurs,
> l'accueil qu'elles vous font, les discours qu'elle vous tiennent ... les insinuations
> de Mme de Sainte-Hermières ... tout vous y porte et vous allez vous engager
> dans notre état sur la foi d'une vocation que vous croyez avoir, et que vous
> n'auriez peut-être pas sans tout cela. Prenez-y garde! (Deloffre 458–9)

The young nun confesses that she herself had entered the convent without a true
vocation, and did not realize her mistake until too late.

This cautionary tale had the effect on Tervire that she wishes to have on
Marianne: "she frightened me at that very moment" ["elle m'effraya dans ce
moment-ci"]. But there is more: in a state of extreme agitation, the young nun
confesses to Tervire her love for a dissolute abbé who frequents Mme de Sainte-
Hermière's circle. She has just received a letter from this abbé asking her to run
away with him. Like Guilleragues's Marianne, the nun's passion for her "ennemi
mortel" almost reaches the level of madness: "I can't promise anything if I see
him again; I am capable of following him, of shortening my life. I see only terrible
things ahead; I envision nothing but bottomless pits; and it is certain that both
of us would perish" ["Je ne réponds de rien, si je le revois; je suis capable de le
suivre, je suis capable d'abréger ma vie, je suis capable de tout; je ne prévois que
des horreurs, je n'imagine que des abîmes, et il est sûr que nous péririons tous
deux," Deloffre 461]. Tervire helps the nun to discourage the abbé's attentions
by polite blackmail; for herself, she is "entirely cured of the desire to be a nun"
["entièrement guérie de l'envie d'être religieuse," Deloffre 462].

This narrative reiterates Marivaux's criticisms of the undue influence convent
women can exert on inexperienced young girls in order to convince them to
profess. He also attacks the hypocrisy of some self-proclaimed religious people.

When Tervire tells Mme de Sainte-Hermières that she no longer wishes to take the veil, she is immediately dropped by her *dévot* circle (Deloffre 466). Worst of all, of course, is the behavior of the abbé: "The nun was merely led astray; the abbé was perverted" ["La religieuse n'était qu'une égarée; l'abbé était un perverti," Deloffre 464]. However, Marivaux's criticism stops short of attacking religious life itself. The young nun tells Tervire that life in a convent without a vocation brings misery; on the other hand, if you have a true calling, "you will live tranquil and contented" ["vous vivrez tranquille et contente," Deloffre 458]. Even the nun's tale has a "happy ending," or at least an edificatory one. After the abbé's visits cease, she eventually cures herself of her passion: "gradually she became attached to her duties, and her piety made her an example to her convent" ["insensiblement elle s'affectionna à ses devoirs et devint l'exemple de son couvent par sa piété," Deloffre 464].

Whatever its larger moral, the imbedded nun's tale has the desired effect of curing Marianne of the desire to become a nun herself. Having accomplished this aim, Tervire's own tale takes on a life of its own, becoming gradually more formulaic and melodramatic.[58] In the last two parts of the novel, all that remains of its original structure is the double frame of Marianne's narrative and the convent setting: for example, at the end of part 11, the story is interrupted by the bell calling the nuns to prayer (Démoris 579). We never learn why Tervire finally took the veil; but she appears oddly responsible for her own downfall, having high-mindedly and naively orchestrated a reconciliation between her aunt and cousin just before the former's death. In "Aux frontières de l'impensé," René Démoris speculates that Tervire may have staged this reconciliation in order to rewrite the story of her father and grandfather, this time with a happy ending. In any case, Tervire's history emphasizes the role of what Démoris calls "family hell" ["l'enfer familial," Deloffre 80] in unhappy convent professions. As Diderot's *La Religieuse* will show far more blatantly, dysfunctional families can lead to involuntary monachization.

If Marivaux's text ends without the reader learning how Tervire ended up in a convent after all,[59] Riccoboni's continuation abandons the nun's tale completely, finding it "long" (Deloffre 586).[60] While shifting the focus back to Marianne, the

---

[58]   The inferior level of Marivaux's last three chapters is also suggested by the fact that they were less well received by the public (Deloffre 561n1).

[59]   From the direction the narrative is taking in part 11, we can speculate that Tervire will lose both her inheritance and her lover after the death of her aunt, and that these circumstances may have forced her into a convent (Deloffre 532–4).

[60]   The *Suite de Marianne qui commence où celle de M. de Marivaux est restée* was composed in approximately 1750. First published anonymously in 1761, it appeared under Riccoboni's own name in 1765. In a prefatory letter, Riccoboni claims the sequel was a "society joke" ["plaisanterie de société," Deloffre 582] rather than a serious attempt to rival Marivaux; nevertheless, the *Suite* was well received by the contemporary public (Deloffre 627n1). Deloffre's and Jin Lu's judgments of the Riccoboni sequel are more critical, with Jin Lu considering it an inferior pastiche of Marivaux (Jin Lu 87–8). My reading emphasizes the *Suite*'s significant differences from Marivaux's novel.

new author retains the convent setting, even developing it further in conformity with her narrative aims. Riccoboni reintroduces the option of monastic profession, but for a different reason: by taking the veil, Marianne wants to make Valville regret her loss. "I flattered myself that the sacrifice I was preparing to make would spread eternal bitterness over the entire life of an ungrateful man; that he would incessantly regret the tender, the unfortunate, the courageous Marianne" ["Je me flattais que le sacrifice où je me déterminais répandrait une amertume éternelle sur tous les instants de la vie d'un ingrat; qu'il regretterait sans cesse la tendre, l'infortunée, la courageuse Marianne," Deloffre 588]. In this passage, Marianne's rhetoric, which usually serves to further her ends, is turned into self-satire. After receiving the count's offers, she states: "I was more determined than ever to take the veil" ["j'étais plus que jamais dans le dessein de me faire religieuse," Deloffre 198]. But she soon questions this romantic fantasy, reflecting that her retreat would only make things easier for Valville and his new love: "So I was preparing to bury myself forever, to renounce the world in order to draw a few sighs from a treacherous soul, to provoke a passing regret in a fickle heart. Mademoiselle Varthon would gain from what I was giving up; I would work for her, I would make her happy …" ["J'allais donc m'ensevelir pour jamais, renoncer au monde pour arracher quelques soupirs à une âme perfide, pour exciter un regret passager dans une âme légère. Mlle Varthon jouirait des biens que j'abandonnais, je travaillerais pour elle, je la rendrais contente …" Deloffre 614].

Thus, in Riccoboni's continuation, the issue of monastic profession is completely secularized and placed under the aegis of the love plot. While Marivaux's Marianne had expressed some longing for tranquility after Valville's betrayal, the only motivation of Riccoboni's heroine to enter a convent is: "he'll be sorry." This same secularization is evident in the representation of the convent itself. Riccoboni's text contains several parlor scenes, including a visit from Marianne's suitor le conte de Saint-Agne (Deloffre 593) and a long conversation with Valville (Deloffre 600–607). In these scenes, the interactions are less melodramatic and more realistic psychologically than in the later Marivaux episodes. In fact, the greatest strength of Riccoboni's narrative lies in its depiction of the conflicted feelings of a jilted girl. While speaking to Valville, she punishes him by feigning indifference, even showing off her "charms" through the convent grill; but once she is alone again, she regrets her cold behavior and her love for him returns.

The role of the convent as a setting for a love story is also confirmed in Marianne's own words. When she is out in society, she confides to the reader that "the hours seem long to me; I wait impatiently for the time I will regain the freedom to think about what interests me, I'm dying to return to my convent" ["les heures me paraissent longues; j'attends impatiemment celle qui me rendra la liberté de penser à ce qui m'intéresse; je brûle de retourner à mon couvent," Deloffre 612]. But what draws her back there? Valville, whom she had just left in the convent parlor.

The function of the convent in the secular love plot is also enabled by the lay sisters who continually bombard Marianne with messages from the outside.

Instead of protecting her privacy, they insist she come immediately to the parlor or send an answer to a letter: "A lay sister comes to torment me: 'come on, Miss, the bell keeps ringing, that servant is getting impatient'" ["Une converse vient me tourmenter: Allons donc, mademoiselle, on sonne à chaque instant, ce laquais s'impatiente," Deloffre 619]. The turnstile, a device for sending messages in and out of the convent meant to limit contact with the outside, becomes a depository for Marianne's correspondence with Valville: "my note was in the turnstile; the slightest sound agitated me" ["Mon billet était au tour, le moindre bruit m'agitait," Deloffre 621]. The love plot even invades Marianne's room [*chambre*, not *cellule*]: steps in the corridor announce the entrance of her rival, Mlle Varthon, come to pick a quarrel with her. Though Marianne's friendly nun finally enters the room to reproach Mlle Varthon for her attitude and put an end to the argument, nothing is explicitly said to suggest that this type of conversation is out of the ordinary in a convent chamber. On the contrary, it is Mlle Varthon's presence that gives Marianne the strength to refuse to see Valville:

> Things were at this point when a lay sister came to tell me that Mme de Miran's son was waiting in the parlor, and begged me to come down right away. … "Be so kind as to tell M. de Valville that I neither can nor wish to speak with him; I sent his letter to Mme de Miran. Say that, and give him to understand that I absolutely refuse to receive him without his mother."

> Nous en étions là quand une converse vint me dire que le fils de Mme de Miran m'attendait au parloir, et me suppliait de descendre à l'instant. … Ayez la bonté de dire à M. de Valville que je ne puis ni ne veux lui parler; j'ai envoyé sa lettre à Mme de Miran. Ajoutez cela, et faites-lui bien entendre qu'absolument je ne le verrai point sans sa mère. (Deloffre 622–3)

In conclusion, the convent in *La Vie de Marianne*, whatever its flaws, is portrayed as an integral and functional part of the social fabric. As in the domain of women's political rights, Marivaux's position remains essentially conservative. Paul Pelckmans justly observes: "Criticism is certainly not absent; it even recurs quite regularly. The essential, in this context, is that such criticism hardly ever goes beyond what an informed and minimally strict religious person would disapprove of, as more or less common failures to meet his ideals" ["Le mot critique n'est certes pas absente; elle revient même fort régulièrement; l'essentiel, ici, est qu'elle ne déborde guère ce qu'une piété avertie et tant soit peu strict pouvait désapprouver comme autant de manquements plus ou moins coutumiers à son idéal," 30]. Marivaux does criticize the psychological manipulations of wily nuns, meant to bring about improper vocations; but his reformist criticisms are situated within the system, not without. To indicate the possibility of internal reform, both Climal and Mme de Themières repent their religious hypocrisy in exemplary fashion. Most important, the greater part of the novel, discreetly and with little ado, takes place in a convent, and this setting is more of a help than a hindrance to Marianne.

In contrast, Riccoboni's *Suite de Marianne* retains the convent setting and leaves out all criticism. Indeed, narrative comments make us aware of the conventual location more frequently than in Marivaux; but these comments only show how thin the walls between convent and world have become. Lay sisters play the role of stage servants, carrying messages and forwarding flirtations; the individual convent room even functions as a "parlor" where a jealous argument between two women can takes place; and none of this is shown as out of the ordinary. Yet in the end, though to differing degrees and in different ways, both of Marianne's chroniclers portray the convent as affording women some measure of individual freedom. In Chapters 5 and 6, the focus will shift from the convent parlor to the cell, with all its negative and sinister connotations.

Chapter 5
Cells I:
Forced Enclosure, Erotic Disclosure

CELL n.f. diminutive of Celle which is no longer in use. Small room of a monk or nun. A monk's cell; I went to see him in his cell (CELLULE. f.f. diminutif de Celle qui n'est plus en usage, Petite chambre d'un Religieux ou d'une Religieuse. La cellule d'un Religieux, je l'ai esté voir dans sa cellule).
—*Dictionnaire de l'Academie française* 1694

Leur couvent est une prison.
—Diderot, *La Religieuse* 310

Our gradual penetration of the convent has finally led to the inmost space of religious retreat: the cell. As indicated in the definitions above, the late seventeenth century inherited and passed on the meaning of *cellule* current since the time of early Western asceticism. Then, in the early nineteenth century, the word suddenly began to denote a very different site of solitary enclosure: a prison. This dramatic shift in meaning will be explored in the next two chapters. Chapter 5 will begin by considering the multiple meanings of the convent cell on the semantic and the architectural levels. Then, through readings of lesser-known early modern fiction, we will explore representations of forced enclosure and unbridled sexuality: the two main criticisms that gave the convent cell a negative connotation even before it became a prison cell.

A Cell of One's Own: Religious Meanings and Practices

The mixed etymologies of the word "cell" forshadow some of the ambiguities that will appear in its literary representations. In Greek, *kellia* simply denotes the small huts that housed early monks. But the Latin word *cella*, despite its phonetic similarity, has a different origin. It is derived from the verb *celar*, "to close": those in convent cells, therefore, are not only housed but locked up. Despite this potentially carceral association, for over two millennia the cell was simply considered to be the basic unit of a monastery, like the biological cell of a body or the wax divisions of a beehive. In fact, for early ascetics, the cell *was* the monastery, the dwelling of a single hermit (or *monial* in French). Both cell and monastery initially designated the living quarters of Jewish hermits who went off into the desert to be alone with God. This call to the solitary life also resonates in the sayings of the early Christian fathers: "Abba Allois said: 'Unless a man say in his heart, "Only I and God are in the world," he shall not find rest'" (Chadwick 132).

In keeping with this imperative for isolation, the first monastic cells were located at a great distance from one another (*Encyclopedia of the Early Church*, s.v. "Egypt"). However, the association of the cell with monastic solitude was not constant through time. In Pacomius's coenobitic communities, first founded in the fourth century, the degree of individual isolation varied with time and place: "The first cenobitic [sic] monasteries of Egypt, Palestine and Syria, where monasticism began, were composed invariably of the monks' cells (replaced later with common dormitories)" (*Catholic Encyclopedia*, "Monastic Art and Architecture" 1024). Excavations of one eighth-century coenobium in Egypt revealed rows of individual dormitory rooms opening onto a central corridor. In other coenobitic communities, monks lived in great complexes, often three to a cell. And for St. Benedict, the great founder of Western monasticism, the imperative of spiritual isolation seemed to vie with, and eventually lose out to, an overriding necessity for disciplinary surveillance. Hence Section 22 of the Benedictine rule, "How the Monks are to Sleep," specifies that "Each monk shall sleep in a separate bed. … If possible, everyone shall sleep in the same room. But if their numbers do not permit; then they shall sleep by tens or twenties, with their seniors among them to take care of them. A lamp shall burn in the room throughout the night. … The younger brothers shall not have their beds near each other, but split up among the seniors" (Chadwick 310). Variations on this arrangement reappeared in dormitories, orphanages, boarding schools, medieval colleges or other forms of collective housing for boys.[1] According to Philippe Sellier, individual cells did not reappear in France until the fifteenth and sixteenth centuries, and then only in monasteries under strict rule like Port-Royal ["Port-Royal: un emblème de la Réforme catholique" 36n11].[2]

What about nuns, whose rule was often modeled on the Benedictines'? Did they have their own cells, or sleep, like many monks, in dormitories? This question is an important one, if only for the frequent satires of convents as places of sexual license; but it is difficult to answer definitively. If little is known about the living arrangements in early male monasteries, there is even less information available concerning women's religious communities of the time. Moreover, some of the assumptions made by modern historians have been shown to be invalid. According to John Nichols, "two recent books on medieval monasticism state that the life of the nuns was the same as the monks, yet neither author could prove his statement or for that matter cite his source" (*Distant Echoes* 3). The paucity of accurate information is due to the fact that, as previously stated, far fewer women's convents were built than men's, and fewer still survive, even as ruins. The traces of their

---

[1]	Historically, however, living patterns in the monastery swung from isolation to community and back again to solitude, following the opposing imperatives of surveillance and contemplation. While early medieval monks seem to have shared common dormitories, according to the *Catholic Enyclopedia* the large sleeping spaces in English Benedictine abbeys were later divided into compartments.

[2]	In the same Sellier article, see also 20–21.

existence that do remain are mainly in the form of written sources, such as charters and gifts to nunneries, rather than material relics.[3] For example, we know how many women joined the convent of Marcigny in a given year, what proportion were widows, and how large a dowry their families gave the monastery (*Distant Echoes* 99); but whether early medieval nuns slept in dormitories or single cells remains a mystery.

By the thirteenth century, however, more evidence is available, especially concerning larger and richer women's convents such as Fontevraud. Following the Benedictine model, the Rule of Fontevraud prescribes that the nuns "sleep alone, each one in a single bed and all in the same room" ["se couchent seules chacune en un lit et toutes en un même lieu"], and that a central light be kept burning all night (*Règle de Fontevraud*, quoted in Lusseau 170). But the excavation and restoration of the convent buildings still standing at Fontevraud suggests that these "lieux"—three large dormitory floors—were subdivided into single cells (see *The Abbaye de Fontevraud* 13). Eighteenth-century descriptions of Fontevraud confirm this arrangement: "The dormitories, three in all, have nothing grand about them but their length and the number of cells; everything is simple and expressive of religious modesty" ["Les dortoirs, au nombre de trois, n'ont rien de grand que la longueur et le nombre de cellules, tout y est simple et se ressent de la modestie religieuse"].[4] In 1790, inventories were made of the monastery and its contents by the Revolutionary authorities, as of all monastic property in France. (Ironically, these inventories, undertaken to implement the governmental policy of dismantling monasteries, often provide the best source for information on the living conditions of nuns at the end of the Old Regime.) The report on Fontevraud confirms the large scale of the dormitories, which are divided into a total of 230 cells. The Revolutionary officials also note that the novices slept in three rooms, each containing five beds (Lusseau 118). Whether this arrangement reflected a lack of space, a perceived need for greater supervision of novices, or a desire to let the novices adjust to the solitary conditions of convent life more slowly, is not clear.

This issue is clarified, at least on paper, by an edict of the Council of Trent which forbade two or more nuns from sleeping in the same room. Single cells were prescribed in St. Teresa of Avila's rule and in the convents of the new French teaching orders. However, the archives of the Monastère Ste-Claire indicate that sleeping alone in separate rooms or beds was not a familiar or comfortable practice for the local girls sent to board there. For example, a document in the Clares' archives recounts that homesick new boarders whose older sisters were nuns at the convent would go upstairs and climb into bed with them; the Abbess had to issue an order specifically forbidding this practice (Sister Elizabeth, "Les Origines de notre

---

[3]   It is only in the last decade that serious archeological excavations have been undertaken at the sites of women's convents. See Roberta Gilchrist, *Gender and Material Culture: The Archaeology of Religious Women*.

[4]   *Histoire de l'ordre de Fontevraud: 1100–1908* (Auch: Impr. de L. Cocharaux, 1911–15), vol. 2, 391 (quoted in Lusseau 114).

monastère," 26). Thus, while public morality and popular imagination see women sleeping together as a shocking or exciting perversion, cultural history suggests otherwise. We will return to this question in the context of Diderot's *Religieuse*.

One of the most complete and enlightening sources on convent women's living conditions in the seventeenth century, and the rationale behind them, comes from the *Constitutions de Port-Royal*, published in 1665. Chapter 22, entitled "Du Dortoir," is entirely devoted to sleeping arrangements at the convent. Like the Superior of the Monastère Ste-Claire, Mother Agnès, who edited the final version of the work, insists that each sister sleep alone in her own cell, or at least separately; if there is a shortage of rooms and two nuns must share a cell, "elles ne seront jamais dans un même lict" (3). This explicit proscription against sleeping together in one bed, found in many monastic rules, doubtless expresses a desire to avoid scandal or any appearance of it. Then again, the fact that the policy needed to be stated indicates that sleeping alone was not a universal practice in the seventeenth century, even in convents. The *Constitutions* of Port-Royal further state, as in Benedictine rule, that except in cases of emergency, the nuns cannot go into one another's cells without the express permission of the superior. When the nuns are not required to be together in community, they must retire to their cells to read. Any extra time must be spent performing "some kind of useful and necessary work" ["quelque oeuvre utile & necessaire," 3]. When together, the sisters will observe silence, except for fixed hours every day devoted to speaking of "necessary matters" ["choses necessaires," 46].

The rigor of the Port-Royal rules arises from two sources: its history and its new leadership and orientation. Port-Royal des Champs was an ancient Cistercian house, founded by Bishop Odo in the twelfth century and reformed according to Jansenist principles in the early seventeenth century. The creator of the Cistercian order, Bernard de Citeaux, had modeled his rule on the ascetic and solitary life of the desert recluses, and the rules imposed by Mother Agnès on her reformed community were intended to return Port-Royal to this original pure state: in her words, "to bring back to life in this house the early spirit of St. Bernard which was almost extinct throughout the entire Cistercian order, equally among men and women" ["faire revivre dans cette maison le premier esprit de St-Bernard qui estoit presque éteint dans tout l'ordre de Cisteaux aussi bien parmi les hommes que parmi les filles," 3–4]. What this spirit consists of is made clear in the last part of the *Constitutions*, "L'Esprit du Monastère de Port-Royal": "What best maintains the spirit of this religion is the small amount of communication with those outside and those within … . The maxim of a prophet is practiced there: *my secret is for me*; for the spreading of good thoughts dissipates them. …" ["Ce qui maintient le plus l'esprit de cette Religion, c'est le peu de communication avec les personnes du dedans & du dehors … L'on y pratique la maxime d'un Prophete: *mon secret est pour moy*; parce que l'epanchement des bonnes pensées les dissipe … ," 402; italics in text]. Even when virtuous thoughts are being expressed, the very act of conversational interchange decreases spiritual concentration and energy. Only by withdrawing, physically and psychically, into one's *intérieur* can one hope to approach the divine. As Agnès explains: "retired into their cells, the sisters will regard them as oratories or temples where they may always offer the sacrifice of prayers made in private to their Lord and father who sees in secret"[5] ["Les Soeurs retirées en leur cellule, elles la regarderont comme une Oratoire, ou un temple où elles puissent toûjours offrir à leur Seigneur & leur pere qui voit en secret, le sacrifice des prières qu'elles feront en leur particulier," 44]. The English expression "in private" has no exact equivalent in French; in classical usage, the nominalized adjectival phrase "en leur particulier" is as close an approximation as one can find. Because of its abstractness, the referent of this "particular" space is ambiguous: it combines the cell as a metaphoric temple or oratory with a metonymic projection (or protection) of the inner, spiritual self. As Sellier states in reference to the early church, "The cell is the image of the Heart" ["La cellule est l'image du Coeur," in "Port-Royal: emblême de la Réforme Catholique" 21]. The strict practices of silence, veiling, praying alone in one's cell, and avoiding unnecessary conversation and even parlor visits with close relatives, are all pursuant to one goal, which Agnès expresses in a beautiful image: "We desire to be neither known nor noticed in the convent, to be as if hidden under the shadow of God" ["L'on desire n'estre ni connuë, ni appercuë dans la maison, d'estre comme cachée sous l'ombre de Dieu," 403]. Thus, in keeping with its reformist project, Port-Royal seeks to return to the fundamental purpose of monastic community: to create for its members a refuge under the protection of God. And a basic necessity for this project is a cell of one's own.

Mother Agnès was twice depicted in her convent by the Jansenist artist Philippe de Champaigne, who also contributed paintings to the Paris Grand Carmel (see above, Chapter 2). One of Champaigne's most famous works, *Ex voto or Two Nuns of Port-Royal*, 1662 (Fig. 5.1) was offered in gratitude when the painter's daughter, a nun at Port Royal, recovered from paralysis after Mother Agnès declared a novena for her cure. The painting depicts the convalescent nun stretched out on a chair in her cell, while Mother Agnès kneels behind her. Revealing the utmost Jansenist simplicity, the cell furnishings consist only of two chairs and a stool made of wood, with a large wooden cross hanging on the wall behind. The stone walls are a dark gray, the nuns' habits a lighter shade of grayish white, their coiffes black, their faces pale. The only touch of color comes from the red crosses sewn on the front of the nuns' robes. The cell has no windows; crypt-like, it appears completely cut off from the outside world except for a shaft of light descending from above. This beam appears of supernatural rather than natural origin. Champaigne depicts the miraculous light of God entering into the nun's cell, which is closed to any natural illumination; rather, its very closure allows the light to penetrate. The artist's vision portrays the encounter between soul and God that can only take place in enclosed isolation; it also suggests symbolically the inner self of mystical writing—dark, hidden, yet lit as by divine flame—revealed in Arnaud d'Andilly's translation of Augustin's *Confessions* (Paige 54).

---

[5] Matthew 6:1.

Fig. 5.1   Philippe de Champaigne, *Ex Voto: Mother Catherine Agnès Arnauld and Sister Catherine de Sainte Suzanne*. 1662. Paris, Louvre. Photo: Franck Raux. Réunion des Musées Nationaux/Art Resource, NY.

Locked in the Cell: The Debate over Forced Profession

By the late seventeenth century, neither Mother Agnès's eloquent expression of the uses of solitude nor Champaigne's vision of enlightenment within enclosure represented the mainstream view of convent life. While the nationalization and abolishment of French religious houses would not take place for over a hundred years, it was preceded and prepared by a long and fierce attack on monastic enclosure, particularly for women. We often identify these attacks with eighteenth-century liberal opposition to absolutism; and they did become more explicit and virulent at that time. But the *philosophes'* critique of monastic life arose in the context of a long-standing and broad-based dissatisfaction with ecclesiastic privilege, both on the part of the larger population and, less expectedly, of the monarchy itself. While early seventeenth-century monasteries and other religious institutions had ridden a wave of Counter-Reformation fervor, by the reign of Louis XIV some secular critics were losing patience with a rich church which enjoyed taxing privileges and tax-exempt status at a time of financial strain in the nation as a whole—a strain exacerbated by continual wars and poor harvests. Quoting one anonymous report, Rapley observes: "the proliferation of monks and nuns, at a time when the economy was under stress, seemed to more critical minds to be tantamount to the creation of a new class of expensive idlers—'much like fleshy excrescences, which drain nourishment from a body of which they are an integral part'" (translated and quoted in *A Social History* 20). Louis XIV, like his forbears, certainly defined France as a Christian monarchy and himself as a Christian king, consecrated by God; but Louis's pragmatic minister Jean-Baptiste Colbert also judged all institutions by their usefulness to the state. As early as 1664, Colbert was looking for ways to cut down the size of a population of "monks of both sexes, who only produce useless people in this world and, often enough, devils in the next" (*Lettres*, in *Mélanges Colbert* 369; quoted in Rapley 20). His success, while only partial, contributed to the impoverishment and even the disappearance of some women's convents by the early eighteenth century (see below, Chapter 7, 283–5).

Thus, the Enlightenment opposition to monasticism and to the church as a whole, which was portrayed as a greedy, superstitious, tyrannical and generally useless institution, was not a radically new attitude. Even the main argument against the enclosure of nuns—the "unnaturalness" of locking up women with other women and preventing them from performing their basic functions as wives and mothers—had its antecedents: seventeenth-century critics argued that through celibacy, monks and nuns were depriving the state of much-needed citizens at a time of population decline through war and famine. However, Enlightenment texts militating against celibacy and enclosure for nuns rely on different arguments from these. Instead of concentrating on the convent's effect on society as a whole, they depict it as a place of forced cloistering and sexual abnormality or excess. In the first instance, anti-monastic literature promotes a negative view through descriptions of sinister convent premises where women are incarcerated involuntarily: in the 1792 Revolutionary decree abolishing monasticism, nuns are referred to as a "mass of victims." Since, with few exceptions, the views of the individual nuns themselves are absent from history, most conclusions must be drawn from indirect evidence, the actual number and proportion of these so-called "victims" is, and will probably remain, a matter of debate among historians. One such debate concerns the medieval convent of Marcigny. While in theory, abuses such as families "giving" girls to convents at the age of seven were forbidden by the church as early as the eleventh century, Jean Verdon suggests that many nuns were still compelled to enter Marcigny at that time, or else entered too young to have a true vocation (252). Taking the opposite position, Mary Skinner sees "little evidence" of forced vocations at Marcigny (96). According to Skinner, the convent explicitly refused to take postulants under the age of 20, and many older women joined the order, presumably after they had been widowed. Skinner continues, on somewhat weaker ground: "I sense a tremendous enthusiasm in the charters on the part of women who founded and entered the new Benedictine houses of the eleventh century" (97).

A similar enthusiasm seemed to possess the post-Trent founders of women's convents; yet at the same time, the Council of Trent sought to guarantee freedom to enter or not to enter those convents. One provision raised the age of profession to 16 and required a probationary period of at least one year (*Canons and Decrees of the Council of Trent*, 25th session, XV, 226). Like earlier medieval decrees, this reform was designed to prevent the placing of female children in convents at an age when they were not yet able to make a rational decision—which suggests that such placements might still have occurred at the beginning of the seventeenth century. The original rule of the Abbaye de Fontevraud had prevented the order from receiving novices who were less than 10 years old. As the novitiate usually lasted three years, the girls would have taken their final vows at 13, while the average marriage age for medieval women was closer to 19. In the seventeenth and eighteenth centuries, profession, like marriage, took place later, with some women wedding at the ripe old age of 24. According to Rapley, however, "An aristocratic girl married much younger than her counterpart in the lower classes; sometimes at the age of 12, more often at 16 to 18, when—according to some learned opinion—she was most likely to produce strong (and male) children" (*Dévotes* 14). In addition, numerous professants had lived at Fontevraud from early childhood. Thus the last abbess, Julie-Sophie d'Antin, had entered the convent as a boarder at the age of two (Lusseau 41–5, 87–8). Despite their entering and professing at an early age, I have seen no evidence of Fontevraud nuns who had been enclosed against their will.

Unlike Mary Skinner's work on Marcigny, Francesca Medioli's study of seventeenth-century Italian nuns is strongly critical of conventual enclosure. In support of her position, she cites the Roman Cardinal de Luca, who in 1675 expressed his sympathy for the unfortunate women who were "imprisoned for life." De Luca also asserted: "it is often the case that young women are induced to take this course (to wit, taking the vow of enclosure) by force" (quoted in Medioli,

168–9). The proportion of enforced monachization is particularly great in one of the convents Medioli studies, the Convertite, whose population included a number of former prostitutes. These women were indeed treated like criminals: formal consent was not required for their enclosure, and many were made to enter the Convertite "by little short of brute force" (174). The Council of Trent decrees state that "No one shall, except in the cases permitted by law, compel a woman to enter a monastery or prevent her if she wishes to enter" (*Canons and Decrees of the Council of Trent*, 25th session, XVIII, 228); the inmates of the Convertite appear to have been among those (hopefully) exceptional cases. While Medioli does "examine briefly the other side of the coin," she concludes that strict enclosure contributes nothing to the spiritual aims of monastic retreat. Rather, it is a purely disciplinary measure, directed only against women. Thus, "A woman who for whatever reason did not wish to remain in a convent had no reason to perceive strict enclosure as anything other than a form of imprisonment" (174).

Elizabeth Rapley takes a more balanced view of forced vocations than either Skinner or Medioli. In her study of women's teaching orders in seventeenth-century France, Rapley finds that at least the letter of the rules for convent entry laid down at Trent was generally observed. However, the decision to enter into religion, like the choice of marriage partners, was not generally made by the girls themselves, who were considered to play little role in their fate, but by their families. The cloister was often a convenient, or perhaps unique, option for orphans, or for parents who were "burdened with many children" (*Social History* 149). Rapley reminds us that there is no way of knowing the intimate feelings of these young postulants as they pronounced their final vows: "how joyful they were, how content, how resigned, or how resentful they were" (177). Evidence Rapley examines for the seventeenth century indicates it was very difficult for nuns to be absolved from their vows.[6] She also cites a small number of eighteenth-century cases where nuns succeeded in leaving the cloister, either because their profession had been fraudulently exacted or because undue force had been exerted against them (178–9). According to records consulted by Rapley, only a tiny minority of nuns brought complaints and asked for release from their vows; but again, we cannot know how many more would have tried to leave if they had had a viable alternative in the outside world: "The rarity of appeals by religious women for annulment of their vows may indicate the great majority's contentment in religion, but it may equally reflect a practical reality—that there was no longer anywhere for them to go" (178).

---

[6] According to the *Decrees of the Council of Trent*, those who wish to repudiate their vows must make an appeal to the Superior within five years of their day of profession, giving their reasons. But anyone who has "laid aside the habit" without following this procedure loses the right to have her/his case considered, and "shall be compelled to return to his monastery and be punished as an apostate" (*Canons and Decrees of the Council of Trent*, 25th session, "Reform of Regulars;" Chapter XIX: "Deserting an Order" 229).

Finally, in "Fantasy and Reality in Fictional Convents of the Eighteenth Century," Katherine M. Rogers presents a mixed view of clausura at the end of the Old Regime. On the one hand, she agrees with some novelists that forced vocations were a "real abuse in traditional French society," especially for upper-class girls (306). The stereotype of noble families locking their daughters up in convents in order to preserve the inheritance for their sons is prevalent in late seventeenth- and early eighteenth-century fiction; but as we will see in connection with Diderot's *La Religieuse*, abuses apparently took place in bourgeois families as well (see below, Chapter 6, 276–7). On the other hand, Rogers asserts that "nuns were generally contented" with their lot: "Evidently most nuns, even if their vocations had been helped along a little, were able to adjust to life in the convent and become sufficiently happy there" (309). This "contentment," if real, may reflect the growing secularization (or laxness, depending on one's point of view) of religious rule in the eighteenth century, which could have made convents a more comfortable place in which to live. Like Rapley, Roberts bases part of her argument on the fact that most nuns stayed in their convents during the Revolution. Roberts concentrates on the period between 1790, when nuns were given the choice to leave the premises, and 1792, when all were forced to vacate. In the great majority of these cases, the nuns wished to stay where they were; some resisted, even violently, being evicted (see Chapter 7, below). Again, the reasons for this reaction are mixed and imperfectly understood. Some nuns expressed a strong desire to live out the rest of their lives in the cloister as their vows had committed them to do. In other cases, it may be that those women who had been cloistered for a period of years had lost all connection with the world outside and could no longer reestablish themselves in society. This group may have included the many girls who entered a religious order after the premature death of their parents; if they had had no other option as children, they would certainly have none as older women. Once more, we are brought up against the ambiguity of the cloistered space: convents, whatever their defects, offered a place for women who had no other place to go. We will now examine how these historical facts square with their representation in fiction.

Anti-Convent Fictional Narratives: Forced Vocation in Castelnau's *Mémoires de Madame la comtesse de M****

The theme of forced vocation plays a central role in the *Mémoires de Madame la comtesse de M*** avant sa retraite* (1697), an autobiographical novel by Henriette de Castelnau, Comtesse de Murat. Murat, like Villedieu, enjoyed the doubly dubious reputation of an adventuress in life and fiction: in the preface to the *Mémoires*, she is forced to refute the criticism that her work is merely a collection of events from novels—"a Collection of Adventures drawn from several Novels" ["un Receuil d'Avantures tirées de plusieurs Romans," Avertissement ii]. Written in a more serious tone than Villedieu's playful *Mémoires de Henriette-Sylvie de Molière*, Murat's novel may give a more realistic picture than Villedieu's of the life of a woman who has no social place of her own. In this respect, her work recalls the memoirs of Hortense Mazarin. However, unlike either Villedieu or Mazarin, Murat's heroine claims she is writing her life not primarily to defend herself, but "in order to justify through my example those Women who have been so cruelly attacked for some time" ["pour justifier par mon exemple les Personnes de mon sexe qu'on a si cruellement décriées depuis quelque-tems," Castelnau vol. 1, 5]. She offers her story as an exemplary tale for other women on what to do, and especially what not to do, if they wish to conserve their fragile reputations. This feminist thrust—in fact, the full title of the novel is *La Défense des Dames ou les Mémoires de Madame la comtesse de M*** avant sa retraite*—makes the work of interest to modern readers.

The narrator's troubles begin at her brother's birth, when she is 11 years old. In order to keep the family fortune intact for the male heir, and to remove a daughter whom her mother does not much care for, the narrator is persuaded against her will to join a convent. She first enters a house where the abbess is her father's cousin. This convent is portrayed by the narrator as a "bad" (i.e., undisciplined) establishment, where the sisters spoil her character with flattery and expose her to worldly influences. She is given little substantive instruction in religion, which she sees only as an "exercise de mémoire" (Castelnau 16), but is left free to read love stories! As a result, by the age of 12, the vain and precocious girl is writing love letters to a friend of her family, the marquis de Blossac, imitating the style of her favorite novelists. When the abbess discovers these letters hidden in a pile of religious books, she tells the girl she deserves to be "locked up between four walls" ["enfermée entre quatre murailles," Castelnau 1.14]—a threat of conventual incarceration already familiar to us. Mainly out of spite, the comtesse announces her decision to become a nun and requests transfer to a "good" convent, where all is regularity and holiness. In the new house, she reports that "each Nun appeared content with her state" ["chaque Religieuse paraissoit contente de son état," Castelnau 63], but still criticizes the nuns for the pride they take in their own austerity. Thus, rather than offering a consistent argument, the narrator vents her general hostility against convents by piling up a series of criticisms—forced enclosure, laxness, proud asceticism—that do not necessarily support one other.

At this point, her father, who is heavily in debt, decides to take her out of the convent and marry her off to a rich man. Since her mother, still hostile to her, wishes her to become a nun rather than to wed, her father arranges a false abduction: "my father took me by the hand while my mother was speaking to the nuns and led me into the courtyard. At the same time, three men approached me; taking me in their arms, they carried me to the gate, and threw me into a six-horse coach. The Coachman immediately struck the horses and separated me from my father" ["mon pere me prenant par la main, pendant que ma mere entretenait les Religieuses, me conduisit dans la cour. En même-tems, trois hommes s'approcherent de moy; & me prenant entre leurs bras, ils me porterent jusqu'à la porte, et là me jetterent dans un carosse à six chevaux. Le Cocher toucha en même-tems, & me separa de mon père," Castelnau 1.25.] Since the story of her love letters is known to everyone by this time, the abduction is blamed not on the father, but on the girl herself.

In an entertaining letter to her daughter, Mme de Sévigné recounts such a "love abduction." One M. de Bethune, a tall, thin, eccentric gentleman whom Sévigné calls "the crazy shepherd of Fontainebleau,"[7] arranges to elope with Mlle de Vaubrun, a daughter of friends who may have entered the convent to facilitate the elopement. Sévigné recounts with gleeful malice:

> So this little girl of seventeen apparently loved this Don Quixote character, and yesterday he went with five or six of M. de Gêvres's guards to break down the convent grill with a log and many blows. He entered the convent with one of his men, found Mlle de Vaubrun who was waiting for him, took her, carried her off, performed a "soldier's marriage," slept with her, and before dawn the next morning they had both disappeared.[8]

> Cette petite fille de dix-sept ans a donc aimé ce Don Quichotte, et hier il alla, avec cinq ou six gardes de M. de Gêvres, enfoncer la grille du couvent avec une bûche et des coups redoublés. Il entra avec un homme à lui dans le couvent, trouve Mlle de Vaubrun qui l'attendait, la prend, l'emporte, fait un mariage sur la croix de l'épée, couche avec elle, et le matin, dès la pointe du jour, ils sont disparus tous deux … . (Sévigné to Mme de Grignan, March 25, 1689. *Correspondance* 3.557)

It would not be surprising if such a romantic scenario were read by the Comtesse's de Murat's fictional public into her abduction as well. In the Comtesse's case, unfortunately, romance plays no role: the man her father forces her to marry, a wealthy counselor in a provincial Parlement, turns out to be cruel and jealous, as well as "naturellement débauché" (Castelnau 1.104). Like Hortense Mazarin, the Comtesse runs away from her husband's house with a single servant, both disguised as peasant women, and takes refuge in an abbey: "After walking all night, we arrived at an abbey where the abbess had offered me asylum" ["Après avoir marché toute la nuit, nous arrivâmes le lendemain à une Abbaye dont l'Abbesse m'avoit offert un azile," Castelnau 1.124]. But again like Mazarin, she quickly learns that "of all the actions that an innocent or guilty Woman can take, the worst is to leave her Husband's House" ["de tous les partis que puisse prendre une Femme innocente ou coupable, le plus mauvais est de sortir de la Maison de son Mari," Castelnau 1.129–30]. The capitalization of "Femme," "Maison" and "Mari," standard typographical practice at the time, accentuates the momentous nature of her error. Yet while the Comtesse cautions other unhappy wives against following her example, her caution is expressed in the form of a wish rather than

---

[7]   A reference to Charles Sorel's popular novel, published in 1633 under the title *Anti-Roman*.

[8]   A *mariage sur le croix de l'épée*, or "soldier's promise of marriage," refers to the cross formed by the transverse grip at the top of a sword. The quote from Sévigné is the most frequent example given for this expression.

a precept, qualified by the sad reflection that women usually lack other choices: "I wish for women in the same circumstances not to follow my example, if, indeed, there are any who could act otherwise" ["Je souhaite que les Femmes qui se trouveront dans les mêmes circonstances ne suivent pas mon exemple, si toutefois, il y en a quelqu'une qui puisse faire autrement," Castelnau 1.134].

The rest of volume 1 recounts the Comtesse's many comings and goings, abductions and escapes after leaving her marital home. At one point, a reconciliation is arranged; but before it can take place, she is abducted by Sauvebeuf, a friend of her husband to whom she had given some unwise encouragement. The Comtesse manages to convince Sauvebeuf to return her to the abbey, a safe space for a woman's reputation; but her husband believes that she had connived in the abduction. And when she finds herself pregnant, he claims that Sauvebeuf is father to her child. She reports of her stay in her husband's house: "I suffered all that cruelty and contempt can invent to torment a Woman. In the end ... fearing for myself and the child I was carrying all the fatal consequences I was justified in fearing, I thought again of running away" ["je souffrois tout ce que la cruauté & le mépris peuvent inventer pour tourmenter une Femme. A la fin ... craignant pour moy et pour l'enfant dont j'étois grosse, toutes les suites funestes que j'avois lieu de craindre, je songeay encore une fois à prendre la fuite," Castelnau 1.180–81]. Allegedly out of respect for her husband, the Comtesse does not reveal his name; nor does she go into the details of these "suites funestes," but the expression certainly points to physical abuse or even death.

Counterbalancing the Comtesse's self-portrayal as an innocent victim, however, are the confessions she makes of what one might now call "poor life choices." Composing love letters to an older man may be seen as the prank of a girl on the verge of puberty, for whom love is still a game learned from books. But the mistakes she makes as a young woman are more serious. For example, after leaving her husband for the second time, instead of following a friend's advice and bringing her case to the Parlement de Bordeaux, she foolishly takes refuge "in a Rival's house" ["chez une Rivale"] to wait for Sauvebeuf, with whom she has become inexplicably infatuated. Yet these actions, while later regretted by the heroine/narrator herself, are not portrayed as the result of "sin" or even bad character. From a privileged inside view, the reader sees the Comtesse as a vain, impulsive young woman, rejected by her mother, avid for attention and admiration, and lacking any positive guidance. For this, the moral condemnation she receives from society is vicious and irrevocable.

When she does not hear from Sauvebeuf, the Comtesse leaves for Paris, even though she is in the last stages of pregnancy. On the way, she gives birth to a son. Upon her arrival in Paris, her husband and mother-in-law try to obtain a *lettre de cachet* to lock her up ["un Ordre du Roy pour me faire enfermer," Castelnau 1.204]. While fighting off her relatives' legal attempts to imprison her, the Comtesse leads a gypsy-like existence in a series of private houses and furnished rooms (*hotels garnis*). She enters a convent again briefly, but is tricked into leaving by a debauched abbé. In this completely unprotected situation, men offer her money which, like Marivaux's Marianne, she refuses; but unlike Marianne, though she constantly declares her virtue and innocence, no one believes her.[9] Even the magistrate whose role it is to defend her against her family's legal action ends up pursuing her. However, the magistrate plays a positive role: through him, she meets his son, the marquis de St-Albe, the first man to woo her respectfully and truly win her heart.

After many more adventures, the novel ends happily, or at least conventionally. Due to a woman friend's influence, the Comtesse receives immunity from prosecution while seeking a separation from her husband. (Like Villedieu, Murat emphasizes the importance of women's mutual support for their survival.) While still in the process of recruiting false witnesses against her for a new order of imprisonment, the Comtesse's husband fortunately dies, leaving behind a declaration of "repentance" ["repentir"] for his cruel treatment of his wife. Her brother's death soon makes her heir to the family estate, and she is able to wed her true love, St-Albe. Sadly, he soon goes off to war and, after a sentimental farewell scene, dies from a wound suffered in battle. The Comtesse laments: "Since then, I have only been occupied with regrets at losing a husband who was so beloved and so worthy of my grief" ["Je n'ay été occupée depuis ce tems-là, que du regret d'avoir perdu un epoux si cher, & si digne de ma douleur," Castelnau 2.372]. She adds: "since then … I have entirely renounced society" ["depuis … j'ay entièrement renoncé au monde," Castelnau 2.394]; but in her retreat, she promises to write more stories in an "aim to justify women" ["dessein de iustifier les femmes," Castelnau 2.395].

In sum, the *Mémoires de la Comtesse de M**** offer an ambivalent view of the cloister. The opening portion focuses critically on involuntary monacization and a complementary topos, abduction from the convent. Murat also satirizes the limited education offered girls in religious establishments, although opportunities for them to study outside hardly existed. However, the convent is also portrayed as an "azile;" at one point in book 1, the Comtesse takes refuge from her husband in an abbey. Similarly, at the end of the novel, the heroine receives the news of her husband's and brother's deaths while living in a "Communauté" of some kind; but no details are given as to its nature. Although the novel and its title end with the Comtesse's withdrawal from society, the phrase *avant sa retraite* creates a false impression of spirituality. Aside from temporary moments of refuge, convent life is not an option the Comtesse takes full advantage of or shows much interest in. Good or bad, the convent is simply taken for granted, as part of contemporary

---

[9] An early twentieth-century example of a woman without a place of her own is Lily Bart, the penniless, orphaned heroine of Edith Wharton's *The House of Mirth*. After her aunt evicts her from her home on false rumors of scandal, Lily lives in a rooming house and fruitlessly attempts to earn her living as a milliner while being pursued by predatory men; finally, penniless and her reputation destroyed, she commits suicide. Wharton's tragic tale, situated in a closed, upper-class New York milieu, echoes early modern women's complaints of abuses suffered by "Filles de Qualité." Published in 1905, it remains a powerful evocation of society's power to destroy "unplaced" women only 100 years ago.

female life. The heroine's retreat, unlike that of Henriette-Sylvie de Molière or the Princesse de Clèves, is both completely secular and conventionally feminine: having married, then lost, the man she loves, she exits the world a decorous and inconsolable widow. Villedieu's and Lafayette's widows exhibit no such conventional motivations (see above, Chapter 4).[10] We never find out why Mme de Chartres had retreated from court; there is no description of her husband or married life. And although M. de Clèves's death was certainly a main factor in the Princesse's retreat, she suffers more from guilt than from traditional wifely grief. As for Henriette-Sylvie de Molière, long before taking up residence in a convent she had outgrown any interest in past or future marriages.

Murat's perspective is quite different from that of these other two women writers. While the *Mémoires de la Comtesse de M**** begin and end in a convent, its main focus is on matrimony. Once the heroine is married, the critique of forced monachization fades into the background, and the *chanson de nonne* modulates into a *chanson de mal mariée* until the heroine finds true love with the comte.[11] What is interesting, however, is that Murat portrays both forced marriage and involuntary religious vocation as examples of the same abuse suffered by girls of good family, whose lives are sacrificed for purely financial motives ["Filles de Qualité que l'on sacrifie à l'interest," Castelnau 1.194]. And of the two, forced marriage is seen as the more pernicious. In appearance, married women have more freedom of movement than cloistered nuns (though this is not always the case). But their freedom is often an illusion, because they are still trapped behind the mutually reinforcing bars of public opinion, patriarchal authority and governmental force.

Venus in the Cloister: Confined Sexuality in *Galant* Fiction

—On Thursday the fifteenth, I bought four new comic pieces that cost me six sous, namely: three pleas, one tale about the principality of fools, of whom there are as many in the world as in the place you might go, and the other on transporting the relics of a penitent nun, of whom there are very few.

—Le jeudi 15, j'ai acheté quatre bagatelles nouvelles qui m'ont cousté six sols, à scavoir: trois plaidoiers, l'un sur la principauté des sots, dont il y en a au monde autant qu'en lieu où vous scauriés aller. L'autre sur la translation d'une religieuse pénitente, dont il y a fort peu.

—Pierre de l'Estoile, *Mémoires et registre-journal de Henri III, Henri IV et de Louis XIII: Roy de France et de Navarre* (1608, pub. 1837), 459.

---

[10] For more on Villedieu's widows, see Donna Kuizenga, "'Fine veuve' ou 'veuve d'une haute vertu'? Portraits de la veuve chez Mme de Villedieu." *Cahiers du Dix-Septième* [Spring 1997] 227–39.

[11] The nun's song and the song of the unhappy wife were both medieval lyrical genres. See below, n20.

Along with forced monachization, sexual license is probably the most common criticism aimed at women's monasteries; in anti-convent writing, these two arguments are often inseparable. While hard historical evidence is rare in the first case, it is even harder to come by in the second. Even if the debate over involuntary monachization may never be fully resolved, the question is at least subject to historical investigation: infrequent though they may be, legal records do exist of nuns appealing to have their vows annulled. On the other hand, hints of *galanterie monastique* are mostly found in letters and memoirs. One instance is the story of Mme de Sévigné's wayward son Charles. In addition to carrying on with Ninon de Lenclos as his father did before him, Charles reportedly had relationships with two highly-placed nuns: Charlotte-Marguerite de Lenoncourt, abbesse de Saint-Goey d'Epinal, and Marie II Ragier de Poussée, abbesse de Sézanne. The first time Sévigné mentions Charles in a letter to her daughter, she also alludes to Charlotte-Marguerite de Lenoncourt: "Charles aroused fears for his health because he was unhappy in Nancy since Mme de Madruche's departure" ["(Charles) faisait peur de sa santé, parce qu'il s'ennuyait à Nancy depuis le départ de Mme de Madruche," *Correspondence* 1.169; February 25, 1671]. "Mme de Madruche" is none other than Charlotte de Lenoncourt, daughter of Charlotte de Madruce and also the abbesse de Saint-Goey d'Epinal.

The second abbesse, Ragier de Poussée, is alluded to when Sévigné speculates about Charles's whereabouts: "Where can he be? For my part, I am not at all perplexed, and I'm sure that he is singing vespers with his pretty abbess: you know that he always finds her house to be on his way" ["Où pourrait-il être? Pour moi, je n'en suis point en peine, et je suis assurée qu'il chante vêpres auprès de sa jolie abbesse: vous savez que c'est toujours son chemin de passer chez elle," *Correspondance* 2.172, November 27, 1675]. Though this is the first time l'abbesse de Sézanne is mentioned in the letters, Sévigné seems to indicate that Charles's visits to her are already an established routine.[12] The granddaughter of Mère Chantal, the first abbess of the Visitation, Mme de Sévigné was personally devout and admired instances of true piety. Nevertheless, Sévigné is rather playful in her descriptions of convent antics. For example, she writes Mme de Grignan concerning a handsome young doctor who treats the nuns at the strict convent of Chelles: "I believe that several good sisters seek him out at their pleasure and tell him their ills, but I would swear that he will not cure one of them except according to the rules of Hippocrates" ["Je crois que plusieurs bonnes soeurs le trouvent à leur gré, et lui disent leur maux, mais je jurerais qu'il n'en guérira pas une que selon les règles d'Hippocrate," *Correspondance* 2.294, May 6, 1676]. On the surface, Sévigné also treats her own son's monastic distractions with cynical tolerance. As she remarks to Mme de Grignan, at least his liaison with the abbesse de Sézanne does not put him in danger of marriage: "my son … left earlier, and comes back later than the others; we think that it is because of a friendship he

---

[12]   This observation was suggested to me by Marc Landry, whose assistance with the *abbesses galantes* is greatly appreciated.

has in Sézanne, but since there is no question of marriage, I put my mind at rest" ["mon fils … est parti plus tôt, et revient plus tard que les autres; nous croyons que cela roule sur une amitié qu'il a à Sézanne, mais, comme ce n'est pas pour épouser, je m'en mets l'esprit en repos," *Correspondance* 2.681–2, January 26, 1674].

In contrast to Sévigné's delicate raillery, the duc de Saint-Simon's account of the misadventures of the aptly named abbesse de la Joye falls completely into the category of farce. Saint-Simon recounts the abbess's acquaintance with the marquis de Ségur, a captain of musketeers who was appointed governor of Foix by Louis XIV for his prowess in battle. According to Saint-Simon, Ségur was "gentle, polite and well-spoken" ["doux, poli et galant"] as well as being a skilled lute player. As a result, and despite having lost a leg at the battle of Marseilles, Ségur "charmed her so well by the ears and the eyes that he got her pregnant" ["la charma si bien par les oreilles et par les yeux qu'il lui fit un enfant"]. Miscalculating the baby's arrival date, the abbess had to give birth in a public inn at Fontainebleau, in close proximity to the court. Her own father, M. d'Aignan, ignorant of the identity of the woman in question, initially spread the story as a fine joke. But the comedy had a serious ending: the abbess spent the rest of her life hidden away in another convent, where she died in 1734 (St-Simon, *Mémoires* 2.26–7).

However good a story it makes, the precise facts of the abbess's adventure are in doubt. St-Simon was not an eyewitness of the affair; Anne du Noyer's *Lettres historiques et galantes*, a probable source for his *Mémoires*, places the child's birth at Versailles, not Fontainebleau, and even suggests that the "jeune nonette" was the author of "those very passionate letters that appeared in society under the name of Portuguese Letters" ["ces lettres si passionnées qui ont paru dans le monde sous le nom de Lettres portugaises," 2.1193n27]. According to du Noyer, the unfortunate author of the letters would have somehow managed to escape her Portuguese convent only to become impregnated by a second French officer! In a final avatar of this tale, du Noyer's *Lettres historiques* were known by Stendhal, and may have played a role in the composition of his *Mémoires d'un touriste* and *Abbesse de Castro*. While something may have occurred between the musketeer and the abbess, it appears that in their eagerness to tell a spicy tale, letter- and memoir-writers, not to mention novelists, hardly distinguish between reality and fiction.[13] Thus, Roger Duchêne proceeds with appropriate caution in regard to the abbesse de Saint Goey d'Epinal: "perhaps she is the one with whom Charles had an intrigue" ["peut-être est-ce avec elle que Charles avait une intrigue," *Correspondance* 1.1005n6].

Whatever the truth of such stories, in the domain of fiction, religious satire has always enjoyed an intimate relation with sex: since the early Middle

---

[13]   Further information on these two abbesses can be found in François Weymuller, *Histoire d'Epinal des origines à nos jours* (Le Coteau: Ed. Hovarth, 1985); and Edouard André, *Histoire de l'abbaye du Bricot en Brie* (XIIème siècle–1792) (Paris: Alphonse Picard & fils, 1895). Marie II Raguier de Poussée had been abbesse at Notre-Dame des Bois and Le Bricot as well as Sézanne.

Ages, scandalous tales of nuns and priests have been told and listened to with delight. In these tales, the simple pleasure of hearing a dirty story is enhanced by the undermining of powerful institutions and supposedly austere reputations. As Bakhtine has shown, medieval and Renaissance satire and farce turn "the world upside down," reversing common hierarchies of male-female, spirit-body, order-disorder. In a fifteenth-century saying, "le bas fait tomber le haut."[14] This heels-over-head tumble is even more pleasurable to hear about when it happens to holy men and women. The prestige of Catholic clerics rests, at least in part, on their celibacy, which sets them apart and marks them as spiritually superior to ordinary mortals; so what could be more enjoyable than hearing tales of these clerics getting up to all kinds of naughty antics in their cells and sacristies?

In addition to the pleasure of power reversal, tales of lascivious nuns feed the latent (or not so latent) misogyny of the time. As daughters of Eve, all women were considered innately licentious and dominated by their sexuality; however, cloistered women were seen as a hundred times worse off because of the sexual frustration they endured. According to a medieval rhyme, "A girl's desire is a fire that devours / A nun's desire is a hundred times worse" ["Désir de fille est un feu qui dévore / Désir de nonne est cent fois pis encore"].[15] The scabrous nun stories which formed part of the oral tradition found their way into writing through late medieval fabliaux, such as the *Cent Nouvelle Nouvelles*, and later through Rabelais's novels and Boccacio's *Decameron*. In the seventeenth century, one of Boccacio's tales of convent debauchery is reprised by La Fontaine in "Le Muet de Bocasse."[16] This licentious anti-clerical tradition was also exploited in the *galant* fiction that came to the fore in the latter part of the seventeenth century: as Geneviève Reynes points out, "Throughout the whole Old Regime, the nun continues to be the favorite subject of love novels, because she exercises a great power of seduction on the imagination" ["Durant tout l'Ancien régime, la religieuse continue pourtant à être le sujet de prédilection de la littérature galante et romanesque, car elle jouit d'un grand pouvoir de séduction sur les imaginations," 186]. The letters of Eloise and Abelard had been republished in Latin in 1616, and appeared in French translation at the end of the century (see below, Chapter 6, n3). Were depictions of love in the cloister, as Reynes suggests, more a source of entertainment than a serious attack on monastic institutions? We will attempt

---

[14]   For more on the comic tropes of the upside-down world and the woman on top, see Mikhael Bakhtine, *Rabelais and His World* (Bloomington: Indiana University Press, 1984); and Natalie Z. Davis, "Women on Top," in *Society and Culture in Early Modern France* (Stanford: Stanford University Press, 1975), 125–51.

[15]   Ruth Graham, "The Married Nuns before Cardinal Caprara" 327. Quoted in Rapley 115.

[16]   La Fontaine, *Contes et nouvelles* (Paris: Nouvelle Librairie de France, 1959). Other bawdy nuns' tales by La Fontaine include "L'Abbesse" and "Les Lunettes," from the third edition of the *Contes*. On the general topic of seventeenth-century erotic convent stories, see Adrienne E. Zuerner, "An Unholy Trinity: Sex, Politics and Religion in Villedieu's *La Religieuse*" 194–5.

to answer this question by examining a series of *romans galants* dating from the seventeenth and early eighteenth centuries.[17]

Catherine de Villedieu, "La Religieuse"

Both male and female *galant* writers incorporated monastic love intrigues into their works. Among these is Catherine de Villedieu. While most *galant* nun's stories did not appear before the 1680s, Villedieu's 1672 collection of short pseudo-historical tales, *Les Annales galantes*, already contains a short story called "La Religieuse."[18] The not-very-serious thesis of Villedieu's *Annales* is that love supplies the secret motor for great historical events. "La Religieuse" follows this scenario: "Set in twelfth-century Italy against the backdrop of the dynastic ambitions of the Holy Roman Emperor, Frederick Barbarossa, "La Religieuse" traces the cause of the Guelph Wars to the rivalry between the emperor and his son over the hand of a woman."[19] For the most part, however, "La Religieuse" is a light-hearted love intrigue, with scabrous and satirical seasonings added to heighten its savor. The story begins when Henry, the emperor's son, is captivated by a beautiful singing voice he hears while attending a public celebration in a Roman convent. In *Invisible City*, Helen Hills writes eloquently of the power of nuns' tantalizingly absent "presence": "the promise of their presence was constantly suggested by angelic singing from the choir, sounds muffled behind screens, an indistinct glimpse snatched between grilles … conventual architecture served to shatter and fragment, to tantalize and obscure, to disembody and to mystify" (Hills 181).

Mesmerized by this disembodied voice, Henry sets out to discover its owner, who turns out to be the Pope's niece Constance. Constance's attraction for Henry is also enhanced by her nun's garb: as Villedieu comments, "he was not the only one to be excited by the simplicity of the veil. There are men with whom love can only find a weak point under this guise" ["il n'a pas été le seul qui se soit fait un ragoust de la simplicité du voile. Il y a des gens dont l'amour ne trouve le foible que sous cette figure," 113–14].

Villedieu observes correctly that Henry is not alone: the seduction exercised by the veil is a common theme in *galant* and *libertin* fiction. In *La Fausse Abbesse ou*

---

[17] *Galant* is a word with wide-ranging meanings. In this context, it broadly refers to the discourse and practices of love. A *lettre galante* is a love letter; a *galanterie* can be anything from a pretty speech to a flirtation to a sexual affair. While it is difficult to draw a firm line, *galant* novels let the reader know that sexual actions have taken place without going into detail. *Libertin* texts are more erotic, though they also display a range: while some contain explicit language, others rely on allusions, metaphors and innuendoes to convey a clear sexual meaning.

[18] An earlier *galant* story concerning a nun, not included in this study, is *Galanteries d'une religieuse* (anon. 1666). For further titles of *galant* novels, see the Works Cited.

[19] Adrienne Zuerner, "An Unholy Trinity" 192. For more on the political aspects of this work, also see Zuerner's very comprehensive article.

l'Amoureux dupé (1681), a character falls in love with a nun: "The air, the grace, the modesty of this young girl, and something sweet about a tight neck-cloth had made a deep impression on my soul" ["L'air, la grace, la modestie de cette jeune fille & je-ne-sçay-quoi de doux, que donne une guimpe bien tirée avait fait une profonde impression dans mon ame," 10–11]. Furthermore, he confesses:

> The intense attraction I felt for this young Nun is aroused in me by the presence of all veiled women who have some features of passable beauty. That is what often attracts me to Parlors and makes me frequent [convent] Churches on the pretense of extreme piety, especially when the sermon gives me the opportunity to observe them in the Choir.

> Cette violente inclination que je pris pour cette jeune Religieuse se renouvelle toujours en moy à la presence de toutes les Voilées, qui ont quelques traits d'une beauté passable. C'est ce qui m'attire souvent aux Parloirs & qui me fait hanter par le principe d'une devotion extravagante leurs Eglises, particulierement lorsque la predication me donne la commodité de les envisager dans le Chœur. (*La Fausse Abbesse* 16)

His claustral obsession is so strong, the character admits, that rather like Sévigné's son "I have never passed by a Convent without dropping in" ["Je n'ay pas rencontré un Couvent en chemin que je n'aye pas visité," *La Fausse Abbesse* 17].

In addition to this fetishistic fascination with the veil, Villedieu's "La Religieuse" presents another theme familiar from monastic satire: the accommodating nature of nuns hidden under a cloak of virtue. According to Villedieu, "Monastic love has its own Rules and regulations; it will endure neither ostentatious entertainments nor obvious attentions; one has to attack the Cloister defenses quietly. But since Religious propriety allows for no vain steps, all the actions one takes arrive at their goal" ["La galanterie Monachale a ses Loix & ses rubriques à part: elle ne souffre ni fêtes d'éclat, ni assiduïtés apparentes: il faut attaquer les places de Cloître à la sourdine. Mais comme la bienséance Religieuse ne permet aucun pas inutile, tous ceux qu'on fait arrivent au but," Villedieu "La Religieuse" 114–15]. However, the "politique de la grille," as Villedieu calls it, limits Henry to a fixed number of parlor visits; and the superior is, unfortunately, not one of those "noble ladies who might have shown some savoir-vivre" by bending the rules ["dames de qualité qui auroit peut-être sçu vivre," Villedieu "La Religieuse" 117]. The expression "qui aurait peut-être sçu vivre" is revealing. *Savoir-vivre* is a quality of worldiness, implying a willingness to compromise, or at least to "parley," with secular behavior. While on the one hand Villedieu satirizes what she calls "la galanterie monachale," she also suggests that some convents, or convent leaders, reject gallantry's dictates and remain faithful to their rule.

Finding the abbess lacking in flexibility, Henry instead enlists the aid of three of his most faithful men, who are also "the most likely to arouse love" ["les plus propres de se faire aimer," Villedieu "La Religieuse" 119]. Henry's strategic plan is simply to have his men seduce, or "entreprendre," three of the key officials in convent security: "the Convent Portress, the Sister who listened to conversations in the Parlors, and the one who was charged with awakening the others" ["la Portière du Couvent, la Soeur qui écoutoit aux Parloirs, & celle qui avoit le soin d'éveiller les autres," Villedieu "La Religieuse" 119]. This aim is quickly accomplished, and Henry and his companions "spent entire nights in the Garden with the four ladies on whom the spell of love had been cast" ["passoient les nuicts entieres dans le Jardin avec les quatre dames sur qui le sort amoureux estoit tombée," Villedieu "La Religieuse" 120]. In her portrait of convent debauchery, Villedieu does, however, draw a distinction between Constance and her companions. Unlike the latter, Constance truly loves her suitor and is equal to him in social rank. She has the additional excuse that she entered the convent unwillingly. But Villedieu's comment on this matter is half-ironic: "Constance had embraced Monastic life by obedience rather than by choice; and in vows made in this manner, one always reserves the right to direct one's intention" ["Constance avait embrassé la vie Monastique par obeissance, plutôt que par choix; & dans les voeux qu'on fait de cette manière, on se reserve toujours le droit de diriger l'intention," Villedieu "La Religieuse" 196]. The fact that Constance did not enter the convent by choice arouses our sympathies and perhaps justifies her behavior to some extent; but in the same sentence, Villedieu introduces a satirical and anachronistic reference to the Jesuit practice of directing one's moral intention, famously satirized in Pascal's *Provinciales* and Molière's *Tartuffe*. For holy vows that are meant to be inviolable and absolute, no such "direction" is possible. This ironic allusion to forced vocation places "La Religieuse" in the realm of light religious satire. Like *Les Memoires de la Comtesse de M****, it is neither a "chanson de nonne" nor a serious criticism of forced vows.[20]

In regard to conventual spaces, it is noteworthy that the quartet of lovers confine their activities to the garden, rather than entering into the convent building and its individual cells as characters from other *galant* works are wont to do. For example, in *La Religieuse penitente* (1649), an early example of this genre, a Captain in love with a nun gets a key made to the *jardin des religieuses* and to her room. The next morning, he writes a triumphant (and bad) poem: "My fate, bound by such cruel laws / Strongly opposed the invincible obstacle / Of these frightful walls, so impossible to attack; / But you speak, Sylvie, and the path is smoothed, / The Cloister opens its bosom, my wishes are granted, / Everything gives way" ["Mon destin attaché è des loix trop cruelles / Opposoit fortement pour obstacle invincible / De ces murs trop affreux l'abord inaccessible; / Mais vous parlez Sylvie & les voies s'applanissent, / Ce Cloitre ouvre son sein, mes souhaits s'accomplissent, / Tout cede," 65]. This example shows an interesting

---

[20]   *Chanson de nonne*: although these medieval songs were written in the voices of unhappy female religious, according to Lisa Colton "the majority were in fact the product of the male, clerical imagination" ("'The Age of Innocence:' Chastity and the Chanson de Nonne in the Montpellier codex." University of Tours. 2005 Medieval and Renaissance Music Conference. http://www.cest.univ-tours.fr/ricercar/medren/Program/Abstracts.pdf).

hybridism: précieux/pastoral rhetoric—"destin ... loix trop cruelles ... Sylvie"—is joined to the metaphoric construction of the convent as a yielding woman's body: "Le Cloitre ouvre son sein ... tout cede."

Villedieu's nuns, however, are not content to remain within the cloister walls; instead of inviting their lovers in, Constance and her three companions contrive to leave the convent to attend a nocturnal celebration put on by the Emperor (Villedieu "La Religieuse" 127). The four nuns change on the way into masquerade dress, leaving their religious garb in the coach. This quick costume switch suggests that the transformation from nun to woman of the world involves no more than a *changement d'habit*. At the festival, Constance meets the Emperor who, in a repeat of his son's adventure, is captivated by her and seeks to learn her true identity. She puts him off, making an appointment for the next day. The four ladies climb back into the coach, again effecting a costume change en route. When they arrive at the rear gate of the convent, a comic scene ensues because the portress cannot remember where she put the key. Villedieu satirically remarks: "not one of our ladies could conceive by what miracle they would be transported from the Coach where they were, into the Cells where they should have been" ["aucune de nos dames ne pouvoit concevoir par quel miracle elles seroient transportées du Carosse où elles estoient, dans les Cellules où elles auroient deu estre," Villedieu "La Religieuse" 137]. It is nearly dawn before the portress finally locates the key. Naturally, "Great prayers of thanksgiving followed this happy discovery" ["Grandes actions de graces suivirent cette heureuse decouverte," Villedieu "La Religieuse" 139].

In order to mislead the Emperor, Constance had agreed to meet him in a garden frequented by courtesans. When she fails to appear, Frederic is furious at being tricked and even more eager to hunt her down. His search is vain until he finds a letter she had written to his son in which she identifies herself. Frederic immediately goes to Constance's convent and demands an interview. When he glimpses her through the bars of the convent parlor, "He saw through her religious habit the form and majesty which had so surprised him under her masquerade dress" ["Il penetra au travers de son habit de Religieuse, cette taille, & cette majesté, qui luy avoient paru si surprenantes sous son habit de masque," Villedieu "La Religieuse," 160]. This sentence emphasizes the erotic power of Frederic's gaze that "penetrates" the convent grill and the masking clothing, whether it be a nun's habit or a masquerade costume, to discern the woman beneath.

Not satisfied with mere visual penetration, Frederick presses Constance to become his lover, threatening to show the Pope the letter she had written to Henry if she does not accede to his demands. As a pretext for visiting the convent frequently, by "divine inspiration" he endows a series of buildings there—including a dormitory. The mercenary superior "now only regards the Emperor as the guardian Angel of her Order" ["ne regarde plus l'Empereur, que comme l'Ange tutelaire de son Ordre," Villedieu "La Religieuse" 175–6]; neither she nor the Pope has any suspicion of Frederic's true motives. Significantly, the construction work under way creates a break (*une brêche*) in the convent wall, just as Frederic's patronage has made a breach in the superior's defenses. Through this break, he enters the garden with his men in order to abduct Constance; but the wily nun convinces him to hand over her letter to Henry, and then screams for help. Her loud cries "persuaded him so strongly that the garden was not a good place for him to be that he left rapidly" ["luy persuaderent si fortement qu'il ne faisait pas bon pour luy dans ce jardin qu'il en sortit en diligence," Villedieu "La Religieuse" 182]. According to Villedieu, the rage and humiliation Frederic feels at this forced retreat provoke him to initiate the long and bloody Guelph war, which in turn leads to the Pope's exile in France, the creation of several "Anti-Popes" and many other religious and civil disorders (Villedieu "La Religieuse" 188).

The tale's love intrigue does not end much more happily. As in the *Mémoires de la vie de Henriette-Sylvie de Molière*, Villedieu subverts the traditional denouement: Constance does marry Henry, but the marriage is a political union arranged by the Pope rather than a love match. By this time, Henry has lost interest in her; as Villedieu states in a cynical maxim: "At the appearance of marriage love must cease, / Disgust is a common ill" ["A l'aspect de l'hymen il faut que l'amour cesse, / Le dégoust est un mal commun," Villedieu "La Religieuse" 195]. Henry's companions, who are not offered any political advantages to sweeten the deal, abandon their own mistresses—fearing that after marriage, the nuns might behave, or misbehave, with other men as they had with them. In any case, as Zuerner points out, none of the love intrigues Villedieu inserts into the story is accurate: the real Constance left her convent with regret, only marrying Henry in obedience to her uncle's order (Zuerner 193).

In conclusion, though "La Religieuse" does not aim much higher than light-hearted entertainment, Villedieu does offer some insights into religious life and identity as well as the abuses of power exercised on women. Zuerner describes the Emperor's pursuit of a cloistered nun as "the deployment of legitimate authority to illegitimate ends" (198); the same description could be applied to the parents and other authorities who order women to enter convents or to marry against their will. And while the multiple disguises in the story mostly serve to add drama and romance, these rapid changes of costume also suggest an identification, even an identity, between the bodies of courtesan, masked lady and nun. This identification radically secularizes the quality of religious existence. While Villedieu's "Religieuse" is a long way, temporally and ideologically, from Diderot's work of the same name, the insistence on the woman's body underneath the habit, and upon the natural sexuality of that body, will play a key role in the Enlightenment argument against conventual enclosure.

Histoire du Comte de Clare

Like "La Religieuse," the *Histoire du Comte de Clare* (published under the name of Madame de Tenain, probably Claudine Alexandrine Guerin de Tencin, in 1695) places comic effect before social comment. While subtitled *nouvelle galante*,

L'Histoire displays something of a crossover between the *galant* and the *libertin* genres. By either name, the characters' behavior is decidedly licentious. The plot of this bawdy novel is double. On the one hand, the comte de Clare is carrying on an intrigue with the marquise de Nerville; when she learns her husband is beginning to suspect her, she enters a convent (Tencin 75). At the same time, Clare's friend Santeüil, a Latin poet who serves as a comic foil to the main plot, is in love with a nun. In one early episode, Clare and Santeüil share a supper with a gluttonous monk. This scene is so quintessentially "eighteenth century" in its combination of religious satire with *joie de vivre* that it could have been a model for Anatole France.[21] The monk, "who was extremely fond of good food, cast his eyes on some little game hens, accompanied by red partridges, whose steam so excited his sense of smell that he had no desire to leave at such a favorable juncture" ["qui aime extrêmement les bons repas, jettant la vûe sur certaines gelinottes du Mans accompagnées de perdrix rouges, dont la fumée lui gagnoit l'odorat, ne voulut point quitter la partie dans une occasion si favorable," Tencin 83].

After the monk invites himself to supper, Santeüil promptly asks him if he knows a nun in a certain convent. The monk replies: "Do you need someone in there? I will give you the Abbess, the Prioress, for that matter the whole Convent, and even, if you want, all their Saints" ["Avez-vous besoin de quelqu'un la dedans? Je vous y donnerai l'Abbesse, la Prieure, & enfin tout le Convent, & méme si vous voulez tous leurs Saints," Tencin 84]. The prepositions "la dedans" and "y" emphasize the priority of the enclosed space over the individual women living in it, who in the monk's hyperbolic statement become almost interchangeable. Since this convent also happens to be the one where the marquise de Neville has taken refuge from her husband, the two friends decide to visit it the very next day, "properly" disguised as monks. As for their supper companion, "this monk disguised himself as an abbé, as those of his order ordinarily do when they go on campaign" ["ce Moine se déguisa en Abbé, comme font ordinairement ceux de cet Ordre, quand ils vont en campagne," Tencin 85].[22] A "very pretty and good-humored" young nun ["fort jolie, & de tres bonne humeur"] comes to meet them in the abbess's place. Although she is not the one he was seeking, in Santeüil's eyes one habit is as good as another, and his interest is immediately aroused. "When he saw that the nun had pretty hands and arms, a slender waist, and admirable eyes, he got down on one knee" ["Ensuite comme il vit que la Religieuse avoit la main & les bras beaux, la taille fine, & des yeux admirables, il mit un genou en terre"] and begins reciting such ridiculous compliments that the nun bursts out laughing. He offers to send her a love poem in Latin, but she objects that she does not understand that language; and in a satirical allusion to the insufficiency of convent

---

[21]   France's delightful *La Rôtisserie de la Reine Pédauque* (1893) features a gluttonous friar, devouring delicious suppers at the *rôtisserie* of the title.

[22]   An *abbé*, in the seventeenth century, was an individual who received revenue from a monastery without actually governing it; the word later came to mean anyone who dressed in clerical garb without having taken vows. Abbés were often lampooned in religious satire.

education, she adds, "I don't believe that out of ten thousand women, there is a single one who understands it" outside of the "nobility of the Latin country" ["je ne pense pas même que de dix mille femmes, il y en ait une qui l'entende … grand monde du Païs Latin," Tencin 90–91].

Accommodating the young nun's ignorance of classical languages, the false monk sends her instead a poem written in French, entitled "Declaration d'amour d'un Moine à une Religieuse." This and the other poems interpolated into the novel cause it to slip from the *galant* into the *libertin* category. The poem begins by comparing the young nun to a cat, and the monk to a friendly rat; but the "rat" quickly becomes a metaphor for the male organ: "I enter everywhere very easily … I slip in with such agility / And the smallest opening / Is where I want to go" ["J'entre par tout bien aisément … Tant j'ai d'adresse à me glisser, / Et la plus petite ouverture / Est celle où je cherche à passer," Tencin 94–5]. As the poem progresses, the phallic metaphor becomes more explicit: "I am most often hidden, / But I appear easily / When the hope of pleasure touches me / And in that sudden moment, / One finds me so tame / That I can be held in the hand" ["Je suis caché le plus souvent, / Mais je parois facilement / Quand l'espoir du plaisir me touche; / Et dans ce moment soudain, / On me trouve si peu farouche / Que l'on me peut prendre à la main," Tencin 96]. The vulgarity of the ending taxes the translating skill of this scholar: "If you value good sex / set out your mousetrap for me. / I'll put it in for the love of you" ["Si vous cherissez les bons coups / Tendez-moi vôtre souriciere. / J'y mettrai pour l'amour de vous," Tencin 97–8]. The nun not only understood the riddle, but "held her sides with laughing" ["se prit par les côtez de rire," Tencin 98].

In the parallel plot, the Comte de Clare gains entry to the convent by bribing the gardener's son. Since the room of the nun Santeüil is courting is located next to the marquise's, her consent is also necessary, but she offers it readily. In a satirical description of convent hypocrisy, the narrator states: "Every night was nothing but joy, pleasure and celebration. During the day these Ladies kept silence with a modest air, like Vestal virgins" ["Ce n'étoit toutes les nuits que joie, que plaisir, que festin. Le jour les Dames étoient dans le silence avec un air de modestie semblables à des Vestales," Tencin 103]. However, Santeüil becomes disenchanted with his nun when she keeps asking for presents; in another set of coarse verses, he compares her to a prostitute: "Don't you know that a woman of pleasure / Thus looks for new prey every day?" ["Ne sçavez vous pas bien qu'une femme de joye / Cherche ainsi tous les jours quelques nouvelle proie?" Tencin 107]. The marquise, in contrast, is disinterested in her passion for Clare, and things go well for them until she learns she is pregnant. Since she is not very far along, she decides the only solution is to write to her husband asking for a reconciliation. He is happy to hear from her after three months of separation, and comes to the convent the very next day. During his visit, the marquise proclaims her virtue and her willingness to spend another three years, even her whole life, encloistered, if necessary to prove her submission to her husband. Delighted, the marquis immediately takes her home with him.

In counterpoint to this relatively legitimate convent exit, Santeüil takes up with a new nun, as attractive and as mercenary as the first, whom he manages to extract from the cloister and set up in "a very nice room" ["une chambre fort propre," Tencin 134]. His annual pension from the King for his Latin verses "allowed him to stuff himself with the nun" ["servit à gonfrer avec la Religieuse," Tencin 135]; but it soon is used up. When the nun sees that Santeüil has no more money, she looks for greener pastures. During a promenade, she encounters a certain chevalier de Belforêt who wins her heart with another set of verses, even lewder and more explicit than Santeüil's. The story ends happily and implausibly: the nun easily obtains freedom from her vows "because she had made them under constraint, and at a very young age" ["pour ce qu'elle les avoit fait par force, & dans une grande jeunesse," Tencin 101]. In reality, since she had deserted the order, probably in disguise, she would have lost any chance to renounce her vows, and been punished severely (see n5). The main plot also resolves itself when the marquis de Nerville dies and Clare is able to marry his widow. The narrator is in accord with Villedieu's cynical view that "possession ... ordinarily diminishes the ardor of Lovers" ["la possession ... d'ordinaire diminuë l'ardeur des Amants"]. But exceptionally in this case, "it only served to increase theirs" ["(elle) ne servit qu'à augmenter la leur," Tencin 203]. Sadly, after a short period of marital bliss, the comte, like the chevalier in the *Mémoires de la Comtesse* ***, dies of a wound received in battle. He leaves half of his wealth to his wife and the remaining half to their child, known as the marquis de Nerville. In the end, even Santeüil consoles himself with another love.

While *Le Comte de Clare*'s depiction of monastic immorality is more complete and graphic than Villedieu's, their immoral tales have a common "moral": "nothing escapes the power of love ... those who should be the most detached from it are often the most compliant" ["que rien n'echape à la puissance de l'amour ... que ceux qui en devroient être les plus detaches y sont souvent les plus obeissants," Tencin 205–6]. In other words, the author of *Le Comte de Clare* exploits the convent setting and the age-old currency of religious satire, like randy nuns and wily wives, simply in order to write an amusing romp. There is no character development in the novel. We do not even learn the names of the holy women Santeüil is pursuing; they are just generically called "nuns." Their attraction is also generic, arising from the mystique of veils and locked gates. This superficiality contrasts with the realism and social criticism found in the *Mémoires de la Comtesse* *** analyzed above; but it might serve as a "well of plots" for novels which are more critical of the institution of monasticism itself.

Convent Criticism and the Catholic-Protestant Debate: *La Religieuse malgré elle*

While the *galant* texts examined thus far satirize women and religious institutions, they do so within traditional limits—mocking the convent without seriously proposing its reform, let alone its abolition. But at the beginning of the eighteenth century, more radical criticisms of monasticism also come into fictional representation. Some of these critiques appear in Protestant texts. Before becoming a theme of the *philosophes*, the condemnation of monastic claustration had been one of the main arguments of the Protestant Reformation against the Catholic Church; and the Revocation of the Edict of Nantes in 1685 revived this debate in France. The issues of monasticism and Protestantism sometimes become confused, however. For example, in the preface to *La religieuse malgré elle, histoire galante, morale et tragique* (1720), Brunet de Brou states as his main intention to show the evil consequences of parents' placing their daughters in convents without their consent; but on the way, the novel becomes embroiled in anti-Protestant polemic. The heroine Florence, like the comtesse de ***, loses her place in the family after a son is born and is forced to enter a convent as a boarder. Later, she is transferred to another house where she is supposed to take vows. Though still a child, she has a "lover" with whom she is able to communicate by letter. Their correspondence paints a dark picture of cloistered life: her friend writes, "you will soon become a prisoner" ["vous allez bientôt devenir prisonniere," Brunet de Brou 98], and Hortense replies, "I am undergoing civil death" ["je suis sur le point de mourir civilement," Brunet de Brou 101]. The couple plan to run away together, but before they can do so, her parents return her to the same monastery where she had first been a boarder, in order to make her final profession. She is only fourteen years old. Hortense's sacrifice is compared unfavorably by de Brou to that of Abraham: whereas the Biblical patriarch agreed to kill his son in obedience to God's will, Hortense is merely sacrificed to her parents' cupidity. In true eighteenth-century style, de Brou declares that such an action violates the "natural ties" binding parent and child. And going beyond the condemnation of forced vocations, de Brou expresses a general hostility to monasticism which echoes some of the language of its seventeenth-century critics: "if [forced vocations] were banned, monasteries would not be so full, and the number of nuns would not be so excessive" ["si l'usage … en étoit banni, les Monasteres ne seroit pas si peuplez, & le nombre des Religieuses ne seroit pas si excessif," Brunet de Brou 110].

After Hortense becomes a nun, her lover enters a Trappist monastery and dies three years later. From this point on, the plot branches (or sinks) into a familiar proliferation of escape attempts and sexual intrigues—both seen as inevitable consequences of forced convent incarceration. Hortense has an affair with a Cordelier monk and disguises herself in a religious habit, in an unsuccessful attempt to escape with her lover and present a brief to the pope asking him to relieve her of her vows (Brunet de Brou 165). After she is returned to her convent, she falls in love with La Roche, a music master who gives lessons to the nuns there. This time her escape, in peasant clothes, is successful. However, the story takes an unexpected turn: the pair make their way to Geneva where Hortense converts to Protestantism, enabling her to marry La Roche. Despite this act of apostasy, all seems to go well for a time. The musician prospers; the couple have a son, Largues, whom they send to Paris at the age of 14 to study. But the "tragique" phase of the novel emerges at this point: the boy learns more from courtesans than from books and becomes a delinquent. He begins with petty theft, stealing torches and spoons from the banker in whose house he is lodging. Buying a horse with the proceeds, he then goes definitively to the bad: he joins a band of robbers in Picardy and kills more than thirty people. Horrifically, Largues is arrested and is broken alive ["rompu vif"] on the wheel.

While the narrator had shown some sympathy for his heroine when she was locked in the convent, his attitude reverses radically after Hortense's conversion. De Brou blames Largues's crimes and terrible end on his mother's "apostasy." As if the horrible death of her son were not punishment enough, Hortense is struck by lightning one day while out walking with her husband. Like Jean-Pierre Camus, De Brou's cruelty towards his heroine reveals a hint of misogyny. De Brou draws the final moral of the tragedy in this way: "Thus ended the life of this infamous Apostate. While human Justice had made all possible efforts to make her return to the righteous path, divine Justice was not satisfied. It wanted to have its vengeance burst forth in this world" ["Ainsi finit la vie de cette infame Apostate. Si la Justice humaine avoit fait tous ses efforts, afin de la faire rentrer dans le bon Chemin, la Justice divine n'étoit pas satisfaite, elle voulut faire éclatter ses vengeances dés ce monde," Brunet de Brou 290]. Shifting from his condemnation of convents at the beginning of the novel, the author condemns Protestantism and its converts far more harshly in the end. While it is difficult to draw much connection between the "morale" and the "tragique" parts of this tale, perhaps its ending can be seen as a worst-case outcome of conventual abuse: whereas most writers relate forced enclosure to debauchery, the supreme sin for de Brou is leaving the Catholic church, even if Florence does so expressly to escape the forced vows de Brou himself has condemned.

Avantures singuliéres de M.C.

An opposing view of the relation between forced vows and Protestantism is proffered in the *Avantures singuliéres de M.C.* (1724), an anonymous text allegedly translated from the Italian. In a reversal of typical gender roles, a younger brother is tricked into entering a monastery by his older sister, who wants to marry. In the end, he flees to "a Country of freedom where he embraced reformed Religion" ["un Païs de liberté où il a embrassé la Religion reformée," *Avantures* title page]. This country is not specified, but since the book was published in Utrecht, it may well be Holland. While de Brou had portrayed conversion to Protestantism, even when performed in order to escape forced monastic vows, as an act of "apostasy" meriting being struck by lightening, the anonymous author of the *Avantures* describes *la Religion reformée* as "free," and the hero's embracing it as a logical solution to his difficulties. However, there is at least one point of resemblance between these two works: the *Avantures* contains seven pages detailing the "disorders that celibacy produced" ["désordres que le célibat a produit," 10–16].

Libertine "Cellibacy" in Barrin's *Vénus dans le cloître*

The disorders of celibacy, which occupy only a small portion of *Avantures*, supply the central focus of *Vénus dans le cloître, ou la religieuse en chemise*. This novel has been attributed to Jean Barrin, writing under the pseudonym of the abbé du Prat. (In a playful self-reference, "l'abbé du Prat" is also listed among the debauched clerics who visit the convent of "Beaulieu.") The first *libertin* tale set within a convent, *Vénus dans le cloître* is also one of the earliest examples of a genre usually associated with the eighteenth century: its first imprint dates from 1682, the latest contemporary edition from 1719.[23] The first conviction for obscenity to be handed down by an English court was pronounced against Edmund Currl, who brought out a translation of the novel in 1727. It is hardly surprising that the *libertin* novel would exploit the erotic possibilities of conventual enclosure. According to Isabel Colegate, "perfervid fantasies about monks and nuns, temptations and seductions, were always the familiar stock in trade of pornographers" as well as authors of *galant* or libertine fiction (Colegate 167–8). Furthermore, as Christopher Rivers points out, "The [convent] setting … heightens the titillation of the presumably male, presumably heterosexual reader of the text, placing him in the ultimate position of voyeurism and scopophilic penetration, the goal of all erotic texts" (391). According to Rivers, in addition to a greater degree of sexual explicitness, *Vénus* exhibits two of the distinctive features of *libertin* as opposed to *galant* convent fiction. The first is an emphasis on passive enclosure within the convent rather than escape from it: though men can, and do, enter frequently, women do not leave. In this respect, *Les Lettres portugaises* resembles an erotic novel more than do the *galant* novels contemporary to it. The second distinguishing feature of the *libertin* genre is its exploitation of homoerotic themes. Rivers concurs that "In the eighteenth-century French libertine universe, the convent is defined by its association with lesbianism" (392).

Vénus dans le cloître illustrates both of these traits. It takes the form of a series of dialogues (*entretiens*) between two young cloistered nuns at the fictional Abbaye de Beaulieu. The elder, Angélique, is a "girl of 19 or 20" who has lived there for seven years. Agnès, the younger, also entered the Abbey at the age of 13; she is now 16. As well as referring to the Lamb of God, Agnès's name recalls the young heroine of Molière's *L'École des femmes*, who was raised in ignorance by her guardian, in the belief that she would thus make a perfect wife for him. But once she meets a young man, Agnès rapidly sheds her naïveté and shows a natural talent for romantic intrigue. Similarly, though on a much more explicit level,

---

[23] French quotations from *Vénus dans le cloître* are from the 1956 edition (Paris: le livre du bibliophile). English versions of the first three dialogues are drawn from a contemporary translation: *Venus in the Cloister, or the Nun in her Smock, In Curious Dialogues, addressed to the Lady Abbess of Loves Paradice, by the Abbot du Prat. Done out of the French* (London: H. Rodes, 1683; Microfilm, Early English Books). A new French paperback edition was issued in 2008 by Hesperus Press (Arles: Actes Sud, preface Matthew Sweet), too late to use in this book.

Sister Agnès is "converted" from repressive religious fervor to sexual freedom and enjoyment—first through dialogue with her older female mentor, then by readings and practical exercises. Towards this pedagogic end, the earliest French *libertin* classics, *L'Ecole des filles* (1655) and *Le Mersius français ou l'Académie des dames* (1660),[24] are assigned as readings for the young girl. For lack of actual precedents, Barrin adds a catalog of piquant invented titles to her reading list, including "The Jesuit Passkey, a gallant play"; "The illuminated Prison, or the Opening of the Little Gate"; and "Collection of remedies for dangerous plumpness, composed for the comfort of the religious ladies of St-Georges" [*Le Passe-partout des Jésuites, pièce galante*; *La Prison éclairée, ou l'Ouverture du Petit guichet*, le tout en figures; *Receuil des remèdes contre l'embonpoint dangereux*, composé pour la commodité des dames religieuses de Saint-Georges; Barrin 76, my translation]. In recounting the "education" of a naïve young woman, *Vénus* thus combines those archetypal figures of sexual fantasy, the schoolgirl and the nun. And like her namesake in Molière, Sister Agnès is a quick learner.

If all the action in the novel takes place among cloistered nuns who never leave their convent, how does their story come to light? "L'Abbé du Prat" answers this question in a tongue-in-cheek dedication to "Madame D.L.R. Most Worthy Abbess de Beaulieu": the dialogues "wherein your society had so great a share" ["où votre communauté a eu si bonne part"] were transcribed at her request and for her eyes only (Barrin 3, English trans. 2). While following her wishes, the abbé expresses a pious fear of the consequences were the tale to get out: "For, in good earnest, if the secret conferences should happen to be made publick, it would occasion no small scandal both to me and your Lady-ship" ["Car, de bonne foi, quelle confusion pour vous et pour moi, si des conferences si secrètes allaient devenir publiques," Barrin 4, English trans. 3]. The abbé adds ironically that she has broken none of her vows; but what if she were exposed "in her Smock, to the sight of all the curious?" ["en chemise à la vue de tous les curieux," Barrin 4, English trans. 3]. Of course, this is exactly what happens in the novel, both figuratively and literally. Agnès's first words, as well as the first words of the novel, are "Ah Lord, Ah Lord! sister Angelica, pray come not into my room" ["Ah Dieu, soeur Angélique, n'entrez pas dans ma chambre," Barrin 7, English trans. 4]. But the rule of Port-Royal and other reformed convents, that individual cells are inviolable, is far from being observed here. Agnès having inexplicably left her cell door open at an intimate moment, Angélique catches her not only half-naked ("en chemise"), but masturbating. Angélique makes this activity clear in her response; at the same time, she reassures her embarrassed sister that the abbess and all the other convent officers do the same:

---

[24]   Like *Vénus*, *L'Ecole des filles* mainly consists of a dialogue between two young women: Suzanne and her inexperienced cousin Fanchon, whom she wishes to initiate into the ways of love. Despite its title, the novel takes place in a bourgeois home rather than a feminotopic locale. For more on these works, see Lynn Hunt ed. *The Invention of Pornography* (New York: 1993); and Rivers, "Safe Sex" 383.

I saw thee in such a Posture and Action as if thou pleas'st I will serve thee in my self; wherein my hand shall at present do thee the Office which thy own a while ago did so charitably render to another part of thy Body; A very great crime indeed that I have discover'd, it is but what my Lady Abbess practices, as she her self says, in the most innocent diversions; It is but what the Prioress does not reject; but what the mistress of the novices calles *The Exstatical Intromission.*

Je t'ai vue dans une action où je te servirai moi-même si tu veux, où ma main te fera à present l'office que la tienne rendait tantôt charitablement à une autre partie de ton corps. Voilà le grand crime que j'ai découvert, que madame l'Abbesse D.L.R. pratique, comme elle dit, dans ses divertissements les plus innocents, que la prieure ne rejette point, et que la maîtresse des novices appelle l'intromission extatique. (Barrin 12, English trans. 8)

This first dialogue sets a pattern for commingling eroticism and voyeurism with religious satire. At the same time the reader enjoys the denuding and exposure of the nun's intimate acts and "parts," the sexual debauchery of the convent is revealed by removing its protective veil of hypocrisy. Angélique observes to Agnès:

Thou couldst not have believed, that such Holy Souls could have been capable of employing themselves in such profane Exercises? Their mean and their outward behavior have deceived thee, and that shew of Sanctity, with which they know so well how to deck themselves upon occasion, has made thee think that they live in their Bodyes, as if they were composed of nothing but the Spirit. Ah my dear Child, I will instruct thee with a Number of things which thou art ignorant of ... .

Tu n'aurais pas cru que de si saintes âmes eussent été capables de s'occuper à des exercises si profanes. Leur mine et leur dehors t'ont décue, et cet extérieur de sainteté, dont elles savent si bien se parer dans l'occasion, t'a fait penser qu'elles vivaient dans leur corps comme si elles n'étaient composées que du seul esprit. Ah! Mon enfant, que je t'instruirai de quantité de choses que tu ignores ... . (Barrin 12–13, English trans. 8–9)

Through Angélique's stories and "philosophy," as well as her own experience, Agnès is rapidly "instructed" in the debauchery rampant among religious persons. In the satirical world of the novel, such debauchery is universal and pansexual. One abbé had observed "there was nothing more dissolute than all the Reclused and Bigots, when they find occcasion to divert themselves" ["il n'y avait rien de plus dissolu que toutes les recluses et bigotes lorsqu'elles trouvaient l'occasion de se divertir," Barrin, Second Dialogue, 58–9, English trans. 72]. But as suggested above, the prime model of dissoluteness at Beaulieu is the abbess herself. Known by the secular title of "madame," she has founded an order, "les chevaliers de la grille," to which 22 clerics belong, enjoying differing degrees of privilege according to their station. In order to receive the visits of her most favored knights, she has had two removable planks installed in her parlor.

While not specifically sexual in nature, a bawdy story recounted in the third dialogue also satirizes the superior's promiscuity. As one of her "divertissements," madame has been raising lobsters and other animals in her room. Unfortunately, one crustacean climbs into her chamber pot and attaches itself to a tender part of her anatomy. When she cries out, all the nuns flock in, adding shame to discomfort. Recounting this story to Agnès, Angélique comments: "Truly a mighty business to be ashamed of, she let nothing be seen but what she had often shown to others" ["Vraiment, il y a bien là de quoi être honteuse! Elle ne fit rien voir qu'elle n'ait souvent montré à d'autres," Barrin 98, English trans. 127]. This punch line, in good medieval tradition, brings the supposed "pur esprit" of the abbess down to the lowest common denominator of bodily functions. But in addition, the phrase "il y a bien là de quoi être honteuse" links up with a recurrent theme in the book: that nudity and physical needs are natural, and therefore nothing to be ashamed of. With somewhat circular logic, Angélique argues that religious vows of chastity are invalid because no one is capable of living up to them. Except for a small minority who receive a special grace from God, those who try to remain chaste are, or will soon become, mad ["fous mélancoliques," Barrin 92, English trans. 119].

As far as male religious are concerned, there is not much danger of them going mad from sexual repression: they are even more lascivious than the nuns. Shortly after their first conversation, Angélique is obliged to go on a retreat. In order that Agnès's education may continue during her absence, Angélique arranges for the younger nun to be visited by a mixed collection of clerics including an abbé and two monks belonging to the Capucin and Feuillantin orders.[25] This variety in status demonstrates the universal licentiousness of male clergy. Their visits also explore the satirical and sexual possibilities (or impossibilities) of the convent space. On his second call, the abbé enters the cloister through the loose planks installed in the superior's parlor and accompanies Agnès to her room where, after offering some resistance, she loses her virginity (Barrin 58). The Capucin, less fortunate, meets with Agnès in another parlor which lacks the convenient removable boards of the "parloir de madame." When he tries to enter the cloister by bending the bars of the grill, he gets stuck—an allusion to monastic gluttony. Other secondary tales exploit the possibilities inherent in the little gate in the parlor grill, intended for passing through parcels. In one of these stories, "Virginie," a nun who is carrying on with a Jesuit, climbs on a stool and lets him "see and grope the parts consecrated to Chastity, and Continency" ["voir et manier les endroits consacrés à la chasteté et à la continence," Barrin 46, English trans. 54]. With playful irony, Barrin uses the euphemisms of devout language to designate the "parts" in question. After exchanging stories with Agnès, Angélique concludes: "there is no Animal in the

---

[25] The Capuchin brothers are an order of minor Friars that branched off from the Franciscans during the sixteenth century. Their name comes from the hood (*capuche* in Italian) they wore. Due to a rocky early history, the morality of the Capuchins was regarded dubiously. The Feuillantin or Feuillant order, a branch of the Cistercians, was dissolved at the time of the Revolution. On abbés in satirical literature, see above, n22.

World more Luxurious than a Monk" ["il n'y a point d'animal au monde plus luxurieux qu'un moine," Barrin 75, English trans. 96].

All of these accounts lead to a heretical claim: "And dost thou not perceive, that those Vows which thou makest in the hands of men, are only Songs?" ["Eh! Ne vois-tu pas bien que ces voeux-là, que tu fais entre les mains des hommes, ne sont que des chansons?" Barrin 90, English trans. 116]. To protect himself from accusations of atheism, the author makes a distinction between human and divine law: monastic vows are *chansons*—nonsense—because they come from the hands of men ["entre les mains des hommes"] rather than from God. Citing the Jesuit priest who "educated" her, Angélique posits the well-known theological doctrine of the two bodies: one "céleste et spirituel," the other "Terrestrial and Corruptible, which is but an invention of Man" ["terrestre et corruptible qui n'est que l'invention des hommes," Barrin 18–19, English trans. 17]. According to her, the present-day church and its institutions, including monasticism, belong to this second body. The original founders of holy orders were motivated by a pure religious zeal, but it faded long ago—so much for the fervor of the Counter-Reformation!—leaving behind only empty forms. This distinguo allows her to reject much of religious practice with impunity. As Angélique puts it, "we can rid ourselves of superstition without falling into Impiety" ["on peut se défaire de la superstition sans tomber dans l'impiété," Barrin Third Dialogue, 114, English trans, 146]. The dualistic separation between the "two bodies" of God and the Church permits the author not only to claim fidelity to true religion, but to broaden the target of his satirical attack from monastic license to the institution of monasticism itself. Angélique blames the continued existence of monasteries on "politique." Although they long ago outlived their usefulness, they could not be eliminated because of "this Bueckler of Religion wherewith they covered themselves" ["ce bouclier de la religion dont ils se couvraient," Barrin 23]. So the authorities developed another strategy: "so such sorts of Companies or Societies might not be entirely useless to the Common Wealth. … Policy has looked upon all those Houses as Common places where it might discharge it self of these following superfluities: It makes use of them for the Ease of Families, which the great number of Children would render poor and indigent, if they had not places to retire to" ["pour que ces sortes de compagnies ne fussent pas entièrement inutiles à la république. La politique a donc regardé toutes ces maisons comme des lieux communs où elle se pourrait décharger de ses superfluités; elle s'en sert pour le soulagement des familles que le grand nombre d'enfants rendrait pauvres et indigentes, s'ils n'avaient des endroits pour les retirer," Barrin 23; English trans. 23–4]. The words "lieux communs," "décharger," "superfluités" and "soulagement" evoke images of social detritus or worse, poured into a kind of public sewer which is the monastery. Furthermore, to prevent "superfluous" people from claiming their inheritances, they are bound by eternal vows of reclusion and deprived of their civil status: "[Policy] makes us renounce likewise the Rights which nature has given us, and separates us so from the world, that we no longer make a part thereof" ["Elle (la politique) nous fait même renoncer aux droits que la nature nous a données, et nous sépare tellement du monde, que nous n'en faisons plus une partie," Barrin 23, English trans. 24]. In other words, religious houses, superfluous in themselves, become depositaries for those whom society considers useless. The vows of poverty and stability, rather than anchored in divine law, are simply the result of connivance among ecclesiastical, civil and family authorities.

Despite these criticisms, *Vénus dans le cloître* is far from being a pure political pamphlet. Lest the tone become too serious or the content too obviously subversive, the author strives to maintain a balance between ideology and erotic enjoyment. Incisive critiques of monasticism are interspersed with kisses, caresses and other loveplay. As a result, the proportion of eroticism in *Vénus dans le cloître* far outweighs that of satire. For the most part, this erotic content is kept "light"; sexual encounters are recounted second-hand, using paraphrases and abstract words like "embrassements" and "attouchements" (Barrin 139), although the latter parts of the novel do contain sadomasochistic episodes of flagellation.[26] However, as in the story of Dorsité, this theme is interlaced with criticisms of ascetic practice. This young nun is one of the "fous," or rather "folles mélancoliques," who try unsuccessfully to live as ascetics: "As it is impossible here below to destroy in us what we call Concupiscence, she was never at peace with herself" ["Comme il est impossible ici-bas de détruire en nous ce qu'on appelle concupiscence, elle n'était jamais en paix avec elle-même," Barrin 108, English trans. 140]. In consequence, Dorsité's self-punishment becomes ever more cruel and frenzied, until a final paroxysm of self-flagellation brings on quite a different kind of paroxysm. The result is described in euphemistic terms by Angélique. Dorsité, yielding to the laws of mere Nature, will lose "maugre all her efforts that Treasure, the keeping whereof had put her to so much pain" ["succomber sous les lois de la nature toute pure, et perdre, malgré ses soins, ce trésor dont la garde lui avait donné tant de peine," Barrin 113, English trans. 145–6]. Asceticism arouses the very sexuality it seeks to repress: mortification of the flesh causes the flesh to take over. But with a naively voyeuristic comment from Agnès, once again the writer changes key from libertine moralizing to *libertinage*: "Well this is what I should have taken delight in, to view her thus all naked, and to observe curiously all the transports, that Love would have caused in her at the moment she was overcome" ["Eh bien! C'est en quoi j'aurais pris du plaisir, de la considérer ainsi toute nue, et de remarquer curieusement tous les transports que l'amour lui causait au moment qu'elle fut vaincue," Barrin 114, English trans. 146]. In a kind of perverse twist on the ancient precept of "plaire et instruire," please and instruct, it is hard to tell where one ends and the other begins.

A second connection between enclosure and female sexuality is made in the novel through lesbian encounters. In Rivers's view, *Vénus dans le cloître* and other libertine novels of the time present lesbianism at best as a "pis aller" for

---

[26]   The most "sadistic" of these episodes is described in the fourth *entretien* as taking place in Italy before Angélique had entered the convent, thus removing it in time and space from French reality. The works of the Marquis de Sade raise psychosexual and philosophical issues that are beyond the scope of the present study.

straight sex, at worst as a "symptom of the disease that is the convent" (396).[27]
Female homosexuality is merely "situational ... a means of satisfying thwarted
heterosexual desire" (397); hence, lesbian practices are *badinages*, a minor
substitute or prelude to the "real thing"—heterosexual activity. Rivers translates
badinage or *badineries* as "foolishness," but a better translation might be "fooling
around," "play" or "foreplay." Thus in Casanova's *Mémoires*, a nun of the
narrator's acquaintance reports that lesbian practices are common in her convent
as an outlet for otherwise unbearable sexual drives: "Alas! Lacking the reality,
we contented ourselves with *badinage*. I will not conceal from you that I love my
young boarder. ... It is a love that feeds my tranquility. It is an innocent passion.
Her caresses dampen a fire that would kill me if I did not weaken its strength by
badinages" ["Hélas! À défaut de la réalité nous nous contentions du *badinage*.
Je ne te cacherai pas que j'aime ma jeune pensionnaire. ... C'est un amour qui
nourrit ma tranquillité. C'est une passion innocente. Ses caresses assouvissent un
feu qui me ferait mourir si je n'atténuais sa force par des *badinages*," Casanova
4.517, quoted in May 126; italics added]. In this passage, sexual practices between
women are clearly denoted as non-serious, "innocent" substitutes for the "réalité"
which is male-female intercourse. Moreover, none of the writers discussed above
envision the possibility of non-sexual, romantic love between women; yet this
ideal of "romantic friendship," epitomized by the Ladies of Llangollen, held a
strong attraction throughout the eighteenth century.[28]

In *Venus dans le cloître* this heterosexist line is not drawn so clearly: the word
badinerie is applied to both homosexual and heterosexual acts short of intercourse.
Among these *badineries* are the "baisers à la Florentine" (French kisses) which
Angélique demonstrates to Agnès (Barrin 119). They also can include touching or
fondling (*attouchements*) or even simple glances (*regards*): in describing another
nun's relationship with a priest, Agnès says "Cecil ... was only culpable before man
of some little wantonings, as of eying and feeling" ["Cécile ... n'était coupable
devant les hommes que de quelques badineries, comme regards et attouchements,"
Barrin 73, English trans. 91]. In the early English translation, the rendering of
badineries by "little wantonings" conveys the tone of the word very well. Agnès
also speaks of *badinerie* when describing her encounter with the Feuillantine monk:
"I was infinitely pleased with his discourse, and his way of *toying and wantoning*,

---

[27]   In *The Telling of the Tale*, Peter Cryle similarly argues that lesbian acts in classical
erotic novels are only a "prelude, or flourish, to adorn the more central, more decisive acts
carried on by males" (324).

[28]   See Elizabeth Mavor, *The Ladies of Llangollen* (Harmondsworth: Middlesex,
England, 1971). "A glance at the more notable correspondence of the period will show
that what we would now associate solely with a sexual relationship; tenderness, sensibility,
shared tastes, coquetry; were then very largely confined to friendships between women"
(Mavor 81). However, recent scholarship has shown that expressions of affection between
men were apparently accepted in the eighteenth century. See Richard Goodbeer, *The
Overflowing of Friendship: Love between Men and the Creation of the American Republic*
(Baltimore: The Johns Hopkins University Press, 2009).

and I made no difficulty of granting him the passage I had so much disputed with our Abbot" ["Son entretien et ses *badineries* me plurent infiniment et je n'eus pas de peine à lui accorder le passage que j'avais tant disputé à notre abbé," Barrin 66, English trans, 82–3; italics added]. Finally, the style of the book is itself *badin*— light, playful, self-consciously implausible. This narrative *badinage* helps open an easier "passage" for both its erotic and its subversive content.

In the sixth dialogue of *Vénus dans le Cloître*, added in the 1719 edition, the light and tolerant attitude toward *badinerie* fades away.[29] While the earlier *entretiens* take a rather indulgent view of the whole spectrum of intramural sex, the sixth dialogue introduces the common anti-convent argument, reprised by Diderot, that lesbianism is one of the "strange" abuses caused by cloistering and mortification of the flesh: "For once it is heated by the violent use of whips, hair shirts, vigils and other forms of penitence that are practiced among you, it is then that terrible assaults and strange rebellions are excited in the flesh by the effervescence of the blood" ["Car quand elle (la chair) est une fois bien échauffée par l'usage violent des disciplines, des haires, des cilices, des veilles et des autres pénitences qui se pratiquent parmi vous, c'est alors qu'il s'excite en elle par les effervescences du sang, de terribles assauts et d'étranges rebellions," Barrin 210].[30] Again, lesbian practice, as well as an abuse, is a poor substitute for the real thing: "a feeble image … a vain phantom of the love that exists between two people of different sexes" ["une faible image … un vain fantôme de l'amour qui se trouve entre deux personnes d'un sèxe different," Barrin 195]. Such passages are quoted by Rivers to support the *pis aller* theory of homoeroticism. In my opinion, however, both the style and content of this dialogue suggest it was added by a different, probably Protestant, author. Instead of Agnès and Angélique, it introduces two new interlocutresses, novices who have not yet taken their vows. They plan to escape the convent, run off to Holland with their lovers, get married and embrace *la religion évangélique*. This introduces a dramatically new note into the novel. The Second Dialogue of the 1683 edition does contain one sympathetic comment about Protestant reform: "We must own, that there are many abuses practised in our Religion, and I am not now at all surprised, that so many Nations have separated themselves from our Church, to apply themselves literally to the Scriptures" ["Il faut avouer qu'il y a bien des abus qui se pratiquent dans notre religion, et je ne suis plus surprise de ce que tant de peuples s'en sont séparés, pour s'attacher litteralement aux Ecritures," Barrin Second Dialogue 65, English trans. 81]. But Catholicism remains "notre religion"; the dominant message

---

[29]   This dialogue is not included in the 1683 English translation *Venus in the Cloister, or the Nun in her Smock*, and translations from this part are my own.

[30]   This argument is also put forth in the *Discours préliminaire* of *Les Delices du Cloitre, ou La None Eclairée* (1742). Convent rigors do not put out "the fire of fleshly desire" ["le feu de la concupiscence," xv]; rather, the frustration of sexual desire leads to "an abyss of impurity and frightful crimes" ["un abîme d'impureté, & de crimes affreux," xvi]. This book is texually identical *Le Triomphe des Religieuses*, discussed below, but the predicatory tone of the preface does not fit the novel's contents.

of the first edition is not how to escape it, but how to seek accommodation with it. Rather than agreeing with St. Paul that it is better to marry than to burn (211–12), Barrin suggests that the convent can be quite a comfortable place for those who know how to bend its rules (or bars). At one point, Agnès criticizes the institution of monasticism in familiar terms: "Alas! There would be but few reclused of either Sex, if those who go into Cloisters had but time given them to reflect upon the Advantages of Civil Liberty, and upon the ill Consequences of a Fatal Engagement" ["Hélas! Qu'il y aurait peu de reclus et de recluses, si on donnait le temps à ceux et à celles qui entrent dans le cloître de réfléchir sur les avantages d'une honnête liberté et sur les suites fâcheuses d'un funeste engagement!" Barrin Dialogue Two, 89, English trans. 115—the English translation supplies "Civil" Liberty, which changes the political tone of the text]. But Angélique counters: "Why dost thou talk at this rate? Cannot we enjoy as perfect Pleasures within the compass of our walls, as those who are abroad?" ["Pourquoi parles-tu de la sorte? Ne pouvons-nous pas goûter des plaisirs aussi parfaits dans l'enceinte de nos murailles que ceux qui sont au-dehors?" Barrin 89–90, English trans. 115]. Thus, one could say that Barrin's is a "convent of pleasure," albeit in a very different sense from Cavendish's. In her utopian creation, women innocently partake of natural enjoyments, removed from social and marital strictures. Cavendish's vision of Nature is in marked contrast to the misogynistic views of women's "natural" lasciviousness which Barrin brings inside the convent walls.

Barrin's depiction of hidden convent pleasures is reiterated in a later libertine novel, *Le Triomphe des Religieuses; ou Les Nones Babillardes* (1720). This work seems to be an imitation of *Vénus dans le Cloître*, and has even been (unconvincingly) attributed to Barrin. Like *Vénus*, it consists of a series of dialogues between two nuns, Agnès and Julie. In one conversation, Agnès shares the advice of her lover, a surgeon brother ["frère chirurgien"]: "Let us enjoy the pleasures of life; the cloister is their home when one knows how to enjoy it. All you need to do is to conceal their appearances" ["Jouissons des plaisirs de la vie; le cloître est leur séjour quand on sçait le goûter, il ne s'agit que de cacher les apparences," *Triomphe* 34]. In one way, this argument seems to support Christopher Rivers's assertion that lesbian sex in libertine convent novels is "safe sex," minimized and controlled within the cloister walls. Barrin's Angélique had also asserted that sexuality enclosed is rendered innocuous: "if there be any hurt in this occupation, yet it is not prejudicial to any Body; and does not any wise disturb the publick tranquility" ["s'il y a du mal à cette occupation, il n'est préjudiciable à personne et ne trouble aucunement la tranquillité publique," Barrin First Dialogue, 31, English trans. 35]. Angélique goes on to argue that keeping these activities within the convent actually performs a social service; such "occupations" would disturb "publick tranquility" a lot more if they were occurring in the outside world. Like Angélique's other arguments, this is a kind of perverse extension of the early modern policy of *renfermement*—locking away anyone whose unconventional behavior is seen as disturbing the surface of social order (see above, Chapter 4, 262–4). This message is conservative, to the extent that authors writing at the turn of the eighteenth century could not have been expected to envision the radical social and political upheavals that would take place in France some decades later. But at the same time, the ironic suggestion that accommodation with convent life can make it quite pleasant is all the more devastating, in a subtle fashion, than the usual imprecations against its horrors.

In conclusion, the radical changes in monastic life over the century following the Counter-Reformation were accompanied by radical changes in conventual representation. Neither process was smooth or linear: arising from disparate sources, representations took disparate and overlapping forms. In the early post-Trent era, religious writing and art often employed the convent cell as a metonymy for the soul seeking solitary communion with God. This discourse was allegorical and Biblical in form, private and meditative in nature. However, the increased participation of women in monastic life after Trent also brought increased public scrutiny. By mid-century, criticism of monasteries enters official French discourse; Louis XIV's ministers feel empowered to portray monastic life as "useless," even abusive. These arguments appear in various guises in anti-monastic fiction. In a satirical vein, *La Religieuse pénitente* and *Vénus dans le Cloître* exploit the tried-and-true combination of anti-clerical content with sexual farce. This ancient combination was still being worked as late as 1861, in works like Lebrun's *Les Amours libertines de religieuses du Couvent des Carmélites*. But it also harks back to Jean-Pierre Camus's racily devout tales from the early century: for Camus, women's sexuality is at fault, and the solution is to lock them away in secure convents. In addition, late seventeenth-century Protestant attacks on monasticism will draw from and contribute to the genre of *galant* and erotic fiction by openly portraying sexual abuses in the cloister. According to Rapley, "no serious historian accuses eighteenth-century nuns, *en masse*, of irregular behaviour" (*Social History* 81). But in certain monastic tales, social criticism is inseparable from the voyeuristic pleasure it affords. Erotic content is heightened; secret places that should evoke reverence call forth prurient curiosity. Less dramatic, but of equal importance in the context of this study, is the migration of traditional anticlericism from the tract or satire to the "modern" literary genre of the memoir-novel. This change brought a larger, mixed readership within the fictional convent walls, including nobles and bourgeois, men and women. In addition to addressing a different audience, works like Murat's *La Défense des dames* offer a new perspective on forced enclosure. More critical than Villedieu's *Mémoires de Henriette-Sylvie de Molière*, Murat's novel still presents the convent as one among the limited field of life alternatives available to women. Murat thus spreads her critique over a larger field; the fault is not solely the convent's, but society's as a whole, for oppressing women. In conclusion, all these widely divergent works have a point in common: when the nuns are locked away, the novel lets its own subversive message out—a message that may have contributed to the dismantling of the monastic system in the tumult of the Revolution.

Chapter 6
Cells II:
Male Appropriations of the Nun's Persona in Guilleragues's *Les Lettres portugaises* and Diderot's *La Religieuse*

La Religieuse, C'est Moi

Many of the works discussed in the previous chapter take an equal opportunity view of religious debauchery: though women are distinguished by their insatiable sexual appetites, monks as well as nuns are caught in the act. In contrast, the two novels to be considered in this chapter—Guilleragues's *Lettres portugaises* and Diderot's *La Religieuse*—concentrate exclusively on the sexual obsessions of women; or more precisely, these works concentrate obsessively on women's sexuality as viewed from within the conventual space. We have seen in Chapter 5 how the eroticism of female enclosed spaces, one of the favorite topics of French erotic literature at least since the fabliaux, was redefined in early modern writing. Indeed, according to Christopher Rivers, "The convent … represents the most eroticized space imaginable in ancien régime France" (386). In the two most famous convent novels of the French canon, the vicarious thrill of entering forbidden female spaces is taken to a new level. Although *Les Lettres portugaises* (1662) and *La Religieuse* (1760) are separated by nearly 100 years and a vastly changed social and intellectual landscape, their similarities, as well as their differences, make for enlightening comparisons. Both novels are authored by men and narrated by first-person female personae. While *Les Lettres portugaises* are wholly composed in an epistolary form, *La Religieuse* is a hybrid epistolary/memoir novel which originated in a unique exchange of letters between an alleged real-life nun created by Diderot and a living person. This phenomenon of "men writing the feminine" is certainly not new; instances range from Ovid's Sappho and Virgil's Dido to the female narrator of Norman Rush's *Mating*. And male authors have intensively identified with their female characters, the most famous example being Flaubert's Emma Bovary. But *Les Lettres portugaises* and *La Religieuse* occupy an extreme point on this narrative continuum: their authors go beyond writing from a female point of view or in a woman's voice to usurp an allegedly real female identity.[1]

---

[1]   In "Poststructuralist Feminism and the Imaginary Woman Writer: The *Lettres Portugaises*" (*Romanic Review*, January 1999), Mary McAlpin rehearses the debate between Peggy Kamuf and Nancy K. Miller concerning the status of the author of the *Lettres*, and subtly questions the postmodern move of "liberating" this text from its male

Both Guilleragues and Diderot asserted that their books were the work of actual nuns, and both assertions were believed to a greater or lesser degree and length of time. In the case of *Les Lettres portugaises*, the hypothesis of a Portuguese nun who wrote her own letters has even been resurrected recently.[2] Why are such claims accepted? One reason may be that the narratives evoke largely traditional images of female subjectivity; another is simply that the public *wants* to believe in their reality. If it is titillating to enter into a fictional convent cell, it is even more exciting to penetrate a real one. And as we will see, this titillation can affect the writer as well as—if not more than—the reader. In addition to the fun of successfully carrying off a literary prank, the authors' motives mirror those of the reader's: the excitement of invading a female setting and persona is heightened by a total identification with that persona as a quasi-real woman. This chapter will analyze the play of desire and fantasy within the conventual and narrative structures the writers have created. It will also explore the meshing of erotic and ideological issues surrounding the convent.

Enclosure and Disclosure in the *Lettres portugaises*

This short novel takes the form of an epistolary "monologue" from a Portuguese cloistered nun to the French officer who had been her lover; his answers, if any, are not included. The novel's structure is founded on the familiar *topos* of the female involuntarily shut up in a convent cell: "I had been shut up in this convent since I was a child" ["On m'avait enfermé dans ce convent depuis mon enfance," Guilleragues Letter Five, 105, Waldman 45].[3] But in a sense, *Les Lettres portugaises*

---

author. In my view, freeing the heroine from a "real," historically based creator reduces, rather than enhances, the meanings of the text. My reading is more in tune with Katherine A. Jensen's in "Male Models of Feminine Epistolarity; or, How to Write Like a Woman in Seventeenth-Century France." In *Writing the Female Voice*, ed. Elizabeth C. Goldsmith (Boston: Northeastern University Press, 1989), 25–45.

[2]   The *Lettres portugaises* were first published in 1669 as Guilleragues's alleged translation of five letters written by a Portuguese nun, Marianna Alcaforado, to her lover, a French officer named Bouton de Chamilly. While Guilleragues's authorship of the letters had long been suspected, convincing textual proof was not brought forth until almost 300 years later. For details of this history, see the preface to the Deloffre edition. The "Alcofobradist" hypothesis of a real Marianne as author of the letters has lately been revived by Miriam Cyr, in her somewhat sensationally titled book, *Letters of a Portuguese Nun: Uncovering the Mystery Behind a 17th Century Forbidden Love* (New York: Hyperion, 2006). This revival has the merit of attracting new readers to the *Lettres portugaises*; but for both historical and stylistic reasons, the claim of real letters translated from the Portuguese remains unconvincing to me. For this reason, I have avoided referring to Guilleragues's heroine as "Marianne."

[3]   French quotations from *Les Lettres portugaises* refer to the Deloffre edition (Paris: Garnier, Folio, 1990). English translations are from *Love Letters of a Portuguese Nun*, trans. Guido Waldman (London: Harvill Press, 1996).

seem more concerned with thresholds than cells: this archetypal convent novel explores the relation of enclosure (walls) to closure (endings), of passages (in and out) to narrative development or stasis. In Guilleragues's masterpiece, spatial relations—up to down, in to out—play an important symbolic and narrative role. It is true that from a realist perspective, Guilleragues's portrayal of the convent setting is minimal, and shows little regard for accuracy or verisimilitude. The classical minimalism of the decor has reinforced an interpretation of *Les Lettres portugaises* as a perfect, detached narrative, à la Roland Barthes's *Fragments d'un discours amoureux*. Long before Barthes, it was read in a similar way by Guilleragues's contemporaries, in the familiar context of the letters and *questions d'amour* composed in salon competitions (Deloffre 31–7). It is interesting that the original title of the novel was simply *Les Lettres portugaises*; *Lettres d'une religieuse portugaise* was introduced by Guilleragues's imitators (Deloffre 16–17). Salon-goers like Mme de Sévigné even referred to a passionate love letter as *une portugaise*, as the English reading public called a thank you letter a "Collins," after the missives written by Mr. Collins to the Bennett family in Austen's *Pride and Prejudice*. In this common reading of the novel, the letters are seen as detached, almost disembodied discourse, recalling models from Ovid to Heloise.[4] Heloise and Abelard's letters can indeed be read as a kind of "shadow text" to *Les Lettres Portugaises*. Although the former consists of an epistolary exchange, Heloise and Abelard's letters often resemble monologues more closely than dialogues, soliloquies in which the separated lovers lament their own woes rather than attempting to connect with each other. In Alexander Pope's 1717 epistle "Eloisa," Abelard's side of the correspondence is removed entirely; according to Judith Mesa-Pelly, this absence of the male voice creates a space into which the (male) author can insert himself—a similar procedure to Guilleragues's in *Les Lettres portugaises*.[5] Finally, what is accented by the title is not so much the fact that the narrator is a nun, but that she is *Portuguese*: hence doomed—or free—to enjoy a degree of southern and female unreason not properly displayed in the country of Descartes, even by women.

While acknowledging the centrality of the epistolary form and tradition, I nevertheless argue that the convent setting plays a key role in *Les Lettres portugaises*. I will first examine its importance to the plot, then its narrative

---

[4]   The 1616 republication in Latin of the letters of Eloise and Abelard aroused interest in this unhappy pair in both France and England. Their letters were translated into French at the end of the seventeenth century. In *Receuil de lettres galantes et amoureuses* (Amsterdam: 1699), the letters of Heloise and Abelard and the Portuguese nun are paired, with volume 1 containing *Héloise et Abailard*, volume 2 *Les Lettres d'une religieuse portugaise*. A paraphrase of two letters of Heloise and Abelard by Bussy-Rabutin was also published in 1697. For more on the history of the Eloise letters, see Linda S. Kauffman, *Discourses of Desire: Gender, Genre and Epistolary Fictions* (84–9) and the introduction to Peggy Kamuf's *Fictions of Feminine Desire: Disclosures of Heloise*.

[5]   Judith Mesa-Pelly, *Fictive Domains: Nostalgic Constructions of Body and Landscape in the Eighteenth Century*, Chapter 3, 1.

function. The love intrigue of the novel strains the bounds of both the convent setting and of credibility. The narrator complains that she cannot leave the convent because of the severity of the laws imposed on nuns (86); yet for a strictly closed convent, it seems to have a lot of openings. She originally catches sight of her lover while she is walking on the convent balcony "with a view over Mertola" ["d'où l'on voit Mertola," Guilleragues Letter Four, 93, Waldman 29]. While this scene violates the reader's conventional expectations—one does not expect to find a nun out on a balcony—it does not entirely lack historical accuracy: convents located in towns with limited land around them did sometimes have terraces or balconies where nuns could take the air (see Foreword). However, in the case of the structure where the story supposedly took place, the convent de la Conception in the city of Beja, the balcony description would be a physical impossibility: Beja is 50 kilometers from Mertola, and the convent de la Conception is not high enough to afford a view of anything. More important, on a literary level, the image of the nun is conflated with the princess locked in her tower and, of course, the Latin beauty on her balcony.

A second sketchy point in *Les Lettres portugaises* plot is that we are never told how the lover gains entry to the convent. The narrator writes: "I was anxious about the dangers you ran when you entered this convent. I was more dead than alive when you were on active service" ["j'étais troublée par le risque que vous couriez en entrant dans ce couvent; je ne vivais pas lorsque vous étiez à l'armée," Guilleragues Letter Five, 103, Waldman 42]. Through its parallel construction, this sentence links the lover's penetration into the convent to a risky military operation: both reveal the courage and daring of a warrior. Again without explanation, we learn that the officer gains entrance to the heroine's room (Guilleragues, like Barrin, uses the word *chambre* rather than *cellule*): "Alas, is my every hope to be in vain, am I never again to see you in my room displaying all the giddy passion you allowed me to witness!" ["Quoi! tous mes désirs seront donc inutiles, et je ne vous verrai jamais en ma chambre avec toute l'ardeur et tout l'emportement que vous me faisiez voir?" Guilleragues Letter Two, 80, Waldman 14]. Once the affair is over, the only contact the nun has with her lover is through the famous letters. At the same time, it is worth noting that a lot of speaking takes place in this convent. In another departure from plausibility, despite what is known about her conduct, the unhappy narrator is made the convent portress. As Rapley points out, according to convent rule "the portress was to be one of the older members of the community. The reason is obvious: an open door and the sight of the world outside might tempt a younger or flightier woman to step across the threshold and thus incur automatic excommunication" (*Dévotes* 121). It would seem that this nun would be the least likely choice for a position usually held by a "wardress, ancient and stony-faced." This public post, which gives her a chance to talk to people, or have them talk to her, only reinforces the heroine's amorous obsession: "this morning a French officer had the kindness to engage me for more than three hours in conversation about you;" "your Lieutenant has come to tell me"; "I heard good reports of you, everyone spoke in your favour" ["ce matin un officier français m'a parlé trois heures de vous," Guilleragues Letter Two, 82, Waldman 16; "votre lieutenant vient de me dire," Letter Four, 89, Waldman 25; "j'entendais dire du bien de vous, tout le monde me parlait en votre faveur," Letter Five, 105, Waldman 45]. The threshold of silence, so important for separating the convent from the sinful world, and doubly important for her peace of mind, is clearly lacking here.

Despite all this talking, the heroine's own voice is expressed in the novel mainly through her letters. These are carried to the French officer not only by his brother soldiers, but by her own brother: she mentions "the occasion furnished me by my brother to write to you" ["l'occasion que mon frère m'a donnée de vous écrire," Guilleragues Letter One, 77, Waldman 10]. Yet the letters are more than a means of communication. Like an author manipulating a character, through writing the letters she conjures up the presence of her absent lover: "I imagine that I am talking to you as I write, and that makes you a little more present to me" ["il me semble que je vous parle, quand je vous écris, et que vous m'êtes un peu plus présent," Guilleragues Letter Four, 96, Waldman 33]. In addition, the letters provide a physical contact between the nun and her interlocutor: they are the only objects that will pass from her hands into his. This near-sensual physicality is emphasized in the text: "Farewell! I cannot be parted from this sheet of paper, it will drop into your hands; how I wished I might enjoy the same good fortune!" ["Adieu, je ne puis quitter ce papier, il tombera entre vos mains, je voudrais bien avoir le même bonheur," Guilleragues Letter One, 78, Waldman 11]. And when she resolves to send all his letters back, her pain mimics that of physical separation: "I placed them resolutely in Dona Brites's hands, at what cost in tears!" ["Je les ai mises entre les mains de Dona Britès; que cette résolution m'a coûtée de larmes!" Guilleragues Letter Five, 105, Waldman 38]. The letters in *La Religieuse portugaise* serve the mediating function performed by physical displacement in *La Princesse de Clèves*, where the Princesse and Nemours frequent locations recently vacated by the other (see above, Chapter 3, 153).

The most important effect of the convent setting, however, is in the area of narrative focus and point of view. The natural limiting of field which accompanies first person narrative—the "I" can only see so far—is further accentuated by the extreme limitation of the convent setting. Since she cannot go out, the nun's knowledge of the outside world is determined by what people choose to tell her. In addition, the convent enclosure causes an extreme feminization of the narrator's subject position. With no outside occupations or distractions, the narrator is "free" to concentrate obsessively on the absent love object: "Nothing prevents [nuns] from devoting unremitting thought to their passion, they are not disturbed by the thousand things that in the world occasion distraction and preoccupation" ["rien n'empêche (les religieuses) de penser incessamment à leur passion, elles ne sont point détournées par mille choses qui dissipent et qui occupent dans le monde," Guilleragues Letter Five, 102, Waldman 41]. In a speech from Jane Austen's *Persuasion*, Anne Elliot makes a similar point:

> We certainly do not forget you so soon as you forget us. It is perhaps, our fate rather than our merit. We cannot help ourselves. We live at home, quiet, confined,

and our feelings prey upon us. You are forced on exertion. You have always business of some sort or other to take you back into the world immediately, and continual occupation and change soon weaken impressions. (*Persuasion* Chapter 23, 363)

Women who lead confined and immobile lives, whether in a convent or at home, can fall prey to stubborn attachments. Yet it is the convent setting that creates the hothouse atmosphere necessary for the unfolding of this particular tale, told in its own particular language. Thus, in Guilleragues's *discours amoureux*, the subject position of the writer is mimicked by her syntax. The Portuguese nun's outpourings evince a kind of openness without vector. Phrases do not fall into regular, canonic periods; rather, they are repetitive and lack closure. This style drew criticism at the time as "sans mesure" (Deloffre, 45). Another "unmeasured" aspect of the writing is its kinetic quality. In this respect, *Les Lettres portugaises* resemble *La Princesse de Clèves*. Within a strictly limited vocabulary, both works are disproportionately rich in terms conveying motion: the word *mouvements* occurs 15 times in *Les Lettres portugaises*, including the last word of the novel: "suis-je obligée de vous rendre un compte exact de tous mes divers *mouvements*," translated as "do I have to give you an exact account of all the various *things I am feeling*?" The meaning range of words like *mouvements*, *transports* (four occurrences) and *emportements* is restricted to a purely metaphorical, emotional domain ["mouvements du coeur"]. This metaphoric lexicon rendered variously, as for example, "I am torn by a thousand conflicting emotions" ["je suis déchirée par mille mouvements contraires," Letter Three, 85, Waldman 21]; "the feelings that you arouse in me are all so extreme" ["tous mes mouvements que vous me causez sont extremes," Guilleragues Letter Four, 90, Waldman 27]. For the heroine, physical movement is forbidden or limited; not only can she not leave the convent, but she does not even want to leave her room. In contrast, *mouvement*, when used in reference to her lover, implies intention and action: "Ah yes, now I am aware of the bad faith in those transports of yours" ["Oui, je connais présentement la mauvaise foi de tous vos mouvements," Guilleragues Letter Three, 85, Waldman 20]. Here, the lack of literal verbs of motion contrasts with *La Princesse de Clèves*, whose heroine is subject to psychological *mouvements* but also free to distance herself physically.

The question mark ending the final letter highlights her incapacity to create closure—to bring the nun's love affair, and the novel, to an unambiguous end. Though she claims it is indeed the last, her own words subvert this claim: "In fact I think I shall not write to you again" ["je crois même que je ne vous écrirai plus," Guilleragues Letter Five, 106, Waldman 46]. Her inability to end the correspondence, or part with the letters, is highlighted by the repetitions of "Adieu": three times in the first letter, twice in the second, five times in the third, four times in the fourth. Thus, in contrast with the officer's freedom of movement, the nun's lament seems to go round in circles; to use an anachronism, she is racing her motor. Or as she realizes herself, "I am mad to keep saying the same things over again" ["je suis une folle de redire les mêmes choses si souvent," Guilleragues Letter Five, 106, Waldman 46].

Bernard Beugnot underscores the double impact achieved when convent setting is compounded with epistolary form: "Marianne enters into … literature and writing within the dual secrecy of a broken emotional intensity and of the cloister. The instrument of this literary ordination is precisely the letter" ["Marianne … naît à la littérature et à l'écriture dans le double secret de l'intensité passionnelle rompue et du cloître. Et l'instrument de cette ordination littéraire est justement la lettre," 183].

In conclusion, Guilleragues constructs a convent setting which is just concrete enough to enable his narration. On the surface, his convent is a purely conventional structure, exploiting the teasing fantasy of a repressed female immured against her will: if only I (the male reader) could get in, too! But closer reading reveals that the Portuguese convent is not completely closed. More accurately, it has a one-way threshold: others can come in—her mother, her relatives, a bunch of soldiers, her lover (of course)—but she cannot go out. In her first letter, the nun writes the officer in frustration: "If it were possible for me to abandon this wretched cloister I would not wait in Portugal for the fulfilment of your promises: I would go, heedless of all restraint, to look for you, to follow you" ["S'il m'était possible de sortir de ce malheureux cloître, je n'attendrais pas en Portugal l'effet de vos promesses: j'irais, sans garder aucune mesure, vous chercher, vous suivre," Guilleragues 77, Waldman 10]. In reality, however, the only things of hers that do exit are her letters. It is pertinent to place this one-way situation in the historical context of convent reform: according to the 25th session of the Council of Trent, "No nun shall after her profession be permitted to go out of the monastery, even for a brief period under any pretext whatever, except for a lawful reason to be approved by the bishop … . Neither shall anyone, of whatever birth or condition, sex or age, be permitted, under penalty of excommunication to be incurred *ipso facto*, to enter the enclosure of a monastery without the written permission of the bishop or the superior."[6]

Some French nuns of the early seventeenth century took the lead in closing their own gates before this edict was officially enforced. As mentioned above (Chapter 4, 187), the most famous instance of this preemptive closing is the Journée des Guichets [day of the gates]: in 1609, Mère Angélique, the Abbess of the convent of Port Royal, refused entry to her own family. This injunction against both egress and ingress is known as "active enclosure." In contrast, the Portuguese nun occupies what I have already called an extreme feminine subject position: receptive, passive, acted upon, but not acting. This position is both mirrored and constructed by Guillerague's conventual space. In talking about "the nun" or "the heroine," it is easy to forget that these letters were written by a man. Usurping the female subject position in this way can be seen as a quintessential crossing of thresholds—the narrative invades the boundaries of the feminine space and of the feminine self.

---

[6]   *Canons and Decrees* 221.

La Religieuse, or Diderot en chemise

Like *Les Lettres portugaises, La Religieuse* examines female sexuality from a two-fold "insider" position: within a woman who is locked within a convent. However, in the usurpation and exposure of the enclosed female subject, as in the criticism of conventual enclosure itself, Diderot goes far beyond Guilleragues. Diderot's intensified scrutiny of female sexuality is abetted by the fact that in the eighteenth century, the age-old misogyny of medieval tales and priestly prejudice was revived in a new scientific form. According to Olwen Hufton, the Enlightenment "immersed woman in nature and made her the creature of her reproductive organs."[7] This sexually deterministic view went on to influence nineteenth-century medicine as well as early psychoanalytic theory. When doctors diagnosed their female patients as "hysterical," they literally postulated that a migrating womb was taking over the women's heads: the medieval maxim that *le bas fait tomber le haut*—sexuality overcomes reason—reappears, dignified by medical language. Taking this premise a step further, if sexual derangement may even affect women living "normal" lives in the world, female passions pent up within convent walls can gain the force of a "volcano."[8] As a materialist, a *philosophe* and the editor of the *Encyclopédie*, Diderot was profoundly engaged in the scientific and medical discussions of his time; the seriousness with which his medical writings were taken is attested by the number of scholarly books devoted to the subject, well into the twentieth century. His opposition to the claustration of women arises from a belief in the physiological differences between the sexes. According to Fein, Diderot "considers that the makeup of the female psyche, when distorted or perverted, leads to socially dangerous and explosive manifestations" (737). Diderot repeatedly expressed his views on women's sexuality, most notably in the 1772 essay "Sur les Femmes" which claims that "'women are ruled by their womb, 'an organ susceptible to terrible spasms, controlling her and creating in her mind all kinds of apparition,' and that they are unusually prone to what he calls 'hystericism' as a result of religious fervor" (quoted in Goulbourne in the introduction to his translation of *The Nun*, xviii). *La Religieuse* places Diderot's patho-physiological views at the service of a radical anti-monastic agenda. In this novel, the "objective description of [female] bodily dysfunctions" (Martin 129) is combined with traditional themes of forced vocation and incarceration in a convent cell to form an eminently powerful critique.[9]

---

[7]   *Women and the Limits of Citizenship in the French Revolution* (Toronto: University of Toronto Press 1992), 101.

[8]   Ponton, *La Religieuse* 20.

[9]   Carole F. Martin examines the pathological aspects of the novel in "Legacies of the Convent in Diderot's *La Religieuse.*" See also Beatrice Durand, "Diderot and the Nun" 104n8. For a general study of Diderot's view of the body, see Angelica Gooden, *Diderot and the Body* (Oxford: Legenda, 2001).

The textual status of *La Religieuse* is even more complex than that of *Les Lettres portugaises*.[10] According to its paratexts, the work we now know as a novel was originally conceived of as a *pièce à conviction*, or supporting document, to accompany a series of letters addressed to the marquis de Croismare.[11] Croismare, a member of Diderot's close circle of *amis intimes*, had left Paris for his family estate in Normandy where he became absorbed in family and country life. Thus, at least according to Grimm's account, the original motivation for the *Religieuse* project was not to militate against convents, but to cause Croismare to return to his friends in Paris. To call Croismare back to the capital, Diderot chose the voice of Suzanne Simonin. Simonin is a pseudonym for Marguerite Delamarre, a nun living at the Longchamp convent who had unsuccessfully attempted to have her vows rescinded a few years earlier.[12] Delamarre's experience at Longchamp, and Diderot's later depiction of it, bear little resemblance to the real convent of that name described in eighteenth-century accounts in Chapter 4 (167). Doubtless, the life of a convent boarder would be quite different from that of a professed nun; in addition, involuntary confinement might make even a relatively comfortable setting feel intolerable.

Without knowing her real identity, Croismare had been actively involved in the lawsuit on Delamarre's behalf. Hence, Diderot and his friends thought an appeal from this unhappy nun, stating that she had escaped from the convent and was requesting Croismare's help, would be an effective enticement. A possible secondary motive for this scenario might have been to punish Croismare for having fallen into devout habits while living in the provinces. According to Grimm's account in the *préface-annexe*, "he liked his priest a lot; he had become a passionate gardener; and since a mind as lively as his needed real or imaginary things to cling onto, he had suddenly thrown himself into a life of the utmost piety" ["Il aimait beaucoup son curé; il s'était livré à la passion du jardinage; et comme il fallait à une imagination aussi vive que la sienne des objets d'attachement réels ou imaginaires, il s'était tout à coup jeté dans la plus grande devotion," *Oeuvres romanesques* 849,

---

[10]   To briefly summarize the textual history: letters between Croismare and a supposed nun were first exchanged in the spring of 1760; the manuscript of the novel we know of as *La Religieuse* was composed later in that year. In 1770, the correspondence, but not the novel, was published in the *Correspondance littéraire*, preceded by an explanatory essay by Grimm, its editor. This dual text is now known as the *Préface-annexe*. *La Religieuse*, followed by the *Préface-annexe*, first appeared in book form in 1796. Most subsequent scholarly editions of the novel have included both parts. For a complete exposition of the manuscript's history and context, see Georges May, *Diderot et la Religieuse*.

[11]   Critics have pointed out that a *mémoire* is also a legal brief presented in support of a lawsuit. Suzanne smuggles such a *mémoire* out of the convent to her lawyer when she initiates an appeal to rescind her vows.

[12]   According to May, Delamarre's suit was actually initiated in 1752 and dragged on for six years until it was finally rejected in 1758. Croismare probably heard about the case by word of mouth in 1757. May was unable to find any written mention of it outside of the official records, which were inaccessible to the public at the time.

Goulborne 153].[13] Perhaps the devout practices Suzanne engages in—even when trying to break her vows, she continues to pray and attend mass—were meant to appeal to Croismare's piety. In any case, upon Croismare's return to Paris eight years later, Grimm reports that "his piety vanishes as everything vanishes in Paris, and today he is nicer than ever" ["sa dévotion s'est évaporée comme tout s'évapore à Paris, et il est aujourd'hui plus aimable que jamais"]. The implication being, of course, that "dévot" and "aimable" are mutually exclusive terms.

However, as Grimm admits, "this infamous trick turned out quite differently" ["Cette insigne fourberie prit tout un autre tour," *Oeuvres romanesques* 850, Goulbourne 154]. The friends' plot backfires when "Suzanne" asks Croismare to help her find work. Instead of rushing back to Paris, he invites her to Normandy as a governess for his daughter, and even begins preparing a room for Suzanne. Once things have reached this point in real life, something must be done. What Diderot does is to kill off his fictional heroine. As the late correspondence reports, Suzanne dies, after a prolonged illness, from the complications of a fall she suffered when climbing over the convent wall to freedom. But what began as a joke in an exchange of letters escaped those confines to grow, almost despite its author's conscious intent, into a full-blown independent narrative, filling 14 notebooks. In a letter to Meister, Grimm's successor as editor of the *Correspondance littéraire*, Diderot reveals: "I wrote this work off the top of my head" ["c'est un ouvrage que j'ai fait au courant de la plume," more literally "this work flowed out of my pen"; Sept. 27, 1780, quoted in May 44]. After the correspondence with Croismare ends, Diderot is still caught up with the fictional memoir; he famously commented that he was moved to tears by his own narrative.

Suzanne, C'est Moi

This disproportion between the rather trivial anecdotal cause and the masterly finished product cries out for explanation. I will offer two. First, Diderot's opposition to convents was plausibly strong and sincere; second, this project afforded him the opportunity to "impersonate" a female character and, in that guise, to "seduce" a close male friend. The *préface-annexe* to *La Religieuse* places its origins in a context of strong male bonding. Grimm, in a coy admission of guilt, characterizes the correspondence as "a horrible plot of which I was the center, in concert with M. Diderot and two or three other bandits of the same temper, among *our intimate friends*" ["un horrible complot dont j'ai été l'âme, de concert avec M. Diderot, et deux ou trois autres bandits de cette trempe de *nos amis intimes*"]. He continues, using the first person plural: "*The most tender friendship* had long bound us to M. de Croismare ... . *This charming Marquis* had left us ... *he still loved us tenderly*"; and, in a phrase already quoted, "today he is more *amiable* than ever"

---

[13]   French quotations are taken from Diderot, *La Religieuse*; *Oeuvres romanesques* (Paris: Garnier, 1962). The English translation is from Diderot, *The Nun*, trans. Russell Goulbourne (Oxford: Oxford University Press, 2005).

["*L'amitié la plus tendre* nous attachait depuis longtemps à M. de Croismare …
. *Ce charmant marquis* nous avait quittés … *il nous aimait toujours tendrement*,
et il est aujourd'hui plus *aimable* que jamais," *Oeuvres romanesques* 847, my
translation; italics added]. The Goulbourn translation renders "il nous aimait
toujours tendrement" by "he was still very fond of us." This phrase is more
in keeping with modern English usage, but it reduces the emotional impact,
and thereby calls into question the need for initiating the "wicked plot" in the
first place. In Grimm's text, the language of *amitié tendre*, which in the salon
discourse of the previous century referred to friendships between men and
women, is transferred to an intimate homosocial group. Miller goes as far as to
speak of homoeroticism ("I's in Drag" 49). This suggestion is consistent with
the pervasively misogynistic tone of the novel: the female narrator, Suzanne,
repeatedly makes traditionally disparaging remarks about her own gender, such
as "I am a woman, and I have the weak mind of those of my sex" ["Je suis une
femme, j'ai l'esprit faible comme celles de mon sexe," *Oeuvres romanesques*
308, Goulbourne 72]. And nuns, as a class, are described as the worst exemplars
of both women and human beings. After hearing of the persecutions Suzanne
endured in her two previous convents, the superior at Ste-Eutrope exclaims: "The
wicked creatures! The wicked creatures! Only in convents could humanity sink
so low" ["Les méchantes créatures! Les horribles créatures! Il n'y a que dans les
couvents où l'humanité puisse s'éteindre à ce point," *Oeuvres romanesques* 348,
Goulbourne 110]. The pitiless campaigns of destruction the nuns wage against
their "sisters" form a marked contrast to the good humor and "amitié tendre" of
the male coterie described by Grimm.

Not surprisingly then, the narrative of *La Religieuse* is also strongly patriarchal.
All of the authority figures in the novel—Suzanne's confessors, her attorney, the
archdeacons and vicars who visit her convents, and, of course, the interlocutor
Suzanne terms her "protecteur" (236)—are male. As Fowler points out, "The father
is always represented as superior in authority to the mother, and no aggression or
hostility is manifested in Suzanne's relations with the father-figures who follow
M. Simonin. Rather, she is consistently submissive, while the male figure is either
authoritative (Hébert), tender (Dom Morel) or both (Lemoine)" (89). Suzanne
follows the instructions of these men even when they are in conflict with those given
by her female convent superiors. It is only in the letters accompanying the novel
that Suzanne receives a female protector, Mme Madin; But Madin is written into
the story mainly to provide an accommodation address where Diderot can receive
Croismare's letters. The real-life Mme Madin had no knowledge of Diderot's plot;
in fact, it was in conversation with her that Croismare first learned of the imposture
six years later, when she denied any acquaintance with a Suzanne Simonin. In this
regard, it is interesting to contrast *La Religieuse* with the memoirs of the Mancini
sisters and the memoir-novels of Villedieu and Murat: in the *Histoire de Henriette-
Sylvie de Molière*, women are helped by other women, not by men, who usually

only cause them more trouble.[14] Suzanne finally runs into that familiar figure of satire, the womanizing cleric, but only after she has fled the convent.

The patriarchal tenor of the novel and its gender stereotyping are fundamental to the seductive strategy of the female narrator (and its male author). Suzanne unabashedly appeals to Croismare as a woman, with a woman's frailty, beauty, innocence and dependency. She reiterates that he is her only hope, the only one who stands between her and death. In agreeing to enter the nunnery, she states: "I began to suspect that I had just signed my own death warrant. And that suspicion will come true, Monsieur, if you forsake me" ["je pensais que je venais de signer mon arrêt de mort, et ce pressentiment, monsieur, se vérifiera si vous m'abandonnez," *Oeuvres romanesques* 255, Goulbourne 22]. Having spent most of her life behind convent walls, she resembles a zoo animal or a long-imprisoned convict who, once released, has no idea how to survive in the outside world: "Because I do not know where to go; because I am young and inexperienced. ... Monsieur, whether or not I know where to go or what to do depends on you" ["C'est que je ne sais où aller; c'est que je suis jeune et sans experience. ... Monsieur, que je ne sache pas où aller, ni que devenir, cela dépend de vous," *Oeuvres romanesques* 258, Goulbourne 24–5]. And despite her assertion that she fears "men and vice," she ends her narrative on a note of coquetry: "I am a woman, perhaps a little flirtatious for all I know. But it is natural and unaffected" ["Je suis une femme, peut-être un peu coquette; que sais-je? Mais c'est naturellement et sans artifice," *Oeuvres romanesques* 393, Goulbourne 152]. These and other self-appraisals reinforce Diderot's ideology of the "natural" woman, naively programmed to charm her male protector. Portraying women as "innocent" (hence potentially corruptible) is also a common ploy in erotic fiction. I agree with Durand, Rustin and others that the implausibilities of the third convent episode, where Suzanne appears unconscious of the lesbian implications of the superior's actions, are "narrative manipulations" designed to maintain the heroine's innocent image (Durand 95–6).[15] These manipulations create the supremely flattering and seductive illusion of a narration customized for an exclusive audience of one—a narrative voice that whispers, "I am made only for you."

At the same time that Suzanne seduces Croismare/the reader by her innocence and ignorance, she must also persuade us by her experience. While Croismare, a man, knows infinitely more about the world than she does—sometimes more than she wants to know—Suzanne, a mere woman, is the inside expert on the horrors of the convent. She writes to Croismare, "Oh! Monsieur, you simply cannot begin

---

[14]   In her article on Diderot, Carole Martin also compares Suzanne's illegitimacy with that of Marivaux's Marianne (118–19).

[15]   For more on the novel's ambiguities, see Armine Kotin Mortimer, "Naïve and devious: *La Religieuse*." *Romanic Review* (88.2 [March 1997] 241–51), as well as Rex (187), J.W. Fowler (75), Hayes (234) and Undank (151). A minority view is expressed by Georges May, who claims that the *Religieuse* is the only one of Diderot's works that is *not* ambiguous in its message.

to imagine how devious these Mothers Superior are!" ["Oh! Monsieur, combien ces supérieures de couvent sont artificieuses; vous n'avez point d'idée," *Oeuvres romanesques* 238, Goulbourne 5]. *He* has no idea; but *she* does (or Diderot does). Suzanne's authoritative knowledge of the convent is sometimes expressed through generalizations and aphorisms at odds with her usual style: "Oh, Monsieur! What wicked creatures they are, those cloistered women who always assist their God by driving you to despair!" ["Ah! Monsieur, les méchantes créatures que des femmes recluses, qui sont bien sûres de seconder la haine de leur supérieure, et qui croient servir Dieu en vous désespérant," *Oeuvres romanesques* 298, Goulbourne 63].

While the rhetorical tone of such statements clashes with Suzanne's normal voice and can strike a modern reader as overwrought, such was not the contemporary response. Indeed, on its posthumous publication in 1796, the novel was almost unanimously praised for its realistic depiction of convent conditions. In an article in *Nouvelles politiques nationales et étrangères*, J. Bluner wrote: "the characters, the events, the speeches are so real that one might be persuaded that the memoirs were written by the nun herself without counsel or exaggeration, if the editor had not put us straight" ["Les personnages, les évènements, les discours sont si vrais qu'on auroit été persuadé que les mémoires auroient été écrites par la religieuse elle-même sans conseil & sans exagération, si l'éditeur ne nous eût pas détrompés," quoted in May, 24]. None of the deviousness and contradictions discerned by modern critics were apparent to Bluner. This is not surprising; for as Natalie Sarraute astutely observed in *L'Ere du soupçon*, popular fiction always strikes its contemporary readers as "real" because it confirms what they expect to see. In this way, *La Religieuse* is less an authentic picture of convent life than a key to some readers' preconceptions at the end of the eighteenth century.

In his 1780 letter to Meister, Diderot had praised his own work in significantly different terms from Bluner's. "It is called *The Nun*, and I do not believe that anyone has ever written so frightening a satire of convents. It's a work that should be constantly leafed through by painters; and if only vanity allowed it, its true epigraph would be: 'I too am a painter'" ["Il est intitulé *La Religieuse* et je ne crois pas qu'on ait jamais écrit une plus effrayante satyre des couvents. C'est un ouvrage à feuilleter sans cesse par les peintres; et si la vanité ne s'y opposait, sa veritable epigraphe seroit: *Son pittor anch'io*," *Oeuvres romanesques* 869; Goulbourne Introduction xxviii]. In claiming *La Religieuse* should be used as a model for painters (of whom he himself was not the least talented), Diderot shows a justifiable pride in the novel's *tableaux*: its striking visual evocations of convent life. The juxtaposition of the two sentences in the quotation above implies a causal connection: *La Religieuse* is "une plus effrayante satyre des couvents" *because* of its "showing"—its graphic representation of the convent— more than its "telling"—the diatribes against the monastic system it contains. Drawing on his experience as a dramatist, as well as his innovative art criticism in the *salons*, Diderot creates an amazingly imaginative evocation of a space its author could not have seen. The dark and infernal atmosphere surrounding *La Religieuse* supplies a more convincing, less ambiguous critique of conventual seclusion than any overt ideological pronouncement can do.

Except for the final scenes, which were merely sketched out by Diderot, the action of *La Religieuse* unfolds almost entirely within walled rooms: as Suzanne writes to Croismare, "j'ai toujours vécu enfermée." The translation, "I have always lived a *sheltered* life," does not convey this concrete sense of enclosure (*Oeuvres romanesques* 258, Goulbourne 24). Most of the rooms described are convent cells: the word *cellule* occurs 80 times, far more often than in any other French novel set in the cloister.[16] However, few of these occurrences bear any relation to the practices of retreat and meditation associated with the cell in monastic spirituality: the first time Suzanne is alone in her cell, shortly after she has taken the habit of a novice, she looks not into her soul but into her mirror, and has to agree with her superior that she makes "une belle religieuse." (In fact, the constitutions of most monastic orders proscribed mirrors in cells.) In the great majority of cases, however, references to cells place them in a penitential or an intimate context: the cell is either a place to enclose and punish unruly nuns or a venue for forbidden encounters. But before arriving at the erotic or nightmarish events to take place within the cell, Diderot already creates a strong sense of claustration simply by tracing the nuns' limited movements. As they go through their daily routine, almost the only displacement is in and out of the cell. To give just a few examples: "I went to her cell. … Early the next morning she [la supérieure] came to my cell" ["j'allai dans sa cellule. … Le lendemain elle entra de bonne heure dans ma cellule," *Oeuvres romanesques* 260–61, Goulbourne 26]. Finally, "and so we locked ourselves away, she in her cell and I in mine" ["Nous nous renfermâmes, elle dans sa cellule, moi dans la mienne," *Oeuvres romanesques* 346, Goulbourne 108].

What other spaces play a central role in the novel? Beside the cells, nuns' choir, refectory and cloister, the conventual space seemingly consists of an endless stretch of corridors. A significant part of the action takes place in these corridors, which are "communicating" in both a spatial and a social sense. As Suzanne explains, to know what is happening in a convent "you have to understand the language" ["il faut entendre le langage," *Oeuvres romanesques* 291, Goulbourne 56]. And much of this language, both verbal and non-verbal, is heard in the corridors: "They were coming and going, whispering to each other, and the dormitory doors were opening and closing; all the signs, as you have already seen, of upheavals in a convent. I was alone in my cell" ["On allait, on venait, on se parlait bas, les portes des dortoirs s'ouvraient et se fermaient; c'est, comme vous l'avez pu voir jusqu'ici, le signal des révolutions monastiques. J'étais seule dans ma cellule," *Oeuvres romanesques* 327, Goulbourne 90]. This corridor communication is one of the aspects of the novel which conveys most clearly the sense of being

---

[16]   This conclusion is based on textual research performed through the ARTFL Frantext database, the result of a collaboration between the French government and the University of Chicago which provides access to a large collection of digitized French resources. Many university libraries subscribe to it.

"inside," in a penitentiary sense of the word. For example, during the period of her persecution at Longchamp, she describes the nuns standing "in the doorways of their cells, talking to one another across the corridors. As soon as I appeared, they quickly went inside their cells, creating a resounding noise as, one after another, they slammed their doors shut" ["sur le seuil de leurs cellules; elles se parlaient d'un côté du corridor à l'autre; aussitôt que je parus, elle se retirèrent, et il se fit un long bruit de portes qui se fermaient les unes après les autres avec violence," *Oeuvres romanesques* 308, Goulbourne 72]. Whereas in the works examined in Chapter 4, "threshold" spaces joined the convent to the outside world, here they only represent a different level of enclosure. However, the quote above does describe a kind of "threshold-crossing" or transgressive behavior. The contrast between the speech (probably gossip) whispered up and down the hall—a double infraction of convent discipline, since nuns are supposed to be silent and stay in their cells when they have no other occupation—and the loud slamming of doors convey with perfect economy the ostracism and violence to which Suzanne is subjected. Later, Suzanne can divine the result of her suit simply by analyzing the sounds of silence filtered through her keyhole: "it seemed to me as if they were deliberately falling silent and tiptoeing past. I had a feeling then that I had lost my case; there was no doubt about it. I started walking silently round and round in my cell, feeling as if I was suffocating …" ["il me parut qu'on se taisait en passant, et qu'on marchait sur la pointe des pieds. Je pressentis que j'avais perdu mon procès … je me mis à tourner dans ma cellule sans parler … ," *Oeuvres romanesques* 313, Goulbourne 76].

Already exhibiting the behavior of a prisoner in solitary confinement, pacing silently up and down her cell, Suzanne in effect becomes one after refusing to take vows. She writes: "From that moment on, I was locked in my cell" ["De ce moment, je fus renfermée dans ma cellule," 243, Goulbourne 11]. When she pretends to acquiesce and then recants publicly during her ceremony of profession, she is immediately locked up again: "as I spoke one of the nuns drew the curtain across the grille … I was taken to my cell and locked in" ["A ces mots une des soeurs laissa tomber le voile de la grille: On me conduisit dans ma cellule, où l'on me renferma sous la clef," *Oeuvres romanesques* 247, Goulbourne 14]. This *voile* or curtain covers the main grill of the convent, which separates the church from the choir where the nuns receive mass. As already noted in *La Vie de Marianne*, when a nun takes her vows, the main grill is opened so that the public gathered in the church can view the ceremony. The lowering of the *voile* marks the curtain falling on the dramatic public scene of Suzanne's resistance; from that point on, her drama and her suffering will take place within impenetrable walls, invisible to all outsiders. In an illustration of this scene from an 1804 edition of *La religieuse*, the nun lowering the curtain is prominently shown (Fig. 6.1).

The artist's choosing to illustrate this particular episode suggests its effectiveness and popularity with readers. It is informative to compare this illustration with other depictions of convent interiors reproduced in this volume. The drawing from the *Religieuse* shows the convent from the *inside*—from behind the scenes—whereas

Fig. 6.1   *Suzanne refuse de prononcer ses vœux*. Diderot, *La Religieuse*, Paris,
1804. Peintre Jacques le Barbier, engraver Jean-Baptiste Dupréel.
Paris, Bibliothèque de l'Assemblee nationale.

the illustration taken from *La Vie de Marianne* shows it from the *outside* (Fig. 4.2, 196). And while Philippe de Champaigne's painting of Port-Royal depicted a light illuminating the convent cell from above (Fig. 5.1, 212), the convent in the *Religieuse* illustration is represented as a place of darkness. The only illumination comes from the grill opening to the outside—a light that will dim as the curtain falls.

Upon her public refusal to profess at Ste-Marie, Suzanne is sent home and locked in her room until she agrees to enter the convent of Longchamp. There, after a relatively peaceful initial stay, a new superior takes over who imposes strict rule. When Suzanne refuses to follow the superior's orders, she is again subjected to penitentiary enclosure: "I was punished in the most inhumane way possible ... I was condemned ... to be locked up in my cell" ["j'en fus châtiée de la manière la plus inhumaine ... on me condamna ... à demeurer enfermée dans ma cellule," *Oeuvres romanesques* 268, Goulbourne 34]. Even worse, she is thrown into a dungeon for three days: "they took out some huge keys and unlocked the door to an underground cell, tiny and dark, and threw me on to some matting half rotten with damp" ["l'on ouvrit avec de grosses clefs la porte d'un petit lieu souterrain, obscur, où l'on me jeta sur une natte que l'humidité avait à demi pourrie," *Oeuvres romanesques* 276, Goulbourne 41]. Following eighteenth-century usage, even in a convent, the penitentiary cell is called a *cachot*, or a prison cell, to distinguish it from a nun's cell or *cellule* (290). The *cellule* as described by Diderot is a penitentiary enclosure as well; but it is more than that. In a complex dialectic, the monastic cell, meant to be a place of retreat from secular life, can be turned into a prison; yet it still remains the only locale for personal privacy—a refuge from the convent itself rather than from the outside world. After her release, Suzanne ironically remarks: "I forgot to tell you that the first sign of kindness shown to me was to allow me to return to my old cell" ["J'oubliais de dire que la première marque de bonté qu'on me donna, ce fut de me rétablir dans ma cellule," *Oeuvres romanesques* 282, Goulbourne 48]. But as we will see later, even this last refuge can be compromised.

In the dialectics of the convent space, *enfermement* finds its counterpoint in escape. During her early days at Longchamp, Suzanne observes a horrifying and prophetic spectacle: that of a mad nun who has broken out of her cell. ["Il arriva un jour qu'il s'en échappa une de ces dernières (folles) de la cellule où on la tenait enfermée. Je la vis," *Oeuvres romanesques* 241, Goulbourne 8]. The night before her profession, Suzanne, in turn, exits her cell in a deranged state: "I cannot remember getting undressed or leaving my cell, but I was found, naked but for a chemise, lying on the ground outside the Mother Superior's room. ... In the morning I was in my cell." She was unaware of how she came there. ["Je ne souviens ni de m'être déshabillée, ni d'être sortie de ma cellule; cependant on me trouva nue en chemise, étendue par terre à la porte de la supérieure. ... Le matin, je me trouvai dans ma cellule," *Oeuvres romanesques* 245, Goulbourne 12.] In this particular context, being "in one's cell" is a metonymy for reason and order; hence, "out of the cell" becomes the equivalent of being out of one's mind. But with cruel circularity, it is solitary confinement in the cell that can lead to nuns' madness and consequent wandering. At Ste-Eutrope, Suzanne will plead in favor of the previous favorite, Soeur Ste-Thérèse, who appears in danger of going mad: "'Oh! Dear Mother,' I said, 'don't ever lock her up'" ["Ah! Chère mère lui dis-je, ne l'enfermez jamais," *Oeuvres romanesques* 358, Goulbourne 120].

A second counterpoint to forced enclosure is forced entry. As indicated above, Suzanne's incarceration in her cell is accompanied by invasions of her personal space. At Longchamp, after she has resisted the new superior's injunction against reading the Bible, the superior enters Suzanne's cell to question her; receiving no satisfactory response, she has the cell searched. One French word for search is "visiter"; thus, the phrase "on visita ma cellule" would make entry synonymous with violation of privacy. This violation becomes more flagrant as Suzanne's persecution begins: "They would come into my cell whenever they wanted, day or night, under any pretext, suddenly and stealthily. They would open my curtains and then leave again" ["on entrait à tout moment dans ma cellule, le jour, la nuit, sous des prétextes; brusquement, sourdement, on entr'ouvrait mes rideaux, et l'on se retirait," *Oeuvres romanesques* 271, Goulbourne 37]. These continual intrusions become even more intolerable after Suzanne, shut up in her cell, breaks the lock on her door in order to be able to attend mass: "Since the door to my cell could no longer be closed, nuns would burst in during the night, shouting, pulling my bed, smashing my windows and doing all sorts of terrifying things to me" ["Comme ma cellule ne fermait plus, on entrait pendant la nuit, en tumulte, on criait, on tirait mon lit, on cassait mes fenêtres, on me faisait toute sortes de terreurs," *Oeuvres romanesques* 294, Goulborne 59]. Thus the cell, as a metonymy for the convent as a whole, is simultaneously both prison and retreat: even after its door no longer locks, it remains a refuge, if a compromised one. As Suzanne pathetically reports: "I went back into my cell, knelt down facing the wall and prayed" ["Je rentrai dans ma cellule; je me mis à genoux contre le mur, et je priai Dieu," *Oeuvres romanesques* 308, Goulbourne 72].

At the same time that it is a site of forced enclosure, Suzanne's cell is also metonymic of her own personal boundaries. As the persecution intensifies, first her cell, then her body, will be progressively denuded: "It even got to the stage of my being robbed and deprived of my belongings, and my chairs, bedding and mattress were taken away. I was no longer given fresh undergarments, my clothes were torn, and I had almost worn out my stockings and sandals" ["On en vint jusqu'à me voler, me dépouiller, m'ôter mes chaises, mes couvertures et mes matelas; on ne me donnait plus de linge blanc; j'étais sans bas et sans souliers," *Oeuvres romanesques* 293, Goulbourne 58]. In the constructions *me voler, me dépouiller, m'ôter mes chaises, mes couvertures*, the percussive combination of infinitives with direct objects or possessive pronouns intensifies and personalizes her *dénûment*. When Suzanne escapes to attend mass, the thievery is exacerbated, striking at her spiritual being as well: "While I was away from my cell, my prayer stool, my portrait of our founder, my other pious images, and my crucifix were all taken away, and I was left only with the crucifix on my rosary, which was also soon taken from me" ["Tandis que j'étais absente, on enleva de ma cellule mon prie-dieu, le portrait de notre fondatrice, les autres images pieuses, le crucifix; et il ne me resta que celui que je portais à mon rosaire, qu'on ne me laissa pas longtemps"]. Reiterating this litany of privation, Suzanne concludes: "So I found myself living within four bare walls, in a room with no door or chair, my only option being to stand or to lie on a straw mattress, with no essential utensils, forced to go out at night in order to meet the call of nature, and accused in the morning of disrupting the convent, of wandering about, and of going mad" ["Je vivais donc entre quatre murailles nues, dans une chambre sans porte, sans chaises, debout, ou sur une paillasse, sans aucun des vaisseaux les plus nécessaires, forcée de sortir la nuit pour satisfaire aux besoins de la nature, et accusée le matin de troubler le repos de la maison, d'errer et de devenir folle," *Oeuvres romanesques* 294, Goulbourne 58–9]. As with the unfortunate nun Suzanne had seen in the corridor at Ste-Marie, wandering outside the cell is equated with madness: "errer et devenir folle." But here, the alienation, or at least its appearance, is deliberately induced.

The metonymy of cell for body also extends to Suzanne's clothing. When an archdeacon finally arrives to investigate the "disorder" in the convent, he asks detailed questions about the abysmal state of her attire:

> "Why are your undergarments and clothes so shabby and dirty?"
> "Because for more than three months now I've been refused fresh undergarments and have been forced to sleep with my clothes on."
> "Why do you sleep with your clothes on?"
> "Because I don't have any curtains, mattresses, blankets, sheets, or nightwear."
> "Why don't you have any?"
> "Because they've been taken away from me."

> —Pourquoi votre linge et vos vêtements sont-ils dans cet état de vétusté et de malpropreté?
> —C'est qu'il y a plus de trois mois qu'on me refuse du linge, et que je suis forcée de coucher avec mes vêtements.
> —Pourquoi couchez-vous avec vos vêtements?
> —C'est que je n'ai ni rideaux, ni matelas, ni couvertures, ni draps, ni linge de nuit.
> —Pourquoi n'en avez-vous point?
> —C'est qu'on me les a ôtés. (*Oeuvres romanesques* 306, Goulbourne 70)

This negative inventory is repeated after the archdeacon visits her cell: "As I have told you, I had no wall hangings, no chair, no prayer stool, no curtains, no mattress, no blankets, no sheets, no utensils whatsoever, no door that could be closed, and hardly a pane of glass in my windows" ["Je vous ai dit que j'étais sans tapisserie, sans chaise, sans prie-dieu, sans rideaux, sans matelas, sans couvertures, sans draps, sans aucun vaisseau, sans une porte qui fermât, presque sans vitre entière à mes fenêtres," *Oeuvres romanesques* 308, Goulbourne 72]. Lacking all belongings associated with "l'état commun des religieuses," living in filth within four bare walls, Suzanne's state during her persecutions recalls the extreme privations some religious ascetics have imposed on themselves. But where the early Desert Fathers, and a few Counter-Reformation nuns, willingly endured hardships in hopes of salvation, Suzanne's privations are not voluntary but involuntary; not penitential, but penitentiary.[17] The parallel drawn between ascetic renunciation and punishment is not coincidental: once again, the convent is represented not as a religious shelter, but as a prison. The technique of enumeration appears one last time, in affirmative form, to indicate that Suzanne's rights have been reestablished: "From that moment on I never heard another word about anything, but I was given some undergarments, other clothes, curtains, sheets, blankets, utensils, my breviary, my devotional books, my rosary, my crucifix, and new panes of glass, in short everything I needed to restore my condition to that of the other nuns" ["Depuis ce temps je n'entendis plus parler de rien; mais j'eus du linge, d'autres vêtements, des rideaux, des draps, des couvertures, des vaisseaux, mon bréviare, mes livres de piété, mon rosaire, mon crucifix, des vitres, en un mot, tout ce qui me rétablissait dans l'état commun des religieuses," *Oeuvres romanesques* 309, Goulbourne 73].[18]

I have quoted these repeated lists verbatim, tedious as they may seem, in order to recreate the impression made by Diderot's distinctive mode of conventual representation. It offers little description in a realist sense; nor, except for the former superior's portrait, does the narrator express much personal interest in the objects she is enumerating. Rather, these lists recall the furnishings for nun's cells prescribed in monastic rules. The *Constitutions de Port-Royal* mandate these cell furnishings in considerable detail, while omitting, perhaps for reasons of *bienséance*, "the most necessary vessels" ["(les) vaisseaux les plus nécessaires"] that were taken from Suzanne along with her other belongings. "The cell furnishings will consist of a small wooden table, a straw-bottomed chair, three planks on trestles or else a little bed without posts, a straw mattress, a covering over it, a straw bedhead, a feather pillow covered with white or grey serge, two large and one small blankets, five images on paper, an earthenware basin for holy water and a lamp" ["Les meubles des Cellules seront une petite table de bois, une chaise de nattes, trois ais sur des traitaux ou bien une petite couche sans piliers, une paillasse, un blanchet dessus, un chevet de paille, un oreiller de plume couvert de serge blanche ou grise, deux grandes couvertures et une petite, cinq images de papier, un bénitier de terre et une lampe," Agnès de St-Paul et al., *Constitutions de Port-Royal*, Chapter 19, "De la pauvreté," 134]. It is noteworthy that the cell furnishings at Port-Royal, though humble in the extreme, do supply a minimum of comfort: each nun has the use of a feather pillow and three blankets to protect her

---

[17]   On self-inflicted penitence by nuns, see Elizabeth Rapley, "Her Body the Enemy: Self-Mortification in Seventeenth Century Convents." British Library 222.bl.uk 25–35.

[18]   It is interesting to note that one of the letters allegedly written by Mme Madin contains an inventory of the "trousseau" she intends to send with Suzanne when the girl takes up a position in Croismare's household. This exhaustive list includes: "fifteen chemises with lace sleeves, some made of cambric, others of muslin … . Two matching bodices, which I had made for my youngest daughter and which turned out to fit her perfectly … . Some corsets, aprons, and neckerchiefs" (Goulbourne 171). Diderot's fixation on women's garments and undergarments merits a separate study.

from the cold. In contrast, Diderot's repeated inventories, void of detail or affect, prefigure the documents that will be prepared by the Revolutionary officials prior to stripping the monasteries of their possessions.[19] It is precisely this blankness, these deadening repetitions, which hammer home the brutality of the events recounted.

Unlike the example from the *Constitution de Port-Royal*, inventories in *La Religieuse* group clothing along with cell furnishings ["ni rideaux, ni matelas, ni couvertures, ni draps, ni linge de nuit"]. By including intimate garments (*linge*) which are worn next to the skin, the narrator emphasizes the continuity between cell and body and the violation of both. The archdeacon's questions to Suzanne reinforce the close connection between her clothing and her cell's furnishings, or lack thereof: in a seamless continuum, the baring of her surroundings also extends to her body. When the superior suspects Suzanne of having written a secret document, Suzanne is subjected to a "strip search":

> Her companions grabbed me, tore off my veil and shamelessly stripped me. They found hanging around my neck a little portrait of my old Mother Superior, which they took from me. I begged them to allow me to kiss it one last time, but they refused. They threw over me a shirt, took off my stockings, covered me with a sack and led me along the corridors, with nothing on my head or feet.

> On m'arracha mon voile; on me dépouilla sans pudeur. On trouva sur mon sein un petit portrait de mon ancienne supérieure; on s'en saisit: je suppliai qu'on me permit de le baiser encore une fois; on me refusa. On me jeta une chemise, on m'ôta mes bas, on me couvrit d'un sac, et l'on me conduisit, la tête et les pieds nus, à travers les corridors. (*Oeuvres romanesques* 275–6, Goulbourne 41)

The word *dépouiller*, to remove or strip, also appears in a passage quoted above describing the plundering of Suzanne's cell: "on en vint jusqu'à me voler, me dépouiller" (*Oeuvres romanesques* 293, Goulbourne 59). This repetition reinforces the identification between cell and person, as well as the parallel between stripping the cell and stripping the body. All of these acts are committed by the superior's favorites; but Diderot's use of the pronoun *on*, instead of the feminine *elles*, makes their actions appear more impersonal and implacable. This effect is reinforced by long sentences filled with brusque verbal clauses: "on me jeta, on m'ôta, l'on me conduisit … ."

After Suzanne loses her suit to have her vows rescinded, she is left in the vengeful hands of her convent "mother" and "sisters." At that point, she is again stripped of her habit. I will quote from this episode at length:

> The next day the Mother Superior came to my cell with a nun carrying over her arm a hair-shirt and the gown made of rough cloth that I had been made to change into when I was taken down to the dungeon. I understood what this meant. I undressed, or rather my veil was torn off me, I was stripped and I put

---

[19] The detached tone contrasts sharply with Mlle de Montpensier's emotional reactions, whether positive or negative, to her own surroundings (see above, Chapter 3).

on the gown. I had nothing on my head or my feet, my long hair fell about my shoulders, and all I had to wear was the hair-shirt I had been given, a very coarse chemise, and the long gown which went from my neck right down to my feet.

Dès le lendemain, la supérieure vint dans ma cellule avec une religieuse qui portait sur son bras un cilice et cette robe d'étoffe grossière dont on m'avait revêtue lorsque je fus conduite dans le cachot. J'entendis ce que cela signifiait; je me déshabillai, ou plutôt on m'arracha mon voile, on me dépouilla; et je pris cette robe. J'avais la tête nue, les pieds nus, mes longs cheveux tombaient sur mes épaules; et tout mon vêtement se réduisait à ce cilice que l'on me donna, à une chemise très dure, et à cette longue robe qui me prenait sous le cou et qui me descendait jusqu'aux pieds. (*Oeuvres romanesques* 317, Goulbourne 81)

To prepare the scene to follow, the narrator repeats that Suzanne is wearing nothing but a chemise under her rough robe. In addition, the rough robe that "qui me prenait sous le cou" foreshadows the rope that will be placed around Suzanne's neck.

Suzanne is forced to remain in this dress throughout the day. Then, in the evening, the entire convent lines up in procession outside her door. A cord is tied around her neck, she is given a torch and a scourge (a small whip used for self-castigation), and dragged between the two lines of nuns to a chapel, where she is ordered to ask the pardon of God and the community:

Then the rope was removed, I was stripped down to the waist, they took my hair, which was hanging down over my shoulders, and pulled it to one side of my neck, they placed in my right hand the scourge I had been carrying in my left, and they started reciting the *Miserere*. I knew what was expected of me, and I did it.

Après cela, on m'ôta la corde, on me déshabilla jusqu'à la ceinture, on me prit mes cheveux qui étaient épars sur mes épaules, on les rejeta sur un des côtés de mon cou, on me mit dans la main droite la discipline que je portais de la main gauche, et l'on commença le *Miserere*. Je compris ce que l'on attendait de moi, et je l'exécutai. (*Oeuvres romanesques* 318, Goulbourne 81)

Although Diderot omits the description of the actual whipping, allusions to Suzanne's loose hair and her partial nudity give the reader's imagination plentiful material for reconstructing the scene. In a final sadistic touch, arrived back in her cell, Suzanne discovers that her bare feet are bleeding from broken glass that had been strewn on her path.

The luridness of this and similar episodes causes Suzanne herself to worry that her tale might appear implausible to her reader. In defense, she argues that the particular persecutions she has undergone represent, in almost Christ-like fashion, the sufferings of all cloistered nuns.[20] Diderot's hyperbolic portrayal of convent

---

[20] Suzanne is explicitly associated with a Christ figure more than once in the novel. In one of the novel's most horrendous scenes, the nuns at Longchamp stage a mock execution. She faints and finds herself on her straw pallet, "with my hands tied behind my

brutality has also been seen as problematic by modern critics. Rogers refers to the novel's more shocking details, such as the broken glass thrown in Suzanne's path, as "sensational fantasies" (308) arising from the excessive zeal of "Enlightenment secularism": "Hostility to monastic ideals caused both French and English writers to distort their pictures of the convent by overemphasizing its austere and extreme aspects" ("Fantasy and Reality" 313).

While this judgment is doubtless accurate as far as it goes, these "sensational fantasies" of stripping and torture are also clearly erotic. Obviously, Suzanne's exemplary victimhood is meant to provoke sympathy for her in particular and hostility to conventual enclosure in general; equally obviously, her disarray offers the reader an exciting spectacle. In the two passages quoted above, the verbs "déshabilla," "dépouilla," "ôta", "arracha," "baisa"; the nouns "sein," "épaule," "cheveux épars" and the repeated "nus"; the intimate evocation of the hairshirt rubbing against Suzanne's bare skin—all these combine into a sadistic fantasy that excites as it shocks. Undank sees eroticism and social criticism as contradictory, arguing that "the ideology of female victimization [that *La Religieuse*] inadvertently supports and draws upon for its very existence and efficacy" undermines the liberal and liberating aims of the text. I would question, however, whether female victimization in the text is "inadvertent" in its erotic implications. Diderot, who was familiar with Barrin's *La Religieuse en chemise* (May 131), repeatedly displays his own *religieuse* "nue en chemise" (14 occurrences indicated in ARTFL). By identifying with the *religieuse*, the writer, like the reader, experiences vicariously both the sadistic and the masochistic sides of the fantasy.[21]

Vicarious eroticism reaches its climax in the famous episode at the Couvent de Ste-Eutrope, where the cell becomes a site of forbidden intimacy between women. Diderot reconstructs the familiar metonymies of cell, corridor, chapel, veil and grill to create one of the most compelling sequences in eighteenth-century fiction. Like earlier scenes, the Ste-Eutrope episode plays itself out entirely within the hermetically closed setting of the convent. However, this part of the novel carries interiorization to a deeper level. Whereas non-verbal signs, like the opening and closing of doors, or movement and speech in the halls, had mostly a social import at Longchamp, at Ste-Eutrope they become charged with psychological meaning.

---

back and a big crucifix on my lap" ["les bras liés derrière le dos, assise, avec un grand Christ de fer sur mes genoux"]. She reflects on the image of the suffering Jesus: "that innocent man, his side pierced, his head crowned with thorns, his hands and feet pierced with nails, and dying in agony, and I said to myself: 'This is my God, and yet I dare to feel sorry for myself!'" ["l'innocent, le flanc percé, le front couronné d'épines, les mains et les pieds percés de clous, et expirant dans les souffrances; et je me disais: 'Voilà mon Dieu, et j'ose me plaindre!'" *Oeuvres romanesques* 300–301, Goulbourne 65].

21 See also Jean-Christophe Abramovici, "A qui profite le vice? Le topos du lecteur jouisseur de roman obscène" in Jan Herman, Paul Pelckmans, Nicole Boursier, eds. *L'Epreuve du lecteur: Livres et lectures dans le roman d'Ancien Régime* (Louvain: Peeters, 1995), 292–9.

For Suzanne, who knows by heart "le langage des couvents," the dumb show of corridor movement reveals unspoken intimate feelings. For example, she recounts how after a gathering of the nuns, "The Mother Superior locked herself away in her cell, and Sister Thérèse paused in her doorway, watching me as if she was wondering what I was going to do. I went back to my cell and it took a little time for the door to Sister Thérèse's cell to be shut softly. It occurred to me that this young woman was jealous of me" ["la supérieure se renferma dans sa cellule, et la soeur Thérèse s'arrêta sur la porte de la sienne, m'épiant comme si elle eût été curieuse de savoir ce que je deviendrais. Je rentrai chez moi, et la porte de la cellule de la soeur Thérèse ne se referma que quelque temps après, et se referma doucement. Il me vint en idée que cette jeune fille était jalouse de moi," *Oeuvres romanesques* 337, Goulbourne 99]. When the superior later orders soeur Ste-Thérèse back into her cell, "[Ste-Thérèse] slammed her door shut" ["ferma la porte avec violence"], signaling her anger and jealousy (*Oeuvres romanesques* 339, Goulbourne 102).

Towards the end of the Ste-Eutrope episode, after the confessor orders Suzanne to stop seeing the Mother Superior alone, the Superior takes to nocturnal wandering: "She used to get up in the night and walk along the corridors, especially mine. I could hear her going up and down, stopping outside my door, moaning and sighing. I would tremble and bury myself under the bedclothes" ["Elle se levait la nuit et se promenait dans les corridors, surtout dans le mien; je l'entendais passer et repasser; s'arrêter à ma porte, se plaindre, soupirer; je tremblais, et je me renfonçais dans mon lit," *Oeuvres romanesques* 373, Goulbourne 135]. As her despair and derangement deepen, the Superior's nightly movements spill over into the day: "At night, she would go down in her nightdress and bare feet. If Ste-Thérèse or I happened to come across her, she would turn away and press her face against the wall. One day, as I was leaving my cell, I found her prostrate, her arms outstretched, and her face to the ground. I stopped and she said to me: 'Carry on, keep walking, walk right over me; it's the only way I deserve to be treated'" ["La nuit, elle descendait en chemise, nus pieds; si Sainte-Thérèse ou moi nous la rencontrions par hasard, elle se retournait et se collait le visage contre le mur. Un jour que je sortais de ma cellule, je la trouvai prosternée, les bras étendus et la face contre terre; et elle me dit: 'Avancez, marchez, foulez-moi aux pieds; je ne mérite pas un autre traitement' *Oeuvres romanesques* 377, Goulbourne 138–9]. This pathetic moment recalls the scene at Longchamp when the superior orders the other nuns to walk on Suzanne's prostrate body: "Walk on her; she's just a corpse" ["Marche sur elle, ce n'est qu'un cadavre," *Oeuvres romanesques* 294, Goulbourne 8]. Unlike Suzanne's, the superior of Ste-Eutrope's abjection is not imposed from the outside, but self-inflicted.

Finally, just before the end of the developed portion of the narrative, the superior, now insane, escapes from her cell: "She had torn off her clothes and was wandering along the corridors completely naked, with just two little lengths of torn rope hanging from her arms" ["Elle avait déchiré ses vêtements, elle parcourait les corridors toute nue, seulement deux bouts de corde rompue descendait de ses deux bras," *Oeuvres romanesques* 387, Goulbourne 147]. This scene adds erotic overtones to the horrifying spectacle of the mad nun Suzanne had recorded earlier. The replay of such vignettes of mad, or allegedly mad, nuns reinforces the apparent inevitability of this cruel end to convent life. Dom Morel, the new confessor, summarizes the nun's unhappy fate in this way:

> "... others look for a deep well, a very high window, or a length of rope, and sometimes they find it; others, who've been anxious for a long time, sink into a kind of daze and remain numb; others, with weak and delicate organs, waste away in languor; and there are yet others whose constitution is upset, whose minds are disturbed, and who go raving mad ... ."

> "And the unluckiest ones," I added, apparently sighing deeply, "are they the ones who experience all of these states in turn?"

> ... d'autres cherchent un puits profond, des fenêtres bien hautes, un lacet, et le trouvent quelquefois; d'autres après s'être tourmentées longtemps, tombent dans une espèce d'abrutissement et restent imbéciles; d'autres, qui ont des organes faibles et délicates, se consument de langueur; il y en a en qui l'organisme se trouble et qui deviennent furieuses ... .

> —Et les plus malheureuses, ajoutai-je, apparemment, en poussant un profond soupir, sont celles qui éprouvent successivement tous ces états. (*Oeuvres romanesques* 382, Goulbourne 142)

Such will be the fate of the superior, due to her guilt and frustrated desire. Such desire is born within the convent cell and spreads through its corridors, like an infection racing unchecked through the human body.

From the beginning of the Ste-Eutrope sequence, the cell is represented in an anomalous and transgressive way. Convent rules forbid nuns from entering one another's cells without the superior's permission, except in extreme emergency. It is clear that Diderot knew this, for he has Suzanne apologize to the superior for going into Ste-Thérèse's cell: "I said to her: 'My dear Mother, please forgive me for coming here without asking permission.'" 'It's true,' she replied, 'that it would have been better if you'd asked'" ["Je lui dis: 'Ma chère Mère, je vous demande pardon d'être venue ici sans votre permission.'—Il est vrai, me répondit-elle, qu'il eût été mieux de la demander," *Oeuvres romanesques* 338, Goulbourne 101]. And during her stricter moments, the superior forbids any nun from visiting another's room. On most occasions, however, the superior not only breaks this rule but orders its infraction. The day of Suzanne's arrival, "she herself came and settled me in my new cell. She did the honors, in her own way: she showed me the oratory and said: 'That's where my little friend will pray to God. We need to put a cushion on this step so that she doesn't hurt her little knees ...'" ["elle vint elle-même m'installer dans ma cellule. Elle m'en fit les honneurs à sa mode; elle me montrait l'oratoire, et disait: 'C'est là que ma petite amie priera Dieu; je veux qu'on lui mette un coussin sur ce marchepied, afin que ses petits genoux ne soient pas blessés ...'"]. The Superior continues to examine the furnishings of the cell, paying particular attention to the bedclothes—mattress, blankets, sheets—with the inhabitant's repose in mind: "She picked up the bolster and plumping it up, said: 'This sweet head of yours will be quite comfortable on this'" ["Elle prit le traversin, et le faisant bouffer, elle disait: 'Chère tête sera fort bien là-dessus,'" *Oeuvres romanesques* 332, Goulbourne 94–5]. The superior's excessive attention to Suzanne's furnishings and physical comfort offers a shocking contrast to the latter's treatment at Ste-Marie, where bed, mattress and linen had all been removed from her cell. Again, Diderot offers an enumeration of the cell's contents; but instead of representing punishment, it is now meant to reveal the superior's sensuality.

Diderot makes another important parallel between the sadistic acts performed at Ste-Marie and the erotic practices at Ste-Eutrope through progressively more explicit descriptions of the superior's removing of Suzanne's clothing. On the very evening of her arrival, "j'eus la visite de la supérieure; elle vint à mon déshabiller; ce fut elle qui m'ôta mon voile et ma guimpe, et qui me coiffa de nuit: ce fut elle qui me déshabilla" ["the Mother Superior came to visit me; she came in as I was getting undressed. It was she who took off my veil and wimple and brushed my hair for bed; it was she who undressed me," *Oeuvres romanesques* 135, Goulbourne 95]. Later in the novel, a much more detailed undressing scene is incorporated into Suzanne's narration of the sufferings she endured at her previous convent. The superior entreats Suzanne to tell her the story of her mistreatment, obviously hoping to find in it a source of erotic excitement: "'Tell me everything, my child,' she said, 'I'm waiting, I'm very much in the mood for emotion'" ["Raconte, mon enfant, dit-elle; j'attends, je me sens les dispositions les plus pressantes à m'attendrir," *Oeuvres romanesques* 347, Goulbourne 109]. Indeed, her sentimental *attendrissement* quickly crosses over into love play, in which process Suzanne is again denuded:

> "How has this delicate machine not been destroyed? ... How has the sparkle in your eyes not been washed away by tears? And she kissed them. "Wringing moans and groans from this mouth! ..." And she kissed it. ... "Daring to tie a rope around this neck and cutting these shoulders with sharp points! ..." And she pushed aside my gimp and wimple and opened up the top of my gown. My hair fell loose over my bare shoulders, my breast was half naked, and her kisses spread over my neck, bare shoulders, and half-naked breast.

> 'Comment toute cette machine délicate n'a-t-elle pas été détruite? ... Noyer de larmes ces yeux! ...' Et elle les baisait. 'Arracher la plainte et le gémissement de cette bouche! ...' Et elle la baisait. ... 'Oser entourer ce cou d'une corde, et déchirer ces épaules avec des pointes aiguës ...' Et elle écartait mon linge de cou et de tête; elle entr'ouvrait le haut de ma robe; mes cheveux tombaient épars sur les épaules découvertes; ma poitrine était à demi nue, et ses baisers se répandaient sur mon cou, sur mes épaules découvertes et sur ma poitrine à demi nue. (*Oeuvres romanesques* 348, Goulbourne 111)

This description draws on memories of torture scenes from Longchamp. Diderot reuses some of the same vocabulary, such as "cheveux ... épars," and has the superior's mouth revisit the same sites of punishment on Suzanne's body. At the same time, Suzanne's account of what is happening to her displays a quality of detached repetition, similar to the earlier inventories of her unfurnished cell; it is as though all these acts, whether punitive or seductive, are inflicted on a passive, somewhat dissociated narrator.

Long before their relationship reaches this point, the growing intimacy between Suzanne and the superior is conveyed by the transgression of cell boundaries: "I saw the affection that the Mother Superior had conceived for me grow day by day. I was constantly in her cell or she in mine" ["Je voyais croître de jour en jour la tendresse que la supérieure avait conçue pour moi. J'étais sans cesse dans sa cellule, ou elle était dans la mienne," *Oeuvres romanesques* 342, Goulbourne 105]. The use of the possessives "sa" and "la mienne" represents their growing intimacy, almost as if they were inside one another's bodies. Thus, it is fitting that the climactic scene of this part, and perhaps the most dramatic of the entire novel, takes place in Suzanne's cell. This is also one of the longest scenes (five pages) in a book more given to short accounts. On the preceding day, the Superior had interrogated Suzanne almost in the style of a confessor to learn if she ever touched herself: "Have you never thought of running your hands over your breast, your thighs, your stomach, your flesh, so firm, so soft, so white?" ["Jamais, vous n'avez pensé à promener vos mains sur cette belle gorge, sur ces cuisses, sur ce ventre, sur ces chairs si fermes, si douces et si blanches?"]. Suzanne replies ingenuously: "Oh, certainly not, for that's sinful, and if I had done, I don't know how I would ever have admitted it in confession …" ["Oh! Pour cela, non; il y a du péché à cela; et si cela m'était arrivé, je ne sais comment j'aurais fait pour l'avouer à confesse … ," *Oeuvres romanesques* 352, Goulbourne 115]. Though Suzanne knows that self-touching is forbidden, she does not seem to know that this proscription extends to being touched by another woman. Ironically, the very innocence that allows the Superior to get as far as she does with Suzanne also prevents her from getting any further.

Suzanne leads up to the climactic events of the next night by recounting the superior's movements: "when everyone was asleep and the convent was silent, she got up. After wandering along the corridors for a while, she came to my cell" ["La nuit suivante, lorsque tout le monde dormait et que la maison était dans le silence, elle se leva; après avoir erré quelque temps dans les corridors, elle vint à ma cellule"]. Three times, the superior approaches Suzanne's door and walks away; finally, Suzanne awakens to find the superior sitting next to her bed. Things progress rapidly: the superior "throws herself" at Suzanne, lying on top of the bed beside her, then asks the young nun to pull aside the covers and let her in. Suzanne is not easily persuaded. Again, while seemingly unaware of her own sexuality— or not possessing any—she knows what is forbidden: "Chère mère, lui dis-je, mais cela est défendue." Again, Suzanne's naive Agnès-like style of narration creates a moment of comic relief. She recounts an anecdote which she seems to understand only imperfectly:

"One night in the convent of Sainte-Marie a nun went into the cell of another nun, her good friend, and I can't tell you just how badly this was viewed. My confessor has sometimes asked me if anyone has ever suggested coming to sleep with me, and he earnestly advised me to say no to anyone who did. I've even told him about your caresses, which I find very innocent, but which he doesn't. I don't know how I forgot his advice, because I'd intended to speak to you about it."

"Il arriva dans le couvent de Sainte-Marie à une religieuse d'aller la nuit dans la cellule d'une autre, c'était sa bonne amie, et je ne saurais vous dire tout le mal qu'on en pensait. Le directeur m'a demandé quelquefois si l'on ne m'avait jamais proposé de venir dormir à côté de moi, et il m'a sérieusement recommandé de ne le pas souffrir. Je lui ai même parlé des caresses que vous me faisiez; je les trouve très innocentes, mais lui, il ne pense point ainsi; je ne sais comment j'ai oublié ses conseils; je m'étais bien proposé de vous en parler." (*Oeuvres romanesques* 355, Goulbourne 117)

How indeed did she forget?

While the confessor had reinforced the conventual rule that nuns should sleep alone, the Superior attempts to enter Suzanne's bed by drawing a parallel with family life:

"Suzanne, did you never share a bed with one of your sisters when you were living with your parents?"
"No, never."
"But if the opportunity had arisen, would you not have done so without any hesitation? If your sister had come, anxious and freezing cold, and asked to lie next to you, would you have turned her away?"
"I don't think so."
"And am I not your dear Mother?"
"Yes you are, but it's still not allowed."

"Suzanne, n'avez-vous jamais partagé le même lit chez vos parents avec une de vos soeurs?—Non, jamais.—Si votre mère alarmée et transie de froid, était venue vous demander place à côté de vous, l'auriez-vous refusée?—Je crois que non.—Et ne suis-je pas votre chère mère?—Oui, vous l'êtes; mais cela est défendu." (*Oeuvres romanesques* 356, Goulbourne 117)

This conversation recalls the incident recorded in the archives of the monastery of Ste-Claire, where homesick young boarders were forbidden to climb into bed with their older sisters (see above, Chapter 5, 209–10). Whereas the abbess of Ste-Claire attempted to enforce the rules, the Superior of Ste-Eutrope tries to subvert them by asserting the "naturalness" of intimacy with Suzanne's "dear mother."

Finally, feeling her superior trembling (with cold), Suzanne lets her into bed and, somewhat uncharacteristically, invites her to go further: "'But,' I said, 'what's stopping you from warming your whole body in that way?' 'Nothing, if you wish.' I had turned back towards her. She had opened up her nightdress, and I was about to do the same when suddenly there were two violent knocks at the door"

["—Mais, lui dis-je, qui empêche que vous ne vous réchauffez partout de la même manière?—Rien, si vous voulez.' Je m'étais retournée, elle avait écartée son linge, et j'allais écarter le mien, lorsque tout à coup on frappa deux coups violents à la porte," *Oeuvres romanesques* 336, Goulbourne,118]. Events are interrupted just at this critical moment by the jealous sister Ste-Thérèse, leaving the Superior—and perhaps the reader—highly frustrated. After this evening, following the orders of her confessor and her own inclination, Suzanne avoids further contact with the superior and refuses to enter her cell. As the superior's love and guilt turn to melancholy, her moaning is audible through the open door of her cell: "She ... went back into her cell, leaving the door open, and started wailing in the most piercing way" ["rentrant dans sa cellule dont la porte demeura ouverte, elle se mit à pousser les plaintes les plus aiguës," *Oeuvres romanesques* 374, Goulbourne 138]. Her penetrating wail recalls Suzanne's own cry while tormented by the nuns at Longchamp: "I gave an inarticulate, broken, painful groan" ["je poussais une plainte inarticulée, entrecoupée et pénible," *Oeuvres romanesques* 300, Goulbourne 64]. Such sounds beyond the reach of language express better than words the sufferings of these enclosed women.

Although less central than the corridor and the cell, four other metonymic settings or objects play a role in the Ste-Eutrope episode: the nun's choir, the parlor, the grill and the veil. One scene that takes place in the choir during morning service, shortly after Suzanne's arrival, mainly serves to illustrate the Superior's subversions of convent discipline. While Suzanne and Ste-Thérèse exchange glances, the superior seems to have fallen asleep in her choir stall. Suzanne comments: "The service was over in the twinkling of an eye. Of all the places in the convent, the choir was not, it seemed to me, the one that the nuns enjoyed being in the most. They left with as much speed and jabbering as a flock of birds escaping from an aviary, and the sisters ran off to each other's cells, laughing and talking" ["L'office fut dépêché en un clin d'œil; le choeur n'était pas, à ce qu'il me parut, l'endroit de la maison où l'on se plaisait le plus. On en sortit avec la vitesse et le babil d'une troupe d'oiseaux qui s'échapperaient de leur volière; et les sœurs se répandirent les unes chez les autres, en courant, en riant, en parlant," *Oeuvres romanesques* 336–7, Goulbourn 99].

Another choir scene is more dramatic. When Suzanne tells her confessor what took place in her cell the night of the Superior's visit, he instructs Suzanne to stop seeing the Superior alone and to spend that night in the choir. The Superior of course follows her, trying to persuade her to return to her cell. Suzanne's efforts to maintain a distance between the two of them create a pattern of flight and pursuit: "I had gathered myself a little and threw myself into a stall. She came over to me and was about to sit in the stall next to me when I stood up and moved to the next stall down. So I travelled from one stall to the next, and so did she, right up to the end. There I stopped and begged her to leave at least one seat empty between us" ["Un peu revenue à moi, je me jetai dans une stalle. Elle s'approcha, elle allait s'asseoir dans la stalle voisine, lorsque je me levai et me plaçai dans la stalle au-dessous. Je voyageai ainsi de stalle en stalle, et elle aussi jusqu'à la dernière: là, je m'arrêtai, et je la conjurai de laisser du moins une place vide entre elle et moi," *Oeuvres romanesques* 370, Goulbourne 131]. On a future night, the Superior will also enter the chapel alone, then prostrate herself on the ground, moaning and sighing ["elle descendit seule à l'église; quelques-unes de nos soeurs la suivirent; elle se prosterna sur les marches de l'autel, elle se mit à gémir, à soupirer, à prier tout haut," *Oeuvres romanesques* 384].

A new stage in the superior's decline is recorded when Suzanne finds a note pinned to the curtain covering the main choir grill: "Dear Sisters, you are invited to pray for a nun who has strayed from her duties and who wants to find her way back to God" ["Chères soeurs, vous êtes invitées à prier pour une religieuse qui s'est égarée de ses devoirs et qui veut retourner à Dieu," *Oeuvres romanesques* 376, Goulbourne 137]. Two more similar messages are left there. The device of attaching a note to the main grill combines anonymity—"une religieuse"— with public confession of an unorthodox kind. The desire for anonymity is also conveyed by the position of the Superior's veil: "The poor Mother Superior only appeared with her veil lowered over her face" ["Cette pauvre supérieure ne se montrait que son voile baissé," *Oeuvres romanesques* 377, Goulbourne 137].

Finally, although the parlor does not play as large a role in the interior drama of *La Religieuse* as in the outwardly directed novels of Villedieu or Marivaux, it is the site of a key scene. While Suzanne is in the parlor with the confessor and several other nuns, "someone could be heard walking up slowly, stopping now and again, and sighing. Listening out, somebody whispered, 'it's her, it's our Mother Superior'" ["on entendit arriver quelqu'un à pas lents, s'arrêter par intervalles et pousser des soupirs; on écouta; l'on dit à voix basse: 'C'est elle, c'est notre supérieure'"]. Attuned to subtle sounds, the nuns can identify the superior by her walk and sighs. The narration continues:

> Indeed it was her. She came in, her veil falling right down to her waist, her arms crossed on her chest and her head bent. I was the first one she saw; instantly she pulled out one hand from under her veil, covered her eyes, and, turning away a little, she gestured with her other hand for us all to leave. We left in silence, leaving her alone with Dom Morel.

> Ce l'était en effet: elle entra: son voile lui tombait jusqu'à la ceinture; ses bras était croisés sur sa poitrine et sa tête penchée. Je fus la première qu'elle aperçut; à l'instant elle dégagea de dessous son voile une de ses mains dont elle se couvrit les yeux, et se détournant un peu de côté, de l'autre main elle nous fit signe à toutes de sortir; nous sortions en silence, et elle demeura seule avec dom Morel.
> (*Oeuvres romanesques* 382–3, Goulbourne 143)

In this dramatic tableau, the superior appears like a specter in a Verdi opera, mutely gesturing with her hands while the rest of her body is completely hidden beneath her veil.

Immediately after this scene, Suzanne violates the secret of the confessional by listening at the parlor door; as she confesses to the marquis, "my curiosity got the better of me" ["ma curiosité fut la plus forte," *Oeuvres romanesques* 383, Goulbourne 144]. It is significant that in this setting, confessional secrets are revealed not in a closed stall, but in the convent parlor, at the threshold between convent and outside world. Suzanne does not hear the Superior's complete confession; nor does she recount what she heard. Instead, she offers a metaphor: "I listened, and the *veil* that had until that point shielded me from the danger I had been in was being ripped asunder, when somebody called me. I had to go, and so I did. But, Oh! I had already heard too much. What a woman, Monsieur le Marquis! What a dreadful woman!" ["J'écoutais; le *voile* qui jusqu'alors m'avait dérobé le péril que j'avais couru se déchirait lorsqu'on m'appela; il fallut aller, j'allai donc; mais, hélas! Je n'en avais que trop entendu. Quelle femme, monsieur le marquis, quelle abominable femme!" *Oeuvres romanesques* 383–4, Goulbourne 145; italics added]. This passage brings to a close the developed portion of the text ["ici les Mémoires de la soeur Suzanne sont interrompus," *Oeuvres romanesques* 384]. Perhaps the narrative has reached the limits of the expressible; perhaps Diderot chose to frustrate the curiosity of the reader after bringing it to a high pitch. In either case (and one does not exclude the other) the torn veil that symbolizes Suzanne's lost innocence also prefigures the breaching of the convent walls whose confines Suzanne will soon leave. Yet in another sense, the veil remains intact, covering over secrets that will remain unseen and unheard.

While *La Religieuse*'s pitiless tableaux of convent life remain riveting today, its overt ideological message now appears fraught with contradictions. Beginning with a relatively narrow criticism of forced vows (*Oeuvres romanesques* 237, 286), this message broadens into a wholesale condemnation of convents in general. Diderot's argument, in brief, is that the incarceration of women in an exclusively female society leads inevitably to perversion, madness and death. Such perversion is not merely, or even primarily, sexual; it permeates the very core of the convent. In this matriarchal domain, a Mother Superior takes the place of the male head of the healthy, "natural" family—a Mother who has nearly absolute control over her "daughters." It is interesting to note that the terms Suzanne uses to address her own problematic mother foreshadow those employed in the convent world. Pleading with Mme Simonin not to return her to the cloister, Suzanne had said: "Very well, Mother … let me experience your goodness again." ["Eh Bien! Maman, lui dis-je, rendez-moi vos bontés," *Oeuvres romanesques* 252, Goulbourne 19]. These sentiments are echoed rather shockingly at Ste-Eutrope by Soeur Ste-Thérèse, the superior's favorite before the arrival of Suzanne. Appealing to the mother/lover who has rejected her, Thérèse says: "I'm having distressing thoughts and I really want to open my heart to my dear Mama" ["J'ai des pensées qui m'inquiètent; je voudrais bien ouvrir mon coeur à maman," *Oeuvres romanesques* 336, Goulbourne 98–9; note that *maman* appears in both quotes in the original French]. But "maman" superior, like Suzanne's biological mother, is deaf to such pleas.

In another reversal, the pleadings of the superior to let her "dear mother" into bed with Suzanne are a perverse distortion of family intimacy.[22]

To push this argument a bit further, Suzanne's tragedy is not so much caused by the convent *per se* as by the dysfunctional family that placed her there against her will. As the "natural" illegitimate daughter of a man who seduced and abandoned her mother—a mother, moreover, who is married to a stern man some years her senior—Suzanne has no place in the Simonin family; hence, she is shunted into the "unnatural" family of the cloister. Faced with Suzanne's continuing opposition to convent life, her mother has a priest inform her of the illegitimacy she had already suspected. After revealing her mother's secret, the priest offers Suzanne this cold comfort: "If you take my advice, you'll make peace with your parents; you'll do what your mother is expecting of you; you'll become a nun; you'll be given a small pension which will enable you to live the rest of your life, if not happily, at least tolerably" ["Si vous m'en croyez, vous vous reconcilierez avec vos parents; vous ferez ce que votre mère doit attendre de vous; vous entrerez en religion; on vous fera une petite pension avec laquelle vous passerez des jours, sinon heureux, du moins supportables," *Oeuvres romanesques* 251, Goulbourne 18].

Viewed from this perspective, the convent is perhaps a lesser evil than "une captivité domestique fort dure" in her parents' house or a life on the streets. As Fowler suggests, "if Suzanne's unhappiness can be said to have an ultimate or at least a principal cause, we must look not to the convent but to the family" (70). Behind the tragedy of convent enclosure thus lies the larger drama of familial disunion and dysfunction; and this latter drama is far from unique to Suzanne's family. As the priest observes: "I see such things all the time: abandoned children, or even legitimate children, supported at the expense of domestic peace" ("Je ne vois que de ces choses-là, ou des enfants abandonnés, ou des enfants même légitimes, secourus aux dépens de la paix domestique," *Oeuvres romanesques* 250, Goulbourne 18). It is again interesting to compare Suzanne's situation to that of the illegitimate Henriette-Sylvie de Molière, who did receive some financial support from her unknown father, but mainly survives, and triumphs, by her own resources and the help of her women friends, many of whom are nuns (see above, Chapter 4). Thus, Diderot's ideology of naturalness ironically destroys itself: natural behavior, producing illegitimate or so-called "natural" children, actually perpetuates the existence of the convent.

In a historical context, the model for Suzanne, Marguerite Delamarre, had stated in her lawsuit that she was illegitimate. There is no evidence to support or refute this allegation; what appears indisputable, however, is that Marguerite suffered the misfortune of having parents, legitimate or not, who wanted to enjoy their improving financial and social status without sharing the benefits with their younger children (see May 60–61). And according to Delamarre, when she refused to enter the convent, the treatment she received at home was crueler

---

[22]   In a letter from the *Préface-annexe*, Suzanne calls Mme Madin a surrogate mother figure, "Mama" (Goulbourne 175).

than that inflicted upon Suzanne; for Delamarre's parents compounded domestic imprisonment with physical abuse. Whether Diderot knew these details of Marguerite's case or not, he was certainly concerned with the widespread problem of illegitimacy, which is the main focus of his "bourgeois drama," *Le fils naturel ou les épreuves de la vertu* (1757).[23] In choosing to make Suzanne an illegitimate daughter, he both lessens her mother's moral responsibility for rejecting her and makes a case for healthy families and "family values"—i.e., the patriarchal family. This ideology fits well with a Revolutionary regime that tried to institute Father's Day as a national holiday along with the Fête de l'Etre Suprême (Didier 202). Neither project was successful.

Diderot's exposés of family dysfunction, however justified, actually weakens the case against monasticism. In the context of the social problem of abandoned, illegitimate or unwanted children, is the convent the disease, the symptom, or, sometimes, even the cure (or palliation)? And if all convent doors were unlocked overnight, as Diderot urges, would Suzanne's situation be improved? On the evidence of the story's suggested ending, this appears unlikely. Upon her escape from Ste-Eutrope, Suzanne literally falls into the hands of a dissolute monk, who takes her in a public coach to a "lieu suspect" which is little better than a house of prostitution (like the cloister, it is a *maison close* or closed house). She remains there for two weeks before she is again able to make her escape. When she is discovered out alone one night, she is warned that unless she finds work, she is in danger of being rounded up and sent to La Salpêtrière. This institution for "criminal, mad or indigent women" ["femmes criminelles, aliénées ou indigents"] is little better than a prison—and worse than a convent (see Chapter 4, 162–3 and *Oeuvres romanesques* 874n204). At this point, Suzanne comments: "If I had been near my convent, I would have gone back there" ["si j'eusse été voisine de mon couvent, j'y retournais," *Oeuvres romanesques* 389 Goulbourne 149]. For a few weeks, she ekes out a miserable living as a laundress;[24] but the injury she suffered when climbing down the convent wall (389) prevents her from standing. Her progressive illness and death are recounted in letters at the end of the text. Suzanne, ever a reluctant nun, never adjusted to convent life; yet at the same time, she was conditioned to it from an early age. In her own words, religion has become a double *habit*: the religious life, like a hair shirt, is transformed into a tormenting

---

[23]   In the eighteenth century, illegitimacy was a major social problem, with more "natural" children being born than legal issue. See Caroline Weber, "The Sins of the Father: Colonialism and Family History in Diderot's *Le fils naturel*." (*PMLA* 118.3 [May 2003]), 488–501.

[24]   In an interesting parallel, when the American woman known as Typhoid Mary was let out of quarantine after repeated attempts to regain her freedom, she was given work as a laundress—apparently the lowest rung on the economic scale for women. Probably because this work was so arduous, she ran away and found employment as a cook in a hospital—again spreading the dread disease. The superior of Ste-Eutrope is also a "carrier" of a deadly infection, a catalyst of dysfunction within the precariously-balanced economy of the convent. But unlike Typhoid Mary, she suffers from the disease as well.

second skin ["ce vêtement s'est attaché à ma peau, à mes os, et ne m'en gêne que advantage," *Oeuvres romanesques* 316, Goulbourne 79]. *Habit* is transformed into *habitude*: accustomed to the hated life of the cloister, Suzanne finds no place either within or without it. Her infirmity and death, while arranged for pragmatic reasons by the author, also demonstrate that she is a creature of the convent, unable to survive outside; after her escape, she is like a bird with a broken wing, a fish out of water. Thus, beyond its obvious attack on the cloister, the novel implies a wholesale condemnation of a society in which women without family, or rejected by their families, had few doors open to them beyond those of the poorhouse, the brothel or the convent. These are the only options available to penniless and unprotected girls in the eighteenth century. And like the nuns who will be expelled from their cloisters a few years later, by the time she leaves, it is too late for her.

In conclusion, what brings *La religieuse portugaise* and *La religieuse* together and what sets them apart? Both novels combine sexual voyeurism with an anti-monastic message; in both, a male author assumes the body and spirit of a female narrator who would normally be hidden from view. As Peggy Kamuf points out, convent narrations like the letters of Eloïse to Abelard, *Les Lettres portugaises* and *La Religieuse* "focus on the constructions which enclose women with their desire" (31). In these extreme representations of women's confinement, the cloistering of the female object/speaker allows her to be enjoyed vicariously by writer and reader. Yet the end products are very different. *Les Lettres portugaises*, a more balanced work, remains perfectly within its self-imposed limits of narrative voice and epistolary genre. The nun's periodic railings against convent life and the severe laws imposed on nuns also stay within conventional bounds, mainly serving as background and justification for the main focus of the novel. In contrast, Diderot's anti-convent message does not always fit comfortably within his own narration: the anti-monastic vituperations uttered on several occasions by Suzanne and other characters can be heavy-handed and incongruous. Yet the troublesome contradictions plaguing Diderot's overt case against the cloister do not detract from the *picture* he paints of the convent as viewed through a nun's eyes. While much has been written on the novel's narrative and psychological complexity, this analysis brings into light the cloister's hidden spaces. By dint of continual, sometimes brutal repetition, *La Religieuse* makes us see everything that is not meant to be seen—whether we wish to see it or not. When read together with *Les Lettres portugaises*, Guilleragues's delicate masterpiece seems to pale in comparison.

Similarly, *Les Lettres portugaises* fall short of *La Religieuse* in its sexual intensity. Again, this difference is partly due to their generic origins. While Guilleragues created a brilliantly discreet example of classical psychological analysis, Diderot, the notorious author of *Les Bijoux indiscrets*, draws unabashedly from the erotic novel tradition while bringing it to a new level. The recurrent motif of stripping or *denûment*—whether of the cell's contents or of Suzanne's body—strengthens and unifies Diderot's vision of the convent as a place of perpetual violation. Yet his own penetration of the female body and psyche has unforeseen consequences. The author's attitudes towards women often reveal sexual stereotyping; yet once he gets inside his female characters, they become real to him and to the reader. The superior of Ste-Eutrope is a case in point: in the end, we know too much simply to regard her, in Suzanne's words, as an "abominable femme."[25] Whereas in earlier libertine novels, lesbian activities merely arouse curiosity or contempt, the superior's unconsummated love for Suzanne attains the level of tragedy: an object arousing pity and terror. In her final madness, the superior sees visions of women being tortured and herself being led to the scaffold, while telling the executioners: "I deserve my fate, I deserve it," *Oeuvres romanesques* 387, Goulbourne 147). In these divagations, the superior identifies both with Suzanne and with her torturers; but unlike Suzanne, she knows herself to be guilty of forbidden desires and acts. Because of the superior's vulnerability, she is the perfect sadomasochistic subject, deriving both pleasure and pain from her own and another's sufferings. She is also Diderot's perfect witness within the novel, serving as a lens to magnify the impact of Suzanne's experience. Scenes from earlier episodes are brought before the reader with heightened impact as the nun's tale is retold and re-experienced through the superior's tormented consciousness.

Given *La Religieuse*'s rhetorical power, it is no wonder the novel was acclaimed by the Revolution and embraced within an overall ideology of liberation and "naturalness." This ideology is strikingly rendered in a drawing by Jean-Jacques Lequeu (1757–1826) which appeared on the cover of the 1990 folio edition of *Les Lettres portugaises*.[26] The drawing (Fig. 6.2) depicts a young nun baring her bosom, with the caption: "We also will be mothers, for …" ["Nous aussi, nous serons mères, car …"]. This image is exemplary of eighteenth-century mixed messages combining liberal ideology with sensuality. The nun's right breast, so rounded it appears distended with milk, reinforces the claims for innocent, "natural" motherhood; in contrast, her full, painted mouth and made-up eyes accentuate her suppressed sexuality as well as providing erotic gratification to the viewer. Looking directly at us, the nun seems to ask for the right to live a "normal" woman's life, with all that implies.

Yet for Lequeu's nun, like Diderot's (and, in a different way, Guilleragues's), the message of female liberation is overshadowed by male identification or intrusion. All three men strip the nun to show the woman underneath: Lequeu's nun removes her wimple or neckcloth with her own hand; Diderot's heroine is undressed by the Longchamp nuns and the Ste-Eutrope superior; and Guilleragues, less openly erotic but more psychologically penetrating, reveals his character's hidden, intimate desires through her own alleged words.

---

[25] For a useful summary of opposing interpretations of Diderot's attitudes toward lesbianism, see Goulbourne, introduction xix–xx.

[26] Lequeu, a "visionary architect" often grouped with Ledoux and other eighteenth-century designers whose projects were never built, also drew graphic images of the sexual parts of adolescent girls. His work and his somewhat bizarre character have attracted current attention. See Philippe Duboy, *Jean-Jacques Lequeu: An Architectural Enigma* (London: Thames & Hudson, 2002).

Fig. 6.2   Jean-Jacques Lequeu, "Et nous aussi nous serons mères; car …!"
Paris, BnF.

The makers of the Revolution, untroubled by such ambiguities, hailed *La Religieuse* as an accurate portrayal of convent imprisonment. The carceral view of the convent, which had become ever more dominant during the last century of the Old Regime, permeates the rhetoric of the Revolutionary decrees abolishing monasticism: "Liberty, or rather life [will be] restored to the mass of victims of both sexes whom the self-interest of families, personal obligation or a passing fervour have cast into the horrors of the cloister and loaded with insupportable chains."[27] In Revolutionary writings, the convent is thus depicted as a kind of ecclesiastical Bastille whose walls and bars must be broken down; and the desire of individuals to live a spiritual life in retreat is dismissed as a "passing fervour."

While the convent cell took on increasingly penitentiary associations by the 1780s, the reverse phenomenon—the word "cellule" itself applied to a prison room—does not appear until the early nineteenth century: the earliest examples I have found, in St-John de Crèvecoeur's *Voyage Pennsylvanie*, date from 1801.[28] Diderot's lexical practice is in keeping with both eighteenth-century usage and Enlightenment opinion: while the denotation of *cellule* in *La Religieuse* is exclusively religious, its connotation is overwhelmingly carceral. As Suzanne says, what "they"—the religious authorities—term a convent is really a prison

---

[27] Quoted in Rapley, *Social History* 26. She adds that "the same language of victimization was used up and down the country" (293n66).

[28] Searches in French dictionaries and other database sources from the seventeenth and eighteenth centuries have revealed no mention of *cellules de prison*; in all cases, *cellule* is defined as a "little room for a monk or a nun" ["petite chambre d'un Religieux ou d'une Religieuse," *Académie française*], and what we now call a prison cell was designated a *prison, une chambre de prison* or a *cachot* (*prison basse et obscure*). Many nineteenth-century instances of the word *cellule* still refer to monasteries or monastery-like dwellings: monastic cells abound, for instance, in the romantic novels of Balzac (*La Duchesse de Langeais*), George Sand (*Lélia*) and Victor Hugo (*Notre Dame de Paris*), not to mention Chateaubriand. At the same time, however, references to prison cells begin to appear. According to the Robert *Dictionnaire français*, the first use of *cellule* in a penitentiary context dates from the 1840s; but in the ARTFL database, I have found occurrences from the early nineteenth century. As noted, the earliest examples come from *Voyage Pennsylvanie*, a travel account which excoriates prison conditions in America. Further references are found in Emmanuel Las Cases's *Mémorial de Sainte Hélène* (1823) and Balzac's *Episode sous la Terreur* (1846). Lexical searches for "cell" in English give similar results as for "cellule." The English word comes from the Old French *celle*, and its earliest meanings designate a monastery room. In the on-line *Oxford English Dictionary*, the first references to a prison cell appear in the late eighteenth century; a little earlier than in France, but it is not certain that no similar examples were to be found across the channel at that time. Indeed, the context of the word in Crevecoeur's *Voyage*, with no explanation offered, indicates the usage was already expected to be understood by 1801: "As soon as a prisoner has been brought in, his hair is cut, he is washed, given new clothes, and locked up in the sort of *cell* prescribed by the tribunal that condemned him" ["Aussi-tôt qu'un prisonnier est entré, on lui coupe les cheveux, on le lave, on lui donne des vêtemens nouveaux, et il est enfermé dans l'espèce de *cellule* prescrite par le tribunal qui l'a condamné," 237; italics added].

for the unlucky woman condemned to spend her entire life there ["passer toute sa vie à se frapper la tête contre les barreaux de sa prison!" *Oeuvres romanesques* 316]. While it is unclear exactly how or when the shift in semantic emphasis from convent to prison cell took place, it more or less coincided with the French Revolution and its immediate aftermath; that is, with a time when monasteries in France, closed and appropriated by the Revolutionary state, were often being turned into prisons—giving the word "cell" its new meaning. In his humanitarian desire to abolish monastic and other "prisons" and liberate their occupants, Diderot surely did not envision that the effect would be to exchange one jail for another— sometimes with the same occupants.

Nor did the Revolutionary regime foresee what Diderot implicitly revealed in his novel: that the problem of forced monachization could not be solved merely by the dissolution of the convents, because the root of the problem was a lack of social options and support for unprotected women. The revolutionaries did not think—nor, apparently, much care—about what would happen to the nuns who were freed or expelled from their cells in 1792. Their fate will be examined in the concluding chapter.

Chapter 7
Tombs/Closing

In 1768, Paris was a thriving Catholic city, containing 53 parish churches, 47 monasteries, 60 convents and a clerical population of approximately 8000 (Aston, *Religion and Revolution in France* 51). By 1792, "The religious landscape of France was in meltdown" (Aston, *Christianity and Revolutionary Europe* 189).[1] Aston's metaphor is scarcely exaggerated: while the intellectual climate of the eighteenth century had been growing increasingly anticlerical, no explanation can readily account for the scope and rapidity of this cataclysmic process of destruction. In the space of a few years, churches, monasteries and synagogues were closed and converted into stables, granaries or prisons; alternative patriotic cults were promoted; parodic Christian rituals were performed in streets and churches. While the Revolution was ultimately unsuccessful in extirpating Christianity from France, the Catholic Church's character and its relation to society would be changed forever. This concluding chapter will begin by surveying the effects of the Revolution on the Church, with a particular focus on women's communities and actions. We will rapidly review the state of religious institutions before the Revolution, the abolition of the established Catholic Church and its monasteries, resistance to the Revolutionary project and the fate of monastic buildings. A second part of this chapter will explore the "Tombs" of conventual representation in post-Revolutionary and contemporary literature. In conclusion, we will ask what the representation of conventual spaces meant for early modern culture and what its import is for us, its inheritors.

Church and Convent Prior to the Revolution

Like the state, the conventual system found itself in financial crisis for most of the eighteenth century; and these two crises are linked. A century earlier, Louis XIV's ministers had already expressed their frustration with religious institutions that, in their view, produced no revenue and little social benefit (see above, Chapter 5). The monarchy did not succeed in taxing the First Estate directly; but beginning in 1689, religious organizations were required to pay *amortissement* on all investment property they had acquired since 1641.[2] The demand that this payment be made immediately, in one lump sum, put extreme stress on weaker ecclesiastical bodies—notably, women's convents. For example, Louis XIV

---

[1] References to Aston's two books in the following pages will be made using the abbreviations *RRF* and *CRR*.

[2] *Amortissements* were payments due on the purchase of property.

continued for years to demand heavy *amortissement* payments from the Ursulines of Nantes, even on the property expansions he had himself approved in the 1680s. The sisters tenaciously appealed for dispensations and tax reductions; at one point, their mother superior, Anne d'Arthenaise, was pursuing six lawsuits against the Crown at the same time (*Les Ursulines à Nantes* 18). Their financial problems were aggravated by the economic depression of Louis XIV's late reign, brought on by the monarchy's colossal war debt. The financial crisis was worsened by the collapse of John Law's paper money and investment schemes, which made it extremely difficult to collect *rentes*, a main source of convent income.[3] As a result, "many communities found their revenues reduced by as much as one-third or one-half" (23). Because of their patient resistance, the Ursulines of Nantes survived the crisis somewhat better, but their number of boarders had decreased from 40 or 50 in 1682 to 30 in 1727. In order to make ends meet, communities were obliged to take in more adult boarders and to seek professants from lower class backgrounds. Both these measures lowered their social standing.

Somewhat paradoxically, women's monasteries in financial distress also sought aid from the Crown. In response, the government created in 1727 a "Commission des secours" which paid pensions to 558 houses in its first five years; but it was also instructed to reduce "the excessive number of female communities with which the kingdom is burdened." The reference to the "burden" imposed by women's convents reflects a consistent policy going back at least to 1666, when Colbert published an edict "ordering a country-wide investigation into religious houses, with the intention of reducing their numbers where possible" (Rapley, *Social History* 21). In pursuit of this mandate, the Commission imposed quotas on the number of residents allowed in convents, banned the reception of novices, eliminated 244 female monasteries and reduced the size of many more, regardless of their financial condition (Rapley 23, 85). Partly as a result of the Commission's actions, "between 1720 and 1789 the population of nuns in France was reduced by about one-third" (*Social History* 24). Thus, Colbert's desire to get rid of "useless" cloistered religious and to make monasteries pay their share of the national debt was finally realized; and Diderot's *La Religieuse*, composed in 1760, ironically portrayed women's monasteries as a grave threat to society at a time when their power had been waning for decades.

The material distress experienced by many women's religious communities belies the stereotype of fat lazy monks and nuns leading an easy life. This view is expressed by the laundress with whom Suzanne briefly works at the end of *La Religieuse*. Without knowing she is speaking to the escaped nun herself, Suzanne's co-worker declares her lack of compassion for cloistered women: "You must really

---

[3]   A *rente*, or *rente constituée*, is basically a loan on which the borrower is required to pay a fixed yearly income. Many French bourgeois, as well as institutions, relied on income from *rentes*. With the inflation and bankruptcies of the early eighteenth century, *rentiers* often went unpaid or were paid in devalued paper money. While this situation was not specific to convents, it had a disastrous effect on their solvency.

be very sympathetic. All she had to do was drink, eat, pray to God, and sleep. She was fine where she was. Why didn't she stick with it? If only she'd be down to the river three or four times in this weather, that would have made her appreciate her way of life" ["Il faudrait que vous eussiez bien de la compassion de reste. Elle n'avait qu'à boire, manger, prier Dieu et dormir; elle était bien où elle était, que ne s'y tenait-elle? Si elle avait été trois ou quatre fois à la rivière par le tems qu'il fait, cela l'aurait raccommodée avec son état," *Oeuvres romanesques* 391, Goulbourne 150]. The hard-working laundress expresses an opinion widely held in the second half of the eighteenth century (Rapley, *Social History* 93). Indeed, some male monks and ecclesiastics could have been counted among "the idle rich"; the disparity in income between monasteries and working country priests was one of the reasons why many priests initially supported the Revolution (see below, 287). But for the majority of cloistered women, life was far from easy. The Commission des secours investigating the condition of convents in the 1720s, though hardly favorable to monasteries, found many nuns "in the direst need, living on the charity of families and friends, even begging their bread from door to door" (Rapley 47). Nor did this situation improve in the early nineteenth century; the first community of nuns to move back into the Monastère Ste-Claire after the Restoration found a collapsed roof and earthen floors. These deplorable conditions forced them to vacate the building after seven years of struggle ("Monastère Ste-Claire" 19 and conversation with archivist). Thus, while Diderot's critique of the convent reflects intellectual attitudes of his time, he is also in a sense beating down an open door— or grate. The anti-monastic goals of Enlightenment writers and revolutionaries had been initiated, and to some degree achieved, by the regime they so detested.

If the financial and physical condition of many convents was precarious, what can be said about the spiritual attitudes of the country as a whole? According to a widely-held view, pre-Revolutionary France was already on the way to becoming a secularized, even "dechristianized," society.[4] Among other historians, Nigel Aston questions this theory, preferring to "dechristianization" terms like "laicization" or "enlightened piety" (55). Even those people who did not attend church regularly would not have considered themselves "dechristianized," a concept that held no currency at the time. While the forms of worship may have become more individualized, Catholicism in eighteenth-century France maintained an established and even dynamic presence. This presence is attested to by a number of factors. Despite a gradual decline in Easter attendance in the 1770s and 1780s, a statistic often used to measure level of religious observance, both men and women still came to Easter services in significant numbers (Aston, *RRF* 52); and 60 percent of the books purchased in provincial France concerned religious subjects. Excluding variations by region, the bourgeoisie and people generally remained attached to Catholic faith and practice. The greatest signs of disaffection were, not surprisingly, among elite metropolitan men. According to Rapley:

---

[4]   For this perspective, see Dale K. Van Kley, *The Religious Origins of the French Revolution* (New Haven and London: Yale University Press, 1996).

> The reconfiguration of the female monastic world—a world that had been shaped during the Catholic Reformation—took place in an atmosphere already steeped in Enlightenment thinking. Not that the women themselves were penetrated by Enlightenment principles—they seem to have been more or less impervious to them—but the men who decided their future, whether laymen or prelates, were decidedly so. (*Social History* 24)

On the other hand, many elite women retained their piety, and sometimes their attachment to the convents where they had boarded as girls: "nunneries continued to provide a depository for the surplus daughters of the nobility down to the revolution," including Louis XVI's aunt, Mme Louise de France, who became a Carmelite nun at St-Denis in 1771 (Aston *RRF* 23).

Indeed, women's religious communities, despite their relative poverty, remained far more numerous than men's: "by the 1770s women outnumbered men in both the active and the contemplative life by three to one" (*RRF* 23). Many of these women belonged to the new orders founded after the Counter-Reformation, including the Carmelites, Sisters of the Visitation, Ursulines, and Sisters and Daughters of Charity. Another manifestation of the vitality of eighteenth-century women's faith was the popularity of orders for lay females (*filles séculières*) founded at the end of the seventeenth century, like the Sisters of Christian Doctrine (1694) and Sisters of Saint-Anne (1707); the Daughters of Wisdom grew from 40 houses in 1759 to 77 in 1789. In other cases, three or four *filles séculières* would set up unofficial "Houses of Charity" in villages, supplying the people's needs. "More than any other group in French society, these congregations bore the burden of caring for the sick and old in hospitals and other charitable foundations" (*RRF* 22–3); they were also the only groups to educate girls. For these reasons, the dispersal of women's religious communities in the 1790s was sometimes regretted by the populations they served. Finally, among lay women, the cult of the Virgin continued to flourish in the eighteenth century, with the foundation of new female confraternities such as the Rosary and the Sacred Heart which would become central elements of nineteenth- and twentieth-century piety.

Given the multiple blows they suffered, how can one explain the continuing strength of religious commitment among eighteenth-century French women? The supposition that women generally receive greater spiritual satisfaction from religious observance than men is impossible to test. Rather, as Aston perceptively observes, women were loyal to the church "because no other public body empowered them in a similar way, and when the Revolution came it offered them nothing like the same participatory possibilities" (*RRF* 42). On the contrary, as many historians have shown, revolutionaries sought to exclude women from political participation. In conclusion, at the eve of the Revolution, "there existed a complex network of relationships centered on the Church, with females playing a full part" (Aston *RRF* 51). As we will see, these women would play an important role in ensuring the survival of Catholicism during the 1790s and in resisting, to the best of their ability, the dechristianizing work of the Revolution.

The Collapse of the Ecclesiastical Order and the Closing of the Convents, 1789–92

The fate of the Revolution, and the religious future of France, were largely set in the early days of the National Assembly by the creation of the Civil Constitution of Clergy. According to Aston, "Gallicism foundered on the rock of the Civil Constitution and so did the nationwide endorsement of the Revolution in 1789–90" (*RR* 162). This measure was presented to the Assembly in May 1789, agreed upon without a vote on July 12, and reluctantly approved by Louis XVI in August of that year. Under its provisions, the old structure of the Gallican church was abolished. Instead of bishops naming priests, all clergy were to become government employees or *fonctionnaires de l'état* elected by the laity and paid by the state. This measure split the country in two, with a narrow majority of the population in favor. Even the clergy was divided. The church hierarchy, unsurprisingly, opposed the Civil Constitution; but it was initially welcomed by some parish priests, either out of patriotism or a hope that their salaries would rise. The division of French opinion was exacerbated in 1791, when by order of the National Assembly all clerics were required to sign an oath of loyalty to the Republic. Approximately half of them signed. Non-compliant priests were removed from their functions; some were sheltered by their congregations, but in anti-clerical areas like the Paris countryside, others were ostracized or even driven from their villages. By 1792, refractory priests and nuns were considered counter-revolutionaries, subject to imprisonment or even execution; many left France to become exiles.

The monastic structure of France fared no better. The closing of French monasteries was a gradual and inexorable process, stretching over a three-year period from 1789 to 1792. On October 28, 1789, the Constituent Assembly forbade the pronouncing of new monastic vows. On January 13, 1790, a new decree abolished all monasteries and convents, except those whose members were dedicated to educational and charitable work. The confiscation and sale of Church property to pay the national debt had already been proposed by Bishop Talleyrand and authorized by the General Assembly. In the same year, a decree approved by Louis XVI gave a pension to those cloistered religious who voluntarily chose to leave their monasteries. Most men left, but the majority of women chose to remain in the religious life. For example, only four of the 515 nuns in the Côtes du Nord department left their convents (Rapley, *Social History* 102). Aston quotes a statement of protest sent to the National Assembly by four Carmelite houses: "People in the world love to say that monasteries only contain victims slowly consumed by regrets; but we protest before God that, if there is true happiness on earth, we enjoy it here in the shadow of the sanctuary" (Aston *RRF* 135). In 1792, a group of Visitation nuns proclaimed: "We ask to live and die in the holy and blissful state that we have freely embraced, that we zealously observe and that constitutes the sole happiness of our days" (137).

Taking no heed of such sentiments, the National Assembly continued to pursue its policy of monastic dissolution; interestingly, the Gallican hierarchy, so vocal in their opposition to the Civil Constitution of the Clergy, remained silent on this issue. Those nuns who refused to depart were forcibly dispersed and sent off to other monasteries, which often grouped together diverse orders in crowded conditions. Despite these moves, some cloistered nuns continued to occupy their houses for another two years. Finally, a decree of August 17, 1792 abolished teaching and hospital orders for women as well, despite their public popularity, and ordered all monastic houses to be evacuated by the first of October. Many nuns returned to their families; some formed small groups and continued their work in their communities. In response, the state forbade women to live together in groups of more than four (Aston *CRE* 284). Some communities managed to evade this interdiction. The nuns of the Visitation of the rue du Faubourg St-Jacques, founded in 1626, did not disperse after they were removed from their convent; they stayed together as a group and moved to their present location, on the rue de Vaugirard, in 1821 (Burns, *Saint-François de Sales* 46). While the Church was under attack, it was often women who played a key role in its preservation, seeking to remain in community and offering resistance to change. According to Aston, "Because women were so tenaciously attached to a religious life and institutions they regarded as distinctively 'theirs,' the task of the Revolutionaries in setting up alternative structures and practices was made infinitely harder" (*RRF* 42).

Individual forms of women's resistance range from the comic to the tragic. As stated above, parish priests who refused to sign the oath of loyalty to the Republic were replaced by juring priests. Women parishioners and nuns were not always welcoming to the "outsiders" who supplanted their own non-juring *curés*. In Caen in 1791, "Two hundred drunken females hurled stones at the altar of one celebrant and nearly killed him" (Aston *RRF* 207). Resistance was also rife within the walls of the Poor Clare's convent in Mur de Barrès. At that time, services at the convent church were open to the public (this custom is again in effect). When the convent chaplain refused to allow a semi-patriotic procession to enter the church, he was removed and a Constitutional priest named Bourran appointed in his place. The sisters refused to accept the new priest, instead performing their own rituals which were attended by the townspeople. When Bourran came to the convent church to serve mass, the sisters refused to supply him with the necessary implements or to ring the bell. Bourran complained of his treatment to the town council. The account of the council meeting of July 3, 1790, makes for entertaining reading. According to Bourran's testimony:

> At the moment he begin to celebrate mass, the nuns who were in their choir withdrew and deliberately made noise, walking and opening and closing doors. After having said mass and removed his implements, M. Bourran walked over to the railing to deliver the prayer of thanksgiving and was assailed by the nuns who insulted him from behind their grill, calling him a thief, a God-stealer.

> Au moment où il a commencé [à servir la messe], les religieuses qui étaient au choeur se sont retirées et ont affecté de faire du bruit dans leur marche et en ouvrant et fermant les portes. Après avoir dit sa Messe et quitté les ornements, le

sieur Bourran s'est retiré au balustre pour faire son action de grâces et a été assailli par des religieuses qui derrière la grille lui ont dit des injures, l'ont traité de voleur, vole-Dieu. (*Le Monastère de Ste-Claire: Un Tricentenaire*, 12; my translation)

The nuns could not do Bourran any physical harm from behind their grill; but at that moment, a lay sister, Jeanne Poulhès, appeared, "who took hold of him and pulled heavily on his arm, telling him to give back the key to the tabernacle … the said Poulhès did not stop pulling on him until he was outside the church, where the said Poulhès addressed insults to him" ["qui l'a pris et tiré lourdement par le bras, en lui disant de rendre la clef du tabernacle … ladite Poulhès n'a cessé de le tirailler jusqu'à ce qu'il ait été hors de l'église où ladite Poulhès lui a dit des injures"].

Bourran's testimony also records the nuns' strong assertion of independence from priestly intervention in their services:

> Monsieur Bourran also said that he had exhorted the said nuns … not to have their services compete with those of the parish; to which they replied that he only had to perform his services when he wanted, that they would do likewise, and that they did not need him for any function. …"

> A dit de plus le sieur Bourran qu'il avait exhorté lesdites religieuses … de ne pas faire concourir leurs offices avec ceux de la paroisse; qu'elles lui ont répondu qu'il n'avait qu'à dire son office quand il le voudrait, qu'elles en feraient de même et qu'elles n'avait pas besoin de lui pour aucune fonction. … (*Le Monastère de Ste-Claire: Un Tricentenaire* 12–13; my translation)

In declaring "qu'elles n'avaient pas besoin de lui *pour aucune fonction*," the nuns of Ste-Claire enacted their own mini-revolution against the regime and against male ecclesiastical authority. Indeed, the report of the town council confirmed that the nuns "receive for the performance of their rituals a large number of residents of the town, both men and women; they even offer to perform pastoral duties [in the chapel], like Evensong and Messes de Confrérie [masses not requiring a consecrated priest] at the same hours as the parish services" ["reçoivent à l'exercise de leur culte une quantité d'habitants de tous sexes de cette ville, qu'elles offrent même qu'on y exerce des fonctions paroissiales telles que le chant des Vêpres aux heures de celles de la Paroisse et la célébration des Messes de Confrérie"]. The sisters were accused of refusing "to render national worship the respect it is due" ["de rendre au culte national l'hommage qui lui est dû"], and of performing, in competition with the parish church, "a different form of worship than that of the nation" ["un culte différent de celui de la nation"]. Judgment was immediate: using as a pretext a danger to health and safety, the town council ordered the convent chapel closed to the public. For more than a year, the Clares continued to live on in their convent; but they were marked women. On October 1, the church was desacralized; the bells and altar were removed and sent to the district administration, and the nuns evicted. Most went to live with families or neighbors, several becoming teachers. Those who had refused to sign the oath of loyalty were imprisoned, one in the convent church.

Other French nuns suffered more tragic fates: the Ursulines of Valenciennes, as well as the famous Carmelites of Compiègne, were executed for refusing to leave their convents. Even after the radical anti-Christian campaign was abandoned in 1795, anticlerical practices continued: refractory nuns were not allowed to claim their pensions, and 143 were imprisoned in a small church in Brouge, along with previously freed non-juring priests. Eighty people died before they were given permission to go outside for air and exercise (Aston *RRF* 282). Yet the less dramatic history of Mur-de-Barrez may be more typical of the reactions of religious women at the height of the Revolutionary attack on Christianity. While they could not stop the government's actions, they resisted to the best of their ability and kept traditions going, performing services as well as catechizing the children and carrying on charitable work. Once attacks against religion eased under the Directory and Consulate, women were the first to campaign to get their churches reopened, "by rioting if necessary" (Aston *CRE* 244). Unsurprisingly, this female activism went unappreciated by either side: neither conservatives nor Jacobins appreciated interfering females! Nevertheless, by filling in the gaps left by the collapse of ecclesiastical structures after 1789, women played an indispensable role in sustaining religious life in France and shaping its future.[5] Their participation would lead to a "feminization" of the church in the nineteenth century; ironically, the opposite effect from what the Revolutionaries would have desired. To conclude in Elizabeth Rapley's words: "Historians are now agreed that there was a long history behind the dechristianization movement of the Revolution; by the same token, there was a long history behind the attachment, manifested during the Revolution, of many people—and more women than men—to the old religion" (*Social History* 107).

The Fate of Religious Buildings

The storm of the Revolution left a swath of destroyed religious property unprecedented since the sixteenth-century Wars of Religion. To give just a few examples, the monastery of Cluny was demolished, as were Royaumont, Longjumeau and Jumièges. In Puy de Dôme, all the church steeples were damaged or destroyed. La Celle contains the ruins of a Benedictine convent of dubious morality, according to local tradition. Little remains of the convent of Sainte-Odile, founded in the seventh century. Many buildings that were not demolished

---

[5]   For more on women's religious participation in the eighteenth century, see Suzanne Desan, *Reclaiming the Sacred: Lay Religion and Popular Politics in Revolutionary France* (Ithaca: Cornell University Press, 1990); and Olwen Hufton and F. Tallet, "Communities of Women: the Religious Life and Public Service in Eighteenth-Century France," in M.J. Boxer and J.H. Quaetert eds, *Connecting Spheres: Women in the Western World 1500 to the Present* (Oxford: Oxford University Press, 1987), 75–85.

were used by the government for a variety of purposes. Other properties were simply "privatized": divided into lots and sold at auction to raise much-needed funds for the Revolutionary government. The Poor Clare convent of Millau was bought in 1792 through a third party, then repossessed by the commune in 1810. At risk of collapse, the property was ordered demolished in 1819. The catalog could continue indefinitely.[6] Given what they went through, it is not surprising how many convent buildings were destroyed; it is astonishing that any survived.

If the history of vanished monastic property has a certain melancholy appeal, the fate of those monastic buildings which came under public control is even more intriguing. The evolving status and needs of the new order often seemed to follow a cycle: formerly "sacred spaces" first became Revolutionary barracks or prisons, granaries or arms dumps; later city halls, law courts or schools. The abbaye de Pentemont, the ambitious plans for which appear in Diderot's *Encyclopedia*, is still in public use after multiple repurposings. During the Revolution, it was transformed into barracks for the National Guard; it housed successive corps of Imperial guards throughout the nineteenth century. The chapel was emptied of its furnishings and divided into two floors to serve as a warehouse. In 1843, it became a Protestant church. In 1915, the remaining buildings were taken over by the War Ministry pensions department; they now contain the Veteran's Ministry. St-Cyr became a hospital in 1793, then a famous military academy which was destroyed by bombardment in 1944.[7] Somewhat ironically, the cloister of Port-Royal de Paris is now a maternity hospital (Reau 20n3). In Tours, a converted convent holds the Prefecture of Police; in Forcalquier in the Alps of high Provence, an old convent contains the town hall and museum. The Musée Greuze is housed in a former convent in Tournus; the ghosts of its former occupants might be scandalized by the innocently erotic works now displayed on its walls.

Returning to Mur-de-Barrez, the Monastère Ste-Claire experienced during its post-conventual history nearly the complete cycle of functions described above. The convent chapel initially became a public assembly room, then a granary: the communion table was removed to allow room for oxcarts to enter and turn. The residential part of the convent was transformed into a barracks, prison and police headquarters. After the prison was disbanded, the police station remained. In 1804, the city created a primary school in the former convent, which later became a well-known boy's boarding establishment. After a catastrophic fire in 1809

---

[6]   Those interested in the destroyed artistic patrimony of France may wish to consult the curious work of Louis Reau, *Les Monuments détruits de l'art français: histoire du vandalisme*. vol. 2: 19e siècle (Paris: Hachette, 1959). For short histories and descriptions of existing Catholic monasteries, some of which receive visitors, see Maurice Colinon, *Guide des monastères* (Paris: Pierre Horay Editeur, 12th edition, 1994). The Guides Michelin are also a useful source of information on the fate of former monastic buildings.

[7]   This famous institution near Versailles was founded in the seventeenth century by Mme de Maintenon, Louis XIV's morganatic spouse, as a school for noble girls of poor family like herself; the first performance of Racine's *Esther* took place in its great entry hall. The school was later reformed into an Ursuline teaching convent.

which lasted four days, the building was repaired but the school declined; it was succeeded in 1840 by a town meeting hall. As mentioned earlier, the premises, in poor condition, were briefly taken over by a convent of the Visitation; finally, the Clares returned to Mur-de-Barrez in 1868, 215 years after the founding of their house. They remain there today.

Each former monastery has a chapter in the history of post-Revolutionary transformation; but the fate of the huge Fontevraud complex could fill many volumes on its own. A visitor to Fontevraud in 1803 remarked that after monastic abolition, the veritable "petite ville" had become a "désert." To fill this void, the municipality asked the government to establish a textile factory or a regional hospice there; but the Napoleonic administration had other priorities: this deserted place, located in an out-of-the-way region of the Loire Valley, was perfect for a prison. A decree of 26 Vendémiaire, An 13 (1804) created a "centre de réclusion" at Fontevraud for prisoners from nine surrounding départements; a new ordinance of 1817 brought that total to 19. The construction costs for this project totaled 2,000,000 francs (Melot and Joubert 16). The penitentiary established by Napoleon at Fontevraud was not abolished until 1963; its last inmate did not leave until September 30, 1985 (Melot and Joubert 16). Fontevraud, through its size, location and closeness to the Old Regime monarchy, probably best exemplifies the prison/enclosure dichotomy running through this book. Illustrations from Chantal Colleu-Dumond and Gérard Rondeau's *L'Abbaye de Fontevraud* juxtapose, on contiguous pages, photographs of the convent parlor and of a prison cell covered with graffiti (86–7). In general, emptied convent spaces either disappeared or filled a series of new social niches. The case of Fontevraud is different. Too isolated to serve local needs, too large to tear down, unconnected to any widespread women's order that might have taken an interest in it, Fontevraud became a vast space of internal exile, and remains a lonely monument to *ancien régime* heterotopia.

The Reopening of the Convents

As indicated above, the end of the Terror saw some easing in anti-Christian policies in France—not that the Thermidorian leaders had any greater respect for religion than their predecessors, but because they realized that these policies had not succeeded. Despite persecutions of clerics and celebrations of the Supreme Being, Christianity had not gone away. In February, 1795, the Constitutional church was separated from the state, and clerics who had been imprisoned for failing to sign the loyalty oath were freed. Napoleon, who took power in the coup of 18 Brumaire (November, 1799), was no more inclined toward religion than his Revolutionary predecessors. He was, however, looking for ways to shore up his fragile political position among the population. With remarkably modern acumen, he commissioned two national surveys of religion which showed the Catholic sympathies of the nation still to be strong. Shortly after, Napoleon entered into negotiations with Pope Pius VII resulting in the signing of the Concordat on July 15, 1801.

This accord brought France back into relation with the Church after over 10 years; but according to Article 13, nothing owned by the clergy before 1789 would be transferred back, not even the monasteries. Napoleon had little sympathy for, or interest in, former nuns who had been ousted from their houses; he simply assumed that they would move back with their families, and gave no help to those who had no family to move back to—although, as we have seen, lack of family support was an important reason why many women had professed in the first place. As a result, "thousands of female ex-religious drifted into the towns and could be found begging on the streets between 1805 and 1815 or, in extreme cases, taking up prostitution" (Aston, *CRR* 284). Despite Diderot's hostility to convents, he foresaw this consequence after Suzanne escapes from her convent at the end of *La Religieuse* (see above, Chapter 6).

Napoleon gave permission for religious orders to be reestablished on a limited basis in 1807. Some women's religious houses had already reappeared before that date; the earliest may be the Dames de la Foi, a new order created in 1800 (Aston, *CRR* 284). Groups like the Ursulines and Visitandines recommenced formal community life shortly thereafter. The Monastery of the Visitation of Macon, dispersed in 1792, was reestablished in September, 1805 in a former Capucin convent of that city dating from 1606. The Visitandines of Troyes were able to return to their own monastery in 1807. As their history proudly states, "They have not left it since" ["Elles ne l'ont pas quitté depuis," Burns, *Saint-François de Sales* 34]. The initiative to reinstitute convents often began with lay women. Thus, in 1807, Mademoiselle de La Fare bought the Monastère de l'Adoration Perpetuelle from its previous owner, in order to house the Sacrementine nuns; they were still there as of 1990. Conventual life resumed more fully after the Restoration in 1815: a census taken at that time shows there were 14,226 nuns in France. This number substantially increased until 1830; but most former nuns did not return to the religious life, and many communities, especially among the contemplative orders, never revived. Nevertheless, the nineteenth century was a time of growth and vitality in women's vocations, particularly for the so-called service congregations: of the 36 Visitation convents still existing in France, nearly a quarter were founded or resettled after 1830 (Burns, *Saint-François de Sales* 35–43). In 1836, a former pupil of the Clares of Mur-de-Barrez, Louise Félicie de Belcont de Malcor, left a sum of 30,000 francs in her will to help reestablish a women's religious and teaching community in the former convent (Taussat, "Saint-François d'Assise en Rouergue" 69). This ambition would be fully realized 32 years later. Thus, nuns were reintegrated into nineteenth-century social and economic structure through their traditional teaching and nursing roles; in addition, female workers in the new industrial economy were housed in Catholic hostels, supervised by nuns (Foucault, *Power/Knowledge* 157).

Thus, for a short time after 1815, Catholic clergy, like Royalists, might have dreamed of a France restored to a pre-Revolutionary order of things; but this dream was never to be realized. For the sacred space, along with the old regime monarchy to which it was joined in an uneasy union, had been shattered by the Revolution; like Humpty Dumpty, the cloister could never really be put back together again. The abolition of the established Church in 1789, followed by the separation of the Constitutional Church from the state in 1795, changed the relation between religion and regime forever: henceforward, though Catholicism remained the faith of the majority of French people, the church was on its own financially and politically. Another factor in the irremediable loss of church strength was the abolition of women's teaching orders in 1792, followed by the creation of secular schools with *instituteurs publics*. By a decree of October 28, 1793, the Convention forbade any male or female cleric from being appointed as a teacher. In 1796, the lay schoolmaster of Mur-de-Barrez was housed by the municipality in a room of the former convent (Delmas, "Une histoire spirituelle en images" 122). Though Napoleon returned girl's education to the hands of the religious orders in the early nineteenth century, where it would remain until the Third Republic, a whole Revolutionary generation had grown up with little or no Catholic training. For this and other reasons, post-Revolutionary regular confession and church attendance dramatically declined, especially among men: "For millions of men, tavern sociability became an acceptable alternative to religious ritual" (Aston *RRF* 343). Many French men and women continued to feel the appeal of Christianity; but the old First Estate, and with it the conventual system, was in its tomb.

Tombs: The Convent and the Restoration Imagination

> … I was called one morning to a convent in the Faubourg Saint Jacques to see a young nun who was ill. Napoleon, by then emperor, had recently sanctioned the reestablishment of some of the convents. The one to which I had to go belonged to the Ursuline order. Part of the building had been destroyed during the Revolution, and the demolition of the ancient church, of which no more than a few vault arches remained, left the cloisters open on one side. It was to these cloisters that I was conducted by a sister. I noticed, as we went through them, that the long flagstones with which they were paved were in fact tombstones, since they bore inscriptions, though most had become illegible with age. Some had been broken during the Revolution, and the sister remarked that they had not yet had time to have them repaired.

> … je fus appelé un matin au faubourg Saint-Jacques, pour voir dans un couvent une jeune religieuse malade. L'empereur Napoléon avait permis depuis le rétablissement de quelques-uns de ces couvents: celui où je me rendais était destiné à l'éducation de la jeunesse, et appartenait à l'ordre des Ursulines. La Révolution avait ruiné une partie de l'édifice; le cloître était à découvert d'un côté par la démolition de l'antique église, dont on ne voyait plus que quelques arceaux. Une religieuse m'introduisit dans ce cloître, que nous traversâmes en marchant sur de longues pierres plates, qui formaient le pavé de ces galeries; je m'aperçus que c'étaient des tombes, car elles portaient toutes des inscriptions pour la plupart effacés par le temps. Quelques-unes de ces pierres avaient été brisées pendant la Révolution: la soeur me le fit remarquer, en me disant qu'on n'avait pas encore eu le temps de les réparer. (*Ourika* 3)

Claire de Duras's *Ourika*, a recently rediscovered masterwork of Restoration fiction, tells the tale of a black girl who becomes a nun because she has no other place in French society. A conventual frame surrounds the story, supplying its beginning and ending. In the passage cited above, a nun conducts a young, anticlerical doctor into the cloister to visit an ill resident—Ourika. The introductory description is striking for its historical accuracy. Duras precisely locates the convent in place and time: the Faubourg St-Jacques, home to so many *ancien régime* convents, shortly after Napoleon authorized the reopening of some monasteries in 1807. The narrator also notes that this particular monastery belongs to a respected teaching order, one of those which received permission to reopen. Moreover, the introduction graphically represents both the meanings and the limits of Restoration. The convent church was destroyed during the Revolution, leaving the cloister literally open to the outside world; the nuns who have recently moved back into these ruins have not yet had time to make many repairs. In this mournful setting, the visiting doctor is "chilled" to discover that the flagstones he is walking on are actually tombstones. Age and the depredations of the Revolution have combined to render the names engraved on the broken tombstones virtually unreadable. It is as impossible to reconstitute the lives of the women who lived, died and were buried in that place as it is to reconstruct the destroyed monastic culture; yet people again walk on those broken stones; the names are still there to be seen, identifying them as tombs. Thus restoration, unlike reconstruction, implies both rupture and continuity. Though the restored place will never be the same, it draws strength from its material presence: having been there all along, it is still there.

The tomb (*tombeau*), as a metonymy of restoration, contains all these complex and bitter-sweet meanings: it is at once the repository of the past dead and, in a figurative sense, a tribute created in the present and stretching into the future. Thus, the composer Jean-Philippe Rameau wrote his "Tombeau de Couperin" as a musical memorial, at once honoring his deceased master and exhibiting his, Rameau's, own mastery.[8] Such broken continuities mark the representation of convents in post-Revolutionary French literature. The first wave of conventual representation numbered writers who had lived through both old and new regimes. The main exemplars of this phase are the close friends but dissimilar writers Alphonse de Chateaubriand and Claire de Duras. The lives of both spanned the pre- and post-Revolutionary period; both lived through exile and return; but their formative experiences were different. From the age of 12 to 14, Duras boarded at the elite convent of Panthemont, where she made friendships which endured all her life. In 1792, the convent was closed by the nation and Duras took refuge with a cousin (Martin and Zimmerman, 153–60). Thus, she brings to *Ourika* a first-hand experience of pre-Revolutionary convent culture and its meaning for women. Both *Ourika* and Chateaubriand's *René* initially approach the convent from the

---

8   For more on the literary meaning of *tombeau*, see Woshinsky, "Tombeau de *Phèdre*: Repression, Confession and Métissage in Racine and Claire de Duras." *Dalhousie French Studies* Special Issue 49 (Winter, 1999), 167–81.

perspective of an outsider looking in, but the resulting effects are quite disparate. The dilapidated convent in the introduction to *Ourika* is described unsentimentally by a young doctor who is not sympathetic to convent life; yet the description creates a hauntingly evocative effect by its very realism. In contrast, Chateaubriand's depiction of the lonely convent on the windswept shores of Brittany, where René spies on his sister in her religious refuge, draws more on Romantic convention than on real experience.

In the main, monastic imagery in Romantic art will hew closer to the model of *René* than to that of *Ourika*. Romantic convent motifs mostly fall into three overlapping categories: the nostalgic, the melancholic and the gothic. Writers and artists from both sides of the Channel were drawn to the enhanced morbidity of tombs located in monastic settings: Fragonard painted *Burial of a Monk* in 1820, and Charles Caius Renoux his *Monks before a Tomb* in 1828.[9] Morbidity, melancholia and nostalgia also dominate convent descriptions in Balzac's 1834 novel, *La duchesse de Langeais*: "They then saw, in the cell's antechamber, the body of the duchess, lying on the ground on a board taken from her bed, and illuminated by two tapers" ["Ils virent alors, dans l'antichambre de la cellule, la duchesse morte, posée à terre sur la planche de son lit, et éclairée par deux cierges," 349]. George Sand's *Lélia* (1839) reveals a greater integration of the convent setting into the novel's themes. Writing from a "post-Catholic" perspective, Sand explicitly places her story at the end of an era: "it was the time of the last gleams thrown by the Catholic faith" ["c'était le temps des dernières lueurs que jeta la foi catholique," *Lélia* 508]. An early scene in the book oddly echoes the allegorical settings of early seventeenth-century religious fiction. Magnus, who had been thinking of leaving the world, wanders alone on a deserted plain. Taking refuge beside an abandoned abbey during a storm, he is nearly buried by the crumbling walls, but providentially rescued just in time:

> A priest, whom the storm had caused to lose his way on these deserted plains, passed by the crumbling convent walls just at that moment. At first, he turned away in fright; then he thought he heard a human voice amid the furious voices of the tempest. He ventured through the new ruins covering the old and found me unconscious under the debris that was about to bury me.

> Un prêtre, que l'orage avait fourvoyé dans ces plaines désertes, vint à passer en ce moment au pied des murailles croulantes du couvent. Il s'éloigna d'abord avec effroi, puis il crut entendre une voix humaine parmi les voix furieuses de la tempête. Il se hasarda entre les nouvelles ruines qui couvraient les anciennes et me trouva évanoui sous des débris qui allaient m'ensevelir. (Sand, *Lélia* 21)

---

[9]   These paintings are reproduced and discussed in Patrick J. Noon and Stephen Bann, *Crossing the Channel: British and French Painting in the Age of Romanticism* (London: Tate Pub.; New York: Distributed in the United States and Canada by Harry N. Abrams, 2003).

This nocturnal scene beautifully epitomizes Romantic and Restoration picturesque. The convent, with its collapsing walls, is portrayed as spooky and dangerous; the "new" ruins, (a compounded result of the Revolution and the storm), join with the old, nearly burying their victim alive.

In the main plot, however, the convent plays a role beyond decor. Lélia, desirous to retain her independence, had refused to marry her lover Stenio. When he turns to another woman, she enters a convent, seeking solace in music, clothing and perfume: as in Cavendish's *Convent of Pleasure*, "luxury and comfort had found their way even into the cloister" ["les luxes et ses douceurs se sont introduits jusque dans le Cloitre," Sand *Lélia* 411], minus the destabilizing presence of men. However, Stenio secretly enters the convent and observes Lélia's profession ceremony. The sense of a post-mortem on Catholicism is again very evident. The Patriarch proclaims, "It seems, then, that the era of great devotion and great acts of faith is about to be reborn" ["Il semble alors que l'ère des grands dévouements et des grands actes de foi soit prête à renaître," Sand *Lélia* 452]. He preaches about the rebirth of faith, but only within the framework of the "grands dévouements" of the past. Moreover, Lélia does not give orthodox answers to his questions during her profession. She later becomes an eloquent and successful abbess, but reveals in a last conversation that while union with men is impossible, life with God alone is insufficient. This ambivalence also informs the novel's dual ending. In the 1833 version, Stenio commits suicide beside the convent wall; Magnus then strangles Lélia over Stenio's corpse. But in the 1839 version, Lélia creates an enlightened community inside and outside the cloister. Thus, rather than using the convent setting merely for local color, Sand appears to have reflected on the meaning of monastic retreat and, like seventeenth-century women writers, to have imagined the women's community as an alternative to marriage.

In general, however, *Lélia* conveys a sense that the convent has ceased to be a dynamic social institution to become a site for romantic or morbid fantasy. A reference to the conventual space at the end of the novel exudes a peculiarly Restoration sensibility of the "living dead." An old abbess speaks of the customs for preparing the bodies of their deceased sisters: "The corpse will sleep forever among the people who will later sleep beside it, and all those who walk on its tomb greet it like a living person" ["Le cadavre doit dormir à jamais parmi des êtres qui dormiront plus tard à ses côtés, et tous ceux qui passent sur sa tombe le saluent comme un vivant," Sand *Lélia* 485]. Like the nun in the introduction to *Ourika*, the abbess in *Lélia* draws disquieting attention to the sisters "sleeping" under their tombs; at the same time that she greets them as living presences, she knows their bones are moldering away. Fantasies of the living dead also enter, albeit in a very different way, into another genre to borrow the convent background: the Gothic novel. Originating in England, the Gothic found its first exemplar in M.G. Lewis's *The Monk: A Romance*, written in 1795 and thus contemporary with the French Revolution. The Gothic was later popularized by mid-Victorian authors of sensation fiction like Mary Ward and Wilkie Collins, one of the first practitioners of the detective story.

Another nineteenth-century genre to exploit the convent setting is the "escaped nun's tale." From the 1830s to the 1860s, intense anti-Catholic feeling in both England and America gave rise to numbers of these popular works. Escaped nun's tales have a hybrid origin, drawing on the Gothic novel as well as on French and Spanish anticlerical fiction. In a typical plot, an innocent Protestant girl is inveigled to join a convent by the beauty of its ritual and decor and the insinuating lies of its nuns. Once incarcerated, she is exploited as a servant and even subjected to persecutions reminiscent of Diderot's *Religieuse*: solitary confinement, starvation, invasion of privacy, imprisonment within penitential cells (Griffin 95). The young victim is sometimes even made to undergo her profession ceremony while unconscious. Maria Monk's *Awful Disclosures* (1836), a best-seller for decades, tells the allegedly true story of the heroine's experiences and escape from the Hôtel-Dieu convent in Montreal (Canada). This tale set the model for numerous others, including *The Chronicles of Mount Benedict*, *The Escaped Nun* and *Six Months in a Convent*. Other nuns' stories of the time were openly fictional or even parodic, like *Six Hours in a Convent*. While both Diderot's *Religieuse* and the American nuns' tales decry the enclosure of girls within evil institutions, there is a marked difference. Suzanne's profession was entirely involuntary; but according to Griffin, underneath their anti-Catholicism, American escaped nun's tales reveal a "cultural anxiety" around girls' growing freedom to make their own life choices, and their perceived incapacity to choose wisely. Examples of all these genres— romance, Gothic, mystery, alone or in various combinations—still enjoy immense popularity; and with its various sinister connotations—destruction, spookiness, melancholy—the monastic setting continues to live a strange half-life.

Avatars of Conventual Spaces in the Twentieth and Twenty-First Centuries

Aside from straightforward historical novels like Françoise Chandernagor's *L'Allée du roi*,[10] how has the fiction of the last century portrayed the convent and other enclosed female spaces? In works from the early twentieth century, a complex gender dichotomy can be observed, a dichotomy that, instead of involving the sex of the author, turns on the sex of the implied reader. For example, in *La Porte étroite* (1909), André Gide paints female retreat as a means of frustrating male sexuality and a destructive impasse leading to death. Like the Portuguese nun's outpourings, the despairing revelations that conclude *La Porte étroite* are written in a female voice ventriloquized by Gide. Colette's example is also complex: her representations of secularized female spaces evolve from a male- to a female-centered perspective. The girls' school of the early Claudine stories, co-authored

---

[10]   (Paris: Juillard, 1981).This engaging memoir-novel, based on period documents, recounts the life of Françoise d'Aubigné from her birth in a debtor's prison to her old age at the St-Cyr convent school near Versailles. An English translation (*The King's Way*, Harcourt Brace Jovanovich) was published in 1984. Chandernagor also co-authored a French film version in 1996.

with her husband Willy, displays a voyeuristic pseudo-feminocentricity reminiscent of Guilleragues. But in the novels Colette wrote alone, like *La Vagabonde* and *La Retraite sentimentale*, she explores the need for a feminine refuge free from heterosexual stresses, and presents a seductive image of female solitude for women who are conditioned to live with, and for, others.

Religious retreat continues to allure or repel women at the turn of the twenty-first century. Isabel Colegate's *Pelican in the Wilderness* (2002) relates with nostalgic charm the history of solitary life, from St. Anthony to contemporary female hermits. In *Dakota: A Spiritual Geography* (1993), Kathleen Norris recounts her life as an oblate: a lay, "threshold" member of a monastic community living in the prairie "desert," as she terms it. In her fictional trilogy *The Summerhouse* (1987–89; 2001) Alice Thomas Ellis recounts with humor and passion a young woman's escape from a disastrous engagement, which allows her to fulfill the deep religious vocation she had discovered during a stay in Egypt: "I thought of rivers, dark faces and the shadowed cloisters of the convent" (22). On the other side of the wall, in *Through the Narrow Gate* (1981), the religious historian and former nun Karen Armstrong chronicles the seven difficult years she spent in a convent. Her more recent memoir, *The Spiral Staircase* (2004), revisits this experience with the insight born of distance. She recalls the sisters as well-meaning, but too rigid, or too frightened, to bring the changes of Vatican II "inside." Like Diderot's Suzanne, Armstrong found that "despite leaving the convent, she remained, in some ways, a nun" (Winner 14). As a student at Oxford, she exchanged one kind of cloister for another; and in the spatial metaphor of her title, reentering "the world" was less a sudden liberation than a slow, arduous climb up a spiral staircase toward self-discovery.

In a different way, contemporary writing has opened up spaces for the female other in African and African American literature. For example, in *Dreams of Trespass: Tales of a Harem Girlhood* (1994), Fatima Mernissi, the Moroccan feminist and sociologist, recalls growing up in a sexually and spatially segregated home in Fez, just before the independence movements of the 1950s brought the era of the harem to a close. Her description of the harem space, with its courtyards and salons, its women's terraces and forbidden terrains, its male doorman who prevented females from going out alone, is juxtaposed with the "harem inside": the rules in people's heads that (still) keep women confined, as well as the inner "dreams of trespass" fostered by her aunts' tales and her own imagination that offer them hopes of freedom. Like the early modern convent, the harem is a vanished world; but women veiled from head to toe and accompanied by men of the family are becoming a common sight on streets around the world. Do they carry their enclosures with them as prison or protection?[11]

---

[11] On Muslim veiling, see Arlene McLeod, *Accommodating Protest: Working Women, the New Veiling and Change in Cairo* (New York: Columbia University Press, 1991); and Saba Mahmood, *Politics of Piety: The Islamic Revival and the Feminist Subject* (Princeton, NJ: Princeton University Press, 2005). While the wearing of the *hijab* is related, or at least

Finally, Toni Morrison's 1998 novel *Paradise* describes a house on the outskirts of an all-black town in Oklahoma which serves as an informal refuge for black and white women. Tellingly, this house is called "the Convent." After the Civil War, freed slaves had moved to the Oklahoma Territory to start their own community where they could live in freedom; but their male descendants see this female space on their borders as a menace. Some of the men finally raid the Convent and kill three of the women inside. In one of the book's most powerful statements, one of these intruders "raises his chin and then his rifle and shoots open a door that has never been locked" (285). Three of the men, viewing the women's drawings on the cellar floor, "observe defilement, perversion and violence beyond imagination" (287), not realizing that the defilement and violence exist only in their own minds and acts. Thus the need, or the threat, of a cell of one's own is still with us in the twenty-first century.

Conclusion: The Convent Difference

A photograph appearing in the "Living Arts" section of *The New York Times* for September 26, 1996, shows a high, empty room, decorated only by bars of light and shadow. The photograph bears the caption and commentary: "'Asylum,' an artwork by the New York artist James Casebere, suggests a welcome refuge or a last resort." This volume, like Casebere's photo, has highlighted the ambiguities of the convent as an "asylum"—often portrayed, even in the same work, as both refuge and lockup. But we have also observed that the successive forms of women's enclosure in the early modern imagination are neither unified nor linear. Hence, in order to enter fully into the conventual space, it is necessary to move beyond simple dichotomies, to explore more complex arrays of meaning. In the terms introduced in the Introduction, a convent is a *heterotopia*—an alternative space affording limited, controlled access to the outside world. It is also a *feminotopia*, or an alternate, exclusively female space; sometimes, though rarely, it can become a *feminutopia*, an ideal feminine domain. But whatever its exact nature, the conventual space is a locus for reflecting on and questioning the social order from a position marginal to that order. Further complicating such reflections, a *represented* conventual space is doubly "hetero-" or other. An actual convent already reproduces certain patterns of the outside world, such as its social and power hierarchies, and reverses others, by placing women in control. The written work may recast dominant social hierarchies in female guise, as with Guilleragues and Diderot; or it can question social hierarchy from a female gender position, as is the case for Villedieu and Lafayette. Thus, the represented convent refers not only to the primary level of the "real" but to the secondary level of the surrounding culture.

Esthetic factors also play a role in the difference(s) representation makes by determining what is left out, added or accentuated. Women's community is a case

---

analogous, to some Catholic and Jewish practices, comparing these would have meant writing a longer, and different, book.

in point. Communal life is perhaps the most important defining characteristic of monasticism, embraced by nuns today as it was by their ancestresses. Despite Mother Agnès's insistence on solitary enclosure, the Institutions of Port-Royal underline the importance of group practices: the gouache by Magdeleine Hortemels decorating the cover of this book depicts the Port-Royal sisters seated in assembly, according to their custom. But the communal note is almost completely absent from the texts we have examined here. This erasure partly reflects the limits of the narrative genre. In fiction, the separate point of view, the individual experience, weighs far more heavily than the group portrait: novels narrated in the third person are rare and, with the exception of Camus's *The Plague*, hardly engaging. Of course there are works in which community is of importance, for example in non-canonical forms like Cavendish's armchair dramas, Montpensier's letters and Scudéry's conversations; communal life is presented, albeit in a rather critical form, in Marivaux's *Marianne*, and in a firmly dystopic context in the case of Diderot. Yet even there, it chiefly serves as a background for first-person narration. On the other hand, while narrative constraints seem to limit the representation of community, the convent setting lends itself admirably to separation. The opening and closing of narrative structure reproduces the opening and closing of convent gates and doors; and metonymies of place—cloister, parlor, cell—perfectly convey the fragmented nature of the conventual space.

In addition to these esthetic factors, the convent setting is extremely sensitive to gender-related distinctions. Relations between gender and narrative may be more complex in the twentieth-century novels discussed above than in earlier fiction; yet it is generally true that the communities depicted by male authors look quite different from those described by women. With the notable exception of Marivaux's *Vie de Marianne*, male-authored convent narratives are skewed toward the melodramatic and the erotic. Whether flaunted, castigated or simply observed, female sexuality is a constant preoccupation in these works. In a related point, the convents depicted in male-authored texts are shown to be more transgressive, a greater threat to the social order, than they appear to be in women's writing, or in fact were. L'abbé de Pure portrays the convent as a haven for sexual play and heretical beliefs; Diderot transforms it into a hotbed of perversity and madness. Such fictional imaginings hardly fit the historical facts: according to Rapley, "No serious historian accuses eighteenth-century nuns of misbehavior" (*Social History* 81). Finally, depictions of convents in works by male writers display a significant time lag between real conditions and their representation. For example, Jean-Pierre Camus's writings castigate so-called lax convents in the mid-seventeenth century, by which date most of them had already been reformed. Analogously, decades of taxation and decreasing income had already diminished the strength and numbers of women's houses by the time Diderot presented his damning exposé in the late eighteenth century. These historical anachronisms contribute to representations which not only demonize convents, but, ironically, assign them more power than they possessed in reality. Perhaps the perceived power is necessary for the demonization.

Early modern women writers, on the other hand, tend to produce more moderate and, perhaps, more realistic pictures of convent life. Their accounts rarely attain the level of sexual suggestiveness displayed by Pure or Diderot. In Villedieu's *Henriette-Sylvie de Molière*, for example, convents are not centers of evil; at worst, they are marginally involved in instances of misconduct that would have taken place anyway (such as a wife escaping into a nearby cloister when found with her lover, or a convent boarder clandestinely meeting her betrothed in town). Moreover, criticisms of the convent in female-authored texts, while certainly present, are less melodramatic, more matter-of-fact than in their male counterparts'. In writing about her boarding school days, Mme Roland remarks: "the house was respectable, the order not too austere; as a result, the nuns dispensed altogether with the excesses and nonsense which are characteristic of most [monasteries]" (Sonnet, *L'éducation des filles* 187, quoted in Rapley, *Social History* 91). Roland's statement encapsulates a view often held by early modern women: namely, that life in a cloistered community was not so much frightening as boring, annoying and sometimes just stupid. But then, as Montpensier was wont to point out, so was marriage (See Chapter 3, 128–31). Male writers have viewed the convent community as a fascinating and horrifying aberration; some female readers may be drawn to it as a place for women to create their own world; but early modern women, living in a much more restricted society, shared a more practical view of its limits and possibilities. The convent path might not have been an *allée du roi*—at times, it was hardly even a *pis aller*—but neither was it a nightmarish *cul de sac*.

In conclusion, while tracing the varied transformations in attitudes and audience from the Catholic Reform to the Enlightenment, this book has offered glimpses of what I term a "convent culture": a complex of ways in which women's enclosure functioned in early modern society. To a certain degree, convent culture resembled the salon culture of the time. Both were female-centered; both influenced and interacted with dominant culture; both were portrayed in exaggerated and sometimes damning ways. But for obvious reasons, the convent remains a more occulted and secret space than the salon. Our main sources of information on its "interior," such as annals and death notices, are narrow in scope; and the documents available become ever more limited and fragmented in the years preceding the Revolution. Readers and writers respond to this monastic secrecy variously, depending on their aims and attitudes. Catholic Reform fiction portrays allegorical isolation as a means to encourage religious retreat. Classical convent satire, like its medieval and Renaissance models, exploits the "mysteries" of the convent to provoke a carnavalesque release, allowing the reader to let off steam while basically leaving the status quo unchanged. In contrast, the radical anti-convent fiction of the eighteenth century draws on the stereotype of unbridled female sexuality to discredit and destroy monasticism as an institution. Yet in the face of all these highly colored images, the information we have gleaned from women's memoirs, letters and fiction suggests that the convent's mystery is really more of a "secret de Polichinelle"—an open secret taken for granted by everyone, or at least by women. The convent setting, like the court background in the *Princesse de Clèves*, requires little description simply because it is so familiar. Akin to a purloined letter gathering dust for centuries, knowledge of convent life is hidden in plain sight; for good or ill, it is interwoven into women's lives as an option for themselves, their aunts, their sisters and their mothers, at a time when few other choices existed.

Works Cited

Primary Sources

Agnès de St-Paul, Gertrude Jaqueline Pascal, and Sébastien Du Cambout de Pontchâteau. *Les Constitutions du monastere de Port-Royal du S. Sacrement.* Mons: chez Gaspard Migeot, 1665.

Les Amans cloistrés, ou L'Heureuse inconstance. Cologne: s.n., 1698.

The American Heritage Dictionary of the English Language. 3rd edition. Boston, New York, London: Houghton Mifflin Company, 1992.

Les Amours de la Magdelene, où l'amour divin triomphe de celui du monde. Paris: Chez N. Rousset, 1618.

Ancrene Riwle. Ed. and trans. Robert W. Ackerman, Roger Dahood. Binghamton: Center for Medieval and Early Renaissance Studies, 1984.

Ancrene Wisse. Parts Six and Seven. Ed. Geoffrey Shepherd. London: Thomas Nelson & Sons, 1959.

d'Angoumois, Philippe. *Les Triomphes de l'amour de Dieu en la conversion d'Hermiogène.* Paris: N. Buon, 1625. 2nd ed. 1631.

Aristotle. *Physics.* Books III and IV. Trans. Edward Hussey. Oxford: Clarendon Press, 1983.

———. *De Anima.* Books II and III. Trans. D.W. Hamlyn. Oxford: Clarendon Press; New York: Oxford University Press, 1993.

Armstrong, Karen. *Through the Narrow Gate.* New York: St. Martin's Press, 1981.

———. *The Spiral Staircase.* New York, Toronto: Alfred A. Knopf, 2004.

Augustine, Bishop of Hippo. *Corpus Augustineanum Gissense ... editum a Pr. Dr. Cornelius Mayer. Opera. De Trinitate.* Past Masters. Intelex Full Text Humanities databases. http://www.nlx.com.

———. *On Christian Doctrine.* Trans. D.W. Robertson, Jr. Indianapolis, New York: The Bobbs-Merrill Company, Inc., 1958.

Austen, Jane. *Northanger Abbey* and *Persuasion.* London and Glasgow: Collins, 1962.

———. *The Trinity. Works of St. Augustine: A Translation for the 21st Century.* Ed. John E. Rotelle. Brooklyn: New City Press, 1991.

Avantures Singulieres de M.C. contenant le récit abregé des désordres qui se commentent dans les couvents. I & II parties. Trad. de l'italien. Utrecht: Chez Pierre Muntendam, 1724.

Balzac, Honoré de. *La duchesse de Langeais.* Paris: Garnier, 1956.

Barrin, Jean. *Vénus dans le Cloître ou la Religieuse en chemise.* Entretiens curieux par l'Abbé du Prat (1682, 1719). Paris: Le Livre du Bibliophile, 1956.

Barrin, Jean. *Venus in the Cloister, or the Nun in her Smock, In Curious Dialogues, addressed to the Lady Abbess of Loves Paradice, by the Abbot du Prat. Done out of the French.* London: H. Rodes, 1683.

Brunet de Brou. *La religieuse malgré elle, histoire galante, morale et tragique.* Amsterdam: C. Jordan, 1720. Amsterdam, 1740, 1761.

Bussy-Rabutin, *Lettre d'Heloïse et d'Abailard* (1697) in *Receuil de lettres galantes et amoureuses.* Amsterdam: chez François Roger, 1699. I. (II = *Lettres d'une religieuse portugaise avec les réponses du chevalier de C*.*)

Camus, Jean-Pierre. *La Mémoire de Darie, où se voit l'idée d'une dévotieuse vie et d'une religieuse mort.* Paris: C. Chappelet, 1620.

———. *Agathonphile ou les martyrs siciliens.* Paris: chez Claude Chappelet, 1621.

———. *Alexis.* Paris: C. Chappelet, 1622–23.

———. *Hermiante, ou les deux Hermites contraires, le reclus et l'instable.* Lyon: Jacques Gaudion, 1623.

———. *Acheminement à la dévotion civile.* Toulouse: R. Colomiez, 1624.

———. *Elise.* Paris: Chez Claude Chappelet, 1624.

———. *La Pieuse Julie, histoire parisienne.* Paris: M. Lasnier, 1625.

———. *Petronille. Accident pitoyable de nos jours, cause d'une vocation religieuse.* Lyon: Jacques Gaudion, 1626.

———. *Les Spectacles d'Horreur. Où se descouvrent plusieurs tragiques effets de nostre siecle.* Paris: André Soubron, 1630.

———. *Les tapisseries historiques.* Paris: J. Branchu, 1644.

———. *Agathonphile: récit de Philargyrippe.* Ed. Pierre Lesage. Geneva: Droz, 1951.

———. *L'Amphithéâtre sanglant.* Paris: Joseph Cottereau, 1630. Geneva: Slatkine reprints, 1973.

———. *Divertissement historique.* Paris: Gervais Alliot, 1632. Ed. Constant Venesoen. Tübingen: Narr, 2002.

Canons and Decrees of the Council of Trent. Ed. Rev. H.J. Schroeder, O.PL. St. Louis and London: B. Herder Book Co. 1941. Rockford: Tan Books and Publishers Inc. 1978.

Casanova de Seingalt, Giacomo. *Mémoires.* Paris: Garnier frères, 1880. 8 vols.

Castelnau, Henriette de: see Murat, Comtesse de.

Cavendish, Margaret, Duchess of Newcastle. *The Convent of Pleasure.* In *Plays, Never Before Printed.* London: A. Maxwell, 1668. Ed. Jennifer Rosewell. Oxford: Seventeenth Century Press, 1995.

Chapelain, Jean. *De la lecture des vieux romans.* Paris: Chez Auguste Aubry, 1870. (Written in 1647 with the title *Dialogue sur la lecture des vieux romans.*)

Chateaubriand, Francois René de. *Atala. René.* Paris: Garnier, 1962.

Cholakian: see Mancini, Marie. *La Vérité dans son jour.*

Cole, Reverend William. *The Blecheley Diary of the Rev. William Cole, 1765–67.* From the original manuscript in the British Museum. Ed. Francis Griffin Stokes. London: Constable, 1931.

Colonna, Marie Mancini. See Mancini, Marie.

Constitutions du monastère de Port Royal: see Agnès de St-Paul.

Le Convent aboli des frères pacifiques. Cologne: Pierre Le Blanc, 1685.

Corneille, Thomas. *Dictionnaire des sciences et des arts.* Paris: chez la veuve de J.B. Coignard, 1694. 2 vols.

Cramail, Adrien de Montluc. *Les Pensées du Solitaire*. [1621] Paris: A. de Sommaville, 1629–30.

Crevecoeur, M. *Voyage Pennsylvanie*. Paris: Maradan, 1801.

Croix, Pierre de. *Le Miroir de l'Amour Divin*. Douai: De l'imprimerie de Balthazar Bellere, 1608.

———. *Le Miroir de l'Amour Divin*. Ed. Lance K. Donaldson-Evans. Geneva: Droz, 1990.

Cuénin: see Villedieu, Mme de.

Les Delices du Cloitre, ou la None Eclairée. Avec un Discours préliminaire. Cologne: Chez Jacques le Sincère. 1742.

Deloffre: see Marivaux, Pierre Carlet de Chamblain de or Guilleragues, Gabriel de.

Démoris: see Villedieu, Mme de.

Dictionnaire de l'académie française. 8th edition. Paris: Hachette, 1932–35. http://artfl-project.uchicago.edu/node/17.

Diderot, Denis. *La Religieuse*. Paris, chez Buisson, 1796. Ed. R. Mauzi. Paris: Colin, 1961.

———. *The Nun*. Trans. Russell Goulbourne. Oxford: Oxford University Press, 2005.

———. *Oeuvres romanesques*. Ed. Henri Bénac. Paris: Garnier, 1962.

Diderot, Denis and D'Alembert. *Recueil de planches sur les sciences, les arts libéraux et les arts mechaniques. Architecture*. Paris: Inter-Livres, 1994.

Donaldson-Evans: see Croix, Pierre de.

Doscot: see Mancini, Hortense and Marie Mancini, *Mémoires d'Hortense et de Marie Mancini*.

Duras, Claire-Louisa-Rose-Bonne Lechal de Kersaint. *Ourika*. Paris, Ladvocat, 1824.

———. *Ourika: The Original French Text*. Eds Joan DeJean and Margaret Waller. New York: MLA, 1995.

Ellis, Alice Thomas. *The Summer House: A Trilogy*. Pleasantville, NY: Akadine Press, 2001.

L'Escole des filles, ou la philosophie des dames. Paris: Louis Piot, 1655. Ed. Pascal Pia. Paris: Cercle du livre précieux, 1959.

Estoile, Pierre de. *Mémoires et registre-journal de Henri III, Henri IV et de Louis XIII. Mémoires pour servir à L'Histoire de France*. Deuxième Série. I. Paris: Chez l'éditeur du Commentaire analytique du Code Civil, 1837.

La Fausse Abbesse ou l'amoureux dupé: Histoire nouvelle. The Hague: Chez Gerard Rammazeyn, 1681.

Furetière, Antoine. *Nouvelle allégorique: Histoire des derniers troubles arrivés au royaume de l'éloquence*. Ed. E. Van Ginnekin. Paris: Droz, 1961. First published 1658.

———. *Dictionnaire universel*. Paris: SNL-Le Robert, 1978. 3 vols.

Genlis, Stéphanie-Félicité Du Crest. *Mémoires inédits de Madame la comtesse de Genlis, sur le dix-huitième siècle et la Révolution française, depuis 1756 jusqu'à nos jours*. Paris: Ladvocat, 1825.

Goulbourne: see Diderot.

Guilleragues, Gabriel de. *Lettres Portugaises traduites en françois*. Paris: C. Barbin, 1669.

————. *Lettres portugaises: suivies de Guilleragues par lui-même.* Ed. Frédéric Deloffre. Paris: Gallimard, 1990.

————. *Love Letters of a Portuguese Nun.* Trans. Guido Waldman. London: Harvill Press, 1996.

Hatzfeld, Adolphe, Arsène Darmsteter and Antoine Thomas. *Dictionnaire général de la langue Française du commencement du XVIIe siècle jusqu'à nos jours, précédé d'un traité de la formation de la langue.* Paris: Librairie Ch. Delagrave. 1964. [1890–93.] 2 vols.

Kuizenga: see Villedieu, Mme de.

La Fontaine, Jean de. *Contes et nouvelles.* Ed. Jacqueline Zeugschmitt. Paris: Nouvelle Librairie de France, 1959.

La Rivière, Louis de. *Histoire de la vie et moeurs de Marie Tessonnière, native de Valence en Dauphiné.* Lyon: C. Prost, 1650.

La Roberdiere, Sieur de. *L'Amant cloîtré ou les Avantures d'Oronce & d'Eugenie.* Amsterdam: Chez Daniel du Fresne, 1683.

La Vallière, Françoise de la Baume Le Blanc, Duchesse de. *Reflexions sur la misericorde de Dieu par une Dame penitente.* Huitiéme Edition augmentée. Paris, chez Antoine Dezallier, 1700. [Paris: A. Dezallier, 1680.]

Lafayette, Marie-Madeleine de. *Correspondance.* Ed. André Beaunier. Paris: Gallimard, 1942. 2 vols.

————. *The Princess of Clèves: Contemporary Reactions, Criticism.* Edited and with a revised translation by John D. Lyons. New York: W.W. Norton, 1994.

————. *La Princesse de Clèves.* in *Romans et Nouvelles.* Ed. Alain Niderst. Paris: Garnier, 1997.

Lebrun. *Les Amours libertines de religieuses du Couvent des Carmélites.* Brussels: Joostens, 1861.

Littré, Emile. *Dictionnaire de la langue française* [1881]. Paris: J.J. Pauvert, 1956–58. 5 vols.

Lourdelot, Jean. *La Courtisane solitaire.* Lyon: Chez Vincent de Coeursilly, 1622.

Macrobius, *Commentarii in somnium Scipionis. Commentary on the Dream of Scipio.* Trans. and ed. William Harris Stahl. New York: Columbia University Press, 1952.

Mailly, Chevalier de. *Avantures & lettres galantes.* Paris: Chez Guillaume de Luine, 1697.

Mancini, Hortense. *La Vérité dans son jour.* Ed. Patricia Cholakian and Elizabeth Goldsmith. Delmar, NY: Scholars' Facsimiles and Reprints, 1998.

————. *Memoirs.* Trans. Sarah Nelson. Chicago: University of Chicago Press, 2008.

Mancini, Hortense and Marie, *Mémoires d'Hortense et de Marie Mancini.* Ed. Gérard Doscot. Paris: Mercure de France, 1987.

Mancini, Marie. *Apologie, ou les Véritables mémoires de Mme Marie Mancini, connétable de Colonna, écrits par elle-même.* Leiden: Van Gelder, 1678.

[————.] *Les Mémoires de M.L.P.M.M. Colonna, G. Connétable du royaume de Naples.* Cologne: P. Marteau, 1676.

Marin, le père Michel Ange. *Adelaide de Witsbury, ou La Pieuse pensionnaire Avec sa retraite spirituelle de 8 jours.* 4th ed. Avignon: Chez Alexandre Giroud, 1750.

——. *Agnes de Saint-Amour, ou La fervente novice.* S.l: s.n., 1761–62. 2 vols.

——. *La Parfaite religieuse.* Avignon: Chez Alexandre Giroud, seul Imprimeur de Sa Sainteté, avec Permission des Superieurs, 1749. (Most recent ed. Lille, 1840.)

Marivaux, Pierre Carlet de Chamblain de. *La Vie de Marianne, ou les avantures de madame la comtesse de* ***. The Hague: Chez Jean Néaulme, 1742–47. Jacobus van der Schley and Simon Fokke, engravers. 12 vols.

——. *La Vie de Marianne.* Ed. Frédéric Deloffre. Paris: Garnier, 1963, 1990.

Mernissi, Fatima. *Dreams of Trespass: Tales of a Harem Girlhood.* Reading, MA: Addison-Wesley Publishing Company, 1994.

Les Metamorphoses de la religieuse. Amsterdam: Chez Schreuder, 1768.

Molière (Jean-Baptiste Poquelin). *Théâtre complet.* Paris: Garnier, 1962. 2 vols.

Montaigne, Michel de. *Essais.* Paris: Garnier, 1962. 2 vols.

——. *Montaigne's Essays and Selected Writings: A Bilingual Edition.* Trans. and Ed. Donald M. Frame. New York: St. Martin's Press, 1963.

Montpensier, Anne-Marie-Louise-d'Orléans, Duchesse de. *Lettres de Mademoiselle de Montpensier, de Mesdames de Motteville.* Paris: Collin, 1806.

——. *Mémoires.* Ed. Adolphe Cheruel. Paris: 1858–59. 4 vols. Charpentier, 1891–1902. Paris: Bibliothèque Nationale, 1978. Microform.

——. *Against Marriage: The Correspondence of la Grande Mademoiselle.* Ed. and trans. Joan DeJean. Chicago: University of Chicago Press, 2002.

Morrison, Toni. *Paradise.* New York: Alfred A. Knopf, 1998.

La Mothe Le Vayer, François. "De la vie privée." *Dialogues faits à l'imitation des anciens.* Paris: Fayard, 1988.

Murat, Comtesse de (Henriette de Castelnau). *La Défense des Dames, ou les Mémoires de la Comtesse de* ***. Paris: Chez C. Barbin, 1697. 2 vols.

Navarre, Marguerite de. *L'Heptaméron.* Ed. Michel François. Paris: Garnier, 1960.

——. *Heptaméron.* Paris: G.F. Flammarion, 1982.

Nelson: see Mancini, Hortense and Marie Mancini, *Memoirs.*

Nervèze, Antoine de. *Les Religieuses amours de Florigene et de Meleagre.* Dernière Edition. Paris: Chez A. du Breuil, 1602.

——. *Victoire de l'Amour Divin ... soubs les Amours de Polidor & de Virginie.* Paris: Antoine Du Breuil et Toussaint Du Bray, 1608.

——. *Les chastes et infortunées amours du Baron de l'Espine et de Lucrèce de la Prade.* Langres, 1598; Paris: 1598; Rouen, 1604. Republished in *Les Amours diverses divisées en sept histoires.* Paris: Toussaincts du Bray, 1605; and in *Les Amours diverses divisées en dix histoires.* Paris: Toussaincts du Bray, 1611, 1617.

——. *Le Iardin Sacré de l'Ame Solitaire* (1602). Paris: Toussaincts du Bray, 1612.

——. *L'Hermitage de l'Isle saincte.* Paris: Chez Antoine du Breuil et Toussaincts du Bray. 1612. Rouen: Chez Nicolas Loselet, 1615.

Norris, Kathleen. *Dakota.* New York: Ticknor & Fields, 1993.

Notes secrètes sur l'abbaïe de Longchamp en 1768. Paris: F. Henry, 1870.

Pascal, Blaise. *Oeuvres complètes*. Ed. Louis Lafuma. Paris: L'Intégrale, 1963.

———. *Pensées*. Ed. Philippe Sellier. Paris: Classiques Garnier, 1999.

Pluche, Antoine. *Histoire du ciel ou l'on recherche l'origine de l'idolâtrie*. Paris: Veuve Estienne, 1740.

Racine, Jean. *Phèdre*. In *Théâtre complet*. Ed. J. Morel and A. Viala. Paris: Garnier, 1995.

Recueil de quelques pièces nouvelles et galantes, tant en prose qu'en vers. Cologne: P. du Marteau, 1667.

La Religieuse esclave et mousquetaire. Histoire galante et veritable. Leipzig: Chez George Wertman, 1747.

La Religieuse penitente, nouvelle d'Artois. 1699.

Robert, Paul. *Dictionnaire alphabétique et analogue de la langue française*. Paris: Le Robert, 1968.

Rush, Norman. *Mating*. New York: Knopf, 1991. New York: Vintage, 1992.

Saint-Simon, Louis de Rouvray, duc de. *Mémoires (1701–07)*. vol. 2. Ed. Yves Coirot. Paris: Gallimard, 1983. Edition de la Pléiade.

Sales, François de. *Oeuvres*. Edition complète. Annecy: Monastère de la Visitation, 1892–1964. 25 vols.

———. *Introduction à la vie dévote*. Paris: Editions du Seuil, 1962.

———. *Traité de l'amour de Dieu*. Ed. André Ravier. Paris: Pléiade, 1969.

Sand, George. *Lélia*. Paris: Félix Bonnaire, 1839.

Segrais, Jean de. *Nouvelles françaises*. Paris: chez Guillaume Saucrin, 1722. vol. 1.

Sévigné, Marie de Rabutin Chantal. *Correspondance* I–III. Ed. Roger Duchêne. Paris: Gallimard, 1973. Edition de la Pléiade.

Schoonenbeck, Adrien. *Courte description des ordres des femmes et filles religieuses, contenant une petite relation de leur origine de leur progres et de leur confirmation et les figures de leurs habits gravés*. Amsterdam: Desbords, 1700.

Shepherd: see *Ancrene Wisse*.

Sorel, Charles. *L'anti-Roman, l'histore du berger Lysis*. Paris: Toussainct de Bray, 1633.

———. *La solitude et l'amour philosophique de Cléomède, Premier sujet des Exercises Moraux de M. Ch. Sorel, Conseiller du Roy & Historiographe de France*. Paris: Antoine de Sommaville, 1640.

———. *Relation véritable de ce qui s'est passé au royaume de Sophie, depuis les troubles excités par la rhétorique et l'éloquence. Avec un discours sur la Nouvelle Allégorique*. Paris: Charles de Sercy, 1659.

Tenain, Mme de. *La Religieuse intéressée et amoureuse avec l'Histoire du Comte de Clare, nouvelle galante*. Cologne, Chez ***, 1695.

Tencin, Mme de. *Mémoires du Comte de Comminges*. Paris: Mercure de France, 1996.

Teresa of Avila, St. *Interior Castle*. Trans. and ed. Allison Peers. Garden City, New York: Doubleday & Company, Inc., 1961.

———. *Constituciones*, 1681. In *Obras completas*. Ed. Efrén de la Madre de Dios and Otger Steggink. Madrid: Biblioteca de Autores Cristianos, 1986.

Thiers, Jean-Baptiste. *Traité de la clôture des religieuses*. Paris: Chez Antoine Dezallier, 1681.

Le Triomphe des Religieuses; ou les Nones Babillardes. Congo: chez Monomatapa, 1748. Préface by Michel Camus. (Same as *Les Delices du cloître*, above).

La Vie de la duchesse de La Valière par ***. Cologne: chez Jean de la Verité, 1665.

[Villedieu, Mme de]. *Mémoires de la Vie de Henriette-Sylvie de Molière* [1702]. Ed. Micheline Cuénin. Tours: Université de Tours, 1977.

———. "La Religieuse." In *Annales galantes* (1670). Ed. René Godenne. Geneva: Slatkine Reprints, 1979, 107–200.

———. *Mémoires de la vie de Henriette-Sylvie de Molière*. Ed. René Démoris. Paris: Editions Desjonquères, 2003.

———. *Memoirs of the Life of Henriette-Sylvie de Molière*. Trans. Donna Kuizenga. Chicago: University of Chicago Press, 2004.

Vitruvius, Pollio. *Les dix livres d'architecture de Vitruve*. 2nd ed. rev. cor., & aug. par M. Perrault. Paris: chez Jean-Baptiste Coignard, 1684. Facsimile ed. Liège: P. Mardaga, 1988.

Waldman: see Guilleragues, Gabriel de.

Secondary Sources

Abbaye Royale de Fontevraud. Centre Culturel de l'Ouest. *The Abbey of Fontevraud and the Fontevraud Order*. S.l: s.n, s.d. (18 p. pamphlet).

Abramovici, Jean-Christophe. "A qui profite le vice? Le topos du lecteur jouisseur de roman obscène." In Jan Herman, Paul Pelckmans and Nicole Boursier, eds. *L'Epreuve du lecteur: Livres et lectures dans le roman d'Ancien Régime*. Louvain: Peeters, 1995, 292–9.

Agrest, Diana, Patricia Conway and Leslie Kanes Weisman, eds. *The Sex of Architecture*. New York: Harry N. Abrams, Inc., 1996.

Ali, Ayaan Hirsi. *Infidel*. New York: Free Press, 2007.

André, Edouard. *Histoire de l'abbaye du Bricot en Brie (XIIème siècle–1792)*. Paris: Alphonse Picard & fils, 1895.

Ardener, Shirley, ed. *Women and Space*. New York: St. Martin's Press, 1981.

Assaf, Francis. "Henriette-Sylvie, objet du désir." *French Review* 73.3 (Feb. 2001), 518–26.

Aston, Nigel. *Religion and Revolution in France 1780–1804*. Washington, DC: Catholic University of America Press, 2000.

———. *Christianity and Revolutionary Europe c. 1750–1830*. Cambridge: Cambridge University Press, 2002.

Auerbach, Nina. *Communities of Women: An Idea in Fiction*. Cambridge, MA: Harvard University Press, 1978.

Bachelard, Gaston. *La poétique de l'espace*. 4th ed. Paris: Presses Universitaires de France, 1964.

Bakhtine, Mikhael. *Rabelais and His World*. Bloomington: Indiana University Press, 1984.

Baldner, Ralph W. *Bibliography of Seventeenth-Century Prose Fiction*. New York: Columbia University Press, 1967.

Bardet, Jean-Pierre. *Rouen aux XVIIe et XVIIIe siècles. Les mutations d'un espace social*. Paris: Société d'édition d'enseignement supérieur, 1983. Collection Regards sur l'histoire. Préface de Pierre Chaunu. 2 vols.

Bazin de Bezons, Jean de. *Vocabulaire de 'La Princesse de Clèves'*. Paris: Nizet, 1967.

Beasley, Faith. *Revising Memory: Women's Fiction and Memoirs in Seventeenth-Century France*. New Brunswick and London: Rutgers University Press, 1990.

Bell, David and Gill Valentine, eds. *Mapping Desire: Geographies of Sexualities*. London and New York: Routledge, 1995.

Ben Salem, Mahdia. *Louise Labé, Marguerite de Navarre et Madame de Lafayette: Trois voix féminines et espaces féminins retrouvés*. Ph.D. Dissertation, University of Tennessee, Knoxville, 1995.

Bernos, Marcel. *Femmes et gens d'église dans la France classique, XVIIe–XVIIIe siècle*. Paris: Les Editions du Cerf, 2003.

Best, Sue. "Sexualizing Space." In Elizabeth Grosz and Elspeth Probyn, eds. *Sexy Bodies: The Strange Carnalities of Feminism*. London: Routledge, 1995, 181–94.

Beugnot, Bernard. "Loisir, Retraite, Solitude: de l'espace privé à la littérature." In Marc Fumaroli et al., eds. *Le Loisir lettré à l'âge classique*. Geneva: Droz, 1996, 173–96.

———. "Pour une poétique de l'allégorie classique." In *Critique et création littéraires en France au XVIIe siècle*. Paris: Editions du C.N.R.S., 1977, 409–20.

———. *La mémoire du texte: essais de poétique classique*. Paris: Champion, 1994, 171–86.

Birely, Robert. *The Refashioning of Catholicism 1450–1700*. Washington, DC: The Catholic University of America Press, 1999.

Biver, Paul and Marie-Louise Biver. *Abbayes, monastères, couvents de femmes à Paris: des origines à la fin du XVIIIe siècle*. Paris: Presses Universitaires de France, 1975.

Bloomfield, Morton. "Allegory as Interpretation." *New Literary History* 3 (1972), 101–71.

Bluche, François. *La vie quotidienne au temps de Louis XIV*. Paris: Hachette, 1984.

Blunt, Anthony. *Art and Architecture in France 1500–1700*. 5th ed., rev. Richard Beresford. New Haven: Yale University Press, 1999.

Boddy, Janice. "Womb as Oasis: The Symbolic Context of Pharaonic Circumcision in Rural Northern Sudan." In Roger N. Lancaster and Micaela di Leonardo, eds. *The Gender/Sexuality Reader*. New York and London: Routledge, 1996, 309–24.

Boinet, Amédée. *Les Eglises parisiennes*. Paris: Editions de Minuit, 1962–64. 3 vols.

Bolton, Brenda M. "Mulieres sanctae," in Susan Mosher Stuard, ed. *Women in Medieval Society*. Philadelphia: University of Pennsylvania Press, 1976, 125–40.

Bourdieu, Pierre. *Outline of a Theory of Practice*. Cambridge: Cambridge University Press, 1977.

Boursier, Nicole. "Le Corps de Henriette-Sylvie." In *Le Corps au XVIIe siècle*. Ed. Ronald W. Tobin. *Biblio 17*, 89 (1995), 271–80.

———. "La Retraite au couvent dans *Les Mémoires de la vie de Henriette-Sylvie de Molière* et *La Princesse de Clèves*." In Colette Piau-Gillot, ed. *Topiques du dénouement romanesque du XVIIe au XVIIIe siècle*. Paris: Sator, 1995, 115–20.

Bradley, Ritamary. "Backgrounds of the Title 'Speculum' in Mediaeval Literature." *Speculum* 29.1 (January 1954), 100–115.

Brémond, Henri. *Histoire littéraire du sentiment religieux en France*. Paris: Librairie Armand Colin, 1967.

Brice, Germain. *Description de la ville de Paris*. 6th ed. Paris: F. Fournier, 1913. 2 vols.

Brugger, Walter. *Philosophical Dictionary*. Trans. Kenneth Baker. Spokane: Gonzaga University Press, 1972.

Brunet, Roger, Robert Ferras and Hervé Théry. *Les mots de la géographie, dictionnaire critique*. Montpellier: Reclus, and Paris: La Documentation française, 1992.

Burns, Sister Marie Patricia. *Saint-François de Sales, Sainte Jeanne de Chantal et la Visitation*. Veyrins: Edition du Champon, 1983.

Butler, Ruth and Parr, Hester, eds. *Mind and Body Spaces: Geographies of Illness, Impairment and Disability*. London: Routledge, 1999.

Carlin, Claire. "The Mancini Sisters and the Subversion of the Marriage Market." Conference paper, Society for Interdisciplinary French Seventeenth-Century Studies. October 1998. 14 pp.

Carrión, María M. *Arquitectura y cuerpo en la figura autorial de Teresa de Jesus*. Madrid: Anthropos, 1994.

Catholic Encyclopedia. New York: McGraw-Hill, 1967. vol. 9.

Cave, Terence. *Devotional Poetry in France c. 1570–1613*. London: Cambridge University Press, 1969.

Çelik, Zeynep. "Gendered Spaces in Colonial Algiers." In Diana Agrest, Patricia Conway and Leslie Weisman, eds. *The Sex of Architecture*. New York: Harry N. Abrams, 1996, 127–41.

Certeau, Michel de. *The Practice of Everyday Life*. Berkeley: University of California Press, 1984.

Chadwick, Owen, ed. *Western Asceticism*. Philadelphia: The Westminster Press, 1958.

Châtellier, Louis. *The Europe of the Devout: The Catholic Reformation and the Formation of a New Society*. Cambridge: Cambridge University Press; Paris: Editions de la Maison des Sciences de l'homme, 1989.

Chilcoat, Michelle. "Confinement, the Family Institution and the Case of Claire de Duras's *Ourika*." *French Forum* 37.3 (Fall 1998), 6–16.

Chill, Emanuel. "Religion and Mendicity in Seventeenth-Century France." *International Review of Social History* 7.3 (1962), 400–425.

Chitty, Derwas. *The Desert a City*. Oxford: Oxford University Press, 1966. London: Mobrays, 1977.

Cholakian, Patricia Francis. "A House of Her Own: Marginality and Dissidence in the "Mémoires" of La Grande Mademoiselle (1627–1693)." *Prose Studies* 9.3 (December 1986), 3–20.

Colegate, Isabel. *A Pelican in the Wilderness: Hermits, Solitaries and Recluses.* Washington, DC: Counterpoint, 2002.

Colinon, Maurice. *Guide des monastères.* Paris: Pierre Horay Editeur, 1994. 12th edition.

Colish, Marcia. *The Mirror of Language.* 1968. Rev. ed. Lincoln: University of Nebraska Press, 1983.

Colleu-Dumond, Chantal and Gérard Rondeau. *L'Abbaye de Fontevraud.* Paris: Robert Laffont, 2001.

Comenius, Johann Amos. *The Labyrinth of the World and the Paradise of the Heart.* Trans. Howard Louthan and Andrea Sterk. New York: Paulist Press, 1998.

Conley, Tom. *The Self-Made Map.* Minneapolis: University of Minnesota Press, 1996.

Copeland, Rita. "Medieval Theory and Criticism." In Michael Groden and Martin Kreiswirth, eds. *Johns Hopkins Guide to Literary Theory and Criticism.* Baltimore: Johns Hopkins University Press, 1997.

Costa, John. *Le Conflit moral dans l'oeuvre romanesque de Jean-Pierre Camus: 1584–1652.* New York: Burt Franklin & Co., 1974.

Couton, Georges. *Ecritures codées: essais sur l'allégorie au XVIIe siècle.* Paris: Klincksieck, 1990.

Cox, Marilyn. "The Bishop's Secret: Jean-Pierre Camus's Unacknowledged Source." *French Studies Bulletin* 77 (2000), 5–7.

Cryle, Peter. *The Telling of the Act: Sexuality as Narrative in Eighteenth- and Nineteenth-Century France.* Newark: University of Delaware Press, 2001.

Cyr, Miriam. *Letters of a Portuguese Nun: Uncovering the Mystery Behind a 17th Century Forbidden Love.* New York: Hyperion, 2006.

D'Monté, Rebecca and Nicole Pohl. *Female Communities 1600–1800.* Houndsmills, Hampshire: Macmillan; New York: St. Martin's Press, 2000.

Danahy, Michael. *The Femininization of the Novel.* Gainesville: Florida University Press, 1991. 101–25.

Davis, Natalie Z. "Women on Top." In *Society and Culture in Early Modern France.* Stanford: Stanford University Press, 1975, 125–51.

DeJean, Joan. *Tender Geographies.* New York: Columbia University Press, 1991.
———. *The Reinvention of Obscenity: Sex, Lies, and Tabloids in Early Modern France.* Chicago: University of Chicago Press, 2002.

Delmas, Claire. "Une histoire spirituelle en images: le retable et le tabernacle du monastère Sainte-Claire de Mur-de-Barrez." In *Sainte-Claire en Rouergue.* Paris: Les Amis de Sainte Claire Aujourd'hui, 1994, 122–9.

DeLorme, Eleanor P. *Garden Pavilions and the 18th Century French Court.* Woodbridge, Suffolk: Antique Collectors Club, 1996.

Delumeau Jean. *Catholicism Between Luther and Voltaire.* London: Burns & Oates, 1977.

Démoris, René. *Le Roman à la première personne*. Paris: Droz, 2002. First published 1975.

———. "Écriture féminine en je et subversion des savoirs chez Mme de Villedieu (*Les Mémoires d'Henriette-Sylvie de Molière*)." In C. Nativel, ed. *Femmes savantes, savoirs des femmes*. Geneva: Droz, 1999, 197–208.

———. "Aux frontières de l'impensé: Marivaux et la sexualité." In Franck Salaün, ed. *Pensée de Marivaux*. Amsterdam and New York: Rodopi, 2002, 69–83.

Desan, Suzanne. *Reclaiming the Sacred: Lay Religion and Popular Politics in Revolutionary France*. Ithaca: Cornell University Press, 1990.

Díaz Balsera, Viviana. *The Pyramid under the Cross*. Tucson: University of Arizona Press, 2005.

Dictionnaire de l'Académie française. 8th ed. Paris: Hachette, 1932. 2 vols.

Dictionnaires du XVIe et XVIIe siècles. CD-Rom. Paris: Champion Électronique, 1998.

Didier, Béatrice. "Images du sacré chez Diderot. " *Travaux de littérature* 6 (1993), 193–209.

Diefendorf, Barbara. "Discerning Spirits: Women and Spiritual Authority in Counter-Reformation France." In Margaret Mikesell and Adele Seeff, eds. *Culture and Change: Attending to Early Modern Women*. Newark: University of Delaware Press, 2003, 241–65.

Domosh, Mona. *Putting Women in Place*. New York: The Guilford Press, 2001.

Dubois, J. and R. Lagane. *Dictionnaire de la langue française classique*. Paris: Belin, 1960.

Duboy, Philippe. *Jean-Jacques Lequeu: An Architectural Enigma*. London: Thames & Hudson, 2002.

Duby, Georges. *Women of the Twelfth Century*. Trans. Jean Birrell. Berkeley: University of California Press, 1997.

Duggan, Anne E. "The Virgin and the Whore: Images of the Catholic Church and Protestant Heresy in Camus." In *Relations and Relationships in Seventeenth-Century Literature*. Ed. Jennifer Perlmutter. Tübingen: Gunter Narr Verlag, 2006, 133–41.

Duncan, Nancy, ed. *Body Space: Destabilizing Geographies of Gender and Sexuality*. New York: Routledge, 1996.

Duport, Danièle. "'De la solitude' ou 'l'arrière boutique' de Montaigne." *Bulletin de la Société des amis de Montaigne* 8.15–16 (July–December 1999), 88–98.

Durand, Béatrice. "Diderot and the Nun: Portrait of the Artist as a Transvestite." In Thaïs Morgan, ed. *Men Writing the Feminine*. Albany: SUNY Press, 1994, 89–106.

[Sister Elizabeth]. *Les origines de notre monastère et un aperçu de son histoire*. Photocopy, Monastère Sainte Claire, Mur de Barrez. n.d. 49 pp.

Elm, Suzanna. *'Virgins of God': The making of Asceticism in Late Antiquity*. Oxford: Clarendon Press, 1994.

Encyclopedia of the Early Church. New York: Oxford University Press, 1962.

Fein, P. L.-M. "The Convent School as Depicted through the Characters of Certain French Eighteenth-Century Novels." *Studies on Voltaire and the Eighteenth Century* 264 (1989), 737–41.

Fiévet, Michel, *L'Invention de l'école des filles: Des amazones de Dieu aux 17ème et 18ème siècles*. Paris: Imago, 2006.

Fletcher, Angus. *Allegory: The Theory of a Symbolic Mode*. Ithaca: Cornell University Press, 1964.

Foucault, Michel. *Histoire de la folie*. Paris: Gallimard, 1972.

———. *Surveiller et punir*. Paris: Gallimard, 1975.

———. *Power/Knowledge*. Ed. Colin Gordon. New York: Pantheon, 1980.

———. "Of Other Spaces." *Diacritics* 16 (Spring, 1986), 22–7.

Fowler, J.E. "Competing Causalities: Family and Convent in Diderot's *La Religieuse*." *The Eighteenth Century* 37.1 (1996), 75–93.

Fragonard, Marie-Madeleine. "La notion d'image: un confluent du discours théologique et du discours littéraire." *Figures* 5 (1990), 67–88.

Franchetti, Anna Lia. "Travestissements romanesques de J.-P. Camus." *Perspectives de la recherche sur le genre narratif français du dix-septième siècle*. Pisa-Geneva: Edizioni ETS-Editions Slatkine, 2000, 107–28.

Frank, Ellen Eve. *Literary Architecture*. Berkeley: University of California Press, 1979.

Freedberg, David. *The Power of Images: Studies in the History and Theory of Response*. Chicago and London: University of Chicago Press, 1991.

Gaines, James F. "Socio-spiritual Suasion: François de Sales and the Bees." In *Relations and Relationships in Seventeenth-Century Literature*. Ed. Jennifer Perlmutter. Tübingen: Gunter Narr Verlag, 2006, 143–52.

Garapon, Jean. "Mademoiselle à Saint-Fargeau: la découverte de l'écriture." *Papers on French Seventeenth Century Literature* 22.42 (1995), 36–47.

Genette, Gérard. *Figures, essais*. Paris: Editions du Seuil, 1966.

———. *Seuils*. Paris: Seuil, 1987.

Gilchrist, Roberta. *Gender and Material Culture: The Archaeology of Religious Women*. London and New York: Routledge, 1994.

Giraud, Yves. "Parlez-nous d'amour: Roman et sentiment chez Nervèze." *Travaux de littérature* 6 (1993), 103–24.

Goebel, Rolf J. "Berlin's Architectural Citations: Reconstruction, Simulation, and the Problem of Historical Authenticity." *PMLA* 118.5 (October 2003), 1268–89.

Gold, Penny Schine. *The Lady and the Virgin*. Chicago: University of Chicago Press, 1985.

Goldsmith, Elizabeth. "Publishing the Lives of Hortense and Marie Mancini." In *Going Public: Women and Publishing in Early Modern France*. Ed. Elizabeth C. Goldsmith and Dena Goodman. Ithaca: Cornell University Press, 1995, 30–45.

Gooden, Angelica. *Diderot and the Body*. Oxford: Legenda, 2001.

Gotter, Léonard. *Livres à figures édités en France de 1601 à 1660*. Paris: J. Duportal, 1914.

Graham, Ruth. "The Married Nuns before Cardinal Caprara." In *Pratiques religieuses mentalités et spiritualités dans l'Europe révolutionnaire (1770–1820)*. Turnhout: Brepols, 1999, 321–31.

Greer, Margaret Rich. *María de Zayas Tells Baroque Tales of Love and the Cruelty of Men*. University Park, PA: Pennyslvania State University Press, 2000.

Griffin, Susan M. "Awful Disclosures: Women's Evidence in the Escaped Nun's Tale." *PMLA* 111.1 (January 1996), 93–107.

Groden, Michael, Martin Kreiswirth and Imre Szeman, eds. *The Johns Hopkins Guide to Literary Theory & Criticism*. 2nd ed. Baltimore, MD: Johns Hopkins University Press, 1997. http://litguide.press.jhu.edu/.

Grosz, Elizabeth. "Bodies-Cities." In Beatriz Colomina, ed. *Sexuality and Space*. Princeton, NJ: Princeton Architectural Press, 1992, 241–53.

Hammons, Pamela S. "Robert Herrick's Gift Trouble: Male Subjects 'Trans-shifting' into Objects." *Criticism* 47.1 (Winter, 2005), 31–64.

Harth, Erica. *Cartesian Women*. Ithaca: Cornell University Press, 1992.

———. "An Official 'Nouvelle." In Marie-Madeleine de Lafayette, *The Princess of Clèves: Contemporary Reactions, Criticism*. Edited and with a revised translation by John D. Lyons. New York: W.W. Norton, 1994, 230–39.

Harvey, Andrew, ed. *The Essential Gay Mystics*. Edison, NJ: Castle Books, 1997.

Hasquenoph, Sophie. "Faire retraite au couvent dans le Paris des Lumières." *Revue Historique* 598 (1966), 353–65.

Hayes, Julie. "Retrospection and Contradiction in Diderot's *La Religieuse*." *Romanic Review* 77.3 (May 1986), 233–42.

Heilbrun, Carolyn. *Writing a Woman's Life*. New York: Norton, 1988.

Hillier, Bill and Julienne Hanson. *The Social Logic of Space*. Cambridge: Cambridge University Press, 1984.

Hills, Helen, ed. *Architecture and the Politics of Gender in Early Modern Europe*. Aldershot, England, and Burlington, VT: Ashgate, 2003.

———. *Invisible City: The Architecture of Devotion in Seventeenth-Century Neapolitan Convents*. Oxford: Oxford University Press, 2004.

Hoffman Philip T. *Growth in a Traditional Society: The French Countryside 1450–1815*. Princeton: Princeton University Press, 1996.

Hufton, Olwen. *Women and the Limits of Citizenship in the French Revolution*. Toronto: University of Toronto Press 1992.

Hufton, Olwen and F. Tallet. "Communities of Women: The Religious Life and Public Service in Eighteenth-Century France." In M.J. Boxer and J.H. Quaetert, eds. *Connecting Spheres: Women in the Western World 1500 to the Present*. Oxford: Oxford University Press, 1987, 75–85.

Hunt, Lynn, ed. *The Invention of Pornography: Obscenity and the Origins of Modernity, 1500–1800*. New York: Zone Books; Cambridge, MA: Distributed by MIT Press, 1993.

Jansen, Guido and Peter C. Sutton. *Michael Swerts 1618–1664*. Amsterdam: Rijksmuseum, 2002.

Jedin, Hubert. "Catholic Reformation or Counter-Reformation?" *The Counter-Reformation: The Essential Readings*. Ed. David M. Luebke. Oxford: Blackwell Publishers, 1999, 19–45.

Jensen, Katherine A. "Male Models of Feminine Epistolarity; or, How to Write Like a Woman in Seventeenth-Century France." *Writing the Female Voice*. Ed. Elizabeth C. Goldsmith. Boston: Northeastern University Press, 1989, 25–45.

Johnson, Penelope D. *Equal in Monastic Profession: Religious Women in Medieval France*. Chicago: University of Chicago Press, 1991.

Jones, Coliny. *The Charitable Imperative: Hospitals and Nursing in Ancien Régime and Revolutionary France*. NY: Routledge, 1989.

Jones, John Paul III, Heidi J. Nast and Susan M. Roberts, eds. *Thresholds in Feminist Geography: Difference, Methodology, Representation*. Lanham, MD: Rowman & Littlefield, 1997.

Jouhaud, Christian. "Roman historié et histoire romancée: Jean-Pierre Camus et Charles Sorel." *XVIIe siècle* no 215, 54e année, no 2 (2002), 307–16.

Julien, Dominique. "Locus Hystericus: L'Image du couvent dans *La Religieuse* de Diderot." *French Forum* 15.2 (May 1990), 133–48.

Kamuf, Peggy. *Fictions of Feminine Desire: Disclosures of Eloise*. Lincoln: University of Nebraska Press, 1982.

Kauffman, Linda S. *Discourses of Desire: Gender, Genre, and Epistolary Fictions*. Ithaca: Cornell University Press, 1986.

Kerr, John M. *Proserpinan Memory in Dante and Chaucer*. Ph.D. Dissertation, University of Notre Dame, 2001.

Kidd, Sue Monk. *The Secret Life of Bees*. New York: Viking, 2002.

Klinkenborg, Verlyn. "The Prairie as an Act of Devotion." Review of Kathleen Norris, *Dakota. New York Times Book Review*. February 14, 1993, 8.

Kuizenga, Donna. "'La Lecture d'une si ennuyeuse histoire': Topoï de la lecture et du livre dans les *Mémoires de la vie de Henriette-Sylvie de Molière*." In Jan Herman and Paul Pelckmans, eds. *L'Epreuve du lecteur: Livres et lectures dans le roman d'Ancien Régime*. Louvain-Paris: Editions Peeters, 1995, 120–28.

———. "'Fine veuve' ou 'veuve d'une haute vertu'? Portraits de la veuve chez Mme de Villedieu." *Cahiers du Dix-Septième* 7.1 (Spring 1997), 227–39.

———. "The Play of Pleasure and the Pleasure of Play in the *Mémoires de la vie de Henriette-Sylvie de Molière*." In Roxanne Decker Lalande, ed. *A Labor of Love: Critical Reflections on the Writings of Marie-Catherine Desjardins (Mme de Villedieu)*. Madison, NJ: Fairleigh Dickinson University Press, 2000, 147–61.

Labarge, Margaret Wade. *A Small Sound of the Trumpet: Women in Medieval Life*. Boston: Beacon Press, 1986.

Lalande, Roxanne Decker, ed. *A Labor of Love: Critical Reflections on the Writings of Marie-Catherine Desjardins (Mme de Villedieu)*. Madison, NJ: Fairleigh Dickinson University Press, 2000.

Laurie, Nina, et al. *Geographies of New Femininities*. Harlow, England: Longman; New York: Pearson Education, 1999.

Lawrence, C.H. *Medieval Monasticism: Forms of Religious Life in Western Europe in the Middle Ages*. London and New York: Longman, 1984.

Lehfeldt, Elizabeth. "Spatial Discipline and its Limits: Nuns and the Built Environment in Early Modern Spain." In Helen Hills, ed. *Architecture and the Politics of Gender in Early Modern Europe*. Aldershot, Hants, England; Burlington, VT: Ashgate, 2003, 131–49.

Lemoine, Dom Robert. *Le monde des religieux: l'epoque moderne*. Paris: Editions Cujas, 1976. Histoire de Droit et des Institutions de l'Eglise en Occident, 15.2: *La Vie Religieuse féminine*.

Lever, Maurice. *La fiction narrative en prose au XVIIe siècle*. Paris: CNRS, 1976.

Lierheimer, Linda. "Redefining Convent Space: Ideals of Female Community among Seventeenth-Century Ursuline Nuns." *Proceedings of the Western Society for French History* 24 (1997), 211–20.

Longhurst, Robyn. *Bodies: Exploring Fluid Boundaries*. London and New York: Routledge, 2001.

Lowe, K.J.P. *Nuns' Chronicles and Convent Culture: Women and History Writing in Renaissance and Counter-Reformation Italy*. Cambridge: Cambridge University Press, 2003.

Lu, Jin. "Ecriture féminine? Marivaux, Mme Riccoboni et leurs 'Marianne.'" *Raison présente* 132 (1999), 87–100.

Lusseau, Patricia. *L'Abbaye royale de Fontevraud aux XVIIe et XVIIIe siècles*. Maulevrier: Herault-Editions, 1986.

Lyons, John D. See Lafayette, Marie-Madeleine de.

McAlpin, Mary. "Poststructuralist Feminism and the Imaginary Woman Writer: The *Lettres Portugaises*." *The Romanic Review* 90 (1999), 27–44.

Macarthur, Elizabeth. *Extravagant Narratives: Closure and Dynamics in the Epistolary Form*. Princeton: Princeton University Press, 1990.

McDowell, Linda. *Gender, Identity and Place*. Minneapolis: University of Minnesota Press, 1999.

McLeod, Arlene. *Accommodating Protest: Working Women, the New Veiling and Change in Cairo*. New York: Columbia University Press, 1991.

Mahmood, Saba. *Politics of Piety: The Islamic Revival and the Feminist Subject*. Princeton, NJ: Princeton University Press, 2005.

Makowski, Elizabeth. *Canon Law and Cloistered Women*. Washington, DC: The Catholic University of America Press, 1997.

Martin, Carole. "Legacies of the Convent in Diderot's *La Religieuse*." *Studies in Eighteenth-Century Culture* 25 (1996), 117–29.

Martin, Eva, and Dorothy Wynne Zimmerman, eds. *French Women Writers*. Lincoln: University of Nebraska Press, 1994. 153–60.

May, Georges. *Diderot et 'La Religieuse': étude historique et littéraire*. New Haven, CT: Yale University Press; Paris: Presses universitaires de France, 1954.

Mayer, Denise. "Mademoiselle de Montpensier et l'architecture." *Dix-septième siècle* 118–119 (1978), 57–71.

Medioli, Francesca. "The Dimensions of the Cloisters: Enclosure, Constraint and Protection in Seventeenth-Century Italy." In Anne Jacobson Schutte et al., eds. *Time, Space and Women's Lives in Early Modern Europe*. Kirksville, MO: Truman State University Press, 2001. Sixteenth Century Essays & Studies, vol. 57, 165–80.

Melnick, Arthur. *Space, Time and Thought in Kant*. Dordrecht and Boston: Kluwer Academic Publishers, 1989.

Melot, Michel. "Le pouvoir des abbesses de Fontevraud et la révolte des hommes." In Kathleen Wilson-Chevalier and Eliane Viennot, eds. *Royaume de fémynie: pouvoirs, contraintes, espaces de liberté des femmes de la Renaissance à la Fronde*. Paris: Champion, 1999, 135–45.

Melot, Michel and C. Joubert. "Abbaye de Fontevraud." *Monuments Historiques de la France* 1973 (3e semestre), 3–16.

Méniel, Bruno. "La disposition des *Amours diverses* d'Antoine de Nervèze." *Etudes françaises* 38.3 (2002), 93–105.

Merlin, Hélène. "Fables of the 'Mystical Body' in Seventeenth-Century France." In *Corps mystique, corps sacré: Textual Transfigurations of the Body from the Middle Ages to the Seventeenth Century*. Yale French Studies 86 (1994), 126–42.

Mesa-Pelly, Judith Broome. *Fictive Domains: Nostalgic Constructions of Body and Language in the Eighteenth Century*. Ph.D. Dissertation, University of Miami, 1999.

Mignot, Claude. "Mademoiselle et son château de Saint-Fargeau." *Papers on French Seventeenth Century Literature* 22.42 (1995), 36–47.

Miller, John Hillis. "The Two Allegories." In Morton Bloomfield, ed. *Allegory, Myth and Symbol*. Cambridge, MA: Harvard University Press, 1981, 355–70.

Miller, Nancy K. "'I's' in Drag: The Sex of Recollection." *The Eighteenth Century: Theory and Interpretation* 22 (1981), 47–57.

Miller, Paul Allen. "Disciplining the Lesbian: Diderot's *La Religieuse*." *Intertexts* 5.2 (2001), 168–81.

Molinié, Georges. "Eros episcopal." *Langue, Littérature du XVIIe et du XVIIIe siècle*. Mélanges offerts à M. le Professeur Frédéric Deloffre. Paris: Sedes, 1990, 55–60.

Le Monastère de Ste-Claire: Un Tricentenaire 1653–1953. Rodez: s.n., 1953. (Pamphlet).

Mortimer, Armine Kotin. "Naïve and devious: *La Religieuse*." *Romanic Review* 88.2 (March, 1997), 241–51.

Nast, Heidi J. and Steve Pile, eds. *Places through the Body*. London and New York: Routledge, 1998.

New Catholic Encyclopedia. New York: McGraw-Hill, 1967–88.

Nichols, John A. and Lillian Thomas Shank, eds. *Distant Echoes*. Kalamazoo: Cistercian Publications, 1984. Medieval Religious Women 1. Cistercian Studies 17.

Noon, Patrick J., and Stephen Bann. *Crossing the Channel: British and French Painting in the Age of Romanticism*. London: Tate Pub., 2003.

Oddo, Nancy. "Antoine de Nervèze: Pieux Protée ou caméléon mondain?" *Littératures classiques* 31 (Autumn 1999), 39–62.

————. "L'Invention du roman au XVIIe siècle: littérature religieuse et matière romanesque." *XVIIe Siècle* n° 215, 54e année n. 2 (2002), 221–34.

Paige, Nicolas D. *Being Interior*. Philadelphia: University of Pennsylvania Press, 2001.

Papasogli, Benedetta. *Le fond du coeur*. Paris: Champion, 2000.

Pelckmans, Paul. "Dieu soit béni qui veut que je vous aime …" in Franck Salaûn, ed. *Pensées de Marivaux*. Amsterdam and New York: Rodopi, 2002, 23–34.

Pitts, Leonard, Jr. "Wedding Bell Blues." *The Miami Herald*, May 19, 2003. B1

Pitts, Vincent J. *La Grande Mademoiselle at the Court of France*. Baltimore & London: The Johns Hopkins University Press, 2000.

Ponton, Jeanne. *La Religieuse dans la littérature française*. Québec: Presses de l'Université Laval, 1969.

Port-Royal et la Vie Monastique: actes du colloque tenu à Orval, Belgique, les 2 et 3 octobre 1987. Paris: Bibliothèque Mazarine, 1997. *Chroniques de Port-Royal* 37.

Pósfay, Eva. *L'Espace architectural et le désir féminin dans les oeuvres de Madame de Lafayette*. Ph.D. Dissertation, Princeton, 1990.

Probes, Christine McCall. "Le Couvent comme prison: l'emprisonnement des femmes et des enfants réformés, leur captivité dans les couvents." In Claire Carlin, ed. *La Rochefoucauld, Mithridate, Frères et soeurs, Les muses soeurs: actes du 29e congrès annuel de la North American Society for Seventeenth-Century French Literature, The University of Victoria, 3-5 avril 1997*. Biblio 17, 111. Tübingen: Narr, 1998, 205–13.

Quilligan, Maureen. "Allegory, Allegoresis and the Deallegorization of Language." In Morton Bloomfield, ed. *Allegory, Myth and Symbol*. Cambridge, MA: Harvard University Press, 1981, 163–86.

Ranft, Patricia. *Women and the Religious Life in Premodern Europe*. New York: MacMillan 1996, 1998.

Ranum, Orest. "The Refuges of Intimacy." In Philippe Ariès and Georges Duby, eds. *A History of Private Life*. vol. III: *Passions of the Renaissance*. Cambridge: Harvard University Press, 1989, 207–63.

Rapley, Elizabeth. *The Dévotes: Women and Church in Seventeenth-Century France*. Montreal & Kingston: McGill-Queens University Press, 1990.

————. "Her Body the Enemy: Self-Mortification in Seventeenth-Century Convents." *Proceedings of the Annual Meeting of the Western Society for French History* 21 (1994), 25–35.

————. *A Social History of the Cloister*. Montreal and Kingston: McGill-Queens University Press, 2001.

Reau, Louis. *Les monuments détruits de l'art français: histoire du vandalisme*. vol. 2: 19e siècle. Paris: Hachette, 1959.

Rex, Walter E. "Secrets from Suzanne: The Tangled Motives of *La Religieuse*." *The Eighteenth Century: Theory and Interpretation* 24 (Fall, 1983), 184–98.

Reynes, Geneviève. *Couvents de femmes: La vie des religieuses cloîtrées dans la France des XVIIe et XVIIIe siècles*. Paris: Fayard, 1987.

Reynier, Gustave. *Le roman sentimental avant l'Astrée.* Paris: A. Colin, 1908. Geneva: Slatkine, 1969.

Rivara, Annie. *Les Sœurs de Marianne: suites, imitations, variations 1731–1761.* Oxford, England: Voltaire Foundation, 1991. Studies in Voltaire and the Eighteenth Century 285.

Rivers, Christopher. "Safe Sex: The Prophylactic Walls of the Cloister in the French Libertine Convent Novel of the Eighteenth Century." *Journal of the History of Sexuality* 5.3 (1995), 381–401.

Robertson, Elizabeth. "An Anchorhold of Her Own: Female Anchoritic Literature in Thirteenth-Century England." In Julia Bolton Holloway, Joan Bechtold and Constance C. Wright, eds. *Equally in God's Image: Women in the Middle Ages.* New York: Peter Lang, 1990, 170–83.

Robic-de Baecque, Sylvie. "*L'Eloge des Histoires dévotes*, ou l'apologétique romanesque de Jean-Pierre Camus." *Cahiers du dix-septième* 7.1 (Spring 1977), 31–45.

———. *Le Salut par l'excès. Jean-Pierre Camus (1584–1652): la poétique d'un évêque romancier.* Geneva: Diffusion Slatkine, 1999.

Rodaway, Paul. *Sensuous Geographies: Body, Sense and Place.* London, New York: 1994.

Rodgers, Silvia. "Women's Space in a Men's House: The British House of Commons," in Shirley Ardener, ed. *Women and Space.* New York: St. Martin's Press, 1981, 50–71.

Rogers, Elizabeth Barlow. *Landscape Design: A Cultural and Architectural History.* New York: Harry N. Abrams, Inc., 2001.

Rogers, Katherine M. "Fantasy and Reality in Fictional Convents of the Eighteenth Century." *Comparative Literature Studies* 22.3 (Fall 1985), 297–315.

Rousseau, François. "Histoire de l'Abbaye de Pentemont depuis sa translation à Paris jusqu'à la Révolution." *Mémoires de la société de l'histoire de Paris et de l'île de France* 45 (1918), 171–227.

Rowan, Mary H. "Between Salon and Convent: Madame de Rohan, a Precious Abbess." In Jean-Jacques Demorest and Lise Leibacher-Ouvrard, eds. *Pascal, Corneille. Désert, retraite, engagement.* Paris: *Papers on French 17th Century Literature*, 1984, 305–21.

———. "The Song of Songs in Conventual Discourse." *Papers on French Seventeenth Century Literature* 22 (1995), 109–17.

Rustin, Jacques. "*La Religieuse* de Diderot: Mémoires ou journal intime?" In *Le vice revisité: Vérité et Mensonge dans le roman des Lumières.* Strasbourg: Presses Universitaires de Strasbourg, 2003, 209–29.

Sainte-Claire en Rouergue. Conférences du Colloque de Millau (29 septembre–3 octobre 1993). Millau: Les Amis de Sainte Claire Aujourd'hui, 1994.

Sarraute, Nathalie. *L'ère du soupçon: essais sur le roman.* Paris: Gallimard, 1956.

Schmidt, Alvin J. *Veiled and Silenced: How Culture Shaped Sexist Theology.* Macon, GA: Mercer University Press, 1989.

Schulenberg, Jane Tibbetts. "Strict Active Enclosure and Its Effects on the Female Monastic Experience (ca. 500–1100)." In John A. Nichols, ed. *Distant Echoes: Medieval Religious Women*. Kalamazoo: Cistercian Publ. 1984. vol. 1, 51–86.

Sellier, Philippe. "Port-Royal: un emblême de la réforme catholique." *Port Royal et la Vie Monastique: actes du colloque tenu à Orval (Belgique) les 2 et 3 octobre 1987. Chroniques de Port-Royal* 37 (1997), 15–26.

———. *Port-Royal et la littérature* I. Paris: Champion, 1999.

Senior, Matt, "Confining Humans, Confining Animals: The Salpétrière and the Ménagerie." Conference paper, SE 17, Society for Interdisiplinary French Studies, 28–30 October 2004, College of William and Mary, Williamsburg, Virginia.

Shoemaker, Peter. "Violence and Piety in Jean-Pierre Camus's *Histoires tragiques*." *French Review* 79.3 (February 2006), 549–60.

Simons, Walter. *Cities of Ladies: Beguine Communities in the Medieval Low Countries, 1200–1565*. Philadelphia: University of Pennsylvania Press, 2001.

Skinner, Mary. "Benedictine Life for Women in Central France, 850–1100: A Feminist Revival." In John A. Nichols and Lillian Thomas Shank, eds. *Distant Echoes*. Kalamazoo: Cistercian Publications, 1984, 87–113.

Smith, Sidonie and Julia Watson, eds. *Women, Autobiography, Theory: A Reader*. Madison, WI: University of Wisconsin Press, 1998.

Soja, E.J. *Postmodern Geographies*. London: Verso, 1989.

Sorabji, Richard. *Matter, Space and Motion*. Ithaca: Cornell University Press, 1988.

Spain, Daphne. *Gendered Spaces*. Chapel Hill: University of North Carolina Press, 1992.

Steiner, Prudence. "A Garden of Spices in New England: John Cotton's and Edward Taylor's Use of the Song of Songs." In Morton Bloomfield, ed. *Allegory, Myth and Symbol*. Cambridge, MA: Harvard University Press, 1981, 27–44.

Sullivan, Andrew. "The Saint and the Satirist." *New York Times Book Review*. May 30, 2004, 11.

Taussat, Robert. "Saint François d'Assise en Rouergue: Frères mineurs, Clarisses et Soeurs Franciscaines, du XIIIe siècle à nos jours." In *Sainte-Claire en Rouergue*. Paris: Les Amis de Sainte Claire Aujourd'hui, 1994, 63–75.

Taveneaux, René. *Le catholicisme dans la France classique*. Paris: Hachette, 1973.

Teather, Elizabeth Kenworthy, ed. *Embodied Geographies: Spaces, Bodies and Rites of Passage*. London and New York: Routledge, 1999.

Thomas, Anabel. *Art and Piety in the Female Religious Communities of Renaissance Italy*. Cambridge: Cambridge University Press, 2003.

Timmermans, Linda. *L'Accès des femmes à la culture (1598–1715)*. Paris: Champion, 1993.

Torres Sánchez, Concha. *La clausura imposible: conventualismo femenino y expansión contrarreformista*. Madrid: Asociación Cultural Al-Mudayna, 2000.

Trabulse, Elías. *La muerte de sor Juana*. Mexico, D.F.: Centro de Estudios de Historia de México Condumex, 1999.

Turner, James. *Schooling Sex: Libertine Literature and Erotic Education in Italy, France, and England, 1534–1685*. Oxford and New York: Oxford University Press, 2003.

Undank, Jack. "Diderot's 'Unnatural' Acts: Lessons from the Convent." *French Forum* 11.2 (May 1986), 151–67.

Les Ursulines a Nantes: de 1627 à nos jours. [Nantes]: [Communauté des Ursulines de Blanche de Castille, Ouvrière Vannetaise], s.d.

Van Dyke, Carolyn. *The Fiction of Truth: Structures of Meaning in Narrative and Dramatic Allegory*. Ithaca and London: Cornell University Press, 1985.

Van Kley, Dale K. *The Religious Origins of the French Revolution*. New Haven and London: Yale University Press, 1996.

Verdier, Gabrielle. "*Lire Nervèze?* Rhetoric and Readability in Early Seventeenth-Century Narrative." *Papers on French Seventeenth Century Literature* 12.23 (1985), 431–49.

Verdon, Jean. "Les moniales dans la France de l'Ouest au XIe et XIIe siècles: Etude d'histoire sociale." *Cahiers de civilisation médiévale* 19.3 (1976), 247–64.

Vernet, Max. *Jean-Pierre Camus: théorie de la contre-littérature*. Paris: Nizet, 1995.

Vessier, Maximilien. *La Pieté-Salpétrière: quatre siècles d'histoire et d'histoires*. Paris: Hôpital de la Piété-Salpétrière, 1999.

Vidler, Anthony. *The Architectural Uncanny: Essays in the Modern Unhomely*. Cambridge, MA: MIT Press, 1992.

Viguerie, Jean de. "Y a-t-il une crise de l'observance régulière entre 1660 et 1715?" In *Sous la règle de saint Benoît. Structures monastiques et société*. Geneva: Droz, 1982, 135–47. Ecole pratique des hautes études: Hautes études médiévales et modernes, 47.

Walker, Claire. *Gender and Politics in Early Modern Europe: English Convents in France and the Low Countries*. Houndmills, Basingstoke, Hampshire and New York: Palgrave Macmillan, 2003.

Ward, William Henry. *The Architecture of the Renaissance in France*. London: B.T. Batsford, and New York: Charles Scribner's Sons, 1911, 2 vols.

Weber, Caroline. "The Sins of the Father: Colonialism and Family History in Diderot's *Le fils naturel*." *PMLA* 118.3 (May 2003), 488–501.

Weinberg, Kurt. "The Lady and the Unicorn, or M. de Nemours à Coulommiers," in Marie-Madeleine de Lafayette, *The Princess of Clèves: Contemporary Reactions, Criticism*. Edited and with a revised translation by John D. Lyons. New York: W.W. Norton, 1994, 190–205.

Weisman, Leslie Kanes. *Discrimination by Design: A Feminist Critique of the Man-Made Environment*. Urbana and Chicago: University of Illinois Press, 1994.

Wetsel, David, and Frédéric Canovas, eds. *Les femmes au Grand Siècle, le baroque, musique et littérature, musique et liturgie: actes du 33e congrès annuel de la North American Society for Seventeenth-Century French Literature, Arizona State University*. Tübingen: G. Narr, 2003.

Weymuller, François. *Histoire d'Epinal des origines à nos jours*. Le Coteau: Ed. Hovarth, 1985.

Whitman, Jon. *Allegory*. Cambridge, MA: Harvard University Press, 1987.

Williams, George H. *Wilderness and Paradise in Christian Thought*. New York: Harper & Brothers Publishers, 1962.

Williams, Ralph C. *Bibliography of the Seventeenth-Century Novel in France*. New York: The Century Co., 1931.

Winner, Lauren F. "Goodbye to God. Also Hello." *New York Times*, Books Section, April 25, 2004 (review of Karen Armstrong, *The Spiral Staircase*), 14.

Wise, Margaret. "Villedieu's Transvestite Text: The Literary Economy of Genre and Gender in *Les Mémoires de la vie de Henriette-Sylvie de Molière*." In Roxanne Decker Lalande, ed. *A Labor of Love: Critical Reflections on the Writings of Marie-Catherine Desjardins (Mme de Villedieu)*. Madison, NJ: Fairleigh Dickinson University Press, 2000, 131–46.

Wolfgang, Aurora. *Gender and Voice in the French Novel, 1730–1782*. Aldershot and Burlington: Ashgate Publishing, 2004.

Woshinsky, Barbara. *La Princesse de Clèves: The Tension of Elegance*. The Hague: Mouton, 1973.

———. *The Linguistic Imperative*. Saratoga, CA: Anma Libri, 1991.

———. "Allégorie et corporalité féminine: les deux Muses de Poussin." In Ronald Tobin, ed. *Le corps au XVIIe siècle: actes du premier colloque conjointement organisé par la North American Society for Seventeenth-Century French Literature et le Centre international de rencontres sur le XVIIe siècle, University of California, Santa Barbara, 17-19 mars 1994*. Paris: Tübingen: Papers on French Seventeenth-Century Literature, 1995, 151–60. Biblio 17.

———. "Tombeau de Phèdre: Repression, Confession and Métissage in Racine and Claire de Duras." *Dalhousie French Studies*, Special Issue, 49 (Winter, 1999), 167–81.

———. "Spatial Ambiguities and Conventual Openings," *Biblio* 17.131 (2002), 113–20.

———. "On the Mirror's Edge: Imagining the Body in Pierre de Croix's *Miroir de l'Amour divin*." *Seventeenth-Century French Studies* 25 (2003), 37–49.

———. "Desert, Fortress, Convent, Body: The Allegorical Architecture of Nervèze's *L'Hermitage de l'Isle saincte*." *Cahiers du XVIIème* 10.1 (2005), 67–74.

———. "Convent Parleys: Listening to Women's Voices in Madame de Villedieu's *Mémoires de la vie de Henriette-Sylvie de Molière*." In *Convent Voices*, ed. Thomas M. Carr. Charlottesville: Rookwood Press. EMF, Studies in Modern France 11, 2007, 167–85.

Yates, Frances. *The Art of Memory*. Chicago: University of Chicago Press, 1966.

Zuerner, Adrienne. "Disclosing Female Desire: Transvestite Heroines in Villedieu's *Mémoires de la Vie d'Henriette-Sylvie de Molière*." In *(Re)constructing Gender: Cross-dressing in Seventeenth-Century French Literature*. Ph.D. Dissertation, University of Michigan, 1993, 98–135.

———. "An Unholy Trinity: Sex, Politics and Religion in Villedieu's 'La Religieuse.'" In La Rochefoucauld: *'Mithridate': Frères et soeurs; Les Muses soeurs*. Tübingen: Gunter Narr Verlag, 1998, 191–204.

Zumthor, Paul. *La Mesure du monde: représentation de l'espace au moyen âge*. Paris: Seuil, 1993.

Index